CLASSIC INDIAN COOKING

Brahma, the supreme Hindu god,
creator of the universe

CLASSIC INDIAN COOKING

JULIE SAHNI

ILLUSTRATIONS BY MARISABINA RUSSO

WILLIAM MORROW AND COMPANY, INC.

New York

Library of Congress Cataloging in Publication Data

Sahni, Julie.
    Classic Indian cooking.

    Includes index.
1. Cookery, Indic. I. Title.
TX724.I4S24   641.5954   80-19475
ISBN 0-688-03721-6

Printed in the United States of America

        4 5 6 7 8 9 10

Book Design by Lydia Link

To my husband, Viraht, whose passion for good food is what launched me into cooking in the first place. Without his loving support and encouragement every step of the way, this book would not have been possible.

Acknowledgments

When I think of all the people who taught me to cook, shared their secret formulas for various cooking techniques, divulged prized recipes, or helped in any small way in the preparation of this book, I am overcome by a sudden burst of emotion. My love and gratitude for all they have done are boundless and shall remain forever.

It seems best to start at the beginning. First I thank my mother, who in an unconscious yet powerful way influenced my senses, my palate and my judgment. She took painstaking care in getting information on various ingredients and sending it to me. My mother-in-law gave me the precious gift of wisdom by reminding me that loving, living, and eating are inseparable and the essence of life. She generously shared many of her treasured family recipes, which have since become my own family favorites and are included in this book. And I thank my family's resident cook, who poured all her love and affection into the food, who filled my life with sweet memories of delicacies, and who taught me many basic skills involved in Indian cooking—including making perfect puffy breads. I would also like to mention my husband's and my own grandmothers, aunts, sisters, and fathers for their advice and help.

I am grateful to Mrs. Moinuddin and Mrs. Salamatullah for their recipe for *Shamme Kabab*. Mrs. Puri and Mrs. Bakshi for their *Channa* recipes. Karim for sharing his family's technique of making *Keema* and *Hussaini Kabab*. Mrs. Uppal for her *Peele Chawal*. And Mrs. Bhatnagar for the Sweet Lemon Pickle recipe. I am indebted to Mrs. B. Singh for showing me the *korma* techniques and exquisite *biriyani* garnishes. Pares Bhattacharji for introducing me to the glorious wealth of fish and shellfish of Bengal, and the many marvelous ways of cooking it. Nazir Mir for giving me insights into the Kashmiri cooking traditions. Asha Vyas for her perceptions about Gujrati food and the general cooking of North India. Saleem Ali of Spice and Sweet Mahal for generously taking time to discuss the food of Pakistan and its various special ingredients. Asha Gokhale for her recipe for *Kajoo Barfi*. And Mrs. Khosla for discussing *Imli Chutney*. I am also grateful to the New York Botanical Garden; Cornell University Cooperative Extension, Ithaca; the United States Department of Agriculture; Adriana Kleiman; and Ruth Schwartz for their help in researching information on spices and grains.

I am thankful to my students for the experience they gave me. Their innumerable questions proved very useful in the writing of this book. I am also grateful to Patricia Wells and Florence Fabricant for their interest, encouragement, and efforts in publicizing my cooking.

I would also like to make special mention of Rayna Skolnik, a student and a dear friend, who took time from her very busy schedule to read the manuscript and make constructive suggestions. Betsy Cenedella for her careful and tireless copy editing, for remaining patient and smiling when changes were made in certain recipes. Rosemary Myers for doing the pronunciation guide. Lydia Link for her magnificent design. Marisabina Russo for her clear and beautiful illustrations. Molly Finn for her support and expert advice. And John Guarnaschelli (Maria's husband), a historian, for coming up with the idea of the spinning wheel as the emblem of India on the cover of the book.

Finally, I wish to thank my editor, Maria Guarnaschelli, who labored over the book with an energy and passion beyond words. For her enthusiastic support and wise guidance all through the book, for her numerous valuable suggestions, superb editing, and for giving form to the book, I express my gratitude and affection forever.

Contents

Introduction

Indian food is the reflection of the heritage of its people. It represents its historical development, religious beliefs, cultural practices, and above all, its geographical attributes. It is, in fact, an amalgamation of the cuisines of many diverse regions. The unifying factor that brings all these varied cuisines under the heading of "Indian food" is the ingenious way that fragrant herbs and aromatic spices are used in all the regions. Indian food is the most aromatic of all cuisines—it is the cooking of captivating fragrances and intriguing flavors. It is crushed cardamom smothering tender young chickens (*Shahi Murgh Badaami*, p. 215), garlic perfuming lamb with cream sauce (*Rogan Josh*, p. 176), bruised carom lacing fish fillets (*Bhoni Machi*, p. 248), and pistachios sweetening the cream sauce for foamy cheese dumplings (*Ras Malai*, p. 465).

Geography

India, Pakistan, Bangladesh, Burma, and Sri Lanka (all of which were once part of the single nation of India) occupy the clearly bounded Indian subcontinent. Sri Lanka is a small separate island to the south in the Indian Ocean. Today, Burma is separated from India by the dense mosquito-ridden jungle that is India's modern eastern boundary. Along the southern part of India's eastern boundary is Bangladesh. Pakistan lies along the northwest border. There is no physical boundary separating Pakistan and Bangladesh from India. India is bounded on the north by the mighty ranges of the Himalayas, beyond which lies the Tibetan plateau. These mountains extend all the way northwest to the Hindu-Kush mountains which, although immense, are passable. Most new waves of invaders entered India through these passes (the best-known being the Khyber Pass). Further to the west lies the Afghanistan plateau bordered by Iran, and Turkmeniya and

Uzbekistan in the USSR. The remainder of the country is bordered by the sea.

The northernmost part of India, embraced by the snow-dusted peaks of the Himalayas, has a temperate climate. Here lies the Valley of Kashmir with its magnificent Persian gardens and terraced lakes. The brisk, cool fresh air in this region is imbued with the fragrance of pines and saffron flowers. Walnut and fruit orchards dot the country side, and morels (*gochian*) and black cumin seeds (*kala jeera*) grow wild. The climate is cool enough for the rearing of sheep; thus lamb (*katch*) forms the basis of many Kashmiri dishes.

As one moves south, the landscape becomes flatter and the climate warmer. The world-famous Indian long grain rice known as *Basmati* is grown in the foothills of these mountains, where the climate and soil are ideal for growing rice. The northern plains, irrigated by the great rivers Indus and Ganges, are rich and fertile. The extreme climate variation, from fierce heat (with temperatures rising to 120° F) to subfreezing cold with dry chilly winds, enables crops of wheat, corn, millet, barley, and innumerable varieties of legumes and vegetables to flourish. Here lie Delhi, Punjab, and Uttar Pradesh, where men are tall and hardy and the diet rich. The cooking fat used here is clarified butter (*usli ghee*). Goat and chicken are the meats eaten here. Even though rice is eaten quite commonly, and with great relish, bread is the primary staple of the people in these regions.

To the east lie the fertile plains of Bengal where the Ganges flows into the Bay of Bengal. The waters here overflow with hundreds of varieties of fish and shellfish, both freshwater and sea. The coastal area is lined with coconut palms, and the fields are covered with the yellow blossoms of mustard plants, looking like golden carpets stretching to the horizon. The climate is hot and humid. Rice grows abundantly here and, together with the abundant fish cooked in mustard oil, forms the daily diet of the people.

Farther to the northeast in the mountains of Assam lies Darjeeling, where the cool air and the seasonal rains that keep the hills perpetually drenched create the ideal conditions for cultivating tea. This is where the famous Darjeeling tea comes from.

Separating the southern regions from the northern plains is the great Deccan plateau. The Deccan is lined on both sides by a chain of hills known as *Ghat* (western *ghats* and eastern *ghats*). The soil along the plateau is not rich and the lack of irrigation further restricts agriculture. The hills taper away to fertile plains near the sea. Gujrat lies to the northwest of the Deccan. Here the soil is rich, which helps the cultivation of cotton, millet, barley, legumes, and many varieties of vegetables. Bread is the staple here. Lentil purees and vegetables cooked in sesame oil are commonly eaten by the primarily vegetarian population.

To the south lie Maharashtra, Goa, and Malabar. In these states tropical conditions prevail, due to their proximity to the equator and because of the monsoon rains. The weather is always warm, wet, and humid. Along the path of the monsoons, rice—the principal staple—is cultivated. The coastal areas yield many kinds of fish. A white non-oily fish called *Pomfret*, which tastes like sole, and a small transparent fish, *Bombil*, popularly known as "Bombay Duck," which is sun-dried and sold as wafers, are most popular. There is also no limit to the variety of shellfish, including prawns, shrimp, crab, lobster, clams and mussels. In addition, banana plants and different varieties of palm, including the coconut and date palms, line the coastline. Fish and seafood cooked with coconut and rice form the daily diet of the people in these regions.

The eastern plains are much wider, flat, and have highly fertile soil. These areas are abundant in limitless varieties of vegetables and greens. The people here are primarily vegetarians; their diet consists chiefly of vegetables, legumes, and rice. Coconut and bananas are used extensively in the preparation of dishes; and coconut or sesame oils are the fats. Here coconut milk substitutes for cow's milk.

Cultural Influence

Even though India is one of the oldest civilizations, it has been enriched over a period of many centuries by the different cultures that were superimposed with each new invasion. These invaders brought with them new ideas and concepts; they introduced new cooking ingredients and techniques which spread to different regions of India, enhancing and refining the local cuisine.

However, this influence was concentrated mainly in the North, where the new hordes primarily settled because of the similarity of the climate and landscape to those they came from. Furthermore, the natural barriers and great distances made migration to the South slow and infrequent. Thus northern cooking evolved far more over the centuries than other regional cuisines and attained unparalleled distinction.

Religious Taboos

India is a country of people of varied race, color, and religion, all bound together by a common culture known as "Indian Culture." The religious differences in particular are extreme—and far too many—and their influence on peoples' lives has been profound, especially in food and eating habits. What is amazing and wonderful is how these people, with their different beliefs, have lived together side by side, tolerating and respecting each other's convictions and practices for so many centuries.

The four major religions that originated and are practiced in India are Hinduism, Buddhism, Jainism, and Sikhism (the last three are offshoots of Hinduism). The Moslem religion is also referred to as one of the Indian religions because it was brought to India nine hundred years ago and has since spread over the entire country, with 65 million followers. India has the second largest Moslem population in the world. The other religions include Christianity, Judaism, and Zoroastrianism (the religion of the Parsees, a sect that emigrated from Persia to escape religious persecution). Each of these groups has its own code and methods of cooking and eating.

The Hindus and Sikhs, for example, are prohibited from eating beef because the cow is a sacred animal in Indian mythology. Lord Krishna was a cowherd who saw the whole universe reflected in the cow's body. Also, Lord Shiva's carrier was the bull *Nandi*. Similarly, Moslems and Jews are for different reasons prohibited from eating pork. There are certain Hindus (Brahmins and Jains) who are strict vegetarians, and who number several hundred million. These groups do not eat meat, which in an Indian context means red meat, poultry, fish, shellfish, eggs, and their products. Certain strict vegetarians won't eat food that resembles meat, such as tomatoes, red beets, and watermelon, because of their fleshlike color. Neither do they use seasonings that are strong and generally associated with the cooking of meat, such as garlic and onion.

While most Hindu Brahmins generally follow these rules, there are two exceptions: the Hindu Brahmins from Kashmir, known as Kashmiri Pandits, follow all the general Brahmin codes of cooking and eating, such as refraining from the use of onions and garlic in dishes, but *do* include meat (except of course beef) in their diet. This is because Kashmir for centuries was (and still is) in political turmoil, shifting constantly between Hindu and Moslem rulers. With each new power came mass conversions. The original people, who were Hindus, were forcibly converted during a Moslem reign and reverted back to Hinduism with the coming of a Hindu king. Since they had assumed a Moslem life-style for many centuries, they maintained several Moslem cultural practices, such as the eating of meat, even after finally becoming Hindu. As a result, the Kashmiri Pandits today eat meat but do not use onion or garlic in their cooking. This cooking is distinctly different from Kashmiri Moslem cooking. Both are famous for their exquisite lamb preparations.

The second exception is the Hindu Brahmins from Bengal. These people include fish, shellfish, and their products in their diet, because they consider them to be *Jal Toori*, meaning cucumbers or vegetables of the sea (or river). These Brahmins eat meat on special occasions, such as during the festival of *Durga Pooja* (worship of the Goddess Durga or Kali) in September and October when animals are ritually sacrificed. The meat of these animals, when offered to the Goddess, is considered holy, and thus a sacred privilege to eat.

All these cultural, religious, and geographical factors have played a great role in influencing Indian food and have shaped and developed it to what it is today.

About Moghul Food

The most popular and refined of all regional styles of cooking is the cooking of North India, which is basically Moghul food. This is the style of food served in most better-quality restaurants, here and in India. It evolved with the coming of the Moghuls in the sixteenth century. The Moghuls were Turk-Mongols by origin and Moslem by religion. The culture they admired most was Persian, since they were influenced by it on their way to India. They settled in the northern plains, with Delhi as their center. This is because Delhi, for strategic reasons (the wide flowing river Jamuna embracing the city, the rich fertile soil surrounding the city, and good landscape providing accessibility and visual security), had for centuries been the capital of the various groups in power. The Moghuls introduced new foods, new ingredients, and new cooking techniques, some of which were their own but most of which were borrowed from the Persians. In time several local herbs and spices found their way into these dishes, thus giving rise to the distinct new style of cooking known as Moghul cooking.

The Moghuls were lovers of nature and the good life, and had a keen sense of beauty, and a passion for elegance. This was reflected in every contribution they made, including art, architecture, painting, landscaping, social attire, mannerism, and most definitely in the presentation of food. For example, elaborate *biriyani* (layered meat and rice pilafs), were put together with meticulous care and presented on three- to four-foot gold and silver platters, garnished with crisp sautéed nuts, crackling onion shreds, and edible pure silver sheets. Many were also given beautiful names to reflect the tastiness of the dish.

Moghul food is famous for its mouth-watering meat preparations and rice pilafs. These include braised dishes called *korma*, pot roasts *(dum)*, kabobs *(kabab)*, kaftas *(kofta)*, and pilafs called *pullao* and *biriyani*.

Moghul cooking is also known for its delicate flavorings and superb silky sauces. The dishes thus created are so subtle that many are often mistaken for Persian. Ingredients such as yogurt, cream, fruit, and nut butters are often incorporated into the food to mellow and velvetize the sauces. The dishes are generally flavored with mild but highly fragrant spices such as cinnamon, cardamom, mace, nutmeg, and clove. There is also extensive use of saffron, especially in the rice pilafs.

The influence of Moghul cooking predominated in the North, especially in Delhi and the areas surrounding it, which are today known as Punjab, Kashmir, and Uttar Pradesh. Moghul cooking also flourishes in Hyderabad, a city in the southern state of Andra Pradesh. It is distinctly different because of regional influences, but is considered just as refined and sophisticated.

All through the centuries, even before the coming of the Moghuls, different cooking styles existed, each highly distinctive and lovely. All these styles flourish today in various parts of the country and each holds a special place in Indian cuisine. The differences among them, however, are great. To describe them would take a volume in itself; such a task is not possible within the scope of this book. What is possible, and what I have tried to do, is to introduce you to most of the important contrasting regional features here and there in the book. This will give you a sense of the fundamental differences that exist in the local cuisines. I want to emphasize that each regional style of cooking is to be appreciated on its own merits, for they all hold a very distinct place in the Indian culinary world.

The Principles of Indian Cooking

Indian cooking is more of an art than a science. It is highly personalized, reflecting individual tastes. It allows the cook to exercise the full range of her or his creative ingenuity. This is because the foundation of Indian cooking rests not so much on special techniques or expensive ingredients as on the flavorings—specifically, spices and herbs. Their uses, in different permutations and combinations, are what give Indian cooking its distinct character. Just as no two pieces of creative work are alike, so the same dish prepared by different cooks exhibits as many individualized flavors as it has interpreters. I am reminded of James Beard who, in his memoir, *Delights and Prejudices,* emphatically defends his food preferences and makes no bones about the things that never quite suit his fancy. Indian cooks generally follow that mode of thinking. In most instances, the Indian cook will add an ingredient or two beyond what is required in a dish, without deviating from the classic flavor, simply to give it his or her own personal stamp. This is commonly referred to in Indian as *Hath ki bat,* meaning "one's touch." These personal touches are what make all the difference and—understandably—are zealously guarded secrets among Indian cooks. That's why a dish never tastes quite the same in any two Indian homes or restaurants, even when it belongs to the same regional style of cooking.

There is no mystical secret behind Indian cooking. It is, in fact, the easiest of all international cuisines; the utensils needed are few and simple and cooking techniques, except for several that are exclusively Indian, are similar to those familiar to Americans and Europeans.

Knowledge of how to use spices and herbs is the key that will unlock the secrets of the seductive flavors and tantalizing aromas in Indian cooking. Knowing the quantities required is only the first step. As you start preparing Indian dishes, you will begin to develop a sense of how the spices and herbs behave with the other ingredients in a dish. Some herbs and spices are used as aromatics, some lend coloring, while others function as souring agents. There are spices that give a hot taste to the food and others that thicken or tenderize a dish. Once you understand the different properties of the various spices and herbs, gain a sense of how they interact, and master the techniques in using them, the classic dishes of India will neither seem a mystery nor be difficult to create.

The role of spices and herbs goes far beyond pleasing the palate and soothing the senses. They have medicinal properties that were known to the ancient Indians. Ayurvedic scripts in the three-thousand-year-old Holy Hindu Scriptures on herbal medicine list the preventive and curative powers of various spices, herbs, and roots in the treatment of common physical ailments. Over many centuries, specific spices were traditionally added to, and thus came to be associated with, certain Indian dishes. Asafetida and ginger root are known to counteract flatulence and colic, so they are added to lentil preparations as a matter of course. Some spices are excellent stimulants of the digestive system, which has a tendency to become sluggish with lack of physical activity. After a meal Indians chew either a betel leaf *(paan)*, a betel nut *(Areca catecha)*, and lime paste, or a few fragrant spices such as fennel, cardamom, or cloves. These are the Indian substitutes for the Western after-dinner mint. In addition to being wonderfully effective mouth-fresheners, they aid digestion, curb nausea, and provide relief from heartburn and acid indigestion. Cloves also act as an antiseptic. Fenugreek water is used as a tonic for gastritis and other stomach disorders. When soaked in water, the seeds soften and swell, and act as a most effective digestive aid. A few fenugreek seeds are always added to starchy vegetables and hard-to-digest legumes, especially when no asafetida or ginger are present. The North Indian appetizer called *chat* is almost always sprinkled with black salt *(kala namak)* and lemon juice, both of which are well-known for stimulating the appetite and increasing blood circulation.

The Holy Hindu Scriptures also document the effect of spices on body temperature. Spices which generate internal body heat are called "warm," and those which take heat away from one's system are called "cool" spices. Bay leaf, black cardamom, cinnamon, ginger powder, mace, nutmeg, and red pepper are "warm" spices and are recommended for cold weather. All the other spices range from "very cool" to "moderately warm" and therefore are suitable at all times in all climates. This is why dishes containing "warm" spices are instinctively prepared by the Indian cook more often during the winter months and avoided during the summer.

In the state of Kashmir where the climate is cool, spices such as cinnamon, nutmeg, mace, black cardamom, and ginger powder are traditionally used in the local specialties. Tea in Kashmir is also often flavored with cinnamon and cardamom. In the Plains, especially during the summer, "cool" spices lace beverages like the delicious cool punch (*Thandai*, p. 490) made with cow's milk, almond milk, sunflower and cantaloupe seeds, fennel, cloves, and green cardamom. The after-dinner spices (fennel, green cardamom, and cloves) are all "cool."

Spices also induce perspiration, which helps one to feel cool and comfortable. This is why Indians prefer to drink piping hot spice-laced tea in hot weather.

When spices and herbs are added to a dish, they act on the ingredients in many specific and wondrous ways. They don't always make a dish spicy and hot, as is widely believed. Except for a few spices that do impart a hot taste, most act as aromatics (to lace the food with a subtle scent), as coloring agents (to make the classic dishes beautiful to behold), as souring agents (to lend piquancy and tartness), as natural tenderizers for meat, and finally, as thickeners and binders for sauces (to give body and texture).

Most spices and herbs possess several properties. Saffron, for example, lends both a lovely orange-yellow color and a hypnotizing aroma to a dish. Coriander thickens a sauce at the same time that it imparts a nutty fragrance. Onions both thicken and perfume Moghul gravies. To give a specific example: In the dish Chicken in Onion Tomato Gravy (*Murgh Masala*, p. 208), the cinnamon, cardamom, and cloves aromatize; the turmeric lends yellow color; the onions, garlic, ginger root, and tomatoes act as thickeners as well as imparting flavor and color to the dish. The tomatoes also function as tenderizing and souring agents.

The secret to mastering the art of classic Indian cooking, then, lies in developing, until it becomes almost instinctive, a knowledge of the specific properties of each spice, herb, and root, and how they behave with other ingredients. For this purpose, I have described in this chapter the different and important properties of each spice, herb, and flavoring used in Indian cooking. Also for your convenience, there is a ready-reference spice chart on page 8.

In sum, to become an experienced and creative Indian cook it is essential to feel at home in your kitchen, surrounded by fragrant spices and aromatic herbs. This confidence will come naturally to you when you develop a working knowledge of these ingredients. This is the first lesson in the process of becoming an expert. Learning the use of spices in Indian cooking is somewhat like learning a new language—practice makes perfect.

A NOTE ABOUT SPECIAL INGREDIENTS

With the increasing acceptance and popularity of Indian food in the United States, more and more Americans are cooking it at home. These well-traveled and enterprising cooks have discriminating tastes and are uncompromising about the authenticity of food and flavors. As a result, several special ingredients needed for Indian dishes that were previously unavailable have recently come onto the market. One is the black cumin seed *(kala jeera)* which is used in India to make delicate pilafs. Although not an absolutely essential ingredient, the black cumin seed is a finer, more subtle variety of cumin and gives the rice the exquisite texture and aroma characteristic of the great Moghul pilafs.

You can find most of the ingredients you will need for Indian cooking in supermarkets or at greengrocers' shops. Only a few special items, such as black cumin, require a trip to a specialty store. This chapter includes a description of all the spices and herbs you will use in Indian cooking, to acquaint you with the multiple roles they play. I have indicated those that are available only in Indian or other specialty stores. Most Indian stores carry all these special ingredients at a fraction of the supermarket price. You would be well-advised to make a complete list of all the ingredients you need and obtain them from these shops. I recommend doing this even if you have to order them by mail, because most will keep indefinitely. (There is a shopping guide and a list of mail-order outlets at the back of the book.) *A word of caution:* Many Indian stores label ingredients by their Indian names only; sometimes they do not label them at all. Be sure to give the Indian name of the ingredient when you order, and request that all orders be labeled, since some ground spices look much like others. I have supplied both the English and the Indian (Hindi) names for all the ingredients.

Spices

Except for a few that are highly aromatic in their raw form, most spices have to be cooked before they release any of their fragrance. All spices, however, release more aroma when slightly crushed. And some are more aromatic than others. Cinnamon is more fragrant than cumin; cardamom is more fragrant than coriander; saffron is more fragrant than turmeric. When cooking Indian dishes, you must make sure that no single spice overwhelms a dish, that each harmoniously blends with the others. There are, however, a few exceptions in which the fragrance of a particular spice is emphasized intentionally. The spice whose aroma is meant to predominate is generally added in large quantity, and the number of additional herbs and spices is reduced to a minimum to support this distinction. For example, in the dish Royal Chicken in Silky White Almond Sauce (*Shahi Murgh Badaami*, p. 215), the fragrance of crushed cardamom in the yogurt-almond sauce is accentuated, whereas in Ground Beef in Cashew Nut Sauce with Chick-peas (*Keema Matar*, p. 162), all the flavorings blend evenly with no one spice dominating.

Spices are dried organic matter such as roots, leaves, barks of trees, buds, stems, and seeds of plants, all of which are difficult to digest in their raw form. The reason people sometimes have digestion problems after eating Indian food is because they have eaten raw spices. The spices used in Indian cooking should be regarded as vegetables to be cooked before being eaten so that they will be easy on your digestive system and give out their maximum flavor. In Indian cooking, spices are always cooked before they go into a dish. They are generally added to the hot oil at the beginning of preparation and cooked for a moment before other ingredients are added. When the spices are incorporated during the final execution of a dish, or used in cold yogurt salads or appetizers (sometimes finished with a sprinkling of cumin and coriander), they should always be dry-roasted before being added.

PROPERTIES OF SPICES

(What Spices Do to Food)

SPICES	Lend Aroma or Fragrance	Lend Taste or Flavor	Lend Color or Visual Appeal	Act as Thickeners
Asafetida *Heeng*	•			
Bay leaf *Tej Patta*	•			
Cardamom *Elaichi*	•			
Carom *Ajwain*	•			
Cinnamon *Dalchini*	•			
Clove *Laung*	•			
Coriander *Dhania, Sookha*				•
Cumin *Jeera*	•			
Fennel *Saunf*	•			
Fenugreek *Meethi*	•			
Ginger Powder *Sonth*	•	sour-hot		
Mace *Javitri*	•			
Mango Powder *Amchoor*		sour		
Mustard *Rai*	•			
Nutmeg *Jaiphul*	•			
Onion Seed *Kalaunji*	•			
Paprika *Deghi Mirch*			red	
Pomegranate *Anardana*		sweetish-sour		
Poppy Seed *Khas-khas*				•
Red Pepper *Lal Mirch*		hot		
Saffron *Kesar*	•		orangish-yellow	
Salt *Namak*	•	alkaline		
Tamarind *Imli*		tangy-sour		
Turmeric *Haldi*	•		golden yellow	
White Split Gram Beans *Urad Dal*	•			
Yellow Split Peas *Channa Dal*	•			

Spices should be purchased whole, to be powdered as needed, because freshly ground spices are always more aromatic. Also, whole spices retain their potency and aroma much longer.

All spices should be stored in airtight containers in a cool dry place, or they will become rancid. If properly stored, ground spices will remain fresh up to three months, and whole ones up to one year (some, such as asafetida, mustard seeds, fenugreek, and onion seeds, stay fresh up to three years).

Asafetida (Heeng)

Asafetida is a combination of various dried gum resins obtained from the roots of certain Iranian and Indian plants. It is available in lump or powdered form at Indian grocery stores. Asafetida lump, brown in color (the powder is buff color), is virtually odorless until it is powdered, when it releases its strong characteristic smell. Asafetida in lump form, its purest state, will keep for years without losing its potency. Yet another reason (though a personal one) for purchasing the lump form: The powerful smell of powdered asafetida takes over the entire kitchen and the aroma lingers on.

For most recipes, you will need a lump of asafetida about the size of a green pea—a size that can easily be crushed. Surprisingly, this strong and overly pungent ingredient, when added to hot oil and fried for five seconds, undergoes a mysterious change: It perfumes the fat with a subtle oniony aroma. Asafetida-flavored oil is the basic ingredient in the cooking of Hindu Brahmins and Jains, whose strict vegetarian diet forbids them to use onions—a flavoring considered too strong and smelly. The Kashmiri Brahmins, who also abstain from cooking with onions, use asafetida in certain kabob preparations. Since asafetida is used as a substitute for onion flavor, it is logical that in Indian cooking the two are never used simultaneously.

Bay Leaf *(Tej Patta)*

There are two types of bay leaves commonly available. The type used in Indian cooking, the Indian bay leaf, is the leaf of the cassia tree *(Cinnamomum cassia)*, native to China, Southeast Asia and northeastern India. The other, known as sweet bay laurel, is the leaf of the bay tree *(Laurus nobilis)*, native to Asia Minor and the Mediterranean. Today bay laurel is grown in many milder regions of the world, including the western coast of the United States. Both trees are evergreen members of the laurel family. The bay laurel leaf, when fully grown, is about five inches long, thick, glossy, and dark green. It has a bitterish taste and a pungent, almost lemony aroma. The Indian bay leaf, on the other hand, is almost seven inches long, thin, dull, and light green, with a sweet taste and a mellow, spicy aroma. Indian bay leaves crumble readily, which is a great asset, as they can easily be powdered and mixed with other spices. One variety may be distinguished from the other in that the Indian bay leaves are broken, dull in appearance, bundled in plastic bags or cardboard boxes, and far less expensive than bay laurel leaves, which are brighter, fresher-looking whole leaves stacked in spice bottles. Indian bay leaves are preferred. If you cannot find them, bay laurel leaves may be substituted. Since bay laurel leaves are much stronger, you will need only half the amount suggested in the recipes. In Indian cooking, the bay leaf is used as a flavoring in preparing meat dishes. It is one of the four essential spices (cardamom, cinnamon, and clove being the others) that give a pilaf the distinctive fragrance associated with Moghul cooking. See Fragrant Pilaf Banaras Style *(Banarasi Pullao*, p. 368).

Cardamom *(Elaichi)*

These are the small, fragrant black seeds of the fruit of the cardamom plant *(Elettaria cardamomum)*, which is native to South India and Sri Lanka. Whole cardamom, known as cardamom pods, comes in two varieties—green and black.

The green cardamom, known as *Choti* (small) *Elaichi*, is

widely available either in its natural green form, or bleached and puffed to give it more esthetic appeal. This beautifying, however, seems somehow to take away that wonderfully intense cardamom aroma, so I recommend you buy it in its natural green form. Green cardamom, a small, quarter-inch-long pod, has a thin pale-green skin and a powerful aroma, but a delicate sweet taste. Green cardamom is available whole or in powder form. In Indian cooking it is used as a flavoring, in both forms, in puddings, desserts, sweetmeats, conserves, and in some very delicate meat and poultry preparations, such as Moghul Braised Chicken (*Mughalai Korma*, p. 206). It is also one of the chief Indian after-dinner mints (clove and fennel being the others).

The second variety is black cardamom, known as *Kali* (black) or *Badi* (big) *Elaichi*, which is available only in Indian and some specialty grocery stores. Black cardamom, a large, one-inch pod, has a thick, husky dark-brown skin. It has a mellow taste, but a nuttier aroma than the green variety. Black cardamom is available only in whole form. In Indian cooking it is used in meat and vegetable dishes, as a flavoring, whole, or it is ground for use in relishes and sweet pickles, such as Sweet and Sour Tamarind Relish (*Imli Chutney*, p. 442). It is another of the four essential spices (with bay leaf, cinnamon, and clove) that give the Moghul pilaf its distinct aroma. It is also one of the main ingredients of the spice mix known as *Mughal Garam Masala* (p. 37). When a recipe calls for black cardamom, the green or bleached cardamom may be substituted if black cardamom is unavailable.

Carom (Ajwain)

Carom, also known as lovage, is the seed of the thymol plant (*Carum copticum*), native to the southern regions of India. The seeds resemble celery seeds. Carom seeds have a sharp and piquant taste and give out an aroma much like thyme when slightly bruised. Carom is available whole in Indian grocery stores. It is used as a flavoring in vegetable preparations, breads, and savory pastries. Carom is essential in the making of the delectable crackers from Punjab called *Matthi* (p. 131). Mixed with garlic and lemon juice, carom transforms simple filets of fish into mouth-watering *Bhoni Machi* (p. 248). Carom is also used in many varieties of pickles, both sweet and hot.

Cinnamon *(Dalchini)*

There are two types of cinnamon that may be used interchangeably. The type used in Indian cooking, the Indian cinnamon, is the bark of the cassia tree *(Cinnamomum cassia)*, a member of the laurel family (see Bay Leaf, p. 10). It is generally referred to as cinnamon even though it is technically "cassia" or "false cinnamon." The cassia bark is peeled in long strips and the corky outer layer is scraped off, leaving the bark in "quills" or "sticks." Cinnamon cassia is reddish brown in color and has a delicate, sweet taste and a captivating aroma.

The other, known as true cinnamon, is the bark of the cinnamon tree *(Cinnamomum zylanicum)*, also a member of the laurel family. Since cinnamon cassia and true cinnamon both come from the same botanical family, *cinnamomum*, they are both sold as cinnamon; therefore, it is not always possible to know which you are buying. (More often than not you are buying cassia, because 90 percent of the cinnamon imported into the United States is cinnamon cassia.) In any event, it matters little, since both varieties look, smell, and taste almost identical, except that cinnamon cassia quills are coarser, thicker, and have a stronger aroma than true cinnamon quills, which are smooth and slender. The textures are different because the true cinnamon bark is fermented for twenty-four hours after being peeled. This enables the corky layer to be scraped off completely, leaving the thin bark to curl.

Cinnamon is available in 3-inch-long quills or sticks, in broken flat pieces or "chips", and in powdered form. In Indian cooking both quills and chips are acceptable, except when whole spices are left in special pilafs as garnish. Here the quills are preferred for purely esthetic reasons; they look handsomer than the broken pieces.

Cinnamon is used as a flavoring, whole as well as in powdered form, in Indian cooking. It is one of the four spices (bay leaf, cardamom, and clove being the others) essential to Moghul pilafs. It is also one of the ingredients of *Mughal Garam Masala* (p. 37). Surprisingly, in Indian cooking cinnamon is never used as it is in the West to flavor puddings, desserts, and sweetmeats.

Clove *(Laung)*

Clove is the dried bud of the plant *Syzygium aromaticum*, native to the Molucca Islands in Eastern Indonesia. Cloves are dark brown in color and have a sharp, pungent taste and fragrant aroma. They are available whole and in powdered form. In Indian cooking cloves are used as a flavoring, whole or powdered, in meat preparations, pilafs, and seafoods. With bay leaf, cardamom, and cinnamon, clove is used to flavor pilafs and is also an ingredient in *Mughal Garam Masala* (p. 37).

Coriander *(Dhania, Sookha)*

Coriander seed is the dried ripe fruit of the coriander plant *(Coriandrum sativum)*, an annual herb of the parsley family, which is native to Asia Minor and Southern Europe but is now cultivated around the world. The coriander seed is round, slightly larger than a peppercorn, light brown in color, and has a strong, nutty aroma and sweetish, piquant taste; it is available whole or powdered. In Indian cooking it is used in both forms. In powdered form it acts as a thickener in sauces and gravies. Roasted ground coriander is frequently added to appetizers called *chat* and yogurt salads known as *raita*, so it is good to keep a supply (a quarter of a cup is fine) of the ground roasted seeds on hand. To roast, grind, and store coriander seeds, follow the instructions on page 66. Coriander is an important spice in cooking throughout India, and an essential ingredient of *Garam Masala* (p. 38).

Cumin *(Jeera)*

Cumin, the dried ripe fruit of the cumin plant, is one of the most important spices throughout India, especially in the northern and western regions. No meal is complete without its use in one form or another. There are essentially three varieties of cumin seeds used in Indian cooking. White cumin—*Safaid* (white) *Jeera*—is the most widely used spice in all regional Indian cooking. The other two varieties, which are similar except that one is brownish-black and the other black, are lumped together under the category of black cumin—*Kala* (black) or *Shahi* (royal) *Jeera*.

White cumin *(Cuminum cyminum)*, generally referred to simply as cumin *(jeera)*, is widely used in many other cuisines, including Mexican, Spanish, African, and Middle-Eastern. It is yellowish-brown in color and resembles the caraway seed in shape but is larger. Cumin seed has a nutty aroma and taste. White cumin, though native to upper Egypt and western parts of Asia Minor, is widely cultivated in various parts of Asia, including India. Cumin is available whole or powdered. In Indian cooking it is used in both forms. Many north Indian recipes, including appetizers *(chat)* and yogurt salads *(raita)*, call for roasted cumin powder to be sprinkled over the dish. Therefore, keep a ¼-cup supply handy. To roast, grind and store cumin seeds, follow the instructions on page 66.

Black cumin *(Cuminum nigrum)* is a rare variety that grows in the mountains of southeastern Iran and along the valleys of Kashmir. Black cumin is sweeter-smelling than the white; it too resembles caraway seed but is smaller. Black cumin costs considerably more than the white, but its delicate texture and mellow flavor are unmatched. Black cumin is available whole in Indian grocery stores, and is generally used whole. Because of its mellow aroma, black cumin does not require roasting. It is an important ingredient in the Kashmiri and Moghul styles of cooking, in dishes such as Lamb in Fragrant Garlic Cream Sauce *(Rogan Josh,* p. 176), and in Moghul pilafs such as Emperor's Pilaf with Black Mushrooms *(Badshahi Pullao,* p. 375) where it gives the dish a more delicate texture.

Fennel *(Saunf)*

Fennel refers to the seedlike fruit of the fennel plant *(Foeniculum vulgare)*, native to the Mediterranean region. Fennel has been cultivated in India since Vedic times. The greenish-yellow fennel seed resembles the white cumin seed but is larger and fatter. It has a sweet licorice flavor, much like anise, and a very appealing aroma.

Recently a finer grade of fennel called *Lakhnawi Saunf*, or fennel from the city of Lucknow in India, has been introduced in Indian grocery stores. It is smaller, thinner, more finely textured, and has a more delicate flavor. It is this variety of fennel which is traditionally served as an after-dinner mint (cardamom and clove being the others). The aroma of this fennel is greatly enhanced when dry-roasted. To roast and store fennel seeds, follow the instructions on page 66.

In Indian cooking fennel is used for its aroma whole as well as powdered in pickles, meat, vegetable preparations, and pilafs. The use of fennel in Indian desserts is rare, with two exceptions: a sweet pastry filled with a mixture of nuts and coconut laced with cardamom, called *Gujjia*, and the seductively delicate fennel-flavored whole wheat crepes studded with pistachio nuts, called *Malpoora* (p. 463).

Anise, also known as *saunf*, can be substituted wherever a recipe calls for fennel, as both anise and fennel are cultivated in India and are used interchangeably in cooking. Anise seed is slightly dull, almost gray in color. The seed, small and crescent-shaped, has a texture like fennel's.

Fenugreek *(Methi)*

Fenugreek *(Trigonella foenumgraecum)* is an annual herb of the bean family native to India and Asia Minor. It has been cultivated in India since pre-Vedic days. Although both the seed and the leaves of the plant are used in Indian cooking, they are not interchangeable because they have different properties and hence impart different flavors and aromas. The fenugreek seed, rectangular and brownish-yellow in color, is actually a leguminous bean like the mung bean, but because of its extreme aroma and bitter taste, it is used as a spice. Fenugreek is available whole in Indian and Middle Eastern grocery stores. In Indian cooking it is used whole as well as powdered. Fenugreek is an important spice throughout India in vegetarian cooking and in pickling. It is an essential spice in the southern lentil-and-vegetables stew called *Sambaar* (see Spicy Brussels Sprouts, Green Beans and Lentils Stew, p. 276).

Dry fenugreek leaves *(kasoori methi)* are the sun-dried leaves of the fenugreek plant; they are used both as herbs and as dried greens. The leaves have a bitter taste and a captivating aroma. Dried fenugreek leaves are available in Indian grocery stores. They are generally cooked with starchy vegetables, like potatoes and yams, used as a stuffing for breads, and as flavoring for crackers such as the delectable Indian Fenugreek Crackers *(Kasoori Mathari, p. 133)*.

Ginger Powder *(Sonth)*

Ginger powder is obtained by drying and powdering fresh ginger root, the pungent aromatic root of the tropical ginger plant *(Zingiber officinale)*. Good quality ginger is light, airy, and buff-colored and has a hottish piquant taste and sweet smell. It is used to lend a woody fragrance as well as a sour taste to a dish. Powdered ginger is used primarily in Moghul cooking. It is also used in sweet pickles and relishes such as Sweet and Sour Tamarind Relish *(Imli Chutney, p. 442)*.

Mace *(Javitri)*

Mace and nutmeg are both part of the same fleshy fruit of the nutmeg tree *(Myristica fragrans)*, native to the Moluccas. When the fruit is ripe it splits, exposing the brown nut (nutmeg) covered with a brilliant red netty membrane (mace). The membrane is carefully peeled off the nutshell and dried until it turns yellowish-brown in color and becomes brittle. These dried membranes are commercially known as mace blades. Mace has a pungent aroma much like nutmeg but is stronger and has a bitter taste. Mace is available in blade or powder form. In Indian cooking it is used as a flavoring, powdered, in Moghul and Kashmiri dishes, certain sweet pickles, and relishes. Though mace and nutmeg belong to the same fruit, they have a slightly different taste and should not be used interchangeably.

Mango Powder *(Amchoor)*

Mango, the fruit of the tropical plant *Mangifera indica*, is native to India but is now grown in many tropical regions of the world. Mango is plucked before it ripens, peeled, sun-dried, and ground to produce a pale buff-colored powder. This mango powder, known as *am* (mango) *choor* (powder), has a pungent aroma and a tangy, sour taste and therefore is used as a souring agent in place of lemon juice. Its primary use is in vegetarian cooking. Because of its dry state, it is preferred over moist souring agents in preparations that will be carried on journeys lasting several days, with temperatures up to 120 degrees Fahrenheit.

Mustard *Rai*

The seed of the mustard plant *Brassica juncea*, an annual herb of the mustard family native to India, is one of the most important spices throughout India. Both the leaves, or mustard greens *(sarsoon)* and seeds *(rai)* are used in Indian cooking, as vegetables and as a spice respectively. Indian mustard seeds are purplish brown, not yellow, and look much like poppy seeds, except larger. They are popularly referred to as black mustard seeds because they look more black than brown. They have a pungent aroma and, when ground and cooked, a sourish, bitter taste. Mustard is available whole in Indian and specialty grocery stores. In Indian cooking it is used as a flavoring whole as well as in powdered form. In northern India mustard seed is used primarily as a pickling spice and in vegetable dishes. In the southern and southwestern regions it is as important as cumin is in the North. In the East the mustard seeds are usually roasted and ground to a powder which is used as an important flavoring spice. (To roast, grind, and store mustard seeds, follow the instructions on page 66.) The oil extracted from mustard seeds is favored over all others for oil-based pickles as well as for deep frying in the northern and northwestern regions of India. Mustard oil is considered an essential ingredient in the famous Goanese dish *Vendaloo* (p. 199), to which it lends its authentic aroma.

Nutmeg *Jaiphul*

As mentioned under "Mace *(Javitri)*" (p. 16), nutmeg is the dark brown shell enclosed within the mace membrane. The shell is dried and cracked open and the oily seed inside, known as nutmeg, is removed. Nutmeg has a gentle aroma and a sweet taste, mellower than mace. It is available whole or powdered (grated). In Indian cooking the reddish-brown powder is used as a flavoring. Nutmeg should be purchased whole and grated as needed. Nutmeg is used primarily in Moghul and Kashmiri cooking. It is one of the ingredients of *Mughal Garam Masala* (p. 37) and is also used in vegetable preparations and relishes.

Onion Seed *(Kalaunji)*

Onion seed, also known as *Nigella*, actually has nothing in common with the onion plant but does resemble an actual onion seed—hence its name. The satiny-black triangular *Kalaunji* has a sweet taste and an aroma much like oregano. It is available whole in Indian and specialty grocery stores. In Indian cooking it is used as a flavoring whole. This spice is used primarily in the northern regions of India, in pickling, vegetable dishes, and for sprinkling on top of the famous *tandoor*-baked bread called *Tandoori Nan*.

Paprika *(Deghi Mirch)*

Indian paprika or *Deghi Mirch* comes from the mild variety of chili pod of the plant *Capsicum*, grown in the valleys of Kashmir. When ripe, the pod is plucked, sun-dried, and ground to produce a mild-tasting, brilliant red powder. *Deghi mirch* has a pungent aroma like red pepper but is sweet-tasting like Hungarian sweet paprika. It is available in powdered form in Indian grocery stores. The common sweet paprika available in supermarket chains is a good substitute. In Indian cooking, *deghi mirch* is used primarily to lend its brilliant red color to the food. It is also extensively used in Kashmiri cooking, specially by Kashmiri Brahmins in making kabobs, kaftas, and other meat preparations.

Pomegranate *(Anardana)*

The brownish-red pomegranate, known as *anar*, about the size of an orange, is the fruit of the tropical tree (or shrub) *Punica granatum*, native to Asia Minor and Mediterranean regions but now cultivated in many warmer regions of the world including India. The thick outer skin is not edible, but the seedlike pulpy interior enclosed in a honeycombed membrane is either eaten fresh as a fruit (see Almond and Rice Dessert [*Firni*], p. 461) or dried and used as a spice called *anardana*. The dried pomegranate is available whole in Indian grocery stores. In Indian cooking it is used in powdered form. Because of their natural piquancy, pomegranate seeds make an ideal souring agent and are frequently used with vegetables and lentils in North Indian cooking. Many chefs prefer pomegranate over mango powder, as pomegranate seeds impart a distinct sweetish-sour taste to a dish instead of just a sour taste. Pomegranate seeds are considered an important ingredient in making the famous chick-pea dish from the Punjab region of India called *Khatte Channe* (p. 271), and in the filling for savory pastries (*Aloo Samosa*, p. 125).

Poppy Seed, White *(Khas-khas)*

The white poppy seed *Khas-khas* should not be mistaken for the black poppy seed that is commonly used as a topping on American rolls, breads, and other confections. Even though the white poppy seed plant, native to Asia Minor but now widely grown in India, belongs to the same family, the seeds do not yield opium. These seeds are off-white, odorless, and flavorless in their raw form. They are available whole in Indian grocery stores, and are used primarily in northern cooking. The seeds are usually ground up with other spices and added to meat, fish, and shellfish preparations as a thickener. Often the seeds are roasted prior to being ground. This not only makes the grinding easier but gives the sauce a wonderful aroma, much like the roasted sesame seed oil used in Chinese cooking. To roast, grind, and store poppy seeds, follow the instructions on page 66.

Red Pepper *(Lal Mirch)*

Indians love red pepper, also known as red chili, not just for its hotness and the flavor it imparts to a dish, but because it enhances the flavor of other ingredients and of the dish as a whole. To Indians, food without chili is like a bride without a veil. In addition to *Lal* (red) *Mirch*, Indian cooking also uses *Kala* (black) or *Gol* (round) *Mirch* and *Safaid* (white) *Mirch*.

The red pepper is the ripe, sun-dried chili pod of the plant *Capsicum*; it is selected for its pungency. Red chili is available commercially under two names, red pepper and cayenne pepper; these can be used interchangeably. Red pepper is available whole, as a pod, or powdered. In Indian cooking both forms are utilized.

Numerous varieties of red pepper are used in India, each with its own distinct aroma, flavor, and pungency. It is this spice that gives a dish the hot taste, so use it with caution. Unless you are an experienced handler of the red chili pepper, this is one spice you should not experiment with, even in its uncooked form. You should not sniff or handle it, because it leaves a burning sensation on the skin that lasts for hours. Hot food is an acquired taste, and its enjoyment is an art in itself. Hot-food lovers believe that unless enough chili is added to the dish, the food tastes bland and insipid. In addition—they rightly claim—the flavors of other spices are enhanced only by the addition of just the right amount (in their estimation, a *generous* amount) of red pepper. And yet there are those (and I include myself in this category) whose senses are numbed when the food is excessively hot. As a result they cannot taste the dish itself, let alone the individual ingredients. So the controversy rages.

Saffron *(Kesar)*

Saffron, known as *Kesar* (sometimes *Zaffran*), is the dried stigmas of flowers of the saffron plant *(Crocus sativus)*, native to Asia Minor and Southern Europe but now cultivated in India in the valley of Kashmir. Saffron is the most expensive spice in the world today—one pound has a retail value of $2,000—for it takes about a quarter of a million dried stigmas collected from some seventy-five thousand flowers to make a single pound of true saffron. Saffron is available in thread or powdered form in Spanish, Middle Eastern, Indian, and some other specialty grocery stores, in plastic bottles containing one twentieth of an ounce (about one tablespoon of threads). Saffron threads, reddish-brown in color and with a sweetish taste, emit a most captivating aroma and impart a beautiful orange-yellow color to a dish. Both thread and powder are suitable for Indian cooking; however, I recommend buying the thread form to avoid the possibility of adulteration of powdered saffron.

Because of its high cost, use this spice sparingly. As little as ¼ teaspoon is usually enough to flavor 1 pound of meat or poultry, or 1 cup (measured uncooked) of rice. Increasing the quantity will not increase the flavor or aroma, and you will only be wasting some of this very precious spice. The best way to use saffron is to powder it with the back of a spoon or your fingertips in a small bowl, soak it in a little hot water or milk for

15 minutes, and then add the solution to the dish you are preparing. This will ensure even coloring and maximum flavoring.

Saffron—utilized for both flavoring and coloring a dish—is extensively used throughout India in desserts such as Saffron Almond Pudding (*Badaam Kheer*, p. 457). It is a favored spice in Moghul cooking, especially in meat and poultry preparations such as Royal Roast Leg of Lamb with Saffron Raisin Sauce (*Shahi Raan*, p. 184), to which saffron gives the brilliant red color and divine aroma characteristic of the dish. Saffron is also an important ingredient in making pilafs and the special casseroles of layered meat and fragrant rice called *biriyani*, such as *Shah Jahani Biriyani* (p. 192). The Moslems in India make a sweet rice pilaf with saffron called *Zarda* (p. 369), which is traditionally served during *Muharram* (the day of observation of Saint Hussain's death).

Salt *(Namak)*

Salt in India is used not only as a seasoning but also as a spice to flavor food. This is because many varieties of salt are used in Indian cooking. Especially in the North, different varieties of salt are used to flavor cold appetizers (*chat*), relishes (*chutney*), and cold drinks. These varieties are not the blends of herbs and spices mixed with salt that are known here as "seasoned" salt, but are spicy salts in their natural form, each with a different taste, aroma, and chemical composition. The most extensively used salts are white salt, commonly referred to as table salt (*Sambhar Namak*), black salt (*Kala Namak*), and rock salt (*Sendha Namak*). Only table salt and black salt are available in the United States.

The black salt is brownish-black when in lump form (hence the name "black salt") but looks pinkish-brown when powdered. It is available in powdered form in Indian grocery stores. Black salt has a pleasant tangy taste and smoky aroma. It is an important ingredient in such famous appetizers (*chat*) as *Aloo Chat* (p. 105), and the delicious Sweet and Sour Tamarind Relish (*Imli Chutney*, p. 442).

Tamarind *(Imli)*

Tamarind is the pulpy pod, resembling a pea pod, of the tropical plant *Tamarindus indica,* native to India. It is brownish-black in color and tastes like a sour prune. Tamarind pods, when fully mature, are plucked, peeled, and pitted, and the pulp is compressed into "cakes." Tamarind is available in cake or juice form in Indian grocery stores. Only the pulp form is suitable for use in Indian cooking, as the juice is too acidic, yet lacks flavor. To extract juice from tamarind pulp, soak a piece of tamarind cake in boiling water for 15 minutes—the rule is a 1-inch-diameter ball of tamarind pulp to ¼ cup of water. Then mash with a fork or your fingers, squeezing out as much juice as possible. Strain and reserve the juice, and discard the dry fibrous residue. Tamarind is used as a souring agent. Its use is more extensive in the southern and southwestern regions of India. But in the North, tamarind is used in relishes, the most famous of which is Sweet and Sour Tamarind Relish *(Imli Chutney,* p. 442), and in vegetable, lentil, and bean preparations.

Turmeric *(Haldi)*

Turmeric is a perennial tropical herb *(Curcuma longa)* belonging to the ginger family and native to India. Like ginger root, the turmeric rhizome resembles a short finger jutting out of the horizontally growing underground stem of the plant. The roots are cleaned, boiled, dried, and powdered to produce a nutty-tasting, aromatic powder. As you may know, turmeric is the main ingredient in commercial curry powder. Good quality turmeric, aside from lending a characteristic yellow color to a dish, also gives a wonderful woody aroma.

Turmeric is used in cooking throughout India, primarily as a coloring agent but also to lend flavor, in various *dal,* vegetable, meat, poultry, and seafood preparations. However, in the northern and northwestern regions, its use is limited; saffron, and other color-imparting flowers, generally replace it. Turmeric is never used in dishes containing cream, because its delicate scent gets masked. On the other hand, it blends beautifully with onion and tomato sauces. It is the most important and sacred spice of Hindus and is used in religious and social rituals. The sacred thread, the marriage symbol that is tied around the bride's neck by the bridegroom during the marriage ceremony, is dipped in turmeric paste.

White Split Gram Bean (Urad Dal)

The white split gram bean is actually a legume (see Legumes [Dal], p. 323), but in the southern and southwestern regions of India it is also used as a spice. It is usually cooked in oil with black mustard seeds, and sometimes yellow split peas; it is then added to flavor various vegetables and legume preparations such as Cauliflower and Scallions with Black Mustard Seeds (Gobhi Kari, p. 301).

Yellow Split Peas (Channa Dal)

The yellow split pea is, in fact, a legume (see Legumes [Dal], p. 323), but in the southern and southwestern regions of India it is also used as a spice. It is generally cooked in oil with white split gram bean and mustard seed, and then used as a flavoring in different lentil and bean preparations, in dumplings, and in stuffings for breads and pastries. It is also ground (raw or roasted) to a powder (or flour) and used as a thickener, or in making sweetmeats and fudge preparations.

Herbs and Seasonings

Basil Leaves   *(Tulsi)*
Coriander Leaves   *(Hara Dhania)*
Garlic   *(Lassan)*
Ginger Root, Fresh   *(Adrak)*
Green Chili   *(Hari Mirch)*
Kari Leaves   *(Meethe Neam ke Patte)*
Mint Leaves   *(Podina)*
Onion, Scallion, and Shallot   *(Piaz, Hara Piaz, aur Chota Piaz.)*

The herbs most frequently used in Indian cooking are coriander, mint, kari, and basil. They are chopped and folded into dishes, or sprinkled over them as a garnish. Herbs may be minced and mixed with ginger root, yogurt, and spices to serve as relishes and dips with appetizers. They are also pureed and cooked with rice to create fragrant herb pilafs, and brewed with ginger root and honey in herbal teas.

Because fresh herbs are essential to vegetarian cooking, they are cultivated all year round in India. Dried herbs are unheard of. In the United States, with the exception of coriander, fresh herbs are not that easily obtainable. Mint and kari leaves, which are more readily available in dried form, can be substituted. I personally have solved this problem by growing my own herbs in pots on my window sills. This way I have a ready supply in any season. I feel there is nothing in the world to compare with the aroma of fresh herbs. Since they are a primary flavoring ingredient in Indian cooking, freshness makes all the difference. Dishes cooked with them are usually more aromatic and flavorful. They have a spring-like bouquet, something always missing in dried herbs.

Basil Leaves *(Tulsi)*

Basil *(tulsi)* is an annual herb of the mint family. The bright leaves have a sharp, biting taste and a distinctly sweet aroma. There are several varieties of basil grown in India. However, three are the most popular: holy basil *(Ocimum sanctum,* known as *Vishnu tulsi),* sweet basil *(Ocimum basilicum,* known as *Biswa tulsi),* and white basil *(Ocimum album,* known as *Ram tulsi).* The three varieties differ in degree of sharpness, holy basil being the sharpest and sweet basil the mellowest; the white basil is somewhere in between. Even though all three can be used interchangeably in Indian cooking and rituals, only sweet basil is available in this country. Some specialty grocery stores do carry dried holy basil, but it is not suitable for use in cooking because basil leaves lose much of their fragrance and bite when dry. Therefore, this herb must be used in its fresh green form. Sweet basil leaves are available at greengrocers' in the summer months.

You can have your own fresh supply always available by growing it at home. Basil is easy to pot. Just cover the seeds (available from nurseries) lightly with soil, and they will be ready to snip in six to eight weeks. In the spring the already potted plants are also available from nurseries.

Basil is one of the oldest herbs known to mankind and different superstitions are associated with it around the world. In India, Hindus have grown and revered basil as a holy plant since Vedic times. Even today, a pot of growing basil is employed in the daily rituals of many Indian homes. Because of the sacred association of basil with the Hindu God Vishnu, the use of this herb in Indian cooking has been severely limited. However, in many Indian homes a delicious brew of basil leaves, shredded ginger, and honey, known as *Tulsi ki Chah,* is served during the winter.

Coriander Leaves *(Hara Dhania)*

Coriander leaves, or *Hara* (green) *Dhania,* come from the same plant *(Coriandrum sativum)* as coriander seeds, but even so, they cannot be used interchangeably. Coriander leaves are available as "cilantro" in Spanish, Mexican, and Portuguese stores, "Chinese parsley" in Chinese and Japanese stores, and "coriander" in Indian and some specialty grocers. Coriander leaves somewhat resemble Italian flat parsley, except that coriander leaves are thinner, lighter green in color, and very fragrant.

Coriander is easy to pot. Just cover the seeds lightly with soil, and the shoots will be mature in six to eight weeks. As you keep snipping, they keep growing.

In the event that you live far from a market where fresh coriander leaves are available and making a trip just for a few sprigs is impractical, I advise you to buy them in large one-pound bunches and store them in the refrigerator. To store, be sure to buy a bunch with the roots still intact. Sometimes the bunch is tied with a cord; this should be carefully removed so that the stems are not damaged. Then wet a couple of paper towels, or a piece of cheesecloth of about the same size, and wrap the towels or cheesecloth around the roots, enclosing them completely. Place the bunch roots down in a large plastic bag. Tie a cord or rubber band around the bag to enclose the wrapped section. This will ensure the retention of moisture in the roots. Place the entire bag in the refrigerator and keep snipping the coriander leaves as you need them. Stored this way, they will keep for eight to ten weeks.

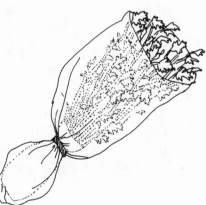

Coriander leaves can also be frozen successfully, which is particularly welcome when coriander is out of season. To store coriander in the freezer, first cut off the roots, then remove the cord. Wash the coriander thoroughly, and coarsely chop the leaves and tender stems. Pack the chopped leaves tightly into a measuring cup. For each cup of coriander add ¼ cup of water. Place the mixture in batches in a food processor with steel blade attached, or in the jar of an electric blender, and process until it is reduced to a coarse puree (you may need to add additional water if chopping in a blender). Spoon the puree into an ice cube tray and freeze. When frozen, transfer the cubes to a plastic bag and seal it tightly. Defrost the cubes as needed. A standard-sized cube of chopped coriander is equal to about 2 tablespoons of chopped coriander leaves. The defrosted coriander may be folded into a dish such as Mint Coriander Dip (*Dhania-Podina Chutney*, p. 437) or it may be dribbled onto a dish as a garnish, just before serving.

Both coriander leaves and stems (the tender part only) are chopped and used as garnish. In addition to their decorative effect, the leaves lend a very distinct flavor to a dish. If you find it hard to acquire a taste for coriander leaves, the world is not going to come to an end. Just omit this herb or substitute parsley, but remember that the taste of the dish will be altered. There is no real substitute for coriander leaves.

Garlic (*Lassan*)

Garlic is the edible bulb of the garlic plant (*Allium sativum*), native to India and other Central Asian countries but widely cultivated around the world. There isn't much I need to say to introduce garlic, as most people have used it at one time or another. The garlic bulb, composed of segments called garlic "cloves," has a strong, pungent aroma and a sharp, hot taste. In Indian cooking only the fresh garlic clove is used; it is peeled, and either finely chopped or ground to a paste. In the event that fresh garlic is not available, freeze-dried garlic flakes may be substituted—2 tablespoons of garlic flakes are equivalent to 1 tablespoon of finely chopped fresh garlic. However, the flakes must be soaked in hot water (they will soak up about 1 tablespoon water for each tablespoon of garlic flakes) for 15 minutes before using; otherwise they will burn almost instantly when added to hot oil and fried. Garlic powder and garlic salt each has a chemistry of its own quite different from that of fresh garlic, and therefore cannot be substituted.

Garlic keeps well when stored in an open jar on the kitchen counter, provided the kitchen is not too warm and dry and there is sufficient air circulation. If your kitchen is too warm, you will be better off keeping the garlic in the refrigerator, loosely wrapped in a plastic bag; otherwise it will dry out in a week to ten days. Ground garlic or chopped garlic can be successfully frozen when sealed in an airtight plastic bag, but must be thawed completely before use. Once defrosted, it cannot be refrozen, so freeze in small portions according to your needs.

In Indian cooking, garlic plays an important role. It is one of the three major seasonings (fresh ginger root and onion being the others) used in making the base for Moghul sauces.

Ginger Root, Fresh *(Adrak)*

Fresh ginger root is the pungent aromatic rhizome of the tropical plant *Zingiber officinale*. Dug up, washed, and scraped, it is sold as fresh ginger root. It is available in Indian, Chinese, and Japanese grocery stores; some supermarket chains also carry it. In Indian cooking the fresh ginger root is first peeled and then either shredded or ground to a paste (one may also finely chop it or grate it) before use. If fresh ginger is unavailable, dry ginger powder may be substituted—1 teaspoon of dry ginger powder is equivalent to 1 tablespoon of finely chopped fresh ginger root. The powder should be added to the dish with other dry spices. Crystalized ginger and candied ginger are completely different products and cannot be used as substitutes.

To store fresh ginger root, follow the instructions given for garlic above.

To grow ginger at home, place a fresh piece of ginger root, at least 2 inches long, into a pot filled with slightly moistened sandy soil, such as cactus soil. The root will begin to grow after four to five weeks, but it will reach maturity only after a full year. Whenever you need ginger, just dig up the root and break off a small portion. The root will keep growing in the soil.

Fresh ginger is one of the three major seasonings (garlic and onion being the others) that form the base of most sauces in North Indian cooking. In addition to flavoring and lending a hot taste to the dish, it also acts as a thickener. Actually, fresh ginger root is valued much more than garlic or onion because of its extensive use in Indian vegetarian cooking; garlic and onion are more commonly associated with nonvegetarian cooking. This is particularly true among the Jain and Hindu Brahmins, whose extensive vegetarian repertoire rarely includes onion and totally omits garlic. (See Cauliflower, Green Peas and Potatoes in Spicy Herb Sauce [*Gobhi Matar Rasedar*], p. 256.)

Green Chili *(Hari Mirch)*

Green chili *(Hari Mirch)* is the young pod of the pepper plant *Capsicum*. It comes in a wide range of strengths, from very mild to devilishly hot. The smaller the size of the pod, the more ferocious it is. You should keep away from the very small ones or use them with caution. Green chilies, I have discovered, get hotter near the stem end, i.e., the portion with the seeds. I personally prefer the medium-to-large size; I slit it open with a sharp knife and scrape out the seeds—the hottest part of the pepper; this way I can use a considerable quantity of the pod for flavor without making the dish too hot. If you like a hotter taste, leave the seeds in. Green chilies are available in Indian, Chinese, Spanish, and Mexican grocery stores. Some specialty grocers and supermarket chains also carry them. Green chilies keep well in the refrigerator for three to four weeks, wrapped loosely in a plastic bag.

Green chili is used primarily in preparing vegetables, lentils, dips, and relishes. It is sometimes used in place of red pepper in other dishes. In Rajasthan, a western region in India, the mildly hot green chilies are turned into a mouthwatering delicacy called *Mirchi ki Bhaji* by cooking them in butter with tomatoes, molasses, and spices. The large variety of chili is slit, stuffed with roasted spices, and pickled in mustard oil to make a pickle called *Mirch ka Achar*, an all-time favorite of the North Indians. This pickle is eaten with griddle-fried Whole Wheat Flaky Bread *(Paratha*, p. 402) and a lump of freshly churned butter. (Chili Pickle is widely available in Indian grocery stores.)

Kari Leaves *(Meethe Neam ke Patte)*

Kari leaves, known as *Meethe Neam ke Patte,* come from the kari plant *(Murraya koenigii),* native to South India and Sri Lanka. The bright green leaves of this tall plant, which grows to a height of six or seven feet, are full of fragrance. The leaves have a bitterish taste and a sweetish, pungent aroma almost like lemon grass. These leaves are used in southern and south-western cooking in the same way coriander leaves are used in the North. They are essential to these regional styles, lending the dishes the characteristic southern flavor. Fresh kari leaves are not yet available in the United States. However, most Indian grocery stores carry the dried variety, which works quite well.

Mint Leaves *(Podina)*

Spearmint *(Mentha spicata)* is an annual herb of the mint family that is native to Europe and the Mediterranean but is now grown in countries around the world, including India. Mint has deep green leaves, reddish-brown stems, and a very appealing taste and aroma. Because mint is an essential herb in North Indian cooking, it is cultivated year round in India; dried mint leaves are unheard of. In the United States, however, fresh mint has limited uses—mainly in teas and drinks—and therefore is hard to find. Some greengrocers carry mint in every season but winter, but the price varies widely. Mint, also known as garden mint, grows wild on the lawns and in the gardens of many homes during the summer months. Those who do not have a backyard can easily grow this herb in a pot on the windowsill. Just plant a cutting 3 to 4 inches into the soil in a pot, and it will grow and spread into a bush ready for snipping in about eight weeks.

Green mint leaves keep well in the refrigerator for five to seven days, wrapped loosely in a plastic bag. To freeze mint leaves, follow the instructions for freezing coriander leaves on page 28, but discard stems and use the leaves only. If fresh mint leaves are not available, dried leaves may be substituted in a recipe. They are available in Middle Eastern, Indian, and some specialty stores.

Mint is used primarily to make relishes (*chutney*) such as Fresh Mint Relish (*Podina Chutney*, p. 436), and cold appetizers such as Cold Minted Potatoes (*Aloo Podina Chat*, p. 103). It is also used in some exceptional lamb preparations, such as Kabob Patties Laced with Ginger and Mint (*Shamme Kabab*, p. 109). Mint has traditionally been preferred over all other herbs to lace pilafs in Moghul cooking, as in the Emperor's Layered Meat and Fragrant Rice Casserole (*Shah Jahani Biriyani*, p. 192) and the famous Mint Pilaf (*Hari Chutney ka Pullao*, p. 377) from the Andra Pradesh, a province in the south.

Onion, Scallion, and Shallot (*Piaz, Hara Piaz, aur Chota Piaz*)

Not much need be said to introduce the onion, the bulbous root of the onion plant *Allium cepa*, belonging to the lily family and used in one form or another around the world. Onion is the most important of the three ingredients (garlic and ginger root being the others) that form the basis of most dishes of North Indian origin. Onions are added to virtually every dish and are also pickled or eaten raw as a relish called *Kachoomar* (p. 432) or *Kache Piaz* (p. 431). *A word of caution:* Onions available in the United States differ from those available in India. Because the Indian climate is warmer, the onion grown there is pungent and less juicy. This is a crucial difference, because Indian recipes specify that onions should be ground to a paste before frying. This is impossible to do with American onions; they become a puree or watery sauce in the process.

Therefore, always finely chop the onions or slice them into thin shreds (never mash) before frying, so that you do not destroy the fibers that contain the moisture. A second point to note is that Indians, particularly northerners, eat raw onions—the pungent ones—with great relish. This is something most Americans would find hard to do, not because the onions are any sharper (on the contrary, American onions are milder and less pungent) but simply because eating onions takes a little learning. Therefore, until you get used to the strong flavor of raw onions, I recommend using large Spanish onions or red Burmuda onions, which are sweet, juicy, and mild, in relishes and cold appetizers. Once you are comfortable with them, you can graduate to the common supermarket variety.

Scallion, also known as green onion, is the young sprout that appears before the onion bulb begins to mature. Shallot, the bulbous root of the plant *Allium ascalonicum*, also belonging to the lily family, is a variety of onion that has a slightly garlicky taste. Shallots are available at greengrocers and some supermarket chains. In North Indian cooking scallions and shallots are virtually unheard of, but in the other regions they hold high places in the culinary world. They are used not only as flavorings, but are cooked as vegetables in such dishes as Cauliflower and Scallions with Black Mustard Seeds (*Gobhi Kari*, p. 301). Shallot is particularly savored by those vegetarians who are forbidden to eat garlic. The southern vegetable-and-lentil stew called *Sambaar*, made with shallots as the only vegetable, is considered a delicacy around the entire country of India.

Special Ingredients

Spice Blends   *(Masala)*
Cooking Fats and Oils   *(Ghee aur Tel)*
Meat Broth   *(Yakhni)*
Vegetable Broth
Coconut   *(Narial)*
Milk and Milk Products   *(Doodh aur Oske Op-phul)*
Flower Essences   *(Ruh)*
Silver Foil   *(Vark)*

Spice Blends

(Masala)

Literally translated, *masala* means a blend of several aromatic spices. *Masala* is usually added to a dish to lend it the distinct flavor characteristic of that dish or of a regional style of cooking. In Indian homes *masala* sometimes refers to a "wet" blend of spices, i.e., spice paste, which is made by grinding herbs and seasonings along with the spices.

The most important of all spice blends is the *garam* (warm or hot) *masala*. It is not just important—it is absolutely essential to most North Indian preparations (its counterparts are *sambaar podi* in the South, and *punch phoron* in the East). *Garam masala* is usually added to a dish at the end, just before serving, to enhance the flavors of the other ingredients. There are, however, recipes that do call for it to be added at the beginning or during cooking. Even though many dishes contain *garam masala*, the additions of extra herbs and ingredients to one's own classic blend and the way one incorporates it into each dish transform the food and make it the distinctly special creation of the individual cook.

There are two types of *garam masala* used in classic Indian cooking. One is the traditional *garam masala*, a blend of four spices—cardamom, cinnamon, cloves, and black peppers (sometimes a little nutmeg is added). This blend of subtle spices has come to be known as *Mughal garam masala*. It is the hallmark of classic Indian cooking, which originated in the North, in the courts and palaces of the great Moghul emperors. *Mughal garam masala* is used in making the classic Moghul dishes Royal Braised Lamb with Fragrant Spices (*Shahi Korma*, p. 174) and Royal Roast Leg of Lamb with Saffron Raisin Sauce (*Shahi Raan*, p. 184).

Over the years large quantities of coriander and cumin have been added to the classic blend. The addition of such spices causes the original subtle *Mughal garam masala* to taste sharp and pungent. This spicy version is usually referred to as *garam masala* (or sometimes *Punjabi garam masala*). It is predominantly used in North Indian cooking today, in dishes such as Green Peas and Indian Cheese in Fragrant Tomato Sauce (*Matar Paneer*, p. 266) and Savory Pastries with Spicy Potato Filling (*Aloo Samosa*, p. 125). This blend of *garam masala* is also used in meat, poultry, and seafood preparations that have a reddish-brown spicy sauce, such as Velvet Butter Chicken (*Makhani Murgh*, p. 225), and Beef in Fragrant Spinach Sauce (*Saag Gosht*, p. 179). Some *garam masala* blends also include several other spices, such as cassia, cassia buds, fennel, and bay leaf. This is attributed to the variations introduced by other regional styles of cooking. Commercial blends often include salt, dry ginger, garlic, or other seasonings, and thickening agents such as poppy seeds, which are quite unconventional and unnecessary. They mask the robust and honest tanginess of the spices.

The *Mughal garam masala* is not available commercially whereas the general *garam masala* is. However, since the commercial blend contains several unnecessary ingredients, in addition to being stale and uncooked (the spices are not roasted), I strongly advise that you make your own blends of both kinds and keep them ready before you start Indian cooking. In case you are wondering whether it is worth the bother of making two separate blends, let me assure you the answer is yes. This is because each *garam masala* imparts a distinctly different fragrance and is used for different types of dishes; hence they cannot be used interchangeably.

(*Mughal garam masala* is a subtle, mellow blend with an accent of cardamom. Its primary use is in cream-, milk-, yogurt-, and fruit-sauce-based dishes. The *garam masala,* on the other hand, is a spicy blend with an accent of roasted cumin and coriander. It is particularly suited for onion and tomato-rich gravies.)

As I mentioned earlier, I love food that is full of aroma and flavor but not hot, and so I have reduced the amount of black pepper in both recipes. If you want, you can always add more black pepper separately. This way, each time I sprinkle a little of either *garam masala* in a dish to perk up the flavors (this is especially necessary when reheating frozen food), I do not have to worry about the dish becoming too peppery.

The following two recipes are my personal blends. The *Mughal garam masala* captures, insofar as possible, the fragrance of the original classic blend that once filled the Moghul courts and perfumed their food. The recipe for the general *garam masala* is popular in Punjab and Uttar Pradesh. Both *garam masalas* will keep fresh for three months in airtight covered containers.

Mughal Garam Masala

Makes ¾ cup

½ cup (about 60) black, or ⅓ cup (about 200) green cardamom pods

2 cinnamon sticks, 3 inches long

1 tablespoon whole cloves

1 tablespoon black peppercorns

1½ teaspoons grated nutmeg (optional)

Break open cardamom pods. Remove seeds, and reserve. Discard the skin. Crush cinnamon with a kitchen mallet or rolling pin to break it into small pieces. Combine all the spices except nutmeg, and grind them to a fine powder (follow instructions on page 66). Mix in the grated nutmeg, if desired. Store in an airtight container in a cool place.

Note: The recipe may be cut in half.

Garam Masala

Makes 1½ cups

3 tablespoons (about 20) black,
   or 2 tablespoons (about 75)
   green cardamom pods
3 cinnamon sticks, 3 inches long

1 tablespoon whole cloves
¼ cup black peppercorns
½ cup cumin seeds
½ cup coriander seeds

Break open cardamom pods. Remove seeds, and reserve. Discard the skin. Crush cinnamon with a kitchen mallet or rolling pin to break it into small pieces. Combine all the spices, and roast and grind them (follow instructions on page 66). Store in an airtight container in a cool place.

Note: The recipe may be cut in half.

You may have noticed that the *Mughal garam masala* doesn't require roasting whereas the general *garam masala* does. This is because the *Mughal* blend primarily consists of what are in English known as "dessert spices" or "sweet spices"; these are very aromatic in their natural (raw) forms, and are also very easy to digest.

The other all-purpose spice blend that is very popular in India is *Sambaar podi*. It is used exclusively in South Indian cooking. *Sambaar podi* (powder) is a hot and spicy blend of turmeric, coriander seeds, red and black pepper, fenugreek, cumin seeds, and several varieties of legume. *Sambaar podi* is available in all Indian grocery stores under the label "Sambaar Powder." It is principally used in flavoring vegetable-and-lentil stews such as Spicy Brussels Sprouts, Green Beans, and Lentil Stew (*Chaunk Gobhi aur Sem Sambaar,* p. 276), and in stir-fried vegetable preparations and other delicacies of South India.

You may have noticed that the *sambaar podi* contains mostly "cool" spices. In addition, the proportion of red pepper in this blend is usually very high, so that the dishes flavored with it turn out fairly hot. Since hot food induces perspiration, it is perfectly suited for the hot and humid climate of the South.

There are several other spice blends that are commercially available today, prepackaged mixes of such popular Indian specialties as *Tandoori masala, Kabab masala, Vendaloo masala,* and *Dhansak masala.* These blends contain all the necessary spices, dehydrated herbs, seasonings, thickeners, and so on. If you want to make *Tandoori* chicken, all you need to do is stir the *Tandoori masala* into the yogurt, marinate the chicken in it, and roast the preparation in the oven. It sounds simple and it is, but bear in mind that there is absolutely no comparison between the fresh blend that you make yourself in your own kitchen with your own spices and commercial varieties that might contain inferior ingredients and have been sitting on a store shelf for months.

Finally, a word about curry powder.

"Curry" is the Western pronunciation of the Indian word *kari,* which can mean one of two things: the sweet aromatic leaves of the kari plant (*meethe neam ke patte,* p. 32) used in southern and southwestern Indian regional cooking, or the southern cooking technique of preparing stir-fried vegetables such as Green Beans with Coconut and Black Mustard Seeds (*Beans Kari,* p. 307). The spice blend used for making kari dishes is called *kari podi* (powder) or curry powder. The South Indian variety is a mixture of several spices varying from one local region to another, but the classic blend essentially contains the following: turmeric, red pepper, coriander, black pepper, cumin, fenugreek, kari leaves, mustard seeds, and (sometimes) cinnamon and cloves—all of which are roasted and ground to a powder.

The earliest British merchants, who arrived with the East India Trading Company, worked and settled along the southeastern coast of India. It is more than likely that they wanted to take back with them to England the familiar aromas, flavors, and colors of the Indian food they had become so passionately fond of. But not having mastered the different Indian cooking techniques or a sense of the spice blends, they in all likelihood just indiscriminately sprinkled *kari podi* over stews and casseroles. This yielded preparations with the familiar golden color, hot taste, and flavor of the dishes known as "curries."

As the British presence spread to the North and East of India, several new spices found their way into the simple *kari podi*. However, the name of the blend, as well as the dishes which contained it, remained the same.

Among the English-speaking Indian middle class, the word "curry" became so popular that in due course a simple everyday dish called *salan* (spicy thin gravy) was renamed *kari*. As a result, chicken in spice gravy, which for centuries was known as *Murghi ka Salan*, came to be called Chicken Kari (or Curry), and shrimp in spicy gravy, known as *Jheenga ka Salan*, became Prawn Kari. In North Indian cooking, no real equivalent to the Western or English curry powder (or, for that matter, any dish known as a curry) exists.

Mind you, the Indian *kari* bears no resemblance whatsoever to the English curry, which is made without using Indian cooking techniques and with packaged curry powder. The other points of difference are that *salan* dishes often contain cardamom, an essential Indian spice that is never found in curry powder—probably because cardamom is not used in the cooking of savory dishes in the South. Also, curry powder contains fenugreek, mustard seeds, and turmeric—the first two never and the third seldom found in the spice blends for *salan* dishes. Finally, the spices for these karis (or *salan*) are mixed individually, with the same judicious care that is taken for any other Indian dish. Today, the name *kari* has totally replaced the name *salan* in all of India and is applied to dishes with a wide variety of ingredients.

Cooking Fats and Oils

(Ghee aur Tel)

The two basic fats used in Indian cooking are butter, known as *usli ghee* (*ghee* means fat; *usli* means pure, but in everyday Indian usage the word *usli* refers to butter), and vegetable shortening, known as *vanaspati* (vegetable) *ghee*. There are several different kinds of vegetable oils *(tel)* used in Indian cooking, the popular ones being sesame, peanut, mustard, coconut, corn, and sunflower. Butter and shortening are generally used for all-purpose cooking. Oils are reserved for frying, deep frying, and pickling. Animal fats, such as lard and suet, are *never* used as a cooking medium in India because of the religious convictions of the Hindus and Moslems. They are also unacceptable to vegetarians since they are considered a meat product.

You may wonder how a vegetarian can consider lard and suet meat products and yet accept butter, which is also an animal fat. The explanation is very simple. The vegetarians believe in and practice *A-himsa* (*A* means no; *himsa* means violence), which forbids the killing of a living creature. To obtain lard or suet, the life of an animal has to be taken. So the vegetarians abstain from eating it just as they do the animal's flesh. Butter, on the other hand, is the gift of the animal, or of nature. To obtain it the animal does not have to be killed. On the same principle, several vegetarians have recently started including unfertilized chickens' eggs (known as vegetarian eggs in India) in their diet, since they contain no life and are therefore a vegetarian product.

Until recently, *usli ghee* was the only cooking medium used in North India. But as the price of butter has skyrocketed, shortening and oils have replaced it.

Indian vegetable shortening, or *vanaspati ghee*, unlike the chalk-white, neutral-tasting American equivalent, has a light lemon color, grainy texture, and a faint nutty-lemon aroma. It is almost identical in appearance and flavor to *usli ghee*. Indians have used *usli ghee* for centuries and would never accept a substitute unless it reproduced the good taste of butter as closely as possible. Therefore, Indian vegetable shortening, a product of highly saturated oils such as coconut, cottonseed, rapeseed, and palm, is not only hydrogenated, but is also specially processed to look, smell, and taste almost like its rival—*usli ghee*. Those accustomed to its flavor prefer it to *usli ghee*.

In the last decade in India, just as in Western countries, there has been a growing awareness of the possible harm in consuming excessive quantities of highly saturated fats (which includes both butter and shortening). As a result, many Indians today who find that food cooked with fat is too rich, heavy, and difficult to digest have substituted unsaturated oils for saturated fats in much of their cooking. There still exists a segment of the population that feels otherwise. The vegetarians, which include Hindu Brahmins, Jains, and Buddhists, and the people from Kashmir (both Brahmins and Moslems) do not like substitutes. For vegetarians, *usli ghee* is the primary source of nutrition. The Brahmins consider it brain food with supernatural powers, and attribute the development of one's intelligence to it. Even today, young Hindu children, particularly males, are given a spoonful of *usli ghee* every day to sharpen their intelligence. The old Brahmin ritual of feeding a newborn infant a spoonful of *usli ghee* within minutes of his birth is still followed by all Indians. Kashmiri cooking, known for its delicate preparations and haunting flavors, uses *usli ghee* as one of its chief ingredients.

Many parts of India have used oil in general cooking for centuries, except for flavoring legumes and desserts. In the southern and southwestern regions, many foods are traditionally cooked in sesame or coconut oil, and mustard oil is used in the central and eastern regions of India.

I personally prefer to use such light vegetable oils as sunflower and soybean for most of my cooking, because they are easy to digest and impart a mellow taste—they do not subdue or overwhelm the subtle flavors of herbs and spices. There are, however, a few Moghul and Kashmiri dishes where *usli ghee* is one of the primary flavoring elements and for these dishes nothing but *usli ghee* should be used. I make a special mention in the recipe when such a situation arises. I am also particularly fond of Indian vegetable shortening, especially for vegetarian main dishes and bread preparations in which it acts as one of the ingredients rather than just as a cooking fat. For deep frying, I use peanut or corn oil because they withstand heat well without burning (the boiling temperature of these two oils is high). To bring out authentic flavors in regional specialties, I like to use the oils popular in those regions, for example, light sesame oil in *Sambaar* (p. 276) from the South, and mustard oil in *Vendaloo* (p. 199) from Goa in the Southwest.

Usli (butter) *ghee,* and *vanaspati* (vegetable) *ghee,* and different *tel* (oil) are available in Indian grocery stores. For those who would like to make *usli ghee* at home, see instructions under "Milk and Milk Products" on page 50.

Meat Broth

(Yakhni)

The highly aromatic broth used in the cooking of Indian dishes plays an important role in the creation of captivating flavors. The meat broth *yakhni* is made by simmering meat and chicken parts and a few vegetables with several fragrant spices and seasonings. It is used primarily in making pilafs, and enriching sauces for meat and poultry dishes. The practice of using meat broth is common among the Moslems, especially in the region of Kashmir, where a robust broth is almost essential to several of the regional specialties. In other parts of India, a cook may simply add a few meaty bones or some boned meat directly to a dish during cooking rather than preparing a meat broth.

Meat broth is extremely simple to make. It is not essential to make it only when you have a quantity of fresh bones on hand. The bones can be kept frozen until you have the time and the inclination to make the broth. The broth itself may be kept indefinitely in the refrigerator, provided it is boiled for five minutes every four days, or it may be stored in the freezer.

Meat Broth

(Yakhni)

Makes 1½ quarts

2 to 3 pounds lamb bones or chicken parts, or a combination of them, cut into 2-inch or 3-inch pieces
1 small unpeeled onion, quartered
1 large unpeeled garlic clove, crushed
1 slice fresh ginger root, ¼ inch thick

1 cinnamon stick, 3 inches long
8 whole cloves
½ teaspoon black peppercorns
1 bay leaf
1 teaspoon Kosher salt

(continued)

Place all of the ingredients in a 3-quart stockpot or any deep saucepan with a lid. Add enough cold water to cover the bones by at least one inch. Bring to a boil over medium heat. Lower heat so that the liquid is barely simmering, and for the next 5 minutes, skim off the scum that rises to the surface. Then cover the pot partially with the lid and let simmer for at least 2 hours, preferably 4. Keep adding boiling water as the liquid in the pot evaporates so that the bones are fully immersed throughout cooking. When cool, strain the broth through several layers of cheesecloth into a container and refrigerate for 2 hours, or until the fat on the surface solidifies. Scoop off the fat, leaving perhaps a teaspoon, and check broth for taste. If desired, add more salt.

Note: Cooks around the world will agree that one can never oversimmer a broth; the longer the simmering, the richer the broth. That's why in restaurants, broth is left to simmer overnight. Two hours of simmering I have found to be the bare minimum required to produce a rich and flavorful broth. An additional two hours of simmering, as well as enriching the broth further, mellows the flavors of the spices and blends them with the flavor of the meat.

Vegetable Broth

Vegetable broth, commonly used by vegetarians, evolved mainly as a base for the vegetarian counterparts of the famous Indian meat and poultry preparations. For example, vegetarian Mulligatawny Soup (p. 143), which has the same ingredients as the classic preparation except for the broth, is just as interesting in taste. The vegetable broth contains the same ingredients as the meat broth except that additional spices and vegetables are added to replace the bones.

Vegetable Broth

(Akhni)

Makes 1½ quarts

3 tablespoons *usli ghee* or light
  vegetable oil
2 small unpeeled onions,
  quartered
1 carrot, cut into 1-inch slices
1 large unpeeled garlic clove,
  crushed
1 slice fresh ginger root, ¼ inch
  thick

1 teaspoon cumin seeds
2 teaspoons coriander seeds
1 cinnamon stick, 3 inches long
3 black (or 6 green) cardamom
  pods
8 whole cloves
1 teaspoon black peppercorns
1 teaspoon Kosher salt

Heat butter or oil in a 3-quart stockpot or deep saucepan, and add all other ingredients. Fry the vegetables and spices over medium heat for 10 minutes, or until the onions are wilted and begin to brown. Add 2 quarts (8 cups) of cold water and bring to a boil. Lower heat, cover the pot partially with the lid, and let simmer for at least 1 hour, preferably 2. When cool, strain the broth through a double layer of cheesecloth into a container, and refrigerate or freeze as described under meat broth.

Coconut

(Narial)

Coconut, the fruit of the coconut palm tree *(Cocos nucifera)*, growing along the coastal regions of many parts of India, is available year-round at greengrocers' and some supermarket chains. The edible white meat is enclosed in a hard, brown, husky shell.

Buying a coconut: Care must be taken when you select a coconut for freshness because, externally, fresh and stale ones look alike. A fresh coconut is usually heavy because of the liquid inside it. This may be checked by shaking it. Also, the shell should not have cracks, because they expose the meat inside and cause it to rot.

Opening a coconut: To get to the meat of the coconut, you must first crack the outer shell. The common way to do this is to whack the coconut with a cleaver or a hammer until the shell cracks open, then scoop out the meat with a curved knife. This procedure is tricky and can be dangerous. It should be done only by those who are veterans at coconut cracking. I suggest you follow this simple and safe technique:

Preheat oven to 375°F. Pierce the "eyes" of the coconut with a knife or a sharp pointed object such as an ice pick or skewer, and drain off the liquid. Taste the liquid—it should be sweet-tasting and pleasant-smelling. (It is a favorite drink of Indian children.) If it tastes sour and smells oily, the coconut is rotten. Place the coconut in the oven for 25 minutes or until the shell cracks. Remove the coconut from the oven and tap it all around with a kitchen mallet or hammer to release the meat from the shell. Then give it a hard whack to crack open the shell. The white meat with its brown skin should fall away from the shell. If it doesn't, use a sharp knife to release the meat.

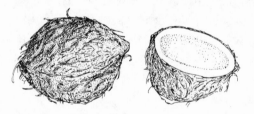

Grating a coconut: Peel the brown skin off the coconut meat. Cut the meat into 1-inch pieces. Grate the coconut, about one cup at a time, in a blender or food processor, or simply use a hand grater. An average-sized coconut will yield about 3 cups of tightly packed grated coconut.

The dry, grated, unsweetened coconut that is widely available in plastic bags in supermarkets can be substituted in an emergency, but remember that it will not be as delicate, moist, and aromatic as freshly grated coconut.

Making coconut milk: To each cup of tightly packed coconut, add

1 cup of boiling water (or milk if you want it richer). Cover and soak for half an hour. Pour the coconut pulp, along with the water it's soaking in, about 3 cups at a time, into the container of an electric blender or food processor and puree for 1 minute. (This will extract every speck of juice from the coconut pulp, thus making the coconut milk much richer and more flavorful.) Strain the liquid through a double layer of cheesecloth, squeezing the pulp as much as possible. (In India, to economize, this process is repeated, over and over with each new batch yielding thinner, less aromatic milk. The different batches of milk are then mixed together and used in cooking.) An average-sized coconut will yield about 3 cups of coconut milk.

The use of coconut is more extensive along the coastal regions of India where coconut trees grow. In the South where there is a lack of cow's (or buffalo's) milk, coconut milk is used as a substitute in general cooking as well as in desserts and sweetmeats. One of the delicacies from the coastal area of Malabar is prawns simmered in fragrant coconut-milk sauce laced with fresh herbs called *Yerra Moolee* (p. 243). In the North it is used in certain famous lamb dishes, pilafs, and to make relishes, the most famous of which is Coconut Relish (*Narial Chutney*, p. 438). It is also used in the preparation of the delectable Coconut Fudge (*Narial Barfi*, p. 476).

Milk and Milk Products

(Dooth aur Oske Op-phul)

Of all the wonderful gifts of nature, there is none more important or more sacred to an Indian than cow's (or buffalo's) milk. The ancient Vedic literature lists milk and clarified butter as the principal foods of an Aryan. In a country of 675 million people, where more than half are vegetarians, milk and milk products comprise the chief source of protein and energy. The five main products of milk are yogurt (*dahi*), Indian clarified butter (*usli ghee*), Indian cheese (*chenna or paneer*), thickened milk sauce (*rabadi*), and milk fudge (*khoya*). Although these products are all derived from the same source, their flavors, textures, and uses are distinctly different.

Milk is often drunk straight in India, but not the way it is in the United States. Indians always drink milk warm and sweetened with a little sugar or honey. Milk is frequently used in cooking vegetables, *dal*, and meat, and in making puddings, desserts, and sweetmeats.

Yogurt

(Dahi)

Yogurt is indispensable to Indian cooking. It is a staple, especially among India's hundreds of millions of vegetarians. In Indian households, yogurt is made every day with fresh milk purchased in the morning. Only when one runs out of the homemade supply does one buy the commercially made yogurt from the local pastry shop.

To describe the multitude of ingenious ways yogurt is used in Indian cooking would take volumes, but this brief list points out some of the important uses: it is used in making yogurt salads (*Raita*, p. 341) and yogurt drinks, including *Lassi* (p. 488), as a meat tenderizer, thickening agent, souring agent, and flavor enhancer. It is added to special pilafs, such as Chicken Pilaf (*Murgh Biriyani*, p. 228), and to various relishes and dips, including Mint Coriander Dip (*Dhania-Podina Chutney*, p. 437). It is used in preparing seasoned gravies for lentils and vegetables and subtle sauces for fish and shellfish. Mixed with peas, it is turned into delicate dumplings (*Kadhi*, p. 284); mixed with dried fruits and honey, it makes delicious desserts, such as *Srikhand* from the Maharashtra-Gujrat area.

Yogurt is available in almost any supermarket. You need to note the crucial difference between the commercial and the homemade varieties. The yogurt used in India is made with buffalo's milk, which is richer than cow's milk because of the full fat content. Indian yogurt is therefore thick, sweet, and rich-tasting. Some supermarket chains carry a special brand of yogurt made with whole milk. This is often unsuitable for Indian cooking because of its tanginess and tartness. The common commercially available yogurt, on the other hand, is made with low-fat or skimmed milk and is thin and watery. It lacks the creamy consistency of whole-milk yogurt and, as a result, Indian sauces made with it do not have enough body and flavor. I have come up with a minor modification: a mixture that is ¾ yogurt and ¼ sour cream.

Or you may prefer to make your own full-fat yogurt as I do. This way I have total control over its quality and freshness. Yogurt is very simple to make—all you need is a thermometer to measure the temperature of the milk, some whole milk, and some plain yogurt (if you are making yogurt for the first time, you will have to buy a small container of commercial plain yogurt) to use as a starter. Once you have made your own yogurt, you can use a bit of your first batch as a starter. Always save a few tablespoons to make the next batch. The quality of the first starter is clearly crucial, since it will eventually control the quality of all your future batches. Therefore, take particular care while buying the plain yogurt. Read the expiration date on the container to make sure you are buying the freshest yogurt possible. Also, when you've brought it home, taste and smell it to make sure that it is sweet, or you may end up with an entire batch of sour yogurt.

Yogurt can be made at home, using any commercially available yogurt maker and following the manufacturer's directions. It is not essential, however, to have a yogurt maker; you can make it as described below.

Making yogurt: Bring 1 quart of milk to a boil in a heavy-bottomed 3-quart pan, stirring constantly to prevent a skin from forming on the surface. Let it cool to a warm temperature. (About 115° to 130°F is the ideal temperature range for the yogurt culture to germinate. If the milk is less warm, the yogurt will set but it will take much longer, allowing time for the yogurt to turn sour. If, on the other hand, the milk is too hot, it will kill the yogurt culture altogether.) If a skin forms on the surface, carefully remove it with a spoon. Add 2 tablespoons of plain yogurt; stir well with the same spoon and transfer it to a 2-quart bowl. Cover the bowl loosely with a piece of cheesecloth or a kitchen towel and set it in a warm place that is at least 80°F but not more than 115°F. An oven with a pilot light is a good place. Or wrap the bowl in a large terry towel and put it in an insulated food cooler. (If the temperature is too low the yogurt will not set. On the other hand, if the temperature is too high the milk will turn sour before the yogurt is set.) It will take anywhere from 10 to 16 hours for the milk to thicken into yogurt, depending upon the surrounding temperature. Once it thickens, transfer it to the refrigerator. The longer you let the yogurt stand, the thicker and more tart it will be. For some reason yogurt made in unglazed clay pots (available only in India) has the best texture and also picks up the earthy aroma that Indians love. However, yogurt can be made in any glass, china, Pyrex, stainless steel, or enamel-coated bowl, or in a commercial yogurt-maker. Yogurt keeps well for several days in the refrigerator but tends to get tangy and sour with time. That's why yogurt should always be tasted before use. For best results, yogurt should be used within 72 hours of making it. After that time it begins to lose much of its lovely unique flavor.

Indian Clarified Butter

(Usli Ghee)

Usli ghee is made by separating the clear butterfat from the milk solids and moisture. Even though *usli ghee* is referred to as clarified butter, it is quite different from the French version. The French clarified butter is made by melting fresh butter, then straining the clear butter off from the milk residue that has settled at the bottom of the pot. *Usli ghee* is also begun by melting fresh butter, but it is then kept at a simmer for a long time, to allow the moisture present in the milk solids to evaporate. This process gives it its characteristic nutty aroma. Sometimes coriander, kari, or basil leaves are added at the end to further perfume the *ghee*. *Usli ghee* is a popular cooking medium in India. In addition it is used to light holy lamps in temples and homes and as an offering to the fire *(Agni)* during religious ceremonies invoking the gods.

Making Indian clarified butter: In a heavy-bottomed 3-quart saucepan heat 1 pound of sweet butter (preferably cut into tiny pieces) over low heat—it should not sizzle—until it melts completely. This will take anywhere from 5 to 15 minutes, depending upon the size of butter pieces. Increase heat to medium. A thin layer of white foam will form on the top and the butter will begin to crackle as moisture is released from the milk solids. Let it simmer, crackling, for about 10 minutes. It is not necessary to stir during this period. The crackling will gradually stop and the foam will subside, indicating that there is no more moisture left in the milk solids. From this point on it must be watched carefully and stirred constantly, because the foam will once again cover the liquid, making it difficult to see the butter fat as it is browning. As soon as the solids turn brown (push aside the foam to see), turn off the heat and let the brown residue settle to the bottom. When the melted

1. Butter covered with foam

2. Foam subsiding

3. Moisture-free butter
   covered with white foam

4. *Usli ghee* separating
   from brown residue

butter is cool enough to handle, pour the clear liquid into a jar, taking care that none of the residue gets in, or strain it through a double layer of cheesecloth. Let it cool completely; then cover the jar tightly. To ensure freshness, *usli ghee* should be kept in the refrigerator. *Usli ghee* keeps well on a kitchen counter for 4 to 6 weeks, provided the temperature in the kitchen is not more than 75°F; in the refrigerator for 4 months; and indefinitely in the freezer. One pound of butter will yield about 1½ cups of *usli ghee*.

Indian Cheese

(Chenna ya Paneer)

Homemade Indian cheese is similar to commercially available pot cheese or Italian ricotta, except that the curd is much drier. Indian cheese is one of the primary sources of protein among Buddhists and Jain and Hindu Brahmins, who follow the principles of nonviolence and adhere to a strict vegetarian diet. It is used extensively in cooking throughout India, except in the South where cow's milk is scarce.

Indian cheese in curd form is called *chenna;* when *chenna* is compressed into a cake and cut into small rectangular pieces, it is called *paneer*. *Chenna* is the basis for many of the famous desserts from Bengal, an eastern region of India. It is used in making the famous dessert Cheese Dumplings in Pistachio-Flecked Cream Sauce (*Ras Malai*, p. 465). *Paneer* is used in the preparation of many savory dishes, such as Green Peas and Indian Cheese in Fragrant Tomato Sauce (*Matar Paneer*, p. 266). Indian cheese is not available commercially, but you can easily make it in your own home.

Making Indian cheese: Bring 8 cups of milk to a boil in a deep heavy-bottomed 3- or 4-quart saucepan or casserole, stirring often to prevent sticking. Reduce heat and add one of the following starters: 4 tablespoons lemon juice, or 3 tablespoons cider vinegar mixed with 3 tablespoons water, or one cup (8 ounces) plain yogurt. (I tend to use lemon juice more often than the other starters because I have found the curd produced is much softer and delicate.) Stir gently until the white curd forms and separates from the greenish-yellow whey (about 10 seconds if you are using lemon juice or vinegar and 30 seconds to a minute if you are using plain yogurt). Once the curd begins to form, the contents of the pot should be stirred very slowly and gently, as though stroking it, so that the freshly formed fragile curds do not disintegrate into small pieces. The curd should be in lumps. Immediately turn off the heat. Pour the cheese and whey through a colander or large sieve, lined with a thin fabric or four layers of cheesecloth and placed in the kitchen sink. (If you intend to make the cheese again within 24 hours, save the whey to add to the next batch of boiling milk instead of using lemon juice, vinegar, or yogurt; cheese made with whey has a softer curd and a more authentically Indian aroma. This is what the pastry shops in India use as a starter, day after day.) Hold the colander or sieve under the tap and let cold water run, at a medium flow, through the curds in the cheesecloth for 10 seconds—to wash away whatever remains of the smell of lemon juice, vinegar, or yogurt. Bring up the four corners of the cheesecloth and tie them together. Gently twist to extract as much water as possible, and hang the cheese to drain for 1½ hours (a good spot is the door handle on a kitchen cabinet directly over the sink).

1. Curds forming and
   separating from whey

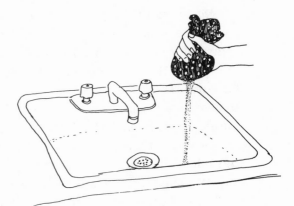

2. Squeezing water from cheese

(continued)

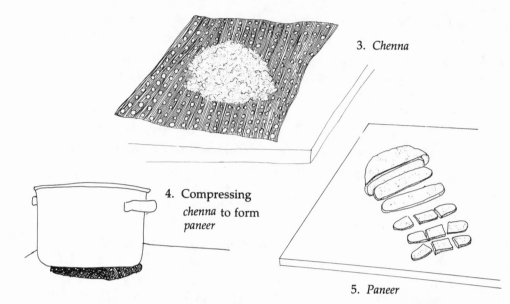

3. *Chenna*

4. Compressing *chenna* to form *paneer*

5. *Paneer*

This drained, crumbly, slightly moist cheese is *chenna*. To make the cheese into cakes *(paneer)*, set the cheese—still in the cheesecloth—on a clean flat surface and place a weight (such as a large pot filled with water) on it for half an hour. Remove the weight, take the compressed cheese out of the cheesecloth, and place it back on the flat surface. With a sharp knife cut the cheese into neat rectangles. *Paneer* keeps well in the refrigerator for 4 days.

Note: Even though exact amounts of lemon juice, vinegar, and yogurt are specified here, you will sometimes find that the curd forms before all the starter has been incorporated. If that happens, do not add the full amount of the starter, as that will only harden the curd. This is a serious matter, especially in delicate desserts such as *Ras Malai*, where soft, moist curds are essential for the dumplings to be soft and fragile.

Or you may find that after you have added the entire suggested amount of starter, the curd still has not formed or has only partially formed and the whey remains milky. There is no need for alarm. All it means is that your starter is not potent enough to do the job. Therefore, add a little more of the same starter until lumps of snow-white curd separate, leaving behind a clear greenish-yellow whey.

Thickened Milk Sauce

(Rabadi)

Rabadi is simply milk that has been cooked down to about a fourth of its original volume. The distinct aroma and pale beige color characteristic of *rabadi* are developed by boiling the milk slowly over low heat. *Rabadi* is essential in making the delectable *Ras Malai* (p. 465). *Rabadi* is also served as a dessert sauce for fruits (see Mangoes with Cream on page 470), and is sweetened and sprinkled with nuts as a pudding called *Basoondi* (p. 455). It is also thinned with water or milk to the consistency of regular milk, sweetened, and served as aromatic milk *(Rabadi doodh)* for a beverage. In India the pastry shops, called *Halwai ki Docan*, sell freshly made *rabadi*. Here, however, such luxuries are not yet available. If you want to make these mouthwatering delicacies, first you have to make *rabadi* at home. Quite honestly, except for the time involved (it takes 1¼ hours to make 2 cups of *rabadi* from 8 cups of milk), it is very easy to do.

Although making *rabadi* requires that you stay in the kitchen for the entire duration of its cooking, the process calls for neither physical exertion nor your undivided attention once the milk has come to a boil. Therefore I suggest that you make the *rabadi* while simultaneously attending to another chore, such as cleaning legumes, cutting and preparing onions, garlic, and ginger, or washing and slicing vegetables. You can even cook another dish, so long as you arrange the timing to be able to return to the *rabadi* full-time during its final ten to fifteen minutes of cooking.

Making thickened milk sauce: Bring 8 cups of milk to a boil in a heavy flat-bottomed 5-quart pan (a ceramic casserole is good for this), stirring constantly with a steel or aluminum spatula, such as a pancake turner or a large metal spoon. This will take about 15 minutes and needs very careful attention so that the milk doesn't stick to the bottom of the pan. Lower heat and simmer 45 to 55 minutes, stirring constantly and scraping down the sides until the liquid is reduced to 2 overflowing cups. Cool for 5 minutes. The consistency will be that of a thick, lumpy cream sauce. Transfer to a bowl and refrigerate. Cooling will further thicken and concentrate the *rabadi*, reducing the quantity to 2 cups.

I have found that a pan with a non-stick surface is best suited for making *rabadi*. In Indian pastry shops, *rabadi* is made in large (30 to 40 inches in diameter) Indian woks *(kadhai)* because the broad surface area aids evaporation. A sharp tool resembling a snow shovel is used for stirring and scraping down the sides. The making of *rabadi* is a common scene in every pastry shop in India in the early morning. When you pass these shops (which are everywhere) on the way to work, you are captured by a whiff of the sweet aroma of milk turning into *rabadi*. From that moment on, the average Indian begins to plan what desserts to buy on the way home. Did I mention that Indians are fond of sweets?

Milk Fudge

(Khoya)

Khoya is the next stage of *rabadi*. When *rabadi* is cooked further and reduced by half, it turns into *khoya*, a thick mass resembling fudge.

Making milk fudge: Follow the preceding recipe for making *rabadi*, but turn down the heat and continue cooking for an additional 15 minutes or so, stirring constantly to keep it from sticking and burning, until the entire mixture resembles a thick paste and comes away from the bottom of the pan when stirred. It will be grainy and very sticky. When cool, this paste develops a fudgelike texture and consistency, and loses its stickiness. Refrigerate after it cools, in a bowl or wrapped in foil. Eight cups of milk will produce 1 cup of pure milk fudge weighing about 12 ounces. *Khoya* is used in making a variety of nut fudges, sweetmeats, and other delicacies such as Almond Milk Fudge (*Badaam Barfi*, p. 479). In the valley of Kashmir, milk fudge grains are fried until they resemble meat and then cooked with green peas in a spicy tomato gravy. This vegetarian dish, called *Matar Shufta*, resembles its meat counterpart, *Keema Matar* (p. 162).

Flower Essences

(Ruh)

Flower extracts are used to perfume many of the classic Moghul dishes. The two most popular are Screw-pine Essence *(Ruh Kewra)* and Rose Essence *(Ruh Gulab)*. Screw-pine essence is extracted from the thick, leathery, yellow-green flower petals. It is used mainly in meat and poultry preparations, in certain special Moghul pilafs, in such Moghul meat and rice casseroles as Emperor's Layered Meat and Fragrant Rice Casserole *(Shah Jahani Biriyani,* p. 192), and in some desserts and sweetmeats. You can find it in Indian grocery stores under the labels "Kewra Water" or "Kewra Essence."

Rose essence *(ruh gulab)* is extracted from small deep-red roses, famous for their fragrance and cultivated solely for this purpose. It is primarily used in flavoring desserts, puddings, sweetmeats, and cold drinks. Rose essence is available commercially in three forms. The first two are available in Indian and Middle Eastern specialty stores; the third type is available only in Indian stores.

Rose water, known as *ruh gulab* or *gulab jal*, is the diluted version of rose essence. It is used, just as rose essence is, in making the rose-flavored yogurt drink, *Lassi* (p. 488) and the luscious Almond and Rice Dessert *(Firni,* p. 461). In India it is considered a good omen to sprinkle rose water on guests arriving at weddings and other religious ceremonies. It is also used as an air-freshener in many Indian homes.

Rose syrup, known as *Gulab Sharbat*, is made by adding rose essence to a heavy sugar syrup. In India it is diluted and served as a cool, refreshing rose drink. The syrup is ideal for making rose ice cream *(Kulfi Ruh Gulab)* and the yogurt beverage *lassi.*

Rose preserve, known as *gulkand*, is made by preserving whole rose petals in heavy syrup. *Gulkand* is an important accompaniment to the betel leaf *(paan)* for cutting bitter aftertastes and refreshing one's mouth.

Silver Foil

(Vark)

Silver foil, known as *vark*, is silver dust pressed to form a foil sheet. Its sole purpose is to adorn sweetmeats, kabobs, and special pilafs. Moghuls used it to decorate their elaborate food preparations, to keep the food at par with their splendorous courts. Today *vark* is used on special occasions such as wedding buffets and religious festivals. I personally like to use *vark* on nut fudges like Almond Milk Fudge (p. 479) and Cashew Nut Fudge (p. 478), and on special Moghul preparations, including *biriyani* (p. 192) and *zarda* (p. 369). *Vark* is perfectly safe to eat. It is tasteless and odorless.

Vark is made by heating and beating pure silver until it resembles cotton candy. A very thin layer of it is then spread on a sheet of paper. Another sheet of paper is placed over that to compress the silver dust into a single long sheet. In the United States, *vark* is available in Indian grocery stores, in packets containing six 2-inch by 3-inch sheets, at a very reasonable price.

To apply *vark*, first peel off the top layer of paper. Lift the bottom sheet, with the silver foil still attached to it, and invert it over the dish to be garnished. Gently peel away the paper. The silver foil will stick to the food.

Two words of caution: Do not work with *vark* in a breezy area, as it may blow away. And, because *vark* is pure silver, store it tightly covered in plastic wrap or in an airtight container, or it will tarnish.

Equipment

There are no special cooking utensils or tools that are absolutely essential to Indian cooking. To give you a sense of things, let me describe the humble setting of the traditional Indian kitchen (*rasooi*). It is really just another room in the house. It is starkly empty and has no counters, cabinets, electrical appliances, or fixtures of any kind—not even a kitchen sink. When a family moves in, it builds a wood- or coal-burning stove (*choolha*) in one corner, which is ritually broken down when the family moves out. The cooking on this stove is done from a squatting position on the floor, or while sitting on one of the low stools.

There is a faucet in or outside the kitchen, or water is brought from the center of town in jugs called *ghara*, and stored. Meat, fish, and vegetables are bought the same day they are cooked. This is because there is no refrigeration, and in the hot climate the meat and fish are apt to spoil, and vegetables wilt in a matter of hours. It is a blessing in disguise, for the meat used in cooking is still warm and sweet-smelling, its juices fully intact, and the vegetables fresh, crisp, and full of their delicate fragrance. The cooked dishes have the wonderful flavor that comes with the freshest of ingredients. This is how food is meant to taste and, therefore, should.

Given this unpretentious set-up, it follows that the cooking equipment will also be simple. The genius of Indian utensils lies in their adaptation to a multitude of functions, thus reducing their number to a bare minimum. These tools are made of all kinds of metal, stone, wood and pottery, and include the following:

- Handleless saucepans with rim (*pateela*) for general cooking
- A handleless flat lid for a saucepan (*dhakkan*)
- Spoons for stirring (*karchi*)
- An Indian wok (*kadhai*) for frying (Indian kitchens usually have two types: one deep, and narrow across the top, used for deep frying; the other shallow, and broad across the top, used for stir-frying.)

• A shallow, flat-bottomed platter *(paraath)*, 12 to 24 inches in diameter with a 3-inch-high rim. This all-purpose utensil is used for preparing vegetables for cooking, cleaning rice and *dal*, and, most importantly, for mixing and kneading bread dough.

• a flat round marble or wooden board *(chakla)*

• a wooden rolling pin *(belan)* for rolling bread

• a handleless iron griddle *(tava)* for making bread

• tongs *(chimta)* for lifting the *tava*

• a flat grinding stone *(sil)* with a triangular stone *(batta)* for grinding herbs and wet seasonings

• a grain-mill *(chakki)* for grinding spices, *dal*, grain, and other dry ingredients

• long, sharp knives *(chakoo)*

• a sieve *(chalni)* for cleaning and sifting ingredients

• a vegetable grater *(kaddoo-kas)*

• a coconut grater *(narial-kas)*

• a pottery or brass jug *(ghara)* used for storing water

• dinner plates *(thali)* and bowls *(katoori)* for serving the meal, made of brass, stainless steel, silver, and even gold

Traditional Indian kitchen

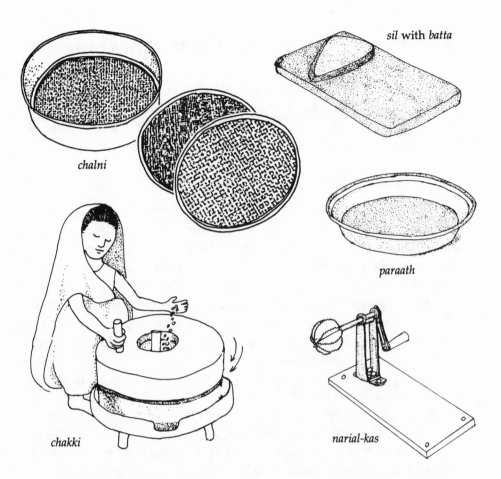

sil with *batta*

chalni

paraath

chakki

narial-kas

In India almost all cooking is done on top of the stove. In classic Indian cooking there is no equivalent to the Western-style oven. There is, however, the *tandoor,* an Indian-style clay oven, a giant barbecue with a small narrow opening at the top, built into the ground. The sides are lined with a special smooth clay and used for baking many kinds of Indian breads. The pit itself is used for roasting the meat.

The *tandoor* is not a feature of most Indian households because it is expensive to build and operate. It is used for bulk cooking, and therefore is found in the neighborhood restaurants of North India and in fancy restaurants throughout India and in other parts of the world.

EQUIPPING YOUR KITCHEN FOR INDIAN COOKING

Most American kitchens are already well equipped for the preparation of Indian food, and are far more functional than most any kitchen in India. Certain utensils and tools, however, lend themselves more successfully than others to Indian cooking.

Pots and Pans

Enamel-coated, heavy-bottomed casseroles and skillets are best suited to Indian cooking. They retain and distribute heat evenly, and you do not have to worry about the ingredients reacting with the metal. They can go directly from the stove top or oven to the table, into the refrigerator, and then into the dishwasher. (Make sure the handles are oven- and dishwasher-safe.) The most versatile sizes are between 3 and 5 quarts. The little ones (¾, 1, and 1½ quarts) are too small for any practical use, and the extra-large ones are too big for household ranges.

A couple of saucepans or casseroles with non-stick surfaces are a worthwhile investment. They are especially good for frying onions, garlic, and ginger; cooking with dried fruits and nut butter; or cooking down milk for milk fudge (*khoya*, p. 56), as all these substances have a tendency to stick to the bottom of the pan. They are also ideal for pot-roasting dishes that have very little liquid.

The Indian wok *(kadhai)*, which looks like a round-bottomed casserole, is immensely useful for deep frying and stir-frying vegetables. It requires much less oil than a deep-fryer or a skillet

because of its shape. But I have found that non-stick frying pans are just as useful for stir-frying; for deep frying, an ordinary skillet or a large pan works well. If you are interested in investing in a *kadhai*, I suggest you buy a heavy cast-iron one (available in Indian stores) that can withstand high heat. A cast-iron *kadhai* needs to be seasoned before being used for the first time, in the same way a wok is for Chinese dishes.

To season a *kadhai:* The *kadhai* usually has a protective coating to prevent rust. You need to wash the *kadhai* thoroughly with dishwashing detergent and warm water, scrubbing it with a steel-wool pad. Wipe dry, and place over medium heat for 1 minute in order to dry it completely. After it has cooled, brush the inside with a little oil (peanut or corn oil will do), and heat again over medium heat until the oil is hot and smoking. Turn off the heat and sprinkle about 2 tablespoons of salt inside. When the *kadhai* is cool enough to handle, rub the salt around the inside with a kitchen towel or a piece of cheesecloth. Wash thoroughly, dry, heat over medium heat for one minute, then let cool. The *kadhai* is now ready for use. This final step (heating over medium heat) ensures thorough drying; it should be followed after every use in order to prevent the *kadhai* from rusting.

Tools

Aside from the usual tools found in the average American kitchen—an assortment of knives, spatulas, peeler, grater, sieve, colander, and beater—you will need special equipment for making bread (described under Bread on page 387). A candy thermometer is essential in making yogurt, sugar syrup, and in heating oil for frying. You will also have to buy a coffee grinder, if you do not already have one, for grinding spices, and an electric blender or a food mill for grinding and pureeing.

I have found that if a single coffee grinder is used for grinding coffee beans as well as spices, it is the coffee whose flavor is altered. This is because the coffee-grinder blades take on the aroma of the spices and not of the coffee beans. Therefore, unless you are willing to drink spice-laced coffee, I recommend keeping a separate grinder just for spices, as I do.

I have also found a small mortar and pestle—preferably made of marble—ideal for pulverizing small quantities of spices. And the marble ones are dishwasher-safe.

Since I discovered the virtues of the phenomenal food processor, I have become a total addict. If properly used, its versatility knows no bounds. Most Indian dishes call for chopped onion, garlic, and fresh ginger. The chopping takes considerable time by conventional methods, but with a food processor the job is done in seconds. A good food processor chops fresh herbs to perfection, powders nuts, and purees fresh tomatoes (with the skin, as I prefer). With a little experience and caution on your part, it will even slice onions to the wafer-thin shreds called for in many Indian dishes. And, to my ultimate delight, it mixes and kneads the dough for Indian breads, pastries, and crackers to perfection.

Techniques

Indian cooking techniques are, for the most part, simple to master. Special skill is required in order to make Indian breads (p. 383), and to prepare certain very delicate Indian desserts such as *Ras Malai* (p. 465). With a little learning and practice, however, you can produce these Indian specialties with ease and pleasure.

In the following pages I have explained the basic techniques used in classic Indian cooking to prepare spices and seasonings, meats and vegetables, and I refer to them again and again in the recipes. You need to understand and master these methods which, coupled with a knowledge of the special spices, herbs, and seasonings, form the backbone of Indian cooking. Once you learn them, you can think, plan, and cook Indian meals with the natural flair of an Indian cook. This means that eventually you will be able to put away this book and start cooking Indian food guided solely by the wealth of your experience, employing your own developed creative skill, improvising confidently and brilliantly where needed. And most important of all, you will know how to rescue dishes when they meet with disaster, which occasionally happens to me. You will be cooking the classic dishes with your own personal touch, tailored to suit your taste. This is the essence of becoming a master Indian cook.

ROASTING AND GRINDING SPICES

(Masala Bhoonana aur Peesana)

Spices are roasted in an Indian wok (kadhai) or a frying pan on top of the stove, and ground by one of the following methods:

To roast spices: Heat a *kadhai* (see description on page 59) or a heavy frying pan, preferably an iron one, for 2 minutes over medium heat. Add the spices and roast over medium heat, stirring and shaking the pan constantly in order to prevent burning. For the first minute or two, nothing will happen—the spices are losing their moisture during this time—and then all of a sudden they will start to brown. This is a crucial period: If you don't watch them carefully and stir them constantly, they will burn almost instantly. As the spices brown they will begin to smoke, releasing the sweet fragrance of roasting spices. Roast them until they turn dark brown. Turn down the heat a little if they seem to be browning too fast. The time will depend upon (1) the spice and (2) the amount of spice being roasted in relation to the size of the pan—the larger the surface area of the pan, the faster the spice will brown. In a *kadhai*, ¼ cup of coriander seeds will take about 6 minutes, ¼ cup of cumin seeds will take about 8 minutes, and 1½ cups of the spice mixture *garam masala* will take about 10 minutes. Take the browned spices out of the pan immediately, and put them into a clean dry bowl to cool completely before using.

To grind spices: Put the spices in the jar of a coffee grinder, a spice mill, or an electric blender, and grind them to a fine powder. The food processor is not suitable for grinding a blend of spices of varying hardness and size. It works well for spices that crumble easily, such as roasted cumin seeds.

For powdering small quantities of spices, such as one-half teaspoon of fennel seeds or a small lump of asafetida, it is best to use a mortar and pestle, a kitchen mallet, or a rolling pin. If you use a mallet or rolling pin, place the spice in a small plastic sandwich bag between two sheets of waxed paper or plastic before grinding it; otherwise the instrument will permanently take on the smell of the spice. Store in airtight containers in a cool, dry place so that the spices do not lose their fragrance.

CRUSHING SPICES

(Masala Musulana)

There are several recipes in Indian cooking which call for crushed, rather than ground, spices to be added. This is because in those dishes a certain amount of the texture of the spice is desired, as in Crab Malabar (p. 101) and Panfried Fillet of Sole Laced with Carom (p. 248). Crushed spices are usually prepared just before the cooking, not too far in advance, because they lose their fragrance. Spices can be crushed between finger and thumb, or with the thumb while holding the spices in the palm of the other hand. To crush spices in a mortar or with a kitchen mallet or rolling pin, follow the instructions above for powdering small quantities, except pound or crush the spices only until they look broken and release their fragrance.

PREPARING ONION, GARLIC, AND GINGER
FOR COOKING

(Geela Masala Tayyar Karana)

Onions, garlic and ginger are the essential ingredients of most Indian main dishes, particularly those of North India. There, the luscious gravies and seductive sauces characteristic of the classic Moghul dishes were created. Onions are usually chopped or finely sliced; garlic and ginger root are usually finely chopped or ground to a paste before they are added to a dish. The texture of each dish, from coarsely grained and crunchy to smooth and velvety, is determined by the degree of fineness of the chopped ingredients.

To slice onions: Peel, and cut the onion in half vertically, beginning at the top end. Place halves on a cutting board, flat side down, and cut off about ¼ inch from the root end, making sure to cut away all of the tough solid stem portion. Slice them lengthwise from top end to root end into paper-thin slices, about ¹⁄₁₆ inch thick. With your fingers, separate the slices.

To chop onions: Follow the instructions given for slicing onions, but do not slice them quite as thin—about ³⁄₁₆ to ¼ inch thick. Then gather the slices and dice them across, into small cubes.

To chop garlic and ginger root: Peel, and slice into thin slices, about ¹⁄₃₂ inch thick. Then stack the slices together, a few at a time and cut into thin strips. Gather the strips and dice across into tiny cubes. You can also crush them to a coarse pulp with a mortar and pestle.

To grind garlic and ginger root to a paste: Peel, place in a mortar, and crush or pound with the pestle until the ingredients are reduced to a fine paste. To ensure smooth texture of the paste, crush garlic and ginger root separately, in small batches.

To chop fresh herbs: Snip off and discard the hard, coarse stems of the herbs. Gather the herbs into a bunch on the chopping board, and chop them into fine pieces.

To chop green chilies: First cut them in half, lengthwise. If you want the chilies to be mild, scrape off the seeds and discard. Gather the halves into a bunch and cut across into thin slices, about ⅛ to ¹⁄₁₆ inch thick. If chilies are hot, wear rubber gloves to protect your hands.

Using the Food Processor

To slice onions: Peel, and cut the onions in half from top end to root end. Cut off the solid stem portion. If the onions are very large, cut into quarters. Attach the serrated slicing disc, preferably fine, on the food processor, and cover the container. Fill the feed tube with onions, standing them on their sides. Slice, using a little pressure on the pusher (you will be able to process 1 or 2 onion halves at a time). When onion slices fill up the workbowl, transfer them to another bowl. Continue with the remaining onions.

To chop onions: Attach the metal cutting blade and add 2 or 3 onion halves at a time to the workbowl. Process, turning the machine on and off rapidly until the onions are finely chopped (about 15 seconds). Transfer the onions to another bowl, and continue with the remaining onions.

To chop garlic, ginger root, and herbs: Attach metal cutting blade, begin processing, and gradually drop peeled garlic, peeled ginger root, green chilies (cut chilies in half; if desired, scrape away the seeds), and fresh herbs (with the coarse stems snipped off) through the feed tube separately, in that order. (If each has to be prepared separately, then remove one from the workbowl before adding the next.) Stop processing as soon as the ingredients are chopped and cling to the sides.

For recipes where several herbs and seasonings are combined with onions and cooked together, it is logical (and easier) to chop all the ingredients at the same time. But always make sure that you chop the garlic, ginger root, and green chilies *before* processing the onions. A little extra processing will not affect the herbs, but it will be disastrous on the onions; they will become a puree and be unsuitable for frying.

FRYING SPICES

(Sookha Masala Bhoonana)

An indispensable process in Indian cooking is the frying of spices in a little hot fat or oil, to release their flavor prior to adding the other ingredients. The secret of success lies in having the fat hot enough so that a green cardamom pod will sizzle gently when put into the pan and will puff and brown in a few seconds. At this temperature most spices will brown almost instantly; watch carefully that they do not burn. It will take a little practice to learn exactly how to fry spices in your own pan on your own stove. Be prepared to lose a few batches and keep trying until you learn how high to turn the heat, how long to heat the oil, and how to lift the pan away from the heat before the spices start to burn. And you must have the next batch of ingredients ready, so that they may be added without interrupting the process. Lift the pan away from the heat and lower the temperature a little before you add more ingredients, and stir rapidly to keep them from burning in the extremely hot oil.

This technique is vital to the flavor of the dish: it removes the raw flavor from the spices at the same time that it perfumes the fat with their sweet scent. As a result, the aromas of the spices penetrate the meat and vegetables much more thoroughly than if the spices had been added after the liquids.

Whole spices, which take longer to brown, should always be added before the ground ones. In dishes that call for ground spices only, the fat should be moderately hot (350°F) so that the ground spices, when added, get a chance to brown without burning.

Whole spices that take a little longer to fry than others should always be added *first*, separately. These include black mustard seeds, sesame seeds, fenugreek, and various legumes used as spices. If a combination of spices includes black mustard seeds, the seeds should be added first and fried until they pop like popcorn. The seeds will not pop evenly if there are other spices present, causing the temperature of the fat to drop. The popping of the seeds is very important: it releases their flavor. Also, unpopped seeds are chewy and bitter. A word of caution: Keep a cover handy, such as the lid of the pan or a spatter screen, since the mustard seeds, while sputtering and splattering, may fly about.

BROWN FRYING ONION, GARLIC, AND GINGER ROOT

(Geela Masala Bhoonana)

An important technique in frying the aromatic seasonings is the brown-frying of onions, garlic, and ginger root, or sometimes only one or two of them. My research has turned up no equivalent process in French or other Western schools of cooking. Brown-frying lies somewhere between sautéing and deep frying.

Most lamb, beef, and chicken dishes, particularly those with golden-reddish gravies, start off with the technique of frying finely chopped or sliced onions in a small amount of fat (use 2 table-spoons of fat to 1 cup of chopped onions) until they lose most of their moisture and turn caramel-brown. The entire process is done over medium high heat. Brown-frying the onions, garlic, and ginger, which takes a little effort and time (at least 20 minutes for 2 cups of onions), is intrinsic to Moghul cooking; these seasonings add both color and fragrance to the dish, and act as thickeners, creating the most wonderful gravies imaginable.

To brown-fry two cups of thinly sliced onions: Heat 4 tablespoons of oil over medium-high heat in a heavy-bottomed pan. Add the sliced onions and stir to coat the slices with oil. Fry the onions, stirring constantly. For the first 5 minutes the onions will steam vigorously, losing much of their excess moisture. As the steam begins to subside, the onions will wilt and begin to fry. In the next 5 minutes they will lose the rest of their excess moisture and turn limp and golden yellow. The aroma of frying onions will begin to fill the air. The oil will now start to separate from the onions, an indication that they are ready to brown. Keep stirring the onions constantly. They will begin clumping together, and in about 5 minutes they will turn light brown. Continue frying until they turn caramel-brown and look shriveled up (about 5 minutes more). Add chopped garlic and ginger midway during the last 5 minutes of frying (or when the onions are 95 percent browned), since they take a very short time to brown. In certain recipes in which the quantity of onions is small, the three seasonings are often combined and fried together. Two cups of sliced onions will yield ½ cup of brown-fried onions.

Note:

1. When onions are added to the hot oil, they often burn unevenly before they finish cooking. To prevent such a disaster, start frying on a lower heat. Heat the oil for ½ minute over medium high heat, and add the onions. In a couple of minutes the oil and the onions will gradually heat up.

2. The onions must be stirred constantly during the entire process to ensure that they brown evenly, or else they will not impart the appropriate caramel color and sweet fried-onion flavor to the sauce. In addition, partially cooked onions will not dissolve into the sauce, thus affecting its texture and consistency.

3. If the onions stick, or fry too rapidly and burn, a little cold water should be added, 1 tablespoon at a time, to slow down the cooking. You should never lower or turn off the heat during the frying process.

4. The last 10 minutes, and particularly the last 5 minutes, of cooking time is a very crucial period in this process. This is because the onions have lost just about all their moisture by this stage, and brown very rapidly. If they are not watched and stirred constantly, without interruption, they burn almost instantly and lend a bitter burnt taste to the dish.

5. To stop any further frying of onions once they are done, add a tablespoon of cold water and stir it in.

6. Brown-fried onions can be prepared in large batches and refrigerated, or frozen and defrosted as needed. Be sure to freeze them in small portions based on your need. Once defrosted they must be used; they cannot be refrozen.

SPECIAL FRIED GARNISHES

(Tadka aur Bhone Piaz ke Lache)

Fried garnishes are as important to Indian dishes as the dishes themselves; they form an integral part of the preparation they adorn. In several dishes, particularly legume preparations, they are considered part of the cooking ingredients and should never be omitted.

In addition to making the dish look attractive and appetizing, fried garnishes lend a very distinct and special aroma, taste, and texture. The two important fried garnishes in Indian cooking are Spice-Perfumed Butter *(Tadka)* and Crispy Fried Onions *(Bhone Piaz ke Lache)*.

Spice-Perfumed Butter

(Tadka)

This is an age-old technique, used since the Vedic times for flavoring all varieties of *dal*, yogurt salads, vegetables, relishes, and meat preparations. *Tadka*, also known as *baghar* and *chaunk*, is the simplest and most effective way of aromatizing food. It is prepared by heating Indian clarified butter to a very hot point (375°–400°F) and frying certain fragrant spices and seasonings, such as asafetida, cloves, cumin, black mustard seeds, ginger root, garlic, onions, or green chilies, to imbue it with fragrance. This perfumed butter is then folded into the dish with the fried ingredients.

In the North, especially in the Punjab region, the preparation of *tadka* for various *dals* has reached the level of a highly refined art. The *dal* in which the *tadka* is to be incorporated is cooked in plain water, with no flavorings added to it except perhaps a little turmeric for color. Nothing must interfere with the seductively teasing fragrance of the *tadka*.

There are regional traditions governing the various combinations of spices that can flavor *tadka*, a different one for each *dal*. In northern cooking, the *tadka* for lentils consists of garlic and red pepper; for mung beans and split peas, cumin and onions; for white split gram beans, asafetida or onions and cloves. Similarly, different combinations of spices and seasonings are used for different legume preparations in all the other regions of India. Recipes for *tadka* can be found as part of each *dal* recipe.

To prepare tadka: First prepare the dish, such as legume *(dal)* puree, and transfer to a serving bowl. In a frying pan, heat the Indian clarified butter, or *ghee*, (oil or vegetable shortening may be used) almost to the smoking point (375°–400°F). Add the whole spices first, and fry until they release their fragrance (about 5 seconds). Add onions, garlic, ginger root, etc., and fry, stirring constantly, until they turn brown. The time will depend upon each seasoning and the quantities used. It can take anywhere from 30 seconds for a few cloves of sliced garlic to 15 minutes for 2 cups of onions. Now add the ground spices. Immediately turn off the heat and pour the entire contents of the frying pan over the *dal* in the serving bowl. Serve immediately.

Crispy Fried Onions

(Bhone Piaz ke Lache)

These crunchy fried onions, a personal favorite of mine, are a delicacy all by themselves. They are primarily used for garnishing pilafs, and meat and rice preparations. This is another Moghul contribution. In addition to the sweet onion flavor they impart, they create an interesting contrast to the pearly white rice in pilafs. There are a great many meat dishes in which these fried onions, also known as *barista*, are crumbled or ground, and folded in just before serving. This is done to keep the flavor of fried onions more distinct in the dish and to lend a sweet flavor to the sauce. In addition, meat cooked with fried onions oftens turns dark. Therefore, to keep the meat light-colored, especially in pilafs like Lamb

Pilaf (p. 189), the fried onions are added at the end, after the meat is cooked.

The process of preparing crisp fried onions is simple to learn. First, slice the onions into thin shreds following the instructions on page 68. Heat vegetable oil in a *kadhai* or frying pan over medium high heat until very hot but not smoking (375°–400°F). Add the onion slices and fry, stirring constantly, until they turn dark brown (watch carefully that they do not blacken and burn, which will make them taste bitter). The time will depend on the quantity of onions being fried. Two cups of thinly sliced onions will take about 25 to 30 minutes.

Drain them on paper towels for 5 minutes, and they will turn crackling crisp. These fried onions keep well for a day if kept in a tightly covered container. If left uncovered, collected moisture will cause them to go limp.

MOGHUL AND NORTH INDIAN COOKING

There are several Indian cooking techniques similar to the ones most of us in the West are familiar with, such as boiling (*oobalana*), stewing (*salan ya kari*), frying (*bhonao aur bhoonana*) and deep frying (*talana*). The braising (*korma*) and pot-roasting (*dum*) are also very similar to familiar methods, with the few minor exceptions that I discuss below. The techniques that owe their origin to the Moghuls are named after the specific method of preparation, or the cooking equipment used to make them. These include kabob (*kabab*), kafta (*kofta*), and the Indian clay-oven-cooked dishes (*tandoori khana*).

Braising

(Korma)

Braising (*korma*) is an important technique in Moghul cooking. It was initially used in cooking meat and chicken dishes, but the technique later found its way into innumerable vegetable preparations, particularly those imitating their nonvegetarian counterparts.

The process of braising is very similar to the Western method, with one difference. The braising liquid used in *korma* is much thicker: it includes yogurt, cream, fruit purees, and nut butters. Indian braised dishes, as a result, often taste as if they had been pot-roasted, and yield thick, velvety sauces that heavily coat the meat pieces.

With a few exceptions, *korma* dishes are begun by marinating the meat in the braising liquid together with the spices and seasonings. The meat is then cooked in the marinade itself, by a slow, prolonged simmering over very low heat on top of the stove. Often a little cream and spice-perfumed butter are incorporated at the end so as to velvetize and aromatize the sauce further.

Korma dishes are generally made with the choicest cuts of meat, because they are traditionally served on special occasions. Furthermore, the *korma* dishes usually contain a very few subtle spices, so as to allow the flavor and texture of the meat to come through and enrich the sauce. A good heavy-bottomed pan with a non-stick surface is essential to successful *korma*. Some classic braised dishes are Lamb in Fragrant Garlic Cream Sauce (*Rogan Josh*, p. 176). Lamb Braised in Aromatic Cream Sauce (*Rogani Gosht*, p. 164), Royal Braised Lamb with Fragrant Spices (*Shahi Korma*, p. 174), and Royal Braised Vegetables in Cardamom Nut Sauce (*Shahi Sabz Korma*, p. 269).

Pot-roasting

(Dum)

Dum is the Indian method of pot-roasting food. *Dum* dishes generally call for a large amount of fat (usually butter) since the basic ingredients (meat, poultry, fish, or vegetables, left whole or cut into large chunks) are literally steamed in the vapor of the butter. A good heavy-bottomed, well-greased pot (such as a heavy casserole with non-stick surface) with a tight-fitting lid is essential to *dum* cooking. To cook any food by the *dum* process, the spices and seasonings must be fried in the butter at the start. The ingredients to be pot-roasted are then added, and lightly browned. (They are often pricked well before being added, to allow the flavors to penetrate fully.) The heat is momentarily increased to high, to create steam (often a little water is sprinkled over the ingredients to speed up this process, especially if they look dry). The lid is placed on and sealed, the heat reduced to the lowest point, and the *dum* cooked slowly in the aromatic vapor.

Traditionally, the pot is sealed with a little dough to prevent the escape of any vapor. The pot is opened only when the cooking is completed. To keep the food from sticking and browning unevenly, the ingredients are stirred by lifting and shaking the entire pot in a circular motion. This is an outdated procedure for which I've devised a simpler and more efficient substitute. I cover the pot with a piece of aluminum foil before putting the lid on. The foil hanging over the lid is then crumpled and pressed against the pot to form a tight seal. The advantage of this method is that the foil can be lifted off, the food stirred with a spoon, and the foil resealed, which is far easier and safer than lifting and shaking the pot. It also allows you to check the *dum* so that there won't be any danger of your overcooking it. (In a sealed pot, you have no way of knowing exactly when the ingredients are done. As a result, you frequently end up with an overcooked dish.)

A classic example of *dum* cooking is Whole Potatoes in Spicy Yogurt Gravy (*Dum Aloo*, p. 258).

The *dum* process is also used extensively in the final execution of Moghul rice pilafs (*pullao*), layered meat and rice casseroles (*biriyani*), and certain braised dishes (*korma*). This is the process that causes grains of rice to develop the exquisite texture and elasticity characteristic of classic Moghul pilafs. It also enhances the flavors of braised dishes, making the meat melt-in-your-mouth tender, and at the same time improves the overall appearance of the dish. These dishes, when 95 percent done, finish their cooking by steaming in their own vapor. *Dum* simply slows the cooking process without stopping it. As a result, meat, chicken, rice, and so on begin to relax in the vapor-filled pot. The juices in the meat and chicken begin to settle, thus making them plump and moist. The starch in the rice forms a permanent bond that enables the grains to expand without breaking or cracking. And the fat mixes with the sauce to give it a velvet glaze and a lovely texture. *Dum* is traditionally done by placing the pot over hot ashes and covering the lid with live charcoal. To do this, you need a charcoal-burning stove, but this step can be successfully duplicated in your own kitchen by placing the pot in a preheated slow oven (300°–325°F) for 20 to 25 minutes. Or the pot may be placed on top of the stove, raised above the burner by means of a pair of tongs or a Chinese wok ring, over very low heat. Since the heat in both cases needs to be very low and gentle, the pot may be left unattended for an extra few minutes without fear of burning the food.

Kabob

(Kabab)

There are special techniques for preparing and cooking meat. *Kabab* generally refers to small pieces of meat that are broiled or fried. *Kabab* is prepared either with ground lamb flavored with spices, herbs, and seasonings and shaped into sausages, patties, or croquettes, or with small chunks of lamb which are marinated in a spicy, fragrant marinade. There are innumerable varieties of kabobs popular in India. Seven (four made with ground lamb, and three with chunks) are considered classics.

Seek Kabab: These kabobs are made with ground lamb, fresh herbs, and only a few spices. The meat is shaped into patties, then wrapped in thin layers around a metal skewer and broiled over a charcoal grill. These soft and moist kabobs are by far the most popular. They are frequently served in restaurants where they are cooked in the Indian clay oven, *tandoor.*

Shamme Kabab: These kabobs contain a large quantity of yellow split peas—a distinctive feature of *shamme kabab*—in addition to spices, herbs, and seasonings. The ground lamb is shaped into patties and shallow fried. *Shamme kababs* are generally very spicy and fragrant with cardamom.

Hussaini Kabab: These kabobs are made with ground lamb and several highly aromatic spices, and are often stuffed with dried fruits and nuts. The meat is shaped into thin sausagelike rolls and panfried or broiled. The flavor is very mild and the texture juicy.

Chapli Kabab: These are very similar to *shamme kabab,* but do not contain yellow split peas and are spicy hot.

Boti Kabab: These kabobs are traditionally made of boneless lamb pieces, usually from the rib. The meat is coated with a thin layer of aromatic yogurt mixture and marinated before being broiled. Kabobs are often sold as roadside snacks in the northernmost regions of India during the cold winter months.

Tikka Kabab: These kabobs are made with lean boneless chunks of lamb, chicken, large pieces of liver, and shellfish. These are the kabobs you see in most Indian restaurants. The meat or fish chunks are marinated in a spicy, ginger-laced yogurt marinade and then broiled. In restaurants they are cooked in the *tandoor.* Their color is usually brilliant orange-red—the characteristic color of all *tandoor*-cooked food (a coloring dye is usually added to the marinade).

Pasanda or *Barra Kabab: Pasanda* or *Barra* means fillet. These kabobs are made with the choicest cuts of lamb (usually from the loin or rib) which are cut into thin strips and pounded until they are reduced to almost paper-thin fillets. (Often lamb breast is substituted for reasons of economy.) The fillets are marinated in a mild fragrant marinade, threaded on bamboo skewers, and broiled over a charcoal grill.

Kafta

(Kofta)

Kofta are very similar to the kabobs that are made with ground meat except, after being broiled or fried, they are simmered in rich sauces and turned into lovely main dishes. The kabobs for kafta dishes are usually shaped into round balls similar to Italian or Swedish meatballs. Of the many different kinds of *kofta* preparations commonly served in India, the following two are the most popular by far and are considered classics:

Malai Kofta: In this dish the meatballs are usually flavored with mild spices and herbs. They are then simmered in butter and cream in an enriched aromatic tomato sauce.

Nargisi Kofta: This *kofta* preparation is somewhat elaborate. First, whole hard-boiled eggs are enclosed in a thin layer of spice-laced ground-lamb mixture and deep fried (they very closely resemble Scotch Eggs at this stage). The stuffed meatballs are neatly sliced to expose the egg, and then simmered in a fragrant onion gravy. The combination of meat and egg looks like a narcissus flower (which, in Indian, is called *nargis*), hence its name.

Indian Clay-Oven Cooking

(Tandoori Khana)

In India the processes of baking, roasting, and grilling are all achieved by *tandoori* cooking. This is because the food is prepared in a *tandoor*, which simultaneously bakes, roasts, and grills.

The *tandoor* is believed to have originated in the northeastern part of Persia (present-day Iran). Its use spread to different parts of the continent with migrations, and as a result, today the *tandoor* is used in all of Central Asia. It is, of course, known by different names, such as *tanoo* in Iran and *toné* in southeastern Georgia in the U.S.S.R.

In India the *tandoor* was initially built for the purpose of baking breads (still its main use). The dough is stretched and shaped into flat breads and smacked onto the sides of the pit, to which it adheres. It puffs up and bakes in 7 to 10 minutes. The cooked breads are then peeled off gently with long metal skewers specially designed for this purpose.

In the earlier part of the nineteenth century, in Peshawar, a city in the northwest frontier region of Pakistan (then part of India), an ingenious method for cooking meat was invented and introduced. Today, it has become one of the most popular cooking methods in India. In this process, whole chickens and large chunks of lamb were threaded on specially designed long skewers, lowered into the *tandoor* pit, and cooked. Any food thus cooked was referred to as *tandoori* food.

The meats cooked in a *tandoor* are generally more moist, and tender (but not dripping juicy) than those cooked by any other method. In addition, they have a special earthy aroma absorbed from the clay lining of the oven.

Just about any meat that can be threaded on skewers can be cooked in a *tandoor*. The most popular is the chicken, called *Tandoori Murghi* (p. 221). The others include *Seek Kabab, Tikka, Boti, or Barra Kabab* (see descriptions on pages 78–79), and *Jheenga* (prawn) *Tikka Kabab*. Chunks of liver and whole fish are also cooked this way. After the main roasting has been finished, the leftover heat in the *tandoor* is used to prepare wonderful delicacies like the pot-roasted leg of lamb with pistachio and raisin-laced saffron sauce, called *Shahi Raan* (p. 184) and Buttered Black Beans (*Kali Dal*, p. 337).

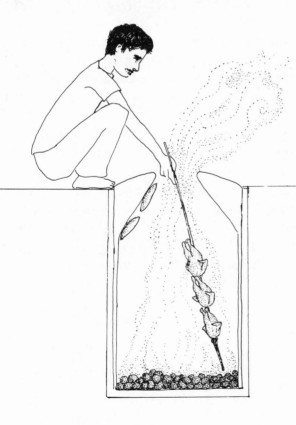

All dishes cooked in a tandoor are first marinated in a special spiced yogurt marinade for a long period, to flavor and tenderize the meat. Chicken is usually coated and marinated in special tenderizers before marinating in a yogurt-spice mixture. (See The Tenderizers on page 83).

The lamb or beef used should always be very lean so that it can be generously basted with butter *(usli ghee)* during cooking. This is because the smoke created by the butter dripping on the charcoal imparts a distinctly sweet aroma, very different from the smoke created by any other fat or oil, and essential to the authentic *tandoori* flavor.

All meats cooked in a *tandoor* have a characteristic bright reddish-orange color, lent by a natural dye called *tandoori rang* that is added to the marinade, so as to give the dishes a strong aesthetic appeal and to distinguish *tandoori* food from all others. Since *tandoori* coloring is a product of nature, it is possible there will be variations in color. Such variations are perfectly acceptable. The coloring of *tandoori* food is not essential to the flavor. You may substitute a little paprika in its place. Some use saffron, but in my judgment it is not a good choice for coloring *tandoori* chicken because its powerful aroma often interferes with and masks the subtle fragrance of the herb marinade. Besides, it is too expensive to waste on color alone.

Unfortunately, there is no way to duplicate the *tandoor* process. Until someone comes up with a modified version of this gigantic clay pit—which is more like a furnace than a barbecue pit—*tandoori* cooking, with its unique flavor, cannot be reproduced in your home. You can, however, get very good results in the meantime by using a charcoal grill (for those of you who are addicted to the charcoal flavor), an electric broiler, or the broiler part of a conventional oven. The recipe for *Tandoori* Chicken is on page 221.

MEAT TENDERIZERS

In Indian cooking the most common method of tenderizing tougher cuts of meat is by marinating them in a spice-laced yogurt mixture. Another traditional Indian method is to add to the meat, while it is cooking, 1 or 2 betel nuts *(sopari)*, known to contain enzymes that break down the muscle fibers of protein. (The tradition of chewing betel leaf *[paan]* with betel nut *[sopari]* among other digestives is common after a heavy meal, and the betel nut performs the same function.) Fillets, chops, and cutlets, which are generally deep fried or broiled, are tenderized by pounding the fibers with a heavy tool until they are broken.

Chicken is usually tenderized with the green papaya *(kacha papeeta)*, the unripe fruit of the papaya plant *(Carica papaya)*. The papaya is usually ground and rubbed onto the pieces of meat to marinate before the grilling process. The enzyme papain, present in the green papaya, breaks up the muscle fibers and makes the chicken tender. This is the source of the special plump, moist, and elastic texture of *tandoori* chicken (see more on *tandoori* cooking on page 80), which cannot be produced by any other process.

The commercially available tenderizer, sold under the brand name Adolph's Natural Meat Tenderizer, is an ideal substitute, as it is nothing but the same enzyme, papain, extracted from the green papaya, dried, and mixed with common table salt. Chicken should be rubbed with this tenderizer and allowed to marinate for ½ hour before the remaining spices are added.

One of the limitations of the enzyme papain is that it does not penetrate deeply enough into the flesh of the chicken (on an average, it penetrates 2 millimeters into the surface of the meat). In order for the tenderizer to be effective, the meat should not be very thick. This is why very young chickens, weighing less than 2 pounds, are chosen for *tandoori* cooking. In addition, they are pricked thoroughly and slashed every 1 to 1½ inches to allow the tenderizer to penetrate as deeply as possible.

ABOUT SALTING FOOD

Salt has been used in food since the beginning of time, not just as a preservative, but to perk up the hidden flavors of other ingredients and to improve the overall taste of the dish. When salting food, two factors must be considered: the strength of the salt itself—different commercial brands available in supermarkets and specialty stores contain varying degrees of alkali—and individual taste.

Most Westerners find Indian dishes, especially those with sauces, somewhat oversalted. This is because they often eat them straight, as they would eat any American main course. This is a mistake. Indian dishes (both main and side) are meant to be eaten with a staple—rice or bread—whose blandness mellows and counteracts the saltiness of the dishes, creating a proper balance. Another factor worth noting is that salt works to subdue the peppery taste in any particular dish. So you must be careful when omitting or drastically reducing the amount of salt in any Indian dish, because you may end up with food that's too hot. For this reason, in every recipe in this book I suggest that you check for salt just before serving.

In Indian cooking, especially in stir-fried vegetable preparations, salt is always added in the beginning of, or during, the cooking process. This allows the flavors to penetrate and distribute evenly. Salt is either omitted or added sparingly in the bread doughs because it produces a tough texture. In yogurt salads salt is always stirred in last, just before serving, because it tends to separate and thin the yogurt.

I always use Kosher salt in all my cooking, because it is milder and more flavorful than other salts. I also happen to like the feel of its granulated texture on my fingers. The recipes in this book have been tested with kosher salt. It is, however, perfectly acceptable to use other salt, as long as you adjust its quantity in the recipe—remember, you need much less of the substitute salt—about half the amount you would use of kosher salt.

REFRIGERATING AND FREEZING

One of the wonderful things about Indian food is that a great many dishes can be prepared well in advance, refrigerated or frozen, and reheated just before serving without losing the main flavoring or original texture.

Almost all the dishes that have gravies or sauces, as well as soups, most pureed vegetables, certain herb relishes, and certain breads can be frozen successfully. The secret of success lies not so much in the freezing as in the defrosting and reheating. One rule for successful defrosting that applies to all dishes is that you must not be in a hurry. The defrosting process needs to be carried out slowly, preferably overnight in the refrigerator. Only when the food has been thoroughly defrosted should it be reheated. In most instances you will find that the liquid has separated and has collected at the bottom of the container in the form of a gelatinous mass. No need for alarm. Do not rush to stir it all up and mix it in; this is a sure way to destroy the fragile texture of the meat and vegetable pieces. Begin by placing the pan on very low heat. When the liquid comes just to a simmer, gently stir the mixture with a fork. This method of slow heating allows the food pieces to absorb the moisture back into their tissues, thus restoring their firmness and body. It is essential that the meat be stirred with a fork, and not a spoon, because it is gentler.

One drawback to freezing food is that most of the fresh herbs, some spices, and salt lose part of their fragrance and potency. Therefore, be sure to taste the dishes and readjust the salt and seasonings before reheating. Usually, a pinch of *Mughal garam masala, garam masala,* or some powdered roasted cumin seeds, and some chopped fresh herbs folded into the dish just before serving, do the trick in reviving all the flavors.

Most fried, grilled, and roasted foods, yogurt salads, puddings, and rice preparations do not freeze successfully; they lose both flavor and texture in the process. Therefore, I caution against freezing them. They can, however, be refrigerated successfully.

THE SENSES

Of the human senses, the visual sense and the sense of smell are the most important in Indian cooking. They are what Indian cooks rely upon most often. This is because Indian chefs, unlike most others, never taste a dish while it is cooking or, for that matter, even after it is cooked, to check for flavors and "doneness." This is because in most parts of India there are religious or social taboos against putting food in one's mouth while it is cooking. Among certain sects the food has to be offered to the gods for their blessings before mortals can consider themselves worthy of putting it in their mouths. Therefore, out of sheer necessity, Indian cooks develop a greater sensitivity to and a deeper understanding of the relationships between aromas, textures, and flavors from a very early age. Indian cooks believe that if a dish looks and smells right, then it has got to taste good. An experienced eye can often gauge exactly whether the onions are fried to the correct degree of brownness, whether the sauce has achieved the appropriate glaze, and if the color and consistency of the gravy are in proper balance. So, too, can a sensitive Indian nose tell whether the spices are cooked and if they are harmoniously blended in the dish.

Equally important is the sense of feel, especially in kneading bread dough and in making sweetmeats, fudges, and meat dishes. With the touch of a finger an Indian cook can tell if enough liquid has been incorporated into the dough and if it has been kneaded enough. Or with a gentle stir of a spoon, know if the pieces of meat are cooked to perfection. (When fully cooked, they move like marshmallows or float like dumplings in the sauce, without any resistance).

Before you start exercising and relying upon the judgment of these senses, you must first familiarize yourself with the dishes and the techniques for cooking them, and develop the tactile ability to know what to expect at the end of any process. In other words, what the dish should smell, look, and taste like. To help you reproduce the dishes exactly as I have prepared them, I have given detailed explanations of each process for each recipe in this book wherever necessary. After you create the dish a few times in your own kitchen, the flavors and the details of the process should register in your mind. Then you will find yourself relying more and more upon your senses, and beginning to cook with the same spontaneity that I do.

A final word of advice:

If you are well prepared, with all the ingredients measured and ready to be added at a moment's notice, the whole process of Indian cooking will be much simplified. This is especially true when preparing dishes that call for adding several dry spices before the liquid. For example, in Broccoli Smothered in Garlic Oil (*Hare Gobhi ki Sabzi*, p. 296), turmeric is added to hot oil and fried for two seconds before you add the broccoli. Unless the broccoli is added almost instantly, the turmeric will burn and the entire dish pick up the burnt-smell flavor. Similarly, in Lucknow Sour Lentils (p. 335), as soon as the spice-perfumed butter is prepared, it is folded into the lentil puree. Any delay will overbrown the cumin or overfry the garlic paste, which in turn will ruin the dish. It is crucial, therefore, to keep the lentil puree fully ready (thoroughly heated, checked for salt and consistency, and transferred to a serving bowl) before you begin preparing the spice-perfumed butter.

Remember always to read the recipe carefully and assemble all the ingredients before beginning the actual cooking.

Read the recipes carefully and fully. Many recipes call for preliminary procedures, such as soaking, resting, and marinating. Therefore, be sure to notice these special considerations and make allowances for time.

The lengths of time suggested in all the recipes are approximate. They will vary depending upon the stove, the burner, the type and size of pan you are using, and also the temperature of the ingredients. Therefore, you should look for the suggested texture, color, or consistency indicated in the recipe.

Until you are thoroughly familiar with the use of Indian ingredients and cooking techniques, always allow yourself more time than is suggested in the recipe.

In many recipes you will notice that the meat is cooked for a long period of time until it is very soft and fragile. *It is not overcooked meat*. This is the Indian style of cooking, tailored especially for the Indian style of eating. Therefore you should throw away your Western concepts when cooking Indian and follow your senses more. With experience you will begin to improvise a lot more than you thought possible.

In order to be consistent, the recipes in this book are worked out in American measurements, in cups and spoons. To help you with shopping, here are some conversions.

1 medium-sized onion	= ¼ pound (⅔ cup finely chopped)
1 medium sized tomato	= ¼ pound (½ cup chopped)
1 medium-sized potato	= ¼ pound
1 garden-pea-sized lump of asafetida	= ⅛ teaspoon ground asafetida
1 inch-round ball of tamarind	= 2 ounces
	(Tamarind pulp is like slightly dry pitted prunes. To measure, pinch a small portion off and press it into a rough ball. If the ball looks too small, add more pulp and re-form the ball. Continue until you have the desired size.)
1 tablespoon finely chopped fresh ginger root	= 1"x1"x1" piece fresh ginger root
1 tablespoon finely chopped garlic	= 3 large cloves garlic
1 teaspoon finely chopped garlic	= 1 large clove garlic
½ teaspoon finely chopped garlic	= 1 medium clove garlic
⅓ teaspoon finely chopped garlic	= 1 small clove garlic

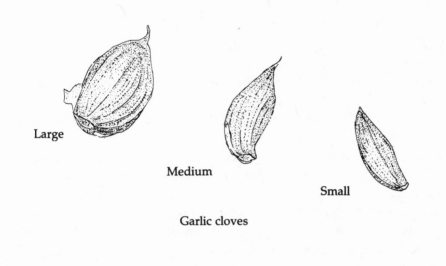

Large

Medium

Small

Garlic cloves

A personal note

Now that you are equipped with all the necessary skills for Indian cooking, let me give you a bit of personal advice. Feel at home in the kitchen, try to be relaxed and handle things with a certain firmness and confidence. To a great extent, cooking is like handling an infant—it blossoms with each gentle caring touch. And most of all, enjoy what you are doing. After all, cooking should be a form of relaxation.

Planning and Serving Indian Meals

There is one fundamental difference between the Western and Indian styles of planning and serving meals. A typical Western meal is planned around a main course consisting of meat, chicken, fish, or shellfish. The size of the main course is governed by various rules of thumb, such as the fact that a whole chicken or a pound of meat serves two to four persons.

A traditional Indian meal, on the other hand, is served all at once and has no such thing as a main course. There is, however, a main dish. This status is given to a particularly elaborate preparation that is a culinary creation in and of itself.

Most nonvegetarian dishes are considered main dishes simply for economic reasons. The cost of meat in India is about five times that of vegetables; poultry and shellfish cost twice as much as meat. The quantity of the main dish is thus based not upon the number of people to be served, as in the West, but upon the family's budget. A pound of meat, or half a pound of fish or shellfish, or one whole chicken is usually cooked for a meal no matter what the size of the family. If company drops by, a few additional side dishes are added and everybody helps himself or herself to a smaller portion of the main dish.

The Western meal, consisting of several courses, is served in various stages. An Indian meal, on the other hand, is served all at once. All the dishes are either placed at the center of the table, so that everyone can help himself to each dish, or served in the classic manner in a *thali*. A *thali* is a large, rimmed metal plate, from fifteen to eighteen inches in diameter, containing several small metal bowls (*katoori*). The various dishes, including soup and dessert, are served in these small bowls. The wafers, relishes, and pickles are put directly in one corner of the plate and the center of the plate is reserved for the staple rice or bread.

Indian food is traditionally eaten with one's fingers. In urban homes, however, spoons and forks are widely used especially in eating rice and soupy dishes. Indians believe that food does not taste quite the same when eaten with a fork or spoon, just as some fervent gourmands adhere to the belief that something is lost when Chinese food is eaten with a fork instead of chopsticks. Using bread as an eating utensil really does seem logical, because Indian breads, unlike French or other Western breads, are highly pliable, the way Mexican wheat tortillas are. It is, therefore, easy to tear a piece of the bread and use it as a scoop or to wrap it around a piece of meat or vegetable. Eating rice with one's fingers, especially when it is mixed with soupy sauces, is a different matter, however. Even experts in this field would agree that it is a very tricky affair for which a long apprenticeship is a prerequisite. I personally prefer to use a fork or spoon. Traditionalists, however, would argue to the contrary.

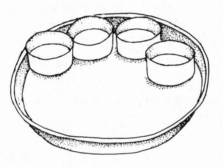

Thali with *katoori*

MENU PLANNING

As you can see, the differences between Western and Indian customs in the planning and serving of meals are not irreconcilable. With minor modifications (such as cooking a larger amount of meat per person to correspond to a typical Western portion), the Indian food plan can easily be adapted for Western-style serving.

An Indian meal essentially consists of three dishes: a main dish, a side dish, and a staple. Of course there is nothing to prevent you serving more than one dish from each category—particularly several side dishes—as is commonly done at parties and feasts. You can also omit a main or side dish altogether for light meals. The important thing to remember is that a staple must accompany an Indian meal.

A *main dish* can either be nonvegetarian or vegetarian. The nonvegetarian main dish can consist of meat, poultry, fish, shell-fish, or eggs, and their products. A vegetarian main dish, on the other hand, consists of vegetables, *dal* of all varieties, or Indian cheese. Vegetarian main dishes usually have gravies and frequently require special preparation. Several of these dishes are expressly created to resemble their nonvegetarian counterparts, a practice also found in Chinese, Greek, and Middle Eastern vegetarian cooking.

A *side dish* can either be vegetables or *dal* or yogurt salads. These vegetable preparations differ from the vegetable main dishes in that they are usually stir-fried and require very little time to prepare. *Dal* preparations are basically soupy purees flavored with fragrant spices and herbs. They are usually used for dipping breads, or they are poured over rice, mixed, and eaten. These *dal* side dishes are very different from the main dish *dals* which are usually cooked with vegetables as stews, or turned into dumplings, kaftas, or rolls.

Yogurt salads consist of various ingredients—such as raw or cooked vegetables, fruits, nuts, dumplings—all or some of which are folded into the yogurt. These salads are very light and can serve as simple unfilling meals, especially good during the summer.

An *accompanying staple* can be either rice or bread. An Indian meal, unlike a Western one, is not complete without a bread or a rice dish. This actually makes a lot of sense, because the consistency of many Indian dishes is much like a thick soup or a stew; both are difficult to eat with a fork. Also, without a staple, you cannot do full justice to the wonderful sauce, which is the best part of the dish. And Indian dishes are spicier than Western dishes, and should not be eaten straight. For this reason, they are either mixed with rice or scooped up with a piece of bread.

Generally rice is served with the soupier dishes, and bread with the drier ones. Rice acts as a sponge to soak up the juices of the sauce, making the dish much easier to handle and eat. A fairly dry piece of meat or vegetable can be scooped up with a piece of bread, but if the sauce is too thin, the bread may fall apart when maneuvered and dipped. This is why most dishes, including the legume preparations served in areas where bread is the staple, as in the North, are much drier and have thick, almost nonexistent gravies. In the South, where rice is the staple, the dishes are soupy and much like broth.

In order to simplify menu planning, the recipes in this book are organized by categories of dishes, as described above: main dish, side dish, accompanying staple, and so on. To plan a meal, simply pick a dish from any category and follow the menu-planning suggestions given at the end of the recipe. Or pick a dish from each category, taking particular care to ensure diversity in flavor, color, and texture, yet blending the dishes so that they complement each other.

Note: In Indian cooking, potatoes, sweet potatoes, yams, and other starchy roots are treated as vegetables; they are not categorized as starches and grouped with rice and bread as in Western cooking. Therefore, an Indian meal may very well be composed of the main dish Whole Potatoes in Spicy Yogurt Gravy (*Dum Aloo,* p. 258), the side dish Lucknow Sour Lentils (*Lakhnawi Khatti Dal,* p. 335), and the accompanying staple Fragrant Pilaf, Banaras Style (*Banarasi Pullao,* p. 368). This is definitely not an example of a well-balanced diet, because all the dishes are high in carbohydrates, but as far as taste, texture, and aroma are concerned, they blend exquisitely.

There are a few general rules worth noting when planning an Indian menu. If the main dish is a *dal,* the side dish should be a vegetable. However, if the main dish is a vegetable, then the side dish could be either a *dal* or vegetables. In other words, it is perfectly acceptable to serve two vegetable preparations, but not two *dal* dishes, as this would make the meal very heavy.

If the main dish is an elegant pilaf, no additional accompanying staple is necessary, because the pilaf contains rice.

If the main dish contains both meat and vegetables, the side dish may be omitted. However, you must be sure to increase the quantity of the main dish to compensate for the omitted dish.

All these dishes, including the staple and such accompaniments as wafers, relishes, and pickles, should be served at the same time. The dishes may either be apportioned on to individual plates and then brought to the table, or placed in the center of the table for buffet serving. Desserts should be served immediately following the meal.

Traditionally in India appetizers and sweetmeats are eaten like snacks, with a beverage, at just about any hour of the day. Among the more affluent Indians, however, appetizers are now served as delectable hors d'oeuvres with cocktails. There are several appetizers that make an excellent first course. They also make a grand opening for an elegant meal. And, even though serving a beverage with sweetmeats at the end of an Indian meal is unconventional, I prefer to do so because it makes a perfect ending to the meal.

WHAT TO DRINK WITH AN INDIAN MEAL

The drink most commonly served with an Indian meal is ice-cold water. Sometimes fresh lemonade, fruit punch, or yogurt drinks are served instead. The tradition of serving wine with a meal does not exist in India. This by no means suggests that there is no liquor in India. On the contrary. India has been producing alcoholic beverages since Vedic times. The ancient Indians brewed and drank *Vasa*, a liquor made from fermented rice. The holy priests and the noblemen drank a more refined brew called *Soma Rasa* (*Soma* means moon; *Rasa* means juice) which was made from the Moon Creeper plant that once grew in the Himalayas. India today produces several varieties of alcohol, including whisky, gin, vodka, and rum. These are consumed primarily by men, because Indian women have, for the most part, traditionally abstained from alcoholic beverages.

What India does not have is good-quality wine. This is because vineyards need high altitudes and a cool dry climate to flourish—

and both are in limited supply in India. Whatever vineyards did exist were originally brought by the Moghuls from Persia; they planted grapes in the cool hills of the North. Unfortunately, the venture was not much of a success, since the wine had often turned to vinegar by the time it reached the Moghul courts in the arid city of Delhi. Also, the Moghuls found that the subtle bouquet of their wine was easily overpowered by the fierce Indian spices. They gradually gave up wine and settled for the cool *Sharbat* (fruit drinks) and fruit punches. Today, with the aid of modern farming techniques and storage equipment, India is producing all varieties of wine, although Indian viticulture has a long way to go.

I have found that beer, ale, and certain wines go well with Indian food. Beer and ale are excellent served with lunch, particularly on hot summer afternoons. In addition to being good thirst quenchers, they add a slight bite and bitterness which is a perfect complement to the spicy food. Sangria is also ideal as a luncheon beverage, if you like a fruity taste. For a nonalcoholic drink, there is nothing better than a homemade punch made with the fruits of the season; this is the official drink served at presidential dinners in India.

For suppers and formal dinners, I prefer to serve wine: chilled rosé with *tandoori* food and dishes that have cream, yogurt, and nut sauces; and hearty reds, such as a Chianti or a California or French Burgundy, for dishes in onion and tomato gravy. I accompany fish and shellfish, no matter how they are prepared, with a chilled Chablis. Chablis also goes beautifully with all appetizers and may be served in place of a cocktail.

One important point to remember while selecting wine for an Indian meal: Indian food is highly fragrant with aromatic spices and herbs. The wine that goes with it, therefore, must be strong enough to stand up to it and not get lost in the strong seasonings. So do not waste money on expensive wines with fine subtle bouquets; not only will they taste bland and flavorless against the food, you will not be doing justice to the fine wine. The wines best suited for Indian food are the moderately priced and inexpensive wines.

Appetizers, Snacks, and Soups

Appetizers and Snacks

(Namkeen)

Crab Malabar   *(Kekada* [Crab] *Chat)*
Cold Minted Potatoes   *(Aloo Podina Chat)*
Cold Potato Appetizer   *(Aloo Chat)*
Fragrant Stuffed Tomatoes   *(Bhare Tamatar)*
Moghul Kabobs with Raisin Stuffing   *(Hussaini Kabab)*
Kabob Patties Laced with Ginger and Mint   *(Shamme Kabab)*
Onion Fritters   *(Piaz Pakode)*
Cauliflower Fritters   *(Gobhi Pakode)*
Indian Cheese Fritters   *(Paneer Pakode)*
Shrimp Fritters   *(Jheenga Pakode)*
Spinach and Mung Bean Dumplings   *(Moong Badian)*
Silky Bean Dumplings   *(Bade)*
Savory Pastries with Spicy Potato Filling   *(Aloo Samosa)*
Savory Meat Pastries   *(Keema Samosa)*
Savory Crackers   *(Matthi)*
Indian Fenugreek Crackers   *(Kasoori Mathari)*

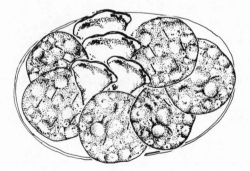

In an Indian meal there is no equivalent to the French hors d'œuvres, the Italian antipasto, or the American fruit cup. Appetizers are traditionally eaten the way *Dim Sum* are eaten in Chinese tea houses—as a snack, at any time of the day, and most always accompanying a beverage. But with the rise of an affluent middle class, appetizers have begun to find their way into Indian meals. Because of this new and great demand, many main-course dishes have been modified slightly and served as first courses. Some of them are so elegant and delicately flavored, I can't think of a more refreshing and delectable way to stimulate the palate. These include Crab Malabar (p. 101), Cold Minted Potates (p. 103), and Moghul Kabobs with Raisin Stuffing (p. 107). Indian Cheese Fritters (p. 117) or Kabob Patties Laced with Ginger and Mint (p. 109) are really finger foods and make excellent hors d'œuvres with cocktails. Many of these appetizers also make lovely individual lunches or light suppers.

Indian snacks are traditionally eaten with a relish. There are different relishes to accompany different appetizers. Although not essential, they do provide an interesting contrast: tangy sweet or soothingly mellow against peppery hot or spicy food. They also perk up rather bland-tasting snacks.

Until recently, a separate soup course would have been completely unthinkable as part of an Indian meal. Today, however, there are several soups, not to mention the famous Mulligatawny, that are often served as a separate first course. In fact, many new soups have been created for just this purpose.

If you are planning to serve a first course with an Indian meal, serve only wafers, crackers, or other similarly light things with the drinks.

Crab Malabar

(Kekada Chat)

Crab Malabar, as the name suggests, is a specialty of Malabar, a coastal region in southern India known for the wealth of its shellfish. Traditionally, the dish is fairly hot and contains a lot of gravy so as to increase the number of servings. My recipe yields just enough subtle fennel-laced, garlicky tomato gravy to coat the shellfish. This way, the tender morsels of crab meat may be enjoyed to their fullest. The crab must be sweet and succulent and the coriander utterly fresh and fragrant for this dish to taste perfect. For a variation, you may substitute cooked lobster meat, which is also very good.

For 6 persons

1 pound fresh or frozen cooked crab meat (preferably Alaska King Crab meat)
3 tablespoons light vegetable oil
¾ cup finely chopped onions
1 tablespoon finely chopped garlic
¼–½ teaspoon red pepper
1½ teaspoons paprika
⅓ teaspoon thyme (or ¼ teaspoon carom seeds, crushed)
¼ teaspoon fennel seeds, crushed
3 cups peeled ripe tomatoes, cut into 1-inch cubes
Kosher Salt
4 tablespoons finely chopped scallions, including the green part
4 tablespoons coarsely chopped fresh coriander leaves

1. Pick over crab meat thoroughly, and cut into large (½-inch to 1-inch) pieces. If using frozen crab meat, thaw following directions on the package. Drain and reserve the juices. Set aside.

2. Heat the oil in a frying pan (one with a lid) and add onions.

(continued)

Cook onions over medium heat until wilted and lightly colored, but not browned (about 5 minutes).

3. Add garlic and cook for an additional minute. Add red pepper, paprika, thyme (or carom), and fennel, stirring rapidly. Cook for 2 more minutes. Add 1 cup of tomatoes (save 2 cups of nicely cubed tomato pieces to be folded in later) and the reserved juices from crab meat (if using frozen crab meat). Lower heat and simmer, covered, until the sauce is reduced to a thick pulp (about 15 minutes). Turn off heat.

4. Fold in the crab meat. Add salt to taste. When cool, carefully fold in tomatoes and scallions, making sure not to break the fragile crab pieces.

5. Cover and refrigerate for at least 4 hours or until thoroughly chilled. Just before serving, fold in chopped coriander leaves, and serve over a bed of shredded lettuce.

Note: The *chat* may be made a day ahead and kept refrigerated. In that case, the chopped coriander leaves should be folded in just before serving so they won't wilt.

This exquisite first course must be followed by an equally elegant and subtle main dish. I prefer to serve yogurt- and cream-based Moghul dishes to contrast with this southern specialty. Examples include Lamb Braised in Aromatic Cream Sauce (p. 164), Lamb Fillets Braised in Yogurt Cardamom Sauce (p. 168), Fragrant Yogurt-Braised Chicken (p. 211), Velvet Creamed Shrimp (p. 245), and Royal Braised Vegetables in Cardamom Nut Sauce (p. 269). This also makes a marvelous light lunch or late supper main course, served hot over a bed of rice and accompanied by a glass of chilled Chablis.

Cold Minted Potatoes

(Aloo Podina Chat)

Chat is Indian salad; it is usually eaten by itself, as a snack or appetizer. There are basically two types of *chat*: one made with vegetables such as potatoes or *arbi*, a variety of starchy root; the other made with fruits such as bananas, guava, papaya, apples, or *chikoo*, an Indian fruit that resembles a kiwi in its shape. Its meat, however, is sugar-sweet, and light brown in color; its texture like an Anjou pear.

Of the many varieties of *chat*, the most popular are two *Aloo Chats*, one flavored with mint and the other with spices. *Chat* is traditionally served on a flat serving plate accompanied by tooth picks for easy buffet serving with cocktails. *Chat*, as a general rule, is eaten cooled—never chilled, because chilling dims the fragrances of spices and herbs.

Red wax potatoes are best for making *Aloo Chat*, because when cooked and while still warm, they retain a tight-grained texture as compared to baking potatoes, which are more porous. When salad dressing is poured over these potatoes, they do not become mushy and fall apart, and they remain firm after being sliced.

For 8 persons

6 medium-sized boiling potatoes (red wax potatoes are best)
2 small cucumbers, 5–6 inches long
2 teaspoons Kosher salt
2 tablespoons lemon juice
1 teaspoon ground roasted cumin seeds (p. 66)
1 teaspoon ground roasted coriander seeds (p. 66)
¼ teaspoon each of black and red pepper
½ teaspoon black salt (optional)
¼ cup firmly packed chopped fresh mint leaves (or substitute 1 tablespoon powdered dry mint leaves)

(continued)

1. Boil potatoes in their jackets in water to cover until tender but firm. Drain and peel them. While still warm, cut them into ½–¾-inch cubes of uniform size.

2. Peel cucumbers, and cut them in half, lengthwise. If the seeds look mature and hard, scrape them out and discard. Cut the cucumbers into ½–¾-inch pieces of uniform size.

3. Put potatoes and cucumbers in a ceramic or glass bowl. Add Kosher salt and lemon juice. Toss briefly to coat all the pieces. Add the remaining ingredients and toss again, carefully, so as not to break the pieces of potato. Cover the bowl and place it in the refrigerator to cool thoroughly (it should not be chilled). Check for salt, and serve heaped on lettuce leaves.

Note: The *chat* may be made several hours ahead and kept refrigerated. Remove from refrigerator about 15 minutes before you are ready to serve. To perk up flavors, sprinkle on a little ground roasted cumin seed.

This fragrant and refreshing appetizer may be followed with any main dish except, of course, those containing potatoes. Try Meat Curry (p. 170), Chicken in Onion Tomato Gravy (p. 208), or Shrimp Laced with Mild Fragrant Spices (p. 240).

Cold Potato Appetizer

(Aloo Chat)

For 8 persons

1 tablespoon *Chat Masala*, homemade (see recipe below), or purchased

⅓ cup cold water

6 medium-sized boiling potatoes (red wax potatoes are best)

2 cups ripe tomatoes, cut into ½–¾ inch cubes

4 tablespoons finely chopped onions

3-4 tablespoons coarsely chopped fresh coriander leaves

1 teaspoon ground roasted cumin seeds (p. 66)

Kosher Salt

Juice of half a medium-sized lemon

1. Mix the *chat masala* with the water and set aside.

2. Boil potatoes in their jackets, in water to cover, until tender but firm. Drain and peel them. Cut the potatoes into ½–¾ inch cubes, put them in a glass or ceramic bowl, and while still warm, pour the *masala* mixture over them. Mix the potatoes, carefully, to distribute the spices. Let rest, uncovered, at room temperature, until potatoes have had time to absorb the spices (about 10–15 minutes), stirring a few times.

3. Add chopped tomatoes, onions, and coriander leaves to the potatoes but *do not stir the mixture.* Cover the bowl and place it in the refrigerator until the potatoes are fully cooled—they should *not* be chilled. This will take about 30 minutes.

4. Take the bowl from the refrigerator and gently stir to mix all the ingredients. Sprinkle the cumin, salt, and lemon juice to taste. Toss and serve over lettuce leaves.

Note: The *chat* may be made several hours ahead and kept refrigerated. Remove from refrigerator about 15 minutes before you are ready to serve. To perk up flavors, sprinkle on a little ground roasted cumin seed.

(continued)

Chat Masala: To make homemade *chat masala*, mix ¾ teaspoon ground roasted cumin seeds with ¼ teaspoon each of red pepper, black pepper, ground asafetida, mango powder, ½ teaspoon black salt, and ¾ teaspoon Kosher salt.

Follow the menu suggestions given for Cold Minted Potatoes *(Aloo Chat)* on page 104.

Fragrant Stuffed Tomatoes

(Bhare Tamatar)

These delightful little tomato cups, bursting with the fragrance of coriander leaves and garlic and shimmering with butter glaze, are perfect for stimulating anyone's appetite. The wonderful thing about this first course is that the stuffing may be prepared ahead and kept frozen until the day you are ready to serve the dish, so that it takes only a few minutes to assemble.

For 8 persons

All the ingredients for making ½ recipe of Dry-cooked Spicy Ground Meat *(Sookha Keema,* page 158.)

48 cherry tomatoes (about one quart or 1½ pounds) or 8 medium-sized tomatoes (about 2 pounds)

4 tablespoons melted *usli ghee* (p. 50) or light vegetable oil

1 teaspoon finely chopped garlic

½ teaspoon Kosher salt

2 tablespoons finely chopped fresh coriander leaves

1. Make ½ recipe of *Sookha Keema* following the instructions on page 158, and set aside.
2. Preheat the oven to 425°F.
3. Rinse tomatoes and wipe dry. Cut the green tops from the tomatoes and, using a small knife or a spoon, scoop out the pulp

into a bowl. Mince the pulp finely with a knife, and stir in *ghee*, garlic, and salt. Set aside.

4. Distribute the *Sookha Keema* filling equally among the tomato cups (about 1 teaspoon of filling for each cherry tomato; 2 tablespoons for medium-sized tomatoes), taking care not to pack the filling down.

5. Arrange filled tomatoes in a greased shallow baking dish in one layer. Dribble the pulpy tomato sauce over the filling in the tomatoes. Pour ⅓ cup boiling water around the edges of the baking dish.

6. Bake in the middle level of the oven, uncovered, until the tomatoes are cooked and look slightly blistered (15 minutes for cherry tomatoes; 25 minutes for medium-sized tomatoes). Serve hot or warm, sprinkled with chopped fresh coriander, on a bed of shredded lettuce.

To maintain an interesting variation in flavors and textures all through the meal, avoid serving a main dish that contains ground meat or tomatoes. Good choices are Chicken in Creamed Coconut Sauce (p. 213), Pan Fried Fillet of Sole Laced with Carom (p. 248), Mung Bean and Cauliflower Stew (p. 278), or Chick-pea Dumplings in Yogurt Sauce (p. 284).

Moghul Kabobs with Raisin Stuffing

(Hussaini Kabab)

These delicate and mellow-tasting kabobs, fragrant with a subtle blend of Moghul spices, are a classic example of Moghul cooking. They are shaped like Italian sausages, stuffed with raisins and almonds, and cooked in a frying pan. To serve these kabobs as hors d'œuvres, roll them into small, cocktail-size sausages (about 1½ inches long and ½ inch thick) and cook them for about 8–10 minutes. And if you finely crush the stuffing, you will find it much easier to stuff the kabobs.

(continued)

For 8 persons (makes 16 kabobs)

THE KABOB

1 pound lean ground beef
     (preferably ground
     round), or lean ground
     lamb
2 teaspoons finely chopped
     garlic
1½ teaspoons finely chopped
     fresh ginger root
1 teaspoon black cumin seeds,
     crushed (or substitute 1
     teaspoon ground cumin)

1 teaspoon ground coriander
1 teaspoon paprika
1 teaspoon *Mughal garam
     masala* (p. 37)
½ teaspoon black pepper
⅛ teaspoon ground asafetida
¼ cup bread crumbs
1 tablespoon sweet butter
1 large egg, lightly beaten
1¼ teaspoons Kosher salt

STUFFING

2 tablespoon blanched
     chopped almonds
2 tablespoons seedless raisins

2 tablespoons light vegetable
     oil for frying

1. Put all the ingredients for the kabobs in a bowl, and mix thoroughly. Cover, and let the mixture rest for ½ hour. (The kabob mixture may be made ahead and refrigerated for up to 2 days, or frozen. Defrost thoroughly before proceeding with the recipe.)

2. Mix almonds and raisins together for stuffing.

3. Divide the kabob mixture into 16 equal portions. Shape each into a "sausage." Make a lengthwise depression in the center of each kabob, and fill with stuffing (about ¾ teaspoon). Pinch meat closed over the stuffing, reshaping each sausage as you go along. Continue with the rest of the meat mixture the same way. (The stuffed kabobs can be shaped several hours ahead and kept covered and refrigerated until you are ready to fry them.)

4. When ready to fry, heat the oil in a frying pan—preferably a non-stick one—for a minute, and add the kabobs. (If the frying pan is not large enough to accomodate all the kabobs in one layer, use two pans.) Fry the kabobs over medium heat, turning them often,

until they are cooked and browned all over (about 15 minutes for beef, 25 minutes for lamb). The kabobs may be cooked under a broiler, or over a grill. (The duration of cooking will depend upon the intensity of heat, the distance between the meat and the source of heat, and whether one wants the meat medium or well-done.) Serve these kabobs accompanied by Raw Onion Relish (*Kache Piaz,* p. 431) or Roasted Onions (*Bhone Piaz,* p. 313).

These kabobs are fairly substantial; therefore the main dish that follows should be very light and contain a lot of sauce. Avoid serving lamb or beef as a main dish. You might try light and subtle fish or shellfish dishes, such as Shrimp Poached in Coconut Milk with Fresh Herbs (p. 243), or Fish in Velvet Yogurt Sauce (p. 253). For a vegetarian meal to follow, try Cauliflower, Green Peas, and Potatoes in Spicy Herb Sauce (p. 256), or Mixed Lentils and Vegetable Stew (p. 280). You can also serve these kabobs as a main dish (this recipe will serve 3–4 persons). To keep the meal light, pair them with a simple lentil puree, such as Lentils with Garlic Butter (p. 332), or Lucknow Sour Lentils (p. 335), and plain cooked rice (p. 357).

Kabob Patties Laced with Ginger and Mint

(Shamme Kabab)

Shamme Kabab, bursting with the fragrance of mint and ginger and laden with hearty split peas, is truly the most exquisitely flavored of all kabobs. For best results, use only fresh mint leaves. Beef cannot be substituted for lamb in this kabob, because the taste of lamb is essential in creating the authentic flavor of this dish.

An important point: the cooked kabob mixture should be fairly thick, like bread dough, before you form it into patties. Before they are fried, the kabobs are coated only with a thin film of egg white to impart a shiny glaze. If the meat mixture is not dry enough to hold its shape, it will splatter and scatter into the oil.

(continued)

These kabobs take a little longer than *Hussaini Kabobs* (p. 107) because the meat mixture is cooked before being shaped into patties and fried. So be sure to allow enough time when planning your menu.

For 8–12 persons (makes 24 kabobs)

FOR COOKING THE MEAT:

1 pound lean ground lamb

½ cup yellow split peas (*channa dal*)

⅓ cup finely chopped onions

2½ tablespoons finely chopped garlic

1 tablespoon finely chopped fresh ginger root

1 teaspoon ground cumin

½ teaspoon ground cardamom

¼ teaspoon ground cloves

1 teaspoon black pepper

½ teaspoon red pepper

1½ teaspoons Kosher salt

1½ cups cold water

FOR FLAVORING MEAT MIXTURE:

1 tablespoon peanut or corn oil

⅔ cup finely chopped onions

1–2 green chilies, seeded, and coarsely chopped

⅓ cup loosely packed fresh mint leaves, coarsely chopped (or substitute 2 tablespoons powdered dry mint leaves)

1 teaspoon lemon juice

Peanut or corn oil, enough to fill a frying pan to a depth of ¾ inch

Whites of 2 medium eggs, lightly beaten

1. Put all the ingredients for cooking the meat into a heavy saucepan. Over medium-high heat bring the mixture to a boil. Lower heat to medium and cook, covered, until the meat is fully cooked and the water totally absorbed into the meat (about 45 minutes). If there is still liquid remaining, uncover, and cook briskly over medium-high heat until the moisture evaporates and the meat mixture looks dry. (It is essential that the meat mixture be

very dry; otherwise the patties will disintegrate during frying. If, for any reason, your meat mixture does not dry during brisk cooking, add ½ cup of bread crumbs to it and mix well. The crumbs will soak up the excess moisture.)

2. In a small frying pan, heat the oil and add onions. Over medium-high heat, fry the onions until they turn caramel brown (about 10 minutes), stirring constantly to prevent burning.

3. Add the fried onions along with the green chilies, mint, and lemon juice to the meat mixture. Grind the mixture in a meat grinder with the fine blade attachment or in a food processor. *Be careful not to make a paste of this.* It should have a coarse grainy texture, yet be smooth enough to be shaped into patties and fried. (The kabob mixture can be made ahead and refrigerated up to 2 days, or frozen. Defrost thoroughly before proceeding with the recipe.)

4. Divide the meat mixture into 24 equal portions. Shape the pieces into 2-inch round patties. (The kabobs can be shaped several hours ahead and kept covered and refrigerated until you are ready to fry them.)

5. When ready to fry, heat the oil in a *kadhai,* chicken fryer, or frying pan until hot (350°F). Dip kabobs in beaten egg whites and slip them into the oil. Add no more kabobs than can easily be accommodated in one layer in the pan. Brown them evenly on both sides (about 1 minute for each side). Take them out with a slotted spoon and drain on paper towels. Continue with the remaining patties. Serve hot accompanied by Roasted Onions (*Bhone Piaz,* p. 313).

Note: The kabobs may be made several hours ahead and, just before serving, reheated, loosely covered·with foil, on the center shelf of a preheated 375°F oven for 12–15 minutes.

These are among my personal favorites. They blend with just about any main dish, though a lamb or beef dish might seem a little redundant. To keep the meal light, try serving a vegetarian main dish, such as Cauliflower, Green Peas, and Potatoes in Spicy Herb Sauce (p. 256), or Round Gourd in Fragrant Gravy (p. 264). Or you may serve these kabobs as a main dish (this recipe will serve 6) over a bed of vegetable pilaf, such as Okra Pilaf (p. 373), or Emperor's Pilaf with Black Mushrooms (p. 375), with a bottle of chilled rosé or burgundy.

FRITTERS

Indian fritters are in a class by themselves. What distinguishes them is their spicy coating of chick-pea flour *(besan)* batter. They are made with vegetables, such as broccoli, cauliflower, eggplant, onions, plantain (green bananas), potatoes, scallions, shallots, spinach, tomatoes, and zucchini; with Indian cheese *(paneer)*; and with chicken, shrimp, and fish.

Fritters are either batter-dipped or spoon-fried. Batter-dipped fritters are made by dipping the pieces of vegetables, cheese, meat, or fish in batter, dropping them in hot oil, and frying. Spooned fritters are made only with vegetables, which are folded into a thick, pastelike batter and then spooned into hot oil and fried slowly over low heat, which enables them to get crisp and crunchy.

Sometimes a little baking soda is added to fritter batter to give the coating a light and fluffy texture; sometimes the fritters are refried to give them an even crisper texture.

A crucial ingredient in successful fritters is the oil. *It must be fresh and sweet-smelling so that it will not mask the subtle flavor of the food.* I never use the same oil twice for frying fritters, because it loses its gentle flavor when exposed to prolonged high heat. After frying the fritters, I strain the oil through a double layer of cheesecloth and use it for cooking robust-flavored dishes that contain onions or tomatoes. Always store used oil in the refrigerator.

Onion Fritters

(Piaz Pakode)

These fritters, spicy and fragrant with cumin, have a lovely crunchy texture on the outside and are soft inside. They are also wonderful when made with shallots.

For 6–8 persons

THE BATTER:

1 cup unsifted chick-pea flour
  (*besan*)
2 teaspoons peanut or corn oil
  or melted vegetable
  shortening

1 teaspoon ground cumin
1½ teaspoons Kosher salt
1–2 green chilies, seeded and
  minced
½ cup warm water (90–100°F)

2 medium-sized onions
  Peanut or corn oil, enough
  to fill a *kadhai*, chicken
  fryer, or large casserole to
  a depth of 2 inches

1. Sift the flour into a large bowl. Rub the 2 teaspoons oil or shortening into it with the fingers, following the directions on page 125–126. Stir in cumin, salt, and chilies. Add water in a thin stream, constantly beating the mixture with an electric beater, wire whisk, or with your hands. The batter should be very thick and smooth. (To make the batter in a food processor or in an electric blender, put all the ingredients into the container of the machine and process until thoroughly blended and smooth. Then transfer the mixture to a bowl.)

2. Beat the batter vigorously for 10 minutes or until it turns pale, light, and fluffy. Cover the bowl and let the batter rest in a warm place (about 80°F) such as an unlit oven with the pilot light on, for ½ hour. (This resting is essential because, in addition to

fermenting the batter, it lightens it to the almost foamy consistency that is necessary if the fritter is to be spongy.)

3. While the batter is resting, peel and thinly slice the onions. When ready to fry, add sliced onions to the batter and mix thoroughly. The mixture will look coarse and lumpy.

4. Heat oil in a *kadhai*, chicken fryer, or frying pan until very hot but not smoking (375°F). Gently drop the onion batter mixture in 2-tablespoon amounts, into the oil. Make about 6–8 fritters at a time. When the fritters are added, the temperature of the oil will drop automatically to around 300°F. Keep the temperature of the oil at this low point by regulating the heat between medium-high and medium-low (the oil should be bubbling gently). This will allow the fritters to cook thoroughly before browning. Also the slow frying enables the fritters to develop a crackling crisp texture. Fry, stirring and turning them, until they are golden brown all over (about 10 minutes). Take out the fritters with a slotted spoon, and drain them on paper towels. Continue with the rest of the onion batter mixture the same way. Serve hot or warm, accompanied by Fresh Mint Relish (*Podina Chutney*, p. 436).

Note: The fritters may be made several hours ahead, and reheated just before serving, by refrying them briefly (about 1 minute) in hot oil (375°F), providing the fritters are a little underdone and pale brown. This last frying will thus both warm and brown them.

There is no appetizer more authentically Indian than these crisp, fragrant fritters. The only thing to remember is not to serve too many of them; they are very filling and can ruin a perfectly planned meal. These fritters can precede almost any main course. They also make an ideal accompaniment to afternoon high tea.

Cauliflower Fritters

(Gobhi Pakode)

These crisp fritters studded with coriander seeds are a sure winner. The batter has no spices except coriander seeds, so as to allow the natural flavor of the cauliflower to emerge. Be sure to buy a head of cauliflower that is young and fresh.

These fritters may also be served in place of a side dish, especially with other fried food.

For 8 persons

1 large head, or 2 small heads, cauliflower

THE BATTER:

1½ cups unsifted chick-pea flour *(besan)*

2 teaspoons peanut or corn oil

2 teaspoons coriander seeds, crushed

¼ teaspoon red pepper (optional)

2 teaspoons Kosher salt

1¼ cups cold water

Peanut or corn oil enough to fill a *kadhai*, chicken fryer, or large casserole to a depth of 2 inches.

1. Break and separate the cauliflower into flowerets. Cut the large flowerets into 1-inch pieces. Wash them under running cold water, drain, and set aside.

2. Sift the flour into a large bowl. Rub oil or shortening into it, following the directions on pages 125–126. Stir in coriander, red pepper (if you are using it), and salt. Gradually add water in a thin, slow, steady stream, beating the mixture all the while with an electric beater, wire whisk, or with your hands. The batter should be thin and smooth, like crepe batter. To make the batter in a food processor or in an electric blender, put all the batter ingredients into

the container of the machine and process until thoroughly blended and smooth. Transfer the batter to a large bowl.

3. Cover the bowl and let the batter rest for at least ½ hour in a warm place (about 80°F), such as an unlit oven with the pilot light on. This will ferment the batter slightly, and make it light and fluffy. (The batter may be made a day ahead and kept refrigerated. Remove from refrigerator and bring to room temperature before use.)

4. Heat the oil in a *kadhai*, chicken fryer, or large casserole, until very hot but not smoking (375°F). Dip a piece of the cauliflower into the batter, and gently slip the coated floweret into the hot oil. When several batter-coated flowerets have been added, the temperature of the oil will automatically drop to around 300°F. Keep the temperature of the oil at this low point by regulating the heat between medium-high and medium-low (the oil should be gently bubbling). This will allow the fritters to cook slowly and brown gently, thus developing a golden, crackling crisp crust. Fry, stirring and turning the fritters until they are pale golden all over—they should not get brown—about 10–12 minutes. Transfer the fritters with a slotted spoon to a cookie sheet lined with several sheets of paper toweling, to drain. Continue with the rest of the cauliflower pieces the same way. Serve hot.

Note: The fritters may be made several hours ahead, and reheated just before serving, either in a 375°F preheated oven (on the center shelf), uncovered, for 5–7 minutes, or by refrying in hot oil (375°F) for one minute. If refried, they must once again be drained on paper towels before serving.

Like Onion Fritters (p. 113), these go well with almost anything, but avoid serving a main dish that contains cauliflower. They are lovely for afternoon tea.

Indian Cheese Fritters

(Paneer Pakode)

These moist and tender fritters, filled with the aroma of fresh cheese, are a true delicacy. Needless to say, the cheese must be as fresh as possible, preferably made the same day you make the fritters.

A Note of Caution: When you dip the *paneer* in the batter, be sure to coat it thoroughly, or the oil will seep through the uncoated portion into the cheese and cause the fritter to taste greasy and heavy. In addition, the moist *paneer* may splatter explosively when it comes in contact with the hot oil.

For 6–8 persons

Indian cheese *(paneer)*, made with 8 cups of milk (p. 52) and cut into ⅛-inch-thick, ½-inch by 1½-inch pieces

1 recipe chick-pea flour batter from the preceding recipe, Cauliflower Fritters (*Gobhi Pakode*, p. 115)

To make Indian cheese fritters, follow the directions given for making the cauliflower fritters, but substitute Indian cheese for the vegetables. Before serving the fritters, sprinkle them with a blend of ¼ teaspoon black pepper, ⅛ teaspoon red pepper, ¼ teaspoon mango powder, and salt to taste. Serve these fritters hot or warm, accompanied by Mint Coriander Dip (*Dhania-Podina Chutney*, p. 437), or Sweet Tomato Relish (*Tamatar Chutney*, p. 440).

Note: The fritters may be made several hours ahead and, just before serving, reheated, loosely covered, in the middle level of a preheated 375°F oven for 5 minutes.

Follow the menu suggestions for Onion Fritters on page 113, but avoid serving dishes that contain a large quantity of Indian Cheese.

Shrimp Fritters

(Jheenga Pakode)

Fragrant with fresh ginger root, garlic, and a hint of green chili pepper, these fritters are among my very favorites. The coating is spicy, light, and fluffy, and the shrimp inside is moist, creamy, and tender. The coating gets its unusual flavor and texture from a batter made with cornstarch, chick-pea flour, and baking powder. This batter, a recent culinary invention in India, is equally suited for crab meat, lobster meat, and firm-fleshed fish.

The shrimps get their piquant flavor and exquisite tenderness from long marination in a blend of ginger root, garlic, green chilies, and a good dose of lemon juice. You should devein the shrimps before cooking them; otherwise the black vein will stand out against the pearly white flesh and make the shrimp look unappetizing.

To devein shrimp: With a sharp-pointed knife, make a ⅛-inch-deep slit down the back of the shrimp from the head all the way to the tail. With the tip of a knife or toothpick, lift out the black vein.

For 6–8 persons

1 pound shrimps, preferably large-medium (about 28–32 per pound)
1 teaspoon minced garlic
1 tablespoon grated or finely chopped fresh ginger root

1–2 green chilies, seeded and minced
½ teaspoon Kosher salt
Juice of ¼ lemon

THE BATTER:

¾ cup corn starch
3 tablespoons unsifted chick-pea flour *(besan)* or all-purpose flour
3 tablespoons peanut or corn oil
¼ teaspoon red pepper
1 teaspoon Kosher salt

1 tablespoon baking powder
2 large eggs
3 tablespoons cold water

Peanut or corn oil, enough to fill a *kadhai*, chicken fryer, or large casserole to a depth of 2 inches.

1. Shell (leaving the tail part on) and devein the shrimps. Rinse under cold water and pat dry with kitchen towels.

2. Place the shrimps in a glass or ceramic bowl. Add garlic, ginger root, chilies, salt, and lemon juice. Mix thoroughly to distribute the marinade evenly over the shrimps. Cover and marinate for 2 hours at room temperature, or overnight in the refrigerator, turning the shrimps from time to time. A longer marinating time is better for flavor.

3. Put all the ingredients of the batter into a bowl and beat, using an electric beater, whisk, fork, or your hands, until thoroughly blended and free of any lumps. (The batter may be mixed in an electric blender or food processor). Cover and let the batter rest for ½ hour.

4. When ready to fry the fritters, heat the oil in a *kadhai*, French fryer, or casserole until very hot (350°–375°F). Hold each shrimp by its tail and dip it into the batter. Hold it briefly over the bowl to let excess drip off, and gently drop the shrimp into the oil. Fry only 6–8 shrimps at a time, so that there is ample room for them to float easily in the oil. Fry the shrimps for 3 minutes, then flip them over with a slotted spoon or tongs, and continue frying until they are light golden on both sides. Take the fritters out with a slotted spoon, and drain on paper towels. Continue with the remaining shrimps the same way. Serve hot, accompanied by Sweet Tomato Relish (*Tamatar Chutney*, p. 440).

These fritters may be followed by any main dish. Try Beef in Fragrant Spinach Sauce (p. 179), Cornish Hens Braised in Fragrant Apricot Sauce (p. 230). Or, for a complete seafood dinner, Lobster in Fried Onion Sauce (p. 247). Or, for a vegetarian meal to follow, Green Peas and Indian Cheese in Fragrant Tomato Sauce (p. 266). For a particularly light meal, omit the main dish, and serve these fritters with a pilaf such as Saffron Pilaf with Peaches (p. 371), or Indian Fried Rice (p. 363), or for a spicier flavor, Vegetable and Rice Casserole with Herbs (p. 379).

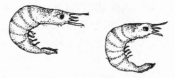

DUMPLINGS

Dumplings in Indian cooking originated to transform the everyday mundane *dal* into something different and interesting. The results were so good that today dumplings are an important part of Indian cooking.

Dumplings are made by soaking dried peas and beans until soft and grinding them into a fine thick paste that looks almost like soft dough. The paste is then set to rise in a warm place. When risen, light and fluffy, it is scooped up with the fingers, shaped into different forms, dropped into the hot oil, and fried. This whole process, a traditional one, is tedious and time-consuming. For this reason, dumpling making in India is not an everyday affair.

Dumplings can be made quite effortlessly in less time (cutting down on the soaking and grinding, and totally eliminating rising time) by using a food processor. The machine not only grinds the beans in a matter of minutes to a smooth, silky, light-textured paste, it also warms the batter, thus aiding the dumplings to puff up while frying. You can use an electric blender to grind the beans, but since it does not beat in air as well as a food processor does, you will need to beat the batter first and then allow it to rise by resting before making the dumplings.

These two dumpling recipes take a little time and effort to make, but the results will prove worthwhile.

Spinach and Mung Bean Dumplings

(Moong Badian)

These golden mung bean dumplings, streaked with shreds of spinach leaves, are absolutely irresistible. A delicacy from the State of Uttar Pradesh, they can be served as a snack at any time of the day, or simmered in fragrant sauce and served as a main dish (see Dumplings in Fragrant Herb Gravy on page 283).

For 4–6 persons (makes twenty-four 1½-inch-round dumplings)

1 cup yellow split mung beans
 (*moong dal*)
½ cup firmly packed shredded
 spinach (about 4 ounces
 fresh, trimmed and
 washed). Or substitute 2
 tablespoons frozen
 chopped spinach,
 squeezed dry.
1 tablespoon finely chopped
 fresh coriander leaves (or
 substitute 2 teaspoons
 dried coriander leaves)

1–2 green chilies, seeded and
 thinly sliced
⅛ teaspoon baking powder
¾ teaspoon Kosher salt

Peanut or corn oil enough to
 fill a *kadhai*, chicken fryer,
 or large casserole to a
 depth of 2 inches.

1. Pick over, clean, and wash mung beans, following the instructions given for cleaning *dal* on page 327.

2. Put the mung beans in a bowl and add enough water to cover the beans by at least 1½ inches. Let them soak for 4 hours. Drain and rinse.

3. *To make the paste in a food processor*: Attach metal cutting blade. Put the drained beans in the container with ½ cup water and process for 5–6 minutes, turning the machine on and off every 15–20 seconds and scraping down sides of container from time to time. Paste made in a food processor is extremely light and fluffy; there is no need to beat it or let it rest before frying.

In a blender: It is more difficult to make the bean paste in a blender, but it can be done. Whether you grind the drained beans first and then gradually add ½ cup water to make a paste, or put the water in the blender container and gradually add the beans, you will have to turn the blender off and on every few seconds, scrape down the sides, and push the paste from the blade with a rubber spatula. Blend until the paste is perfectly smooth (about 4–5 minutes). Do not add any more liquid than necessary, as the paste should be fairly thick, like muffin batter. Transfer to a clean bowl and beat, using an electric beater or a wire whisk, until very pale, light, and fluffy (at least 5 minutes). Cover, and let the paste rest in a warm place (about 80°F), such as an unlit oven with the pilot light on, for at least 2 hours. (The beating and resting steps are not essential but are recommended because they will ferment the paste and cause it to rise, producing an even lighter and fluffier texture.)

4. When ready to fry the dumplings, stir the remaining ingredients, except for oil, into the paste. *Do not overblend or the mixture will become dense, which will in turn make the dumplings hard and chewy.*

5. Heat the oil in a *kadhai*, chicken fryer, or frying pan until very hot but not smoking (375°F). Drop a heaping teaspoon of the bean mixture into the hot oil. Fry 8–12 dumplings at a time, making sure not to overcrowd the frying pan. Fry, stirring and turning, until dumplings are light golden (about 4–5 minutes). Take them out with a slotted spoon, and drain on paper towels. Continue with the rest of the bean mixture the same way. Serve hot accompanied by Fresh Mint Relish (*Podina Chutney*, p. 436) or Mint Coriander Dip (*Dhania-Podina Chutney*, p. 437).

Note: These dumplings can be made several hours ahead and, just before serving, reheated, loosely covered, in the middle level of a preheated 350°F oven for 12–15 minutes.

These fragrant, spongy, and mellow-flavored dumplings should be followed by a main dish containing plenty of spicy sauce. They are particularly good when succeeded by a vegetarian main dish, such as Cauliflower, Green Peas, and Potatoes in Spicy Herb Sauce (p. 256), Round Gourd in Fragrant Gravy (p. 264), or Green Peas and Indian Cheese in Fragrant Tomato Sauce (p. 266).

Silky Bean Dumplings

(Bade)

These dumplings have a silky and fluffy interior, and taste as if they had been made with all-purpose flour dough, instead of with Indian beans called *Urad dal*. The beans are soaked and pureed to a thick paste, which is then formed into small patties with holes in the center. When they are fried, they puff up and look like doughnuts. The shaping of the bean dumplings takes a little time and effort. It is, however, not essential that the dumplings be shaped like doughnuts to taste authentic. A simpler method, followed by many Indian cooks as well, is to dip your hand in cold water, scoop up 2–3 tablespoons of bean paste, shape it into a rough ball, drop it into the hot oil, and fry. They are good to eat by themselves, or soaked in spice-laced yogurt and served as a salad (see Dumplings in Fragrant Yogurt on page 348).

For 8–12 persons (makes 24 dumplings)

1 cup white split gram beans
   (*urad dal*)
2 tablespoons finely chopped
   onions
1 tablespoon finely chopped
   fresh ginger root
2 green chilies, seeded and
   chopped
1 tablespoon ground coriander

⅛ teaspoon baking soda
1⅓ teaspoons Kosher salt
2 tablespoons peanut or corn
   oil

Peanut or corn oil, enough to fill
   a *kadhai*, chicken fryer, or large
   casserole to a depth of 2 inches.

1. Pick, clean, and wash gram beans, following the instructions for cleaning *dal* on page 327.

2. Put the beans in a bowl, add enough water to cover by at least 2 inches, and let them soak for 4 hours. Drain and rinse the beans.

3. *To make the paste in a food processor*: Attach metal cutting

blade. Put the drained beans in the container with ½ cup water and process for 5–6 minutes, turning the machine on and off every 15–20 seconds and scraping down sides of container from time to time. Paste made in a food processor is extremely light and fluffy; there is no need to beat it or let it rest before frying.

In a blender: It is more difficult to make the bean paste in a blender, but it can be done. Whether you grind the drained beans first and then gradually add ½ cup water to make a paste, or put the water in the blender container and gradually add the beans, you will have to turn the blender off and on every few seconds, scrape down the sides, and push the paste from the blade with a rubber spatula. Blend until the paste is perfectly smooth (about 4–5 minutes). Transfer the bean paste to a clean bowl and beat with an electric beater, wire whisk, or fork until light and fluffy. (It will take at least 10 minutes of beating with wire whisk or fork, and 5 minutes with the electric beater.) Cover and let the paste rest in a warm place for at least 4 hours. (The beating and resting steps are not essential, but are recommended, because they ferment the batter, causing it to become even more light and foamy.)

4. When ready to fry the dumplings, stir all the remaining ingredients except any of the oil into the paste. Do not overblend, or the paste will become dense and the finished dumplings hard and tough.

5. Cut 6 squares of waxed paper, 6 inches by 6. Put the 2 tablespoons of oil in a small bowl, fill another small bowl with cold water, and keep these three items close to where you will fry the dumplings.

6. Make one at a time. Place one piece of waxed paper on the work board and brush it with some of the oil. Then, first dipping your fingers in the cold water, scoop up enough of the bean mixture to form a ball the size of a golf ball. Drop it onto the oiled waxed paper. Using your fingers, flatten the ball into a 2-inch-round patty. With your forefinger make a hole in the center of the patty. The patty should now resemble a small doughnut. Make 5 more patties on the 5 remaining pieces of waxed paper in the same manner. When you have formed all 6 patties, you are ready to fry the first batch. (You will make 4 batches altogether.)

7. Heat the large quantity of oil in a *kadhai*, chicken fryer, or large pan until moderately hot (325°–350°F).

8. Lift one piece of waxed paper at a time, with the patty on it, and hold it right over the hot oil. Using a rubber spatula or a wide knife, dipped in water, to guide it, slide the patty gently off the waxed paper and into the hot oil. Slide the remaining five patties into the oil the same way. Fry on one side for 3 minutes, then very carefully flip them over with a slotted spoon, and continue frying until the dumplings are light golden on both sides. Drain the dumplings on paper towels. Continue with the remaining bean mixture the same way. Serve hot with Coconut Relish (*Narial Chutney*, p. 438), or Sweet and Sour Tamarind Relish (*Imli Chutney*, p. 442).

Note: These dumplings can be made several hours ahead and, just before serving, reheated, loosely covered, in the middle level of a preheated 350°F oven for 12–15 minutes.

Follow the menu suggestions given for Spinach and Mung Bean Dumplings (*Moong Badian*, p. 120).

Savory Pastries with Spicy Potato Filling

(Aloo Samosa)

Samosas are the most traditional snacks of India. They are so delicious that Indians often make a meal of them. *Samosas* are stuffed with either potatoes or ground meat *(keema)*, but this *Aloo Samosa* is the more popular.

The unique feature of these *samosas* is their delicious *khasta*, meaning crispy and flaky pastry crust. This special texture is obtained by incorporating fat into the flour before adding the water, by a special technique called *Moyan dena* or "rubbing into it." In this technique—unlike the American method for mixing pastry crust, in which the fat is *cut* into the flour—the fat or oil is *rubbed* into the flour until all the particles of flour are evenly coated with it.

To rub fat or oil into flour: Place the flour in a bowl. Make a well in the center of the flour, and add fat, or oil. Pick up some flour and fat (or oil-coated flour) in one hand. Place the other hand over the flour and fat mixture. Now slide your two hands back and forth from heel to fingertips, rubbing the flour and fat between your palms. This entire motion should be carried out directly over the bowl containing the flour and fat, so that the fat-coated flour may fall back into the bowl as the rubbing continues. When the whole handful of flour has fallen back into the bowl, pick up more flour and fat, and continue until the entire batch of flour in the bowl is evenly coated with the fat or oil, and no more lumps of fat can be seen.

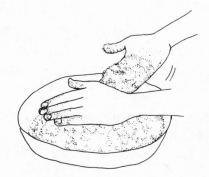

Rubbing fat into flour

Samosas take some time to make, since both the filling and the dough have to be prepared before rolling, filling, shaping, and frying.

Makes 32 savory pastries

PASTRY DOUGH:

1½ cups unsifted all-purpose flour, measured by scooping up with measuring cups and leveling off with a spatula or knife

1 teaspoon Kosher salt
4 tablespoons vegetable shortening
6–7 tablespoons cold water

SPICY POTATO FILLING:

4 tablespoons vegetable
  shortening, or light
  vegetable oil
2 teaspoons coriander seeds
½ cup finely chopped onions
1½ teaspoons finely chopped
  fresh ginger root
7 medium-sized potatoes (1¾
  pounds), boiled till soft,
  peeled, and cut into ½-
  inch cubes
½ cup cooked shelled green
  peas
2–3 green chilies, seeded and
  chopped, or ¼ teaspoon
  red pepper

1¼ teaspoons *garam masala*
  (p. 38)
2 teaspoons ground
  pomegranate seeds, or
  1 tablespoon lemon juice
2 teaspoons Kosher salt

⅓ cup all-purpose flour for
  dusting

Peanut or corn oil enough to
fill a *kadhai*, French fryer,
or large casserole to a
depth of 3 inches.

1. Mix flour and salt in a large bowl. Rub shortening in, following directions on pp. 125–126. Pour 6 tablespoons water over the flour, and mix. Add the remaining tablespoon in droplets, until all the flour adheres together in a mass that can be kneaded.

2. Place the dough on a marble or wooden board. Coat your fingers with a little oil to prevent the dough from sticking, and knead the dough for 10 minutes. This will be a firm but pliable dough, not at all sticky. Cover with a towel or plastic sheet, and let the dough rest for half an hour. (The dough may be made a day in advance and kept refrigerated, tightly sealed in aluminum foil. Remove from refrigerator about 30 minutes before you are ready to roll it out.)

To make the dough using a food processor: Put the flour and salt into the container of the food processor, with steel cutting blade attached. Process for a few seconds to mix them. Add shortening, and process, turning the machine on and off, until the fat is well distributed through the flour. Add the water through the feed tube, with the motor running, until ball of dough forms on blades (about 15 seconds). Take out the dough and gather it into a smooth ball.

(continued)

Coat the ball with a little oil and place it in a bowl. Cover with a moist towel or plastic wrap, and let it rest for ½ hour.

3. To make the filling, heat the shortening or oil over medium-high heat in a frying pan for two minutes. Add coriander seeds and fry until they turn dark brown (about 15 seconds). Add onions and ginger root, and continue frying until the onions turn light brown (about 4–5 minutes). Add potatoes and peas, stir rapidly, and fry until the potatoes begin to become dry and look fried (about 10 minutes). Turn off heat.

4. Add the remaining filling ingredients, mix well, and set aside. (This filling can be made up to 2 days in advance and kept refrigerated until you are ready to make the pastries.)

5. Knead the dough again for a minute, and divide into 2 equal portions. Using your hands, roll each into a ½-inch-thick rope, and cut into 8 equal parts. Roll the small pieces into smooth balls.

6. Working with one at a time, place a ball on your workboard, dust it lightly with flour, and roll it into a 6-inch circle. Cut the circle in half. Now you have two semicircles. Each semicircle will make a *samosa*.

7. Place a small bowl of water next to the workboard. Form a cone: Moisten half of the semicircle's straight edge with water, and bring the other half of the straight edge over it, so that the dry side overlaps the moistened portion by ⅛–¼ inch. Press the overlapped edges securely together to seal.

8. Place a scant tablespoon of filling in the cone. Moisten the open end of the cone, and quickly pinch the open end shut in a straight line, closing the cone into a triangular shape. Press tightly to seal. Moistening is essential to ensure a good seal; otherwise, during frying, oil will seep into both pastry and filling, making it taste greasy, heavy, and rich.) Continue with the rest of the dough and filling the same way. (The *samosa* can be rolled and shaped a few hours ahead of time and kept loosely covered with a piece of paper. Do not worry if they dry out slightly. In fact, for best results they *should* be left out to dry for ½ hour. This makes the crust more crunchy and flaky.)

9. When ready to fry the pastries, heat the oil in a *kadhai*, French fryer, or large pan. When the oil is hot (350°F), drop in about 8–10 pastries. The temperature of the oil will drop automat-

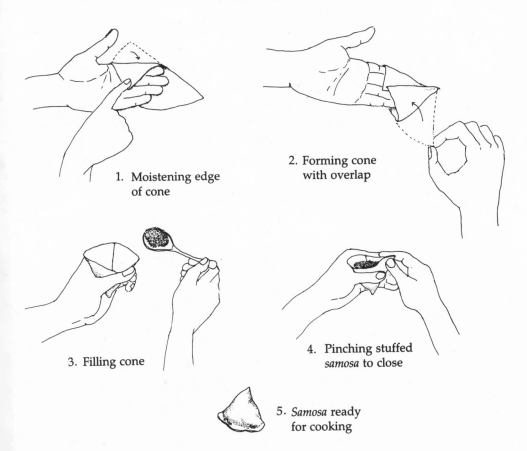

1. Moistening edge of cone

2. Forming cone with overlap

3. Filling cone

4. Pinching stuffed *samosa* to close

5. *Samosa* ready for cooking

ically to around 300°F. Maintain the temperature at this low point by regulating the heat between medium-high and medium-low. This low-temperature cooking is essential for *samosa*, because it enables the pastry dough to brown evenly and become flaky. Fry, stirring and turning the pastries until they are light brown (about 12 minutes). Take them out with a slotted spoon or tongs, and drain on paper towels. Continue with the remaining pastries the same way. Serve hot or warm, accompanied by Sweet and Sour Tamarind Relish (*Imli Chutney*, p. 442), or Fresh Mint Relish (*Podina Chutney*, p. 436).

Note: The pastries can be made several hours ahead, and reheated just before serving by frying them briefly (1½ minutes) in very hot oil (375°F), provided the pastries were left a little underdone and pale. This last frying will thus both warm and brown them. The pastries can also be reheated, uncovered, on the center shelf of a preheated 375°F oven for 8–10 minutes.

These savories may be followed by any dish that does not contain an excessive amount of potatoes. I like to serve broiled or roast meat or chicken to make the meal meaty and simple. Examples include Royal Roast Leg of Lamb with Saffron Raisin Sauce (p. 184), Mint Scented Broiled Leg of Lamb (p. 182), or Tandoori Chicken (p. 221). These pastries also are ideal for afternoon high tea.

Savory Meat Pastries

(Keema Samosa)

Makes 32 pastries

1 recipe pastry dough (p. 126)
1 recipe Dry-cooked Spicy
   Ground Meat (*Sookha Keema*,
   p. 158)

Peanut or corn oil enough to
   fill a *kadhai*, chicken fryer, or
   large casserole to a depth of
   3 inches.

To make savory meat pastries, follow the instructions given in the preceding recipe for Savory Pastries with Spicy Potato Filling, except substitute meat filling for potato filling. Serve these savory pastries hot or warm, accompanied by Fresh Mint Relish (*Podina Chutney*, p. 436) or Mint Coriander Dip (*Dhania-Podina Chutney*, p. 437).

Note: To reheat, follow the instructions given for heating Savory Pastries with Spicy Potato Filling (*Aloo Samosa*, p. 125).

Follow the menu suggestions given for Savory Pastries with Spicy Potato Filling, except avoid main dishes that contain ground meat. I find these quite filling, so I often serve them with a vegetarian main dish, such as Green Peas and Indian Cheese in Fragrant Tomato Sauce (p. 266). They may also be served with afternoon high tea.

Savory Crackers

(Matthi)

These beautiful, light, golden wafer-thin crackers, studded with tiny bubbles, are an absolute delight. They are generally flavored with carom seeds. Traditionally *matthi* are made with a large proportion of fat, which produces crackers that taste like savory short bread. I prefer a less rich taste; therefore I use less fat in the flour.

Makes about 4 dozen crackers

2½ cups unsifted all-purpose flour, measured by scooping the flour up with measuring cups and leveling it off with a spatula or knife.

3 tablespoons warm melted vegetable shortening, plus 1 teaspoon shortening for kneading

¾ teaspoon carom seeds, crushed

2¼ teaspoons Kosher salt

⅛ teaspoon baking soda

2 tablespoons plain yogurt

10 tablespoons warm water (90°–100° F)

⅓ cup all-purpose flour for dusting

Peanut or corn oil enough to fill a *kadhai*, chicken fryer, or any large frying pan to a depth of 1½ inches.

1. Place flour in a large bowl. Rub the 3 tablespoons shortening into it, following the directions on pages 125–126. Stir in carom seeds, salt, and baking soda. Blend the yogurt with the water and pour over the flour in a thin stream, until the dough can be gathered into a mass and kneaded.

2. Place the dough on a marble or floured wooden board. Coat your fingers and palms with the remaining teaspoon of shortening (to keep the dough from sticking) and knead the dough for 10 minutes. This will be a firm but pliable dough. Place the dough in a greased bowl, cover with a towel or plastic wrap, and let the dough rest for at least ½ hour at room temperature. (The dough can be

made a day in advance and kept refrigerated, tightly sealed in plastic wrap to prevent graying. Remove from refrigerator about 30 minutes before you are ready to roll it out.)

To make the dough using a food processor: Mix yogurt and water together. Put flour and three tablespoons of shortening into the workbowl of the processor, with the steel cutting blade attached. Process, turning the machine on and off, until the fat is well distributed. Add the carom seeds, salt, and baking soda, and process for a few seconds to mix all the ingredients. Continue processing, adding yogurt and water mixture in a thin stream through the feedtube, until a ball of dough forms on blades (about 15 seconds). Take out the dough, and gather it into a smooth round ball. Coat the ball with the remaining teaspoon of shortening, and place it in a greased bowl. Cover with a moist towel or plastic wrap, and let it rest for at least ½ hour at room temperature. The ½ hour resting relaxes and softens the dough, thus making it easier to roll.

3. Knead the dough again for a minute. Divide into 8 equal portions, and shape them into balls.

4. Place one ball at a time on the work board. (Keep the remaining balls covered with a plastic sheet to prevent a crust from forming.) Dust generously with flour and roll into a 10-inch circle. Cut round crackers with a plain 2-inch-round cookie cutter. (Reserve the scraps.) With a sharp knife make four to six ¼-inch slashes in the center of the crackers to prevent their puffing up during frying. Continue the same way with the rest of the balls. The reserved scraps may be pressed into different patterns and fried, a few pieces at a time. (These crackers may be rolled an hour ahead of time, as long as they are kept loosely covered with plastic wrap to keep them from drying out.)

5. When ready to fry the crackers, heat the oil in a *kadhai*, chicken fryer, or frying pan until moderately hot (325°F).

6. Drop 6 to 8 crackers at a time into the oil. The crackers will first sink to the bottom of the pan and then rise sizzling, to the surface (about ½ minute). Fry, turning often, until they are cooked through and barely pink (about 3 minutes). Do not let them color too much. They should remain as pale as possible.

7. Take the crackers out with a slotted spoon, and place them on a cookie sheet lined with several layers of paper towels, to drain.

Continue with the rest of the crackers the same way. When cool, store them in airtight containers. These crackers keep for 8–10 weeks.

Cooked *matthi*

Matthi make perfect appetizers when a heavy meal is to follow. They are also a good choice when the rest of the meal takes a little time to prepare. Examples include Emperor's Layered Meat and Fragrant Rice Casserole (p. 192), and Goanese Hot and Pungent Curry (p. 199). They are ideal at afternoon high tea.

Indian Fenugreek Crackers

(Kasoori Mathari)

Because of their beautiful fragrance and slightly bitterish taste, fenugreek *(methi)* leaves are often used to flavor lentils, vegetables, and breads. They are considered a delicacy in the Northern States of India. These crackers can either be deep fried as Savory Crackers (see page 131) or baked by the conventional oven method described in this recipe, which is more popular in India today.

Makes 6–7 dozen crackers

¼ cup dry fenugreek leaves
   (kasoori methi)
2½ cups unsifted all-purpose
   flour, measured by
   scooping the flour up with
   measuring cups and
   leveling it off with a
   spatula or knife

2 teaspoons Kosher salt
4 tablespoons chilled sweet
   butter, cut into tiny cubes
4 tablespoons chilled vegetable
   shortening
½ cup cold water
⅓ cup all-purpose flour for
   dusting

(continued)

1. In a large bowl, crumble the fenugreek leaves to a rough powder with your fingertips. Add flour and salt, and mix to distribute the herb evenly. Add butter and shortening, and mix with your fingertips, or with a pastry blender, until they are evenly distributed in the flour, with no lumps of butter to be seen.

2. Pour the cold water, about 1 tablespoon at a time, over the flour until it can be gathered into a mass. Place the dough on a marble or floured wooden board, and knead briefly (about 1 minute) to make a soft, smooth ball. (Do not overknead or dough will become rubbery and difficult to roll.)

(The dough can be made ahead of time and kept refrigerated for up to 6 hours. Remove from refrigerator 15 minutes before you are ready to roll it out. If, however, you want to roll the dough within an hour of refrigeration, you do not need to take it out ahead of time.)

To make the dough using a food processor: Put the fenugreek leaves into the workbowl and, using the steel cutting blade, process, turning the machine on and off until the leaves are reduced to a coarse powder (about 10 seconds). Add flour and salt and process briefly to distribute the herb. Add butter and shortening, and process, turning the machine on and off, until the butter is cut into very small granules—about the size of rice grains (about 10 seconds). Continue processing, adding cold water through the feed tube, until a ball of dough forms on the blades. Take out the dough and gather it into a smooth round ball.

3. Preheat the oven to 375°F. Line two 12-inch by 15½-inch cookie sheets with aluminum foil.

4. Divide the dough into 4 equal portions, and shape each into a round ball. Place one ball at a time on the work board. (Keep the remaining balls covered with plastic wrap or a moist towel to prevent a crust from forming.) Dust lightly with flour, and roll into a 10-inch circle. Cut crackers with a 1½-inch cookie cutter (round or any fancy shape). With a fork or a thin skewer, prick the crackers all over to prevent them from puffing up during baking. Reserve the scraps. Continue with the rest of the balls the same way. Finally, gather the scraps, press them into a ball, roll, and cut them into crackers until no more scraps remain.

5. Place the crackers ½ inch apart on cookie sheets. Bake the crackers in the middle level of the oven for 10 minutes, or until a few light brown spots appear on the underside. Gently, using a metal spatula or a pair of tongs, turn the crackers, and continue baking for an additional 5 minutes or until they are lightly browned on the edges.

6. Transfer the crackers to racks, and cool thoroughly before storing in airtight containers. These crackers should rest for 2–3 days before being served, for the full-bodied aroma of fenugreek to penetrate.

Follow the menu suggestions for Savory Crackers (Matthi) on page 131.

Soups

(Shorva)

Mysore Spicy Lentil Broth   *(Mysore Rasam)*
Hyderabad Lime Soup   *(Hyderabadi Gosht Shorva)*
Mulligatawny Soup   *(Mullagatanni)*
Cream of Spinach Soup   *(Palak ka Shorva)*
Cucumber Mung Bean Soup   *(Kheera Dal Shorva)*

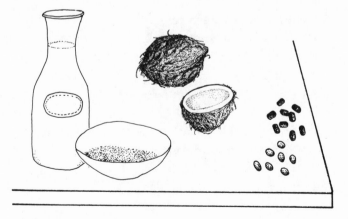

Mysore Spicy Lentil Broth

(Mysore Rasam)

Rasam, a Sanskrit word, literally translated means broth. *Rasam*, a highly seasoned lentil broth, is a Southern delicacy. It is either mixed with rice and eaten, or drunk in cups as a soup. It is the most popular soup in India today. There are innumerable variations, but this version from the State of Mysore is the finest by far. *Rasam* is traditionally made with lentils *(toovar* or *arhar dal)* to give the broth a thick, creamy, almost gelatinous texture. If you cannot get lentils, you may substitute the supermarket variety of yellow split peas. If you use a substitute, follow directions for cooking the different varieties of legumes *(dal)* on page 327.

Tamarind is essential to the authentic *Mysore Rasam* flavor. But tomatoes are often substituted and produce an equally delicious soup, although not the classic one.

For 8 persons

1 cup yellow lentils
  (Toovar dal)
1 teaspoon turmeric
2½ cups chopped fresh ripe
  tomatoes (or substitute 2
  cups chopped canned
  tomatoes)
2 teaspoons finely chopped
  garlic
1 one-inch ball tamarind pulp
1 tablespoon ground coriander
1 teaspoon ground cumin
¼ teaspoon each red and black
  pepper

1 teaspoon molasses or sugar
1 tablespoon Kosher salt
2 tablespoons *usli ghee* (p. 50),
  or light vegetable oil
¾ teaspoon black mustard
  seeds
⅛ teaspoon ground asafetida
2 tablespoons finely chopped
  fresh coriander leaves (or
  substitute 1½ tablespoons
  dry coriander leaves)

1. Pick over, clean, and wash lentils following instructions on page 327.

2. Put the lentils in a deep 3-quart saucepan with the turmeric and 4 cups cold water. Bring to a boil over medium-high heat. Reduce heat and simmer at a gentle bubble, partially covered, until the lentils are tender (about 35 minutes), stirring occasionally to prevent sticking. Set aside.

3. While lentils are cooking, puree tomatoes and garlic with ½ cup cold water in an electric blender or food processor, and set aside.

4. Put the tamarind pulp in a small bowl, add ¼ cup boiling water, and let mixture soak for 15 minutes. Then mash the pulp with the back of a spoon, or use your fingers. Pour the liquid through a strainer into a small bowl, being sure to squeeze as much juice out of the pulp as possible (discard the stringy fiber).

5. Puree the lentils in an electric blender, food processor, or food mill, and return to the pan. Blend in 3 cups hot water with a wire whisk, and mix thoroughly. Let lentils rest, undisturbed, for 15 minutes. Pour the lentil broth that has accumulated at the top into another bowl. (There should be about 4½ cups of broth. If not, add enough water to bring it up to that quantity.) Transfer the thick lentil puree left at the bottom of the pan into a small bowl. (This can be saved and used for making lentil stews [*Sambaar*, p. 276], or enriched with Spice-Perfumed Butter [*Tadka*, p. 73] and served as a side dish.)

6. Return the lentil broth to the pan, and add the tomato puree, tamarind juice, coriander, cumin, red and black pepper, molasses or sugar, and salt. Bring the broth to a boil over medium-high heat. Reduce heat to low and simmer, partially covered, for 15 minutes. Turn off heat. (The lentil broth may be made ahead up to this stage and set aside, covered, for up to 4 hours, refrigerated for up to 4 days, or frozen. Defrost and heat thoroughly before proceeding with the recipe.)

7. Heat the *ghee* over high heat in a small frying pan. When it is very hot, carefully add the mustard seeds. Keep a pot lid or spatter screen handy, since the seeds may splatter and sputter when added. When the sputtering stops and the seeds turn gray (about 5

seconds), add the asafetida. Then immediately turn off the heat, and pour the spiced butter over the lentil broth. Stir to mix. Cover the pan, and let the broth rest briefly (about 5 minutes). When ready to serve, simmer until heated through. Check for salt, and stir in the coriander leaves. Serve piping hot.

Note: This soup should definitely be classified as a clear soup or, even better, as an Indian consommé. Sometimes, however, a little lentil puree or tomato pulp escapes into the clear broth, and this is quite acceptable. The residue usually sinks to the bottom of the pan. So always stir the soup thoroughly before serving, to distribute the residue evenly. Because of its brothlike consistency, this soup is always served in a cup—not in a soup bowl—with a saucer, and a teaspoon to stir the soup frequently, and is meant to be sipped.

This spicy tomato-rich lentil broth will liven up anyone's appetite. It is particularly soothing on cold winter days. To maintain a southern mood, follow this soup with other southern delicacies, such as Spicy Brussels Sprouts, Green Beans, and Lentil Stew (p. 276), or Goanese Hot and Pungent Curry (p. 199). Or if you wish to serve a simple light lunch, omit the main dish and serve an herb-fragrant pilaf, such as Mint Pilaf (p. 377) or Vegetable and Rice Casserole with Herbs (p. 379), accompanied by a cool yogurt salad, such as Tomato and Yogurt Salad (p. 345) or Okra and Yogurt Salad (p. 347)

Hyderabad Lime Soup

(Hyderabadi Gosht Shorva)

This is a classic Indian soup, traditionally made with meat bones, potatoes, spices, and enriched with milk, cream, and nuts. In India, the word *shorva* is used to refer to this soup. It means either a thin broth (a version usually sold by roadside vendors, especially in winter), or a slightly thickened, more meaty version to be eaten as a meal. Because of regional differences, the soup has several variations. This version comes from Hyderabad, a city in the state of Andra Pradesh in the South; it is believed to have originated in the courts of the nizam of Hyderabad.

I personally prefer the soup to be light and velvety smooth, and therefore do not like to add anything to it. If you prefer a heartier version, add one cup of cooked shredded meat (lamb or chicken), or cooked rice before serving.

For 8 persons

1 thin cinnamon stick, 3 inches long, broken into 2–3 pieces
6 whole cloves
3 green cardamom pods
1 teaspoon black peppercorns
4 tablespoons *usli ghee* (p. 50), or light vegetable oil
2 medium-sized onions, peeled and chopped
5 medium-sized potatoes, peeled and cut into 1-inch cubes
¼ teaspoon turmeric
6 cups homemade meat broth (p. 43), or vegetable broth (p. 44), or canned chicken broth

¼ cup firmly packed fresh coriander leaves (or substitute 2 tablespoons dried coriander leaves)
Kosher salt, to taste
⅔ cup coconut milk (p. 46), or almond milk (p. 462), or whole milk
⅓ cup heavy cream juice of one small lime or lemon

(continued)

1. Place a piece of cheesecloth, about 6 inches square, on the chopping board. Put cinnamon, cloves, cardamom, and black peppercorns in the center of the cloth. Bring up the four corners of the cheesecloth and tie the spices into a bag. Bang it lightly with a wooden mallet or any heavy tool, to break up and crush the spices coarsely.

2. Heat the *ghee* in a deep pan. Add the onions and potatoes, and cook over medium-high heat, stirring often, until the onions are wilted and begin to brown (about 10 minutes). Add the turmeric, broth, and the spice bag, and bring to the boil. Reduce heat, and simmer, covered, until the vegetables are thoroughly cooked and tender (about 35 minutes). Turn off heat, and stir in coriander leaves and salt to taste.

3. When the soup is cool enough to handle, remove the spice bag, squeezing out whatever juice remains, and discard. Puree the soup in an electric blender, food processor, or through a food mill. (The soup may be made to this point and refrigerated up to 3 days, or frozen. Defrost thoroughly before proceeding with the recipe.)

4. Heat the soup until piping hot, add coconut milk (or almond or whole milk) and heavy cream, and continue simmering until the soup is heated through. Check for salt, and serve piping hot in warm cream-soup bowls, sprinkled with a little lime juice.

Note: The soup should be creamy and of medium-thick consistency—similar to French potato-leek-based soups. If it is too thick, add some broth or water to thin it to the desired consistency.

This lime-scented Moghul soup becomes more and more flavorful with each sip, and the wonderful taste lingers on for some time. Therefore, so as not to shock the taste buds with a sudden contrast, it should be followed with another subtle Moghul spice-laced delicacy, such as Royal Braised Lamb with Fragrant Spices (p. 174), Lamb Pilaf (p. 189), or Ground Meat with Potatoes in Scented White Sauce (p. 160).

Mulligatawny Soup

(Mullagatanni)

I first tasted this soup sixteen years ago in an elegant restaurant in Frankfurt, Germany, while I was traveling through Europe. Contrary to what the name suggests (*mullaga* means pepper, and *tanni* means water or broth), what I tasted was an exquisitely delicate broth, faintly laced with spices that brought back the familiar aromas of home.

The exact origin of this soup is somewhat sketchy, but one thing is certain: it was created two centuries ago by local cooks in the south of India for their English masters. It is believed that the cooks originally served the South Indian soup *rasam*, made with black pepper known as *Mullaga Rasam*, also known as *Mullagatanni*. With time, however, the ingredients in the soup changed so completely that the present version bears no resemblance whatever to the traditional *rasam*. Today the soup essentially consists of a rich broth (lamb, chicken, beef, or just vegetables) flavored with onions and spices (turmeric for color, coriander for piquancy, and red pepper for a hot taste) and velvetized with coconut milk, almond milk, peanut butter, or sweet cream.

Because of its unorthodox origin, Indian cooks have had a field day exercising their creative genius with it. As a result, there are innumerable interesting variations of this soup around the world today.

Mulligatawny can either be made from scratch—that is, using different spices—or with a commercial curry powder, which is more popular in England and Europe. This is the one occasion on which I set aside my spices and use a commercial curry powder blend, because then only am I able to re-create the flavor and aroma that once captured my senses. There are several brands of curry powder available in the market. All of them are suitable except those containing fennel seeds. Fennel has a strong aroma and a tendency to stand out, or even overpower a dish, and therefore must be avoided in this soup.

(continued)

For 8 persons

3 cups chopped vegetables
(mixture of onions, carrots,
celery, parsnips,
mushrooms)

6 cups homemade meat broth
(p. 43), or vegetable broth
(p. 44), or canned chicken
broth

1 teaspoon finely chopped garlic

1 sprig fresh coriander leaves
(or substitute 1 tablespoon
dry coriander leaves)

¼ teaspoon black pepper

2 tablespoons *usli ghee* (p. 50),
or light vegetable oil

½ cup finely chopped onions

4 teaspoons curry powder

3 tablespoons all-purpose flour

½ cup heavy cream
Kosher salt

2 tablespoons finely minced
fresh coriander leaves (or
substitute 1 tablespoon dry
coriander leaves)

1. Put the vegetables in a deep heavy-bottomed, 3-quart saucepan with the broth, garlic, coriander, and black pepper. Bring to a boil over medium-high heat. Reduce heat and simmer, covered, for 45 minutes or until vegetables are soft. Turn off the heat.

2. When the vegetables in broth are slightly cool, puree the soup (broth and vegetables both) in an electric blender or food processor. Then pass the soup through a fine sieve. This is to ensure that it will be smooth and velvety in texture and free of all fibrous particles. Return the soup to the pan and bring it to a gentle simmer.

3. While the soup is simmering, put the *ghee* and onions in a small frying pan over medium-high heat. Fry onions until they turn caramel brown (about 10 minutes), stirring constantly to prevent burning. Add curry powder and flour, and cook the mixture for 1 minute, stirring rapidly. Turn off heat, and add this mixture to the gently simmering soup, stirring constantly to prevent lumping. Simmer until the soup is thickened (about 2 minutes). Turn off heat. (The soup may be made up to this point and set aside, covered, for several hours, or refrigerated for up to 3 days, or frozen. Defrost, and heat thoroughly before proceeding with the recipe.)

4. *To serve:* Stir in cream, salt to taste, and coriander leaves. Simmer over low heat until warmed through. Serve hot in cream-soup bowls.

This is an incredibly delicate soup, and surprisingly, it goes well with just about any main dish. To provide contrast in flavor and color, I like to serve cream- and yogurt-based dishes, such as Lamb Fillets Braised in Yogurt Cardamom Sauce (p. 168), Fragrant Yogurt-Braised Chicken (p. 211), or Royal Braised Vegetables in Cardamom Nut Sauce (p. 269).

Cream of Spinach Soup

(Palak Shorva)

This lovely, refreshing soup with its appealing green color is ideal for the summer months. It is one of the most popular soups (the others are tomato, pea, and mixed vegetable) created in India in recent years, and one of the easiest and quickest to make. All you need is some precooked spinach, cooked rice, and a lot of rich chicken broth. This soup has an interesting texture because of the cooked rice. You may also try using rice flour (about 2–3 tablespoons) instead of cooked rice; it needs to simmer in the soup for five minutes to cook fully.

For 8 persons

4 tablespoons *usli ghee* (p. 50),
   or light vegetable oil
2 cups thinly sliced onions
1 teaspoon finely chopped garlic
1 teaspoon ground cumin
¼ teaspoon each ground cloves,
   nutmeg, and black pepper
4 cups homemade meat broth
   (p. 43), or vegetable broth
   (p. 44), or canned chicken

broth or 4 bouillon cubes
   dissolved in 4 cups of water
½ cup tightly packed cooked rice
½ recipe Cooked Spinach (*Obla
   Saag*, p. 318)
1 cup milk
   Kosher salt
¼ cup heavy cream
   Juice of ½ lemon
½ lemon, thinly sliced

(continued)

1. Heat the *ghee* in a small frying pan, and add the onions and garlic. Over medium-high heat, sauté until the onions turn golden yellow (about 5 minutes), stirring constantly to prevent burning. Do not let the onions brown, or they will impart a bitter flavor to the soup. Add cumin, stir rapidly for 15 seconds, and add cloves, nutmeg, and black pepper. Turn off heat.

2. Put 1 cup of broth along with the rice in the container of an electric blender, or food processor, and puree until smooth. Add the onion mixture and spinach, and continue processing until the vegetables are reduced to a fine smooth puree, using more broth as needed.

3. Pour the vegetable puree into a 3-quart pan and stir in the remaining broth, milk, and salt to taste. (The soup may be made up to this stage several hours ahead, set aside, covered, or refrigerated for a day, or frozen. Defrost thoroughly before proceeding with the recipe.)

4. When ready to serve the soup, add cream and heat it until warmed through. Check for salt, and serve in cream-soup bowls, sprinkled with lemon juice, garnished with lemon slices and, if desired, a little black pepper.

Note: The consistency of this soup should be thick. If you prefer a thinner soup, add a little broth or water, but do not thin it too much or the spinach and rice will separate.

This simple and hearty nutmeg-laced soup is filling, and therefore needs to be followed by a simple, light main dish consisting of cutlets and/or fried fish. Examples include Meat Cutlets (p. 197), Panfried Fillet of Sole Laced with Carom (p. 248), and Chick-pea Batter Fish (p. 251). For an even lighter meal, omit the main dish and serve the soup with plain or stuffed breads.

Cucumber and Mung Bean Soup

(Kheera Dal Shorva)

This is one of the finest adaptations I know of a lentil dish served as a soup. I first tasted it twenty-five years ago on a visit to my great aunt's home in Calcutta.

Made with shreds of young tender cucumber, potatoes, and onions, all bound together in a thick bean puree, this thick hearty soup is particularly good on a cold winter day. Interestingly, the combination of cucumbers and onions gives the soup a delicate taste much like a cream of fish soup. If you don't like that taste, substitute potatoes for the onions. If you make the soup with pink lentils *(masar dal)* instead of mung beans, you will produce a much heartier soup.

For 8 persons

¾ cup yellow split mung beans (*Moong dal*)	4 tablespoons *usli ghee* (p. 50), or light vegetable oil
⅛ teaspoon turmeric	¾ teaspoon cumin seeds
¾ cup grated potatoes	¼ teaspoon black pepper
¾ cup thinly sliced onions	Juice of ½ lemon
2 cups grated cucumbers (about 2 large cucumbers)	2 tablespoons finely minced fresh coriander leaves
1½ teaspoons Kosher salt	

1. Pick over, clean, and wash mung beans following the instructions on page 327.

2. Put the beans in a 3-quart pan with the turmeric and 2½ cups cold water. Bring to a boil over medium-high heat. Reduce heat and simmer, partially covered, until the beans are tender and cooked through (about 30 minutes). Stir from time to time to keep them from burning. Turn off heat.

3. Beat the cooked beans with an electric beater or wire whisk for a minute, to make a coarse puree. Measure the puree, and add enough hot water to make 5 cups.

(continued)

4. Add potatoes, onions, cucumbers, and salt to the puree, and bring to a boil, stirring, over medium heat. Reduce heat and simmer, uncovered, until the vegetables are cooked but still firm (about 5 minutes). (This soup may be made up to this point and set aside, covered, for up to 4 hours, or refrigerated for a day. Reheat the soup until it comes to a gentle simmer.)

5. While the soup is simmering, heat the *ghee* over high heat in a small frying pan. When it is very hot, add the cumin and black pepper and fry until the cumin turns dark brown (about 5 seconds). Remove from heat and pour this perfumed butter with the spices over the soup. Add lemon juice and chopped coriander, and mix thoroughly. Check for salt and serve hot, sprinkled with a few more coriander leaves.

Note: The consistency of this soup should be like any lentil soup—thick as German split pea or Cuban black bean soup. If you prefer a thinner soup add broth or water to thin to the desired consistency. Be careful not to overthin, or the bean puree and vegetables will separate and begin to float in the liquid, looking quite unappetizing.

This soup is good enough to be eaten as a main dish. It is so substantial, all you need is a simple light meal consisting of pilaf and yogurt salads. A good choice is Chicken Pilaf (p. 228) or Royal Vegetable and Rice Casserole (p. 381).

Main Dishes

Meat

(Gosht)

Dry-cooked Spicy Ground Meat   (Sookha Keema)
Ground Meat with Potatoes in Scented White Sauce   (Safaid Keema)
Ground Meat in Cashew Nut Sauce with Chick-peas   (Keema Matar)
Lamb Braised in Aromatic Cream Sauce   (Rogani Gosht)
Meat Smothered with Onions   (Gosht Do-piaza)
Lamb Fillets Braised in Yogurt Cardamom Sauce   (Khara Pasanda)
Meat Curry   (Gosht Kari or Mutton Kari)
Beef in Spicy Tomato Gravy   (Masala Gosht)
Royal Braised Lamb with Fragrant Spices   (Shahi Korma)
Lamb in Fragrant Garlic Cream Sauce   (Rogan Josh)
Beef in Fragrant Spinach Sauce   (Saag Gosht)
Mint-Scented Broiled Leg of Lamb   (Bhona Gosht or Roast Mutton)
Royal Roast Leg of Lamb with Saffron Raisin Sauce   (Shahi Raan)
Lamb Pilaf with Leftover Roast Lamb   (Gosht Pullao)
Lamb Pilaf   (Mughalai Pullao)
Emperor's Layered Meat and Fragrant Rice Casserole
        (Shah Jahani Biriyani)
Meat-Stuffed Cabbage Rolls with Ginger Lemon Sauce
        (Keema Bhare Bandh Gobhi)
Meat Cutlets   (Gosht Tikka or Mutton Cutlets)
Goanese Hot and Pungent Curry   (Vendaloo)

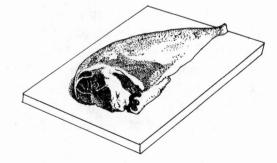

The most commonly eaten red meat throughout India is the meat of goat, a cousin of the sheep, except that it is a much smaller and thinner animal. Goat's meat in India is known as *Bakara* (goat) *ka gosht* (meat) or just *gosht*. In Kashmir, however, where the weather is cool, sheep are raised and so lamb is the traditional meat. The meat of the sheep, or lamb, is known as *Katch* (sheep's) *maanz/gosht* (meat), or simply as *maanz/gosht*. The Anglicized name for both these meats in India is "mutton," which has caused tremendous confusion, because outside of India "mutton" refers to a completely different meat. Consequently, Indians on visits here or recently immigrating go through much grief before they discover the difference. They ask the butcher for mutton, expecting mild and lean goat's meat; instead they are given the aged meat of old sheep, which has a strong and gamy flavor.

HOW TO BUY LAMB FOR COOKING:

The lamb that comes closest to the Indian variety, and also the most widely available here, is the meat of the young sheep (between five months and one year), known as yearling or spring lamb and commercially referred to as lamb or spring lamb. It has pinkish-red flesh, a sweet fragrance, and a mild subtle flavor when cooked. Goat's meat is still in the exotic meats category in this country and therefore it is difficult to find and often very expensive. You can frequently find it in Middle Eastern, Indian, Italian, and Greek neighborhoods in large cities. Or ask your butcher if he will order it for you.

Mutton is the meat of a mature sheep (between two and three years). Its flesh is deep red, and it has a strong flavor for which most of us have to acquire a taste. Mutton became very popular in the last century, particularly in England when there were no facilities for preserving and storing tender juicy young meats. Because mutton is a much drier meat with a tight texture and less prone to spoilage, it became the common meat. With time, people acquired a taste for its strong but unique-tasting meat. Today, it is considered a delicacy and is often one of the more expensive items on the menus of exclusive restaurants.

There are two cuts of lamb most commonly seen in the market: the leg of lamb, which is sometimes cut in half and sold as butt end (next to the loin) or shank end (next to the leg—shaped like a cone); and the chop, from the rib, loin, or shoulder. In the frozen meat section of supermarkets, frozen lamb is labeled "New Zealand lamb." My advice is to buy the fresh cut, since it is of such good quality and available all year long.

Young fresh leg of lamb is available in supermarkets around March, weighing between 4½ and 6½ pounds. A slightly larger leg is found in the fall or winter, weighing 7½ to 9½ pounds. Even though the smaller leg of lamb, known as spring lamb, is considered to be more tender, in Indian cooking the difference is negligible. Just about any cut of lamb can be used in Indian cooking, but I find the meat from the leg to be best. It is almost free of gristle and can be easily boned and cut. Also, because it is one large piece, it is extremely versatile.

In all fried meat preparations and certain pilafs, such as Lamb Pilaf (p. 189), generally the more tender and succulent meat from the rib and loin is used, because it does not become dry, tough, and fibrous in dishes without gravies.

HOW TO PREPARE LAMB FOR COOKING:

It is not essential that you prepare the meat yourself, since most butchers will gladly do this for you. But if you want to do it, use the following procedures.

To prepare a leg of lamb for cooking, you must first remove the fell, the parchmentlike skin that covers the leg. This exposes the thick flaky fat that covers the meat—which brings us to the issue of the difference between goat and lamb. Goat's meat is always lean— the way horsemeat is, whereas lamb is encased in a thick coat of fat. This is because the goat is primarily a warm-climate animal and therefore skinny. The sheep, on the other hand, is a fat, well-fed animal that grazes on higher plains and hills. It develops a thick padding of fat—nature's way of insulating it for long, cold winters. In Indian cooking animal fats (suet and lard) are never used. Lamb fat is particularly frowned upon because it has a very strong and distinct odor that becomes even more intense when cooked. Therefore, before doing anything else, the Indian cook carefully cuts and scrapes away all the fat from the lamb. This is done no matter what Indian lamb dish is being prepared.

Once the fat is removed, place the lean leg of lamb with the top side down (the side that was covered with fat) on the chopping board. With a sharp boning knife held at the tip of the hip bone, cut the leg all the way down from the butt end to the shank end, thus opening the leg and exposing the bone. Separate the bones from the meat by working around them, scraping and pushing the meat away from the bones with the knife. (Reserve the bones for making meat broth.)

This is the trimmed, boned, butterflied leg of lamb, which is now ready to be prepared in one of the following ways:

To prepare for roasts, such as Royal Roast Leg of Lamb with Saffron Raisin Sauce (p. 184), re-form the leg into a cylinder, making sure to tuck in the meat at the shank tip. Secure the leg by tying it with string at several places.

To prepare for barbecues and broiled dishes, such as Mint-Scented Broiled Leg of Lamb (p. 182), lay the butterflied leg of lamb on the chopping board and pound with a kitchen mallet until it is flattened to an approximately even thickness. Scoring the thick parts of the meat usually helps.

To prepare chunks for gravy dishes, such as Lamb in Fragrant Garlic Cream Sauce (p. 176), cut the meat into neat cubes or pieces of the size recommended in the recipe.

To prepare ground meat for kabobs, etc., grind the meat, using the coarse or fine blade of the meat grinder or food processor as recommended in the recipe.

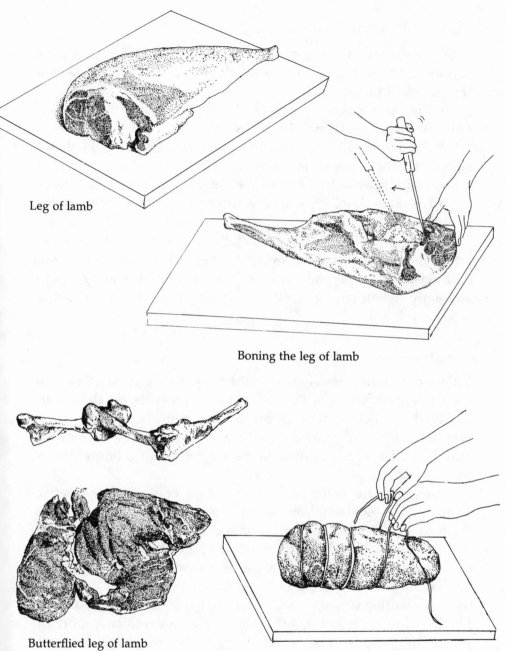

Leg of lamb

Boning the leg of lamb

Butterflied leg of lamb

Re-forming boned leg with string

(continued)

TIPS ON COOKING LAMB:

Lamb, compared to goat's meat, or even beef or pork, is a very juicy and loose-textured meat. To brown the meat, you need to keep a few points in mind:

• The meat pieces should be thoroughly dry and free of all traces of floating moisture, or they simply will not brown.

• The fat or oil for browning must be almost-smoking hot before the meat pieces are added. This is because the sudden contact with intense heat causes the outer layer of the meat pieces to shrivel and close, thus sealing in the juices and aiding quick browning.

• The pan should be large enough to accommodate the meat pieces in one layer without overcrowding; otherwise the pan will cool down and the meat will steam instead of searing. Consequently, when large quantities of meat are to be browned, it is best to do it in batches.

ABOUT SUBSTITUTIONS:

Unless otherwise indicated, in most recipes beef or lamb can be used interchangeably with total success. There is no change in cooking technique, or time, or preparation, provided tender cuts of beef (such as round and rump) are used. But whatever the meat, it must be trimmed of all visible fat before being cubed or ground as the recipe requires.

There is one point of caution. Lamb or goat's meat, after trimming, is essentially lean, whereas even average quality beef is marbled with a certain amount of almost invisible fat that cannot be trimmed away. Therefore, the finished beef dishes very often have a layer of fat, mostly released by the beef, floating on the surface. In the Indian subcontinent, Middle Eastern countries, and the countries of Southeast Asia, excess fat in food has never posed a problem. In fact, it has traditionally been considered an important source of good nutrition and energy. Its lavish use in food symbolizes one's affluence and high status in the society. Often during banquets and wedding receptions, extra fat is folded into a dish for enrichment to pamper the guests and exhibit one's wealth and fortune. Therefore, degreasing a dish before serving is totally unthinkable in India. We have an opposite outlook here: Fat floating on the surface of a dish is considered esthetically unappealing and is often frowned upon as unnecessary calories.

I therefore suggest that you degrease the dish carefully by scooping out the excess fat with a spoon, leaving just enough to coat and glaze the dish. The discarded fat can be used for preparing fried onions for a garnish (see methods on page 73) or for cooking other meat dishes.

In Indian cooking, meat is cooked until very tender. This is essential, as food is traditionally eaten with the fingers and should pull apart at the slightest touch.

Most meat dishes can be stretched to increase the number of servings by adding potatoes while the dish is cooking. Or you can keep the specified number of servings and substitute potatoes for part of the meat. Peel the potatoes, cut them to about the same size as the meat pieces, and add them during the last 30 to 50 minutes of cooking. The potatoes will absorb the wonderful sauce and end up tasting much like meat. In Indian homes this is done very commonly, not just to stretch the dish but because Indians love potatoes braised or stewed in meaty gravies.

A final word of caution: Do not reduce or omit the fat suggested in the recipe on the presumption that if you start off with less, or no fat at all, then there will be no extra fat to degrease. The suggested amount of butter fat or oil is the bare minimum essential for browning and frying all the ingredients properly. Also, for the authentic classic Indian flavoring, the meat must be cooked in *ghee* or oil, not in suet or lard.

Dry-cooked Spicy Ground Meat

(Sookha Keema)

This refreshing, coriander-scented ground-meat dish has as many uses in Indian cooking as the ingenious cook can come up with. It can be served as a main dish in its own right, or for variety mixed with Crisp Fried Okra (p. 310). It is the basic stuffing for a variety of breads, vegetables, and *samosas*. It is used in Savory Meat Pastries (p. 130), Meat-Stuffed Cabbage Rolls with Ginger Lemon Sauce (p. 194). More creative variations: such vegetables as eggplant, green peppers, and zucchini are good stuffed with *Sookha Keema* and then cooked by the *dum* method (see instructions on p. 76). Or, it can be folded into cooked rice and become a *keema pullao*.

For 4–6 persons

  2 tablespoons light vegetable oil
⅔ cup finely chopped onions
  4 teaspoons finely chopped garlic
1½ tablespoons finely chopped fresh ginger root
  2 green chilies, seeded and minced
  1 pound lean ground lamb or beef

¼ teaspoon turmeric
1½ teaspoons Kosher salt
  2 teaspoons *garam masala* (p. 38)
  2 teaspoons lemon juice
  2 tablespoons chopped fresh coriander leaves (or substitute 1 tablespoon dried coriander leaves)

1. Heat the oil in a skillet or large frying pan and add the onions. Fry the onions over medium-high heat until they turn caramel brown (about 10 minutes), stirring constantly to ensure even browning.

2. Add garlic, ginger, and green chilies, and cook for an additional 2 minutes. Add lamb or beef, and cook until the meat loses its pink color and begins to brown. Sprinkle turmeric and salt over the meat, stir for a moment or two, and then add ¼ cup hot

water. Reduce heat, cover, and let the meat cook thoroughly for about 25 minutes, stirring the mixture often to prevent burning. (The moisture should be totally absorbed; if it is not, uncover the pan, increase the heat, and cook until all the moisture has evaporated.) Turn off heat and stir in *garam masala,* lemon juice, and chopped coriander. Serve, if desired, enclosed in a ring of Roasted Onions (*Bhone Piaz,* p. 313) or Crisp Fried Okra (*Bhoni Bhindi,* p. 310).

This *keema* is traditionally cooked very dry—a texture greatly relished by Indians. It is perfectly acceptable, however, if you prefer to leave it slightly wet (cooking it only 15–20 minutes), especially when serving it straight as a main dish. When using it as a stuffing, you *must* cook it dry, as suggested in the recipe, or it will be difficult to fill and seal *samosa* or cutlets.

Note: The cooked *keema* is usually lumpy and coarse and not very pleasing to the eye. I like to mash it with a potato masher, or the back of a measuring cup for a minute to break up the lumps of meat into tiny springy granules. This gives the *keema* a fine silky texture. This final mashing is essential when the *keema* is used as stuffing for Savory Meat Pastries (*Keema Samosa,* p. 130).

(*Sookha Keema* can be made ahead and refrigerated for up to 3 days, or frozen. Defrost thoroughly before reheating. To reheat, simply warm in a frying pan over low heat until heated through.)

Sookha Keema should be served with bread, such as Baked Whole Wheat Puffy Bread (p. 397), Whole Wheat Flaky Bread (p. 402), or Deep-fried Puffy Bread (p. 413). Since both the main dish and the bread are on the dry side, the meal should feature a moist vegetable, such as Buttered Smothered Cabbage (p. 298) or Smoked Eggplant with Fresh Herbs (p. 305). You may also want to add a *dal:* Spice- and Herb-Laced Split Peas (p. 330) or Buttered Black Beans (p. 337) are good choices. For a refreshingly cool touch add a yogurt salad, such as Spinach and Yogurt Salad (p. 344), or Dumplings in Fragrant Yogurt (p. 348). Perfect accompaniments to this meal are Sweet Lemon Pickle with Cumin (p. 447), and an onion relish, particularly the Raw Onion Relish (p. 431).

Ground Meat With Potatoes in Scented White Sauce

(Safaid Keema)

Keema means ground meat. Any dish made with ground meat is also referred to as *keema*. It can be made with a white sauce generally consisting of yogurt and potatoes. Or it can be red in color, and spicy, and contain green peas, tomatoes, fresh coriander leaves, cardamom, cinnamon, and cloves. This white *keema* is my husband's favorite. I make it in large batches, simply doubling or tripling the recipe and freezing it in quart containers. This way I have a ready-made meal on those days when I am running short of time.

For 8 persons

5 tablespoons light vegetable oil
2½ cups finely chopped onions
1 tablespoon finely chopped garlic
2 tablespoons finely chopped fresh ginger root
1½ pounds lean ground beef (preferably ground round) or lean ground lamb
4 medium-sized potatoes (about 1 pound), peeled and cut into halves

1¼ teaspoons black cumin seeds, or 1 teaspoon ground roasted cumin seeds (p. 66)
⅓ teaspoon ground cloves
1 teaspoon ground cardamom
½ teaspoon ground cinnamon
⅓ teaspoon black or red pepper
⅔ cup plain yogurt
½ cup milk
2 teaspoons Kosher salt

1. Heat the oil in a large pan and add the onions. Cook over medium-high heat until the onions turn a light golden brown (about 15 minutes), stirring constantly to prevent burning. Do not let them brown or the sauce will become dark.

2. Stir in the garlic and ginger, and cook for an additional 2 minutes. Add beef or lamb, and cook until the meat loses its pink

color and begins to brown. Add all the remaining ingredients except the cumin powder (if you are using it), stir briefly, and add 1½ cups hot water. Bring the contents to a boil, reduce heat, and simmer, covered, for 35–45 minutes. Check and stir every now and then to keep the sauce from sticking to the bottom of the pan and burning. Be careful while stirring not to break the fragile pieces of potato. Turn off heat. If you are using roasted cumin powder, stir it in now. Check for salt, and serve.

Note: This can be made up to two days in advance and kept refrigerated. The flavor, in fact, improves with keeping. It can also be frozen successfully. However, defrost thoroughly before reheating. To reheat, gently simmer the *keema* over low heat until warmed through. Refrigerating and freezing generally thickens the *keema* and mellows the taste of salt. Therefore, add 3–4 tablespoons of heavy cream or milk to thin the *keema*. Also taste the dish, and if necessary, add a little salt before serving.

Keema is generally served with bread. Good choices are Baked Whole Wheat Bread (p. 393) or Baked Whole Wheat Puffy Bread (p. 397). A lovely vegetable side dish would be either Stuffed Okra with Fragrant Spices (p. 311) or Spicy Baby Eggplant (p. 303). If you want to serve another side dish, choose a yogurt salad, such as Dumplings in Fragrant Yogurt (p. 348) or Cucumber and Yogurt Salad (p. 343). Accompaniments are not necessary with this meal, but if you desire one, Raw Onion Relish (p. 431) is a good choice.

Ground Meat in Cashew Nut Sauce with Chick-peas

(Keema Matar)

This dish is traditionally made with beef or lamb and green peas *(matar)*. I prefer a more robust pea and therefore use chick-peas. Also, in the traditional recipe the *keema* is either left unthickened, causing the meat and the sauce to separate, or thickeners like flour or cornstarch are used, which give the *keema* a pasty look. I have experimented with this recipe and found that nut butter, especially cashew butter, not only functions as a natural thickening agent but also velvetizes the sauce at the same time that it imparts a nutty flavor. Beware of a tendency to be overenthusiastic with the cashew butter: don't increase the quantity, because too much will cause the dish to become too buttery and will also mask the flavors of the spices. *(Note:* Nut butters are available in health food stores. Or you can make your own in the blender or food processor; see the instructions at the end of this recipe.)

For 8 persons

4 tablespoons light vegetable oil

2 cups finely chopped onions

2 teaspoons finely chopped garlic

1 tablespoon finely chopped fresh ginger root

1 teaspoon ground cumin

2 teaspoons ground coriander

1 teaspoon turmeric

½ teaspoon red pepper or more, to taste

2 bay leaves

2 pounds lean ground beef (preferably ground round) or ground lamb

1½ teaspoons Kosher salt

2½ cups fresh, or 2 cups canned, chopped tomatoes

3 tablespoons cashew nut butter, or 4 tablespoons ground roasted cashew nuts

1 twenty-ounce can chick-peas with liquid, or 2 cups cooked chick-peas with ½ cup liquid

2 teaspoons *garam masala* (p. 38) or ground roasted cumin seeds (p. 66)

FOR GARNISH:

1 medium-sized onion, peeled   1 medium-sized tomato, cut
    and thinly sliced   into ½-inch wedges
1 green chili, shredded

· 1. Heat the oil in a large pan and add onions. Over medium-high heat, cook onions until they turn a caramel brown (about 25 minutes), stirring constantly so that they do not burn. (See directions for Brown-frying Onions, p. 71).

2. Add garlic and ginger, and cook for an additional 2 minutes. Add cumin, coriander, turmeric, red pepper, and bay leaves. Stir for a moment or two. Add beef or lamb. Cook the meat, breaking it up with a fork or wooden spoon, until it loses its pink color. Add salt, chopped tomatoes, nut butter, and chick peas with their liquid. Add ½ cup of hot water and bring the contents to a boil. Reduce heat and simmer, covered, for about 45 minutes or until the meat is cooked through and the sauce thickened. Check and stir often to keep the sauce from sticking and burning. Turn off heat, and stir in *garam masala*. Check for salt, and serve in a heated serving bowl. If desired, garnish with onion and chili shreds and tomato wedges.

Note: This dish can be made ahead and kept refrigerated for up to 2 days, or frozen. Defrost thoroughly before reheating. To reheat, gently simmer the *keema* over low heat until warmed through. Refrigeration, and particularly freezing, subdues the fragrance of *garam masala* and of the salt. Therefore, taste the dish, and add a little *garam masala* and salt as needed before serving.

NUT BUTTER:

To make 1 cup of nut butter, place 1½ cups unsalted roasted nuts in the container of a food processor or electric blender and blend for 1 minute, turning the machine off every 10 seconds. The nuts will reduce to a fine powder but will have the texture of coarse meal because of the natural oil still being released. Continue processing, turning the machine off every 30 seconds and scraping down the sides of the container, until the coarse powder becomes a thick fudgelike paste (about 3 minutes in the food processor; 5 minutes in the blender). Add 1½ tablespoons of walnut or other light vegetable oil, and run the machine for an additional 30 seconds, or until the oil is thoroughly blended in.

This *keema* is perfect for picnics and large barbecues, since it looks like an Indian version of the famous Tex-Mex chili dish. It's also excellent for a Sunday brunch. *Keema matar* is best accompanied by a fried bread, such as Deep Fried Puffy Bread (p. 413), but Whole Wheat Flaky Bread (p. 402) is also a fine choice. To balance the spicy flavor of *keema* and soothe the palate, serve a yogurt salad, such as Cucumber and Yogurt Salad (p. 343), and a soothing Onion Vegetable Relish (p. 432). For a more elaborate brunch, include another main dish, especially a vegetarian one. An excellent choice would be Potatoes in Fragrant Gravy (p. 260).

Lamb Braised in Aromatic Cream Sauce

(Rogani Gosht)

This dish represents the subtle flavoring that is the hallmark of Moghul cooking. Tender chunks of lamb and cubes of potatoes are slowly braised in a mellow, wonderfully flavored cream and yogurt sauce until the lamb becomes melt-in-your-mouth tender and the sauce is glazed with a satiny sheen. The best thing about this dish is that it's extremely simple to prepare and can be made quickly. All you need to do is mix the ingredients in a pot and cook them until they are done—no initial frying and no garnishing to worry about.

Since this dish requires expensive ingredients such as heavy cream and almonds, in India it is generally reserved for banquets.

For 6–8 persons

1 cup plain yogurt
2 medium-sized onions,
 peeled and quartered
1½ tablespoons chopped fresh
 ginger root
2 tablespoons slivered
 blanched almonds
2 tablespoons ground
 coriander
2½ teaspoons ground
 cardamom
1 teaspoon black pepper

1 tablespoon Kosher salt
1 cup heavy cream
2 pounds boneless lean lamb
 (preferably from the leg),
 or boneless lean beef
 round, cut into 1½-inch
 pieces
3–4 medium-sized boiling
 potatoes (preferably red
 wax, about 1 pound),
 peeled and quartered
¼–⅓ cup milk (if needed)

1. Put yogurt, onions, ginger, and almonds in the container of an electric blender or food processor, and run the machine until the ingredients are reduced to a fine puree (use a few tablespoons of heavy cream from the one cup in the recipe if necessary).

2. Put the pureed mixture along with the coriander, cardamom, black pepper, salt, heavy cream, and the meat in a large heavy-bottomed pan (preferably one with a non-stick surface). Place the pan over medium-high heat and bring to the boil. Reduce to a simmer, and cook, covered, for 1¾ hours. Add potatoes, and continue simmering until the potatoes are done and the meat is very tender (about 40 minutes). Check and stir often during cooking to keep the sauce from sticking and burning. When stirring, be careful not to break the fragile meat and potato pieces.

3. Degrease the dish, if necessary, as suggested in the introduction to the meat recipes. Check for salt, and serve.

Note: For the best flavor, make the dish several hours before it is to be served and leave it at room temperature. (The resting mellows the sauce and flavors the meat and potatoes more intensely.) It may be kept in the refrigerator for up to 2 days, or frozen. Defrost thoroughly before reheating. To reheat, simmer gently over very low heat until warmed through. If the sauce looks too thick, add a little milk or water.

(continued)

Cream sauce dishes are traditionally eaten with a pilaf. This lovely dish should be accompanied by one that does not interfere with or mask the subtle flavor of the dish. A superb choice would be Saffron Pilaf with Peaches (p. 371). For a side dish, serve a vegetable, such as Glazed Cauliflower with Ginger (p. 299), Broccoli Smothered in Garlic Oil (p. 296), or Smoked Eggplant with Fresh Herbs (p. 305).

For a more elaborate meal include a *dal*, such as Buttered Black Beans (p. 337). On formal occasions, I start with an elegant first course, such as Crab Malabar (p. 101), or Fragrant Stuffed Tomatoes (p. 106) or Mulligatawny Soup (p. 143). Hot Hyderabad Tomato Relish (p. 441) goes particularly well with *Rogani Gosht*.

Meat Smothered with Onions

(Gosht Do-piaza)

This recipe for *Gosht Do-piaza*, a specialty of my mother-in-law, is a far more subtle dish than the common, more popular version consisting of fried onions and several different spices. Here the spicing is kept to a bare minimum; turmeric is used to perfume the meat with its woody scent. Also, to keep the overall flavor mellow and delicate, *raw* (not fried) onions are folded into the meat after it is cooked. The onions lose their raw sharp taste and become sweet and glazed, without losing their crispness, by steaming in the wonderful vapors of the meat. *Gosht Do-piaza*, literally translated, means meat in twice as many onions, and that's exactly what the dish is supposed to be. But most Indian cooks, including myself, add only half the prescribed amount; otherwise the entire dish tastes of nothing but onions.

For 6 persons

½ cup light vegetable oil
2 tablespoons minced garlic
3 tablespoons ground, grated,
   or crushed fresh ginger
   root
2 teaspoons turmeric
1 teaspoon red pepper, or to
   taste

2 pounds lean boneless lamb,
   cut into 1-inch cubes
2½ teaspoons Kosher salt
2 large Spanish onions (about
   2 pounds altogether),
   peeled and sliced into
   ¼-inch slices

1. Heat oil in a large heavy-bottomed pan, such as a 5-quart casserole, and add garlic and ginger. Over medium heat, fry until they turn light golden (about 5 minutes), stirring constantly to ensure even browning. Add turmeric and red pepper, and stirring rapidly, fry for an additional 10 seconds.

2. Add meat, and mix thoroughly. Reduce heat to low, cover the pot tightly, and let the meat cook in its juices for 15 minutes (at the end of cooking, the moisture should be totally absorbed by the meat, leaving behind the oil; the contents of the pan will look quite dry). Check and stir often during this period to ensure the meat is not sticking to the pan and burning.

3. Add salt, along with 2 cups boiling water. Stir well, and simmer, covered, until the meat is very tender and the liquid has turned into a thick sauce (about 1–1¼ hours).

(The meat may be prepared up to this stage and set aside, covered, for several hours, or refrigerated for up to 2 days, or frozen. Defrost thoroughly before reheating and proceeding with the recipe. To reheat, bring the sauce to a gentle simmer over low heat, until thoroughly warmed.)

4. Add onion slices, mix thoroughly to distribute them evenly with meat and sauce, and replace the cover. Increase heat to high for exactly 15 seconds (to build up steam), and turn off heat. Let the onions steam, undisturbed, for 5 minutes. Under no circumstances should the pan be opened during this time, because that would cause the steam to escape, thus leaving the onions raw and hot. Check for salt, and serve.

(continued)

This *Do-piaza* must be served with a bread such as Whole Wheat Flaky Bread (p. 402), Baked Whole Wheat Puffy Bread (p. 397), or Deep Fried Puffy Bread (p. 413). Since the dish contains a lot of onions, you don't need to serve any extra vegetables, but if you want, Smoked Eggplant with Fresh Herbs (p. 305) is an excellent choice.

Lamb Fillets Braised in Yogurt Cardamom Sauce

(*Khara Pasanda*)

This is another exquisite example of classic Moghul cooking: lamb fillets (*pasanda*) gently braised in a cumin- and green cardamom-laced yogurt sauce. In India, lamb fillets are preferred because they cook to a greater degree of tenderness and still remain moist. Lamb in America, however, is naturally tender and juicy, so it is not essential to use such an expensive cut. *Pasanda*, which requires expensive ingredients, is usually reserved in India for special occasions.

For 4–6 persons

8 tablespoons light vegetable oil

2 cups finely chopped onions

4 teaspoons finely chopped garlic

1½ tablespoons finely chopped fresh ginger root

¼ cup slivered blanched almonds

1 teaspoon black cumin seeds (optional)

¾ teaspoon ground cardamom

1 teaspoon black pepper

1 cup plain yogurt

2 teaspoons Kosher salt

2 pounds boneless lean lamb, preferably from the leg or rib, or boneless lean beef round, cut into strips, ¼-inch thick, 2½ inches long, and 1 inch wide

¼–⅓ cup heavy cream

1. Heat 4 tablespoons of the oil in a heavy-bottomed pan (preferably one with a non-stick surface), and add onions. Over medium-high heat, fry the onions until they turn light brown (about 15 minutes), stirring constantly to prevent their burning. (See directions for Brown-frying Onions, p. 71).

2. Add garlic, ginger, and almonds, and fry until the almonds are lightly colored (about 5 minutes). Add cumin, if you are using it, cardamom, and black pepper, and fry briefly to release their fragrance (about 1–2 minutes). Turn off heat.

3. Put the entire contents of the pan into the container of an electric blender or food processor. Add yogurt, salt, and 1 cup hot water, and finely puree the mixture. Set aside.

4. Add the remaining 4 tablespoons of oil to the pan, and turn the heat high. Pat dry the meat pieces on paper towels (or they will not brown), and add when the oil is very hot. Brown them quickly and evenly on all sides (about 3–5 minutes). The pan should not be overcrowded with too many pieces of meat, as crowding will cool the pan and the meat will steam instead of being seared. Therefore, the browning should be done in batches. As each batch is browned, transfer it with a slotted spoon to a bowl. When all the pieces are browned, return them to the pan. Add the pureed mixture and bring to a boil. Reduce heat and cook, covered, until the meat is very tender (about 1¼–1½ hours). Check every 15 minutes to make sure the sauce is not sticking to the bottom of the pan and burning. The sauce should be fairly thick; if it is not, uncover, increase heat, and boil rapidly until it reduces to a thick creamy consistency. Also, if there is excessive fat floating on the surface (particularly if you are using beef), carefully scoop it out. Do not take out all the fat, as there should be a thin film of it left to coat and velvetize the sauce and meat pieces.

5. Stir in the cream, check for salt, simmer until heated through, and serve.

Note: The flavor of this dish improves noticeably with keeping. Therefore, make it at least a couple of hours before you are ready to serve the dish, or a day before and refrigerate. It can also be frozen successfully. Defrost thoroughly before reheating. To reheat, gently simmer over low heat until warmed through. If the sauce looks slightly thick, add a little milk or water. Check for salt before serving.

Accompany this noble dish with a pilaf that is fragrant with Moghul spices, such as The Emperor's Pilaf with Black Mushrooms (p. 375), Okra Pilaf (p. 373), or Patiala Pilaf (p. 366). Or, for a sweeter taste, Sweet Saffron Pilaf (p. 369). For a side dish, serve Spicy Baby Eggplant (p. 303), or Turmeric Potatoes with Green Peppers (p. 316).

For an elaborate meal, serve a *dal* such as Lucknow Sour Lentils (p. 335), and a yogurt salad such as Dumplings in Fragrant Yogurt (p. 348). Hot Hyderabad Tomato Relish (p. 441) goes extremely well with this meal.

Meat Curry

(*Gosht Kari* or *Mutton Kari*)

Gosht Kari is far and away the most popular meat dish in North India. It is an uncomplicated dish in which unboned pieces of lamb are stewed in a turmeric-laced fried onion sauce. Tomatoes are frequently added to enrich the sauce; they also impart a beautiful reddish-brown color.

Unless it is absolutely essential, I avoid using unboned meat in any gravy-based dish, because it makes eating difficult. Since bones are left in essentially to enrich the sauce, I add a few meaty ones at the beginning of cooking and remove them before I serve the dish. Or I make a broth from the bones to use in place of the water.

Note: the quality of the tomatoes is crucial in this dish. They should be fully ripe, red juicy tomatoes. Lovely beefsteak tomatoes that have become so overripe as to be unsliceable for salads are ideal.

For 8 persons

8 tablespoons light vegetable
   oil
3 pounds lean boneless beef,
   preferably beef round, or
   lean boneless lamb, cut
   into 1-inch cubes
3–4 meaty beef bones (if using
   beef) or lamb bones (if
   using lamb) (optional)
4 cups finely chopped onions
4 teaspoons finely chopped
   garlic
3 tablespoons finely chopped
   fresh ginger root
1 tablespoon ground cumin
2 tablespoons ground
   coriander

2½ teaspoons turmeric
¾ teaspoon red pepper, or to
   taste
2 cups finely chopped or
   pureed fresh ripe
   tomatoes, or 1½ cups
   canned tomatoes, chopped
   or pureed
1 tablespoon Kosher salt
4 medium-sized potatoes
   (about 1 pound), peeled
   and quartered
3–4 tablespoons finely chopped
   fresh coriander leaves (or
   substitute 2 tablespoons
   dried coriander leaves)

1. Heat 4 tablespoons of the oil over high heat in a large heavy-bottomed pan. When the oil is very hot, add the meat pieces (and bones, if using them), and brown them. For successful browning it is essential to pat the meat dry of all clinging blood and juices on the surface, with paper towels. Also, the pan should not be overcrowded with too many pieces of meat, as crowding will cool the pan and the meat will steam instead of being seared. Therefore, the browning should be done in batches. As each batch is browned, transfer it with a slotted spoon to a bowl.

2. Add the remaining 4 tablespoons of oil to the pan, along with the onions. Reduce heat to medium-high, and fry the onions until they turn dark brown (about 20 minutes), stirring constantly so that they do not burn. (See directions for Brown-frying Onions, p. 71).

3. Add garlic and ginger, and fry for an additional minute. Add cumin, coriander, turmeric, and red pepper, and continue frying until the spices begin to give out their fragrance (about 10–15 seconds). Return the browned meat (and bones) to the pan, along

with the tomatoes, salt, and four cups of boiling water. Bring to the boil. Reduce heat, and simmer, covered, for 1½ hours. Add potatoes, and continue simmering, covered, until the potatoes are tender and the meat is cooked through (about 30 minutes). Turn off heat, and let the meat rest for at least ½ hour, preferably 2 hours. When ready to serve, first remove the bones and discard, then check for salt, and simmer again until heated through. Fold in the chopped coriander leaves, and serve.

Note: This dish may be made in advance and refrigerated for up to 3 days, or frozen. Defrost thoroughly before reheating. To reheat, simmer gently until warmed through. Also, taste to check the flavors, and if necessary, add a little salt, ground roasted cumin seeds (p. 66), and chopped coriander leaves.

This gorgeous curry with its garnet-colored sauce should be served with a plain cooked rice (p. 357), or a simple baked bread such as Baked Whole Wheat Bread (p. 393) or Baked Whole Wheat Puffy Bread (p. 397). You can serve any of the vegetable side dishes. Good choices would be Buttered Smothered Cabbage (p. 298) or Turmeric Potatoes with Green Peppers (p. 316). For an additional side dish, serve Lentils with Garlic Butter (p. 332) or Lucknow Sour Lentils (p. 335) if you are serving a staple of rice; try Buttered Black Beans (p. 337) if you are serving bread. Consider Indian Cheese Fritters (p. 117) as an appetizer. They go beautifully with this meal.

Beef in Spicy Tomato Gravy

(Masala Gosht)

Masala Gosht is very similar to *Gosht Kari*, except that it contains a few additional spices, and a portion of the tomatoes is replaced by plain yogurt. Here the tomatoes, ginger, and garlic are finely pureed, which is why the gravy has such a smooth creamy texture. The addition of yogurt velvetizes the gravy even more. This dish is served in restaurants more than it is in Indian homes.

For 6 persons

2 medium-sized ripe fresh
    tomatoes (about
    ½ pound), or 1 cup canned
    tomatoes
4 large cloves garlic
1½ tablespoons chopped fresh
    ginger root
⅓ cup plain yogurt
6 tablespoons light vegetable
    oil
2 pounds lean beef round, cut
    into 1½-inch cubes
3 meaty beef bones (optional)
2 cups finely chopped onions

4 black (or 8 green) cardamom
    pods
8 whole cloves
2 teaspoons turmeric
½ teaspoon red pepper, or to
    taste
2 teaspoons Kosher salt
1½ teaspoons ground roasted
    cumin seeds (p. 66)
2 tablespoons chopped fresh
    coriander leaves (or
    substitute 1 tablespoon
    dried coriander leaves)

1. Preheat the oven to 325°F.

2. Put tomatoes, garlic, chopped ginger, and yogurt in the container of an electric blender or food processor, and run the machine until the ingredients are reduced to a fine smooth puree. Set aside.

3. Heat 2 tablespoons of the oil in a large frying pan over high heat until very hot. Pat dry the meat pieces and bones (if you are using them) on paper towels (otherwise the meat will not brown, but steam instead), and add to the pan. Brown them, turning and tossing the pieces, for 3–5 minutes. (The frying pan should be large enough to accommodate the pieces in one layer without overlapping. The best way to brown them is in batches.) Transfer the meat to a heavy-bottomed casserole.

4. Add the remaining 4 tablespoons of oil to the frying pan, along with the onions. Reduce heat to medium-high, and fry until the onions turn caramel brown (about 20 minutes), stirring frequently to prevent burning. (See directions for Brown-frying Onions, p. 71). Add cardamom, cloves, turmeric, red pepper, and salt, and fry for an additional minute. Add the tomato yogurt puree, and continue frying the mixture until it reduces to a thick paste and the oil begins to separate from the paste (about 5 minutes). Turn off heat.

(continued)

5. Add this paste to the meat in the casserole. Add 3 cups of hot water to the frying pan. Scrape the sides and bottom of the pan to release the pieces clinging to it, and pour into the casserole. Stir the meat to distribute the spices and liquid evenly. Place the casserole over medium-high heat and bring the contents to a boil. Place a sheet of foil over the top of the casserole, and cover tightly with the lid.

6. Bake in the middle level of the oven for 2 hours. Check and stir meat every 30 minutes to ensure it won't burn. Turn off the oven. Let the casserole remain in the oven 15 minutes longer.

7. Take the casserole out of the oven, uncover, and remove and discard the bones. Check for salt, and serve sprinkled with ground roasted cumin seeds and chopped coriander leaves.

Note: This is one of those dishes that taste best when allowed to rest for a couple of hours at room temperature or refrigerated for a day or two before serving. It also freezes extremely well; however, defrost thoroughly before reheating. To reheat, gently simmer over low heat until warmed through. As always, check the flavoring, and if necessary add a little salt, ground roasted cumin seeds (p. 66), and chopped coriander before serving.

Follow the menu suggestions for Meat Curry (p. 170).

Royal Braised Lamb with Fragrant Spices

(Shahi Korma)

Korma, or braising, is the classic technique used to prepare lamb in Moghul Cooking (see description on page 75). There are several basic recipes, varying in the spicing. But all korma dishes are essentially butter- or cream-braised meat dishes perfumed with Moghul spices. I like to accentuate the flavor of mace in this recipe because it imparts a lovely sweet fragrance well-suited to this lordly dish (*Shahi* means Royal).

Korma may be served by itself as a main dish or used for making another classic—Emperor's Layered Meat and Fragrant Rice Casserole (p. 192).

For 8 persons

½ cup *usli ghee*, (p. 50) or light
  vegetable oil
1½ cups thinly sliced onions
1 tablespoon finely chopped
  garlic
1½ tablespoons finely chopped
  fresh ginger root
2 teaspoons black cumin
  seeds, or 1½ teaspoons
  ground cumin
1½ teaspoons ground mace
¾ teaspoon ground cinnamon
1 teaspoon *Mughal garam
  masala* (p. 37)

½ teaspoon red pepper, or to
  taste
1 teaspoon paprika
3 pounds lean boneless lamb,
  preferably from the leg,
  cut into 1½-inch cubes
1 cup plain yogurt
1 cup sour cream or heavy
  cream
1 tablespoon Kosher salt
  milk (if needed)

1. Heat the *ghee* in a large heavy-bottomed pan, preferably a non-stick type, and add onions. Over medium-high heat, fry the onions until they turn caramel brown (about 15 minutes), stirring constantly to prevent burning. (See directions for Brown-frying Onions p. 71).

2. Add garlic and ginger, and cook for an additional 2 minutes. Add cumin, mace, cinnamon, *Mughal garam masala*, red pepper, and paprika, and stir rapidly for a moment or two to distribute the spices into the fried onions.

3. Dry meat pieces thoroughly on paper towels. Increase heat to high, add meat pieces, and brown them on all sides evenly, turning and tossing them rapidly (about 5 minutes). Add ½ cup yogurt, ½ cup sour or heavy cream, and salt, and bring to a boil. Reduce heat, and simmer the meat, covered, until very tender (about 2 hours). The meat should be checked and stirred frequently during cooking to keep the sauce from sticking and burning. If the

sauce evaporates too fast while cooking, add a little milk. When the *korma* is fully cooked, it should look quite dry, with just enough gravy to coat the meat pieces. Stir in the remaining yogurt and cream, and turn off heat.

Note: Because the *korma* is practically sauceless, a considerable amount of fat usually separates and floats on the surface. This is characteristic of *korma* dishes. The dishes are traditionally served with the fat. For various reasons, however, I prefer to degrease the dish slightly, leaving just enough fat to coat and glaze the gravy and meat pieces. The scooped-out fat may be used in preparing other dishes or frying onions for garnish.

This dish may be made ahead and refrigerated for up to 3 days. Since it is practically dry, with thick scanty gravy, it does not take well to freezing. To reheat, gently simmer over low heat until warmed through. If the gravy looks a little too thick and dry, add a few tablespoons of milk or water to bring it to the right consistency.

This *korma* perfumed with butter and spices must be matched with an equally fragrant pilaf. What better choice could there be than Sweet Saffron Pilaf (p. 369)! Any vegetable may be served. Particularly good choices are Glazed Cauliflower with Ginger (p. 299), Broccoli Smothered in Garlic Oil (p. 296), or even Cauliflower and Scallions with Black Mustard Seeds (p. 301). For an additional side dish, you may serve Lucknow Sour Lentils (p. 335) or Lentils with Garlic Butter (p. 332).

Lamb in Fragrant Garlic Cream Sauce

(Rogan Josh)

This is truly the finest example of the superb flavoring of Moghul cooking. With its velvety sauce, filled with the aroma of garlic butter, it is every inch an imperial dish. Although there are several versions of *Rogan Josh,* no variation equals this one from Kashmir, the northernmost state of India. For such a special preparation, use only the best: top-quality lamb free of all membranes and tissues, the freshest and sweetest smelling yogurt, and freshly ground spices.

Traditionally, the meat is first marinated for several hours in a yogurt-spice mixture before being cooked in the marinade. This process tenderizes the meat. But I find the lamb in this country so tender and of such good quality that I cut short this step. Instead, I let the cooked meat sit in its sauce for a short time before serving it. This allows the flavors of the sauce to permeate the meat and make it even more flavorful.

For 8 persons

FOR MARINADE:

4 medium-sized onions (about 1 pound), peeled and quartered
2 tablespoons finely chopped fresh ginger root
2 tablespoons ground coriander
¾ teaspoon red pepper, or to taste

2½ cups plain yogurt
½ cup sour cream
1 tablespoon Kosher salt
⅓ cup melted *usli ghee*, (p. 50) or ½ cup (one stick) melted sweet butter

3 pounds lean boneless lamb, preferably from the leg, cut into 1½-inch cubes
4 tablespoons *usli ghee,* or 2 tablespoons sweet butter mixed with 2 tablespoons light vegetable oil
1 tablespoon minced garlic
1 tablespoon black cumin seeds, crushed, or 2 teaspoons ground cumin

2 teaspoons ground cardamom
1 teaspoon *Mughal garam masala* (p. 37)
1 cup heavy cream
Milk or water if needed

(continued)

1. Put all the ingredients of the marinade except *ghee* into the container of an electric blender or food processor, and run the machine until the ingredients are finely pureed.

2. Place the lamb in a large bowl, and pour the marinade and the melted *ghee* over it. Mix thoroughly to coat the meat pieces with the marinade. Cover, and let the meat marinate for at least ½ hour at room temperature, or 2 hours in the refrigerator. (Remove from the refrigerator about 30 minutes before you are ready to cook the meat.)

3. Transfer the meat, along with the marinade, to a heavy-bottomed pan (preferably one with a non-stick surface). Place the pan over medium-low heat, and gently bring the contents to a boil. Reduce heat, and simmer, covered, until the lamb is very tender. The lamb is done when a fork or a thin skewer pierces it without any resistance (about 2–2½ hours depending upon the heat, pan used, and above all, the quality of the meat). Stir frequently to prevent the sauce's sticking to the bottom of the pan and burning.

4. Heat the 4 tablespoons *usli ghee* in a small frying pan over high heat. When it is very hot, add garlic, and stirring rapidly, fry for 15 seconds. Immediately add cumin, cardamom, and *Mughal garam masala*. As soon as the spices begin to sizzle and release their fragrance (about 3–5 seconds), turn off heat and pour the perfumed butter, along with the spices, over the meat. Add cream, and stir to distribute the ingredients. Let the meat rest at room temperature for 2 hours.

5. When ready to serve, check for salt, then reheat the meat until piping hot, and serve.

Note: Sometimes too much moisture evaporates during cooking, causing the *ghee* to separate from the sauce. If that happens, add a little milk or water, a tablespoon at a time, until the fat is incorporated back into the sauce. Do not degrease, as the fragrant *ghee* is one of the primary flavoring ingredients in this dish.

Note: Rogan Josh definitely improves in flavor with keeping. Therefore I would advise you to make it the day before you are planning to serve it. It keeps well in the refrigerator for up to 3 days, and also freezes well. Defrost thoroughly before reheating.

To reheat, simmer gently over low heat until warmed through. As always, taste for salt, and if necessary, add a fresh batch of perfumed butter (using very little butter, of course).

For planning a complete meal, follow the menu suggestions given for Lamb Braised in Aromatic Cream Sauce (p. 164).

Beef in Fragrant Spinach Sauce

(Saag Gosht)

Spinach is used extensively in India, where it's inexpensive and available year-round. But the main reason for its prevalence in Indian cooking is that it can be utilized in so many marvelous ways—for instance, as a sauce. Spinach is a mild green. If it is cooked with a meat that contains a lot of spices, its flavor is likely to get lost, and its lovely bright green color with it. To be sure that the spinach will hold its own in this dish, you must cook it separately and fold it into the meat just before serving.

This beautiful dish—another variation of the Moghul rulers' fine cooking—is based on the use of different greens. You can substitute kale, collard, or mustard greens, or combine any of these with the spinach.

For 8 persons

3 cups cooked spinach (p. 318)
6 tablespoons light vegetable oil
3 pounds lean boneless beef round, or lamb, cut into 1½ inch cubes
3½ cups thinly sliced onions
1½ tablespoons finely chopped garlic

3 tablespoons finely chopped fresh ginger root
1 tablespoon ground cumin
2 tablespoons ground coriander
1 teaspoon turmeric
1 medium-sized ripe tomato, finely chopped, or ¼ cup chopped canned tomatoes

(continued)

3 green chilies, seeded and
    minced, or 1 teaspoon red
    pepper
3 tablespoons plain yogurt or
    sour cream
1 cinnamon stick, 3 inches
    long, broken into small
    pieces
6 black (or 12 green)
    cardamom pods

9 whole cloves
3 bay leaves, crumbled
1 tablespoon Kosher salt
4 teaspoons *garam masala*
    (p. 38), or ground roasted
    cumin seeds (p. 66)
2–4 tablespoons light vegetable
    oil (if needed)

1. Finely puree the spinach, using a food processor or electric blender, or mince it with a knife on a chopping board. Set aside.

2. Preheat the oven to 325°F.

3. Heat 2 tablespoons of the oil in a large frying pan over high heat until very hot. Pat the meat dry on paper towels (or it will not brown), and add. Brown the meat, turning and tossing the pieces, until nicely seared on all sides. (This is best done in batches so that the frying pan is not overcrowded. As each batch is browned, transfer to a heavy-bottomed casserole.)

4. Add the remaining 4 tablespoons oil to the frying pan, and add onions. Reduce heat to medium-high, and fry until they turn caramel brown (about 25 minutes), stirring constantly to prevent burning. (See directions for Brown-frying Onions, p. 71). Add garlic and ginger, and fry for an additional 2 minutes. Add cumin, coriander, and turmeric, and stir rapidly for 15 seconds. Add tomatoes and chilies, and continue frying until the tomato is cooked and the entire mixture is turned into a thick pulpy paste (about 3 minutes). Add yogurt or sour cream, and immediately turn off the heat. When slightly cool, puree in an electric blender or food processor, and add to the meat in the casserole.

5. Place a double layer of cheesecloth, about 6 inches square, on the work surface. Put cinnamon, cardamom, cloves, bay leaves in the center, bring up the four corners of the cheesecloth to wrap the spices, and tie them to form a bag. Crush the bag slightly with a wooden mallet or any heavy tool to break up the spices. Add the spice bag to the casserole.

6. Add 4 cups of boiling water along with the salt, and stir to distribute the meat into the sauce. Place a piece of aluminum foil on top of the casserole, and cover tightly with the lid. Bring the contents to a boil on top of the stove.

7. Place the casserole in the middle level of the oven for 2½ hours. Or alternatively, it may be cooked on top of the stove over low heat for 2–2½ hours, or until the meat is fork tender.

8. Remove the casserole from the oven or turn off the stove, and take off the lid. Remove the spice bag, and squeeze hard to extract as much juice as possible. Discard the bag. Add the cooked spinach and *garam masala*, and blend well, being careful not to break the fragile meat pieces. Cover the pot, return it to the oven or stove, and cook for 5 minutes more. Turn off the oven, and let the pot remain undisturbed for an additional 10 minutes. Check for salt, and if the sauce lacks adequate glaze, stir in a few tablespoons of oil. Serve.

Note: This dish, just like any other braised dish, tastes better with keeping. It is particularly good if made a few hours in advance, and allowed to rest at room temperature before being reheated and served. This dish keeps well in the refrigerator for up to 2 days, and also freezes well. Defrost thoroughly before reheating. To reheat, gently simmer over low heat until warmed through. Before serving, taste for salt, and if necessary, fold in a little *garam masala*.

You can serve this dish with either Fragrant Pilaf Banaras Style (p. 368) or Patiala Pilaf (p. 366). Even simple plain cooked rice goes well (p. 357). For a bread, try Whole Wheat Flaky Bread (p. 402), Baked Whole Wheat Puffy Bread (p. 397), Chick-pea Flour Bread (p. 399), or Deep Fried Puffy Bread (p. 413). For a side dish, serve a yogurt salad like Dumplings in Fragrant Yogurt (p. 348). There is no need for an additional green, but a light stir-fried vegetable, such as Glazed Cauliflower with Ginger (p. 299), Turmeric Potatoes (p. 314), or Cauliflower and Scallions with Black Mustard Seeds (p. 301) would provide an interesting contrast. To complete the meal, serve a spicy appetizer to set the tone of the dinner to follow. A good choice would be Savory Pastries with Spicy Potato Filling (p. 125).

Mint-Scented Broiled Leg of Lamb

(*Bhona Gosht* or Roast Mutton)

If you like the flavor of lamb, you will love this delicious roast oozing with the fragrances of cumin and mint. It is absolutely simple to make and requires very little cooking time. All that you need do is prepare the marinade and add it to the lamb. When you are ready to serve the meal, take the lamb out of the marinade, and broil.

Bhona Gosht belongs to the school of outdoor cooking in which meats are cooked over charcoal or wood fires. The meat can, however, be cooked over an electric grill with very good results. Traditionally, the broiled meat is cut into large chunks and served over a pilaf (to be mixed and eaten), but I prefer to serve it separately. I also like to make a gravy from the marinade and serve it with the lamb, because the meat by itself tends to taste dry.

Before being marinated, the leg of lamb is first butterflied and trimmed of all visible fat (see instructions for preparing lamb on p. 153), which makes carving easier. The leftover broiled lamb can be used in many delicious ways. You can fold it into cooked rice for a pilaf (see Lamb Pilaf with Leftover Roast Lamb on p. 188), or you can add it to an onion and tomato gravy to produce a *kari*, or mince it and use it as a stuffing for *samosas*.

For 8 persons

One 5–6-pound leg of lamb

FOR MARINADE:

1 tablespoon minced garlic	½ teaspoon Kosher salt
1 tablespoon grated or finely chopped fresh ginger root	2 tablespoons minced fresh mint leaves (or substitute 1 teaspoon powdered dry mint)
½ teaspoon red pepper	
2 teaspoons paprika	
2 teaspoons ground cumin	½ cup light vegetable oil
¼ teaspoon ground clove	2 tablespoons lemon juice

1. Bone and butterfly the leg of lamb following the directions on page 154. Or ask your butcher to prepare the leg.

2. Place the meat in a large shallow dish that will hold it snugly without its overlapping or curling. Mix all the ingredients of the marinade in a small bowl, and pour it over the meat. Rub the marinade well to coat the meat thoroughly, turning it often. Cover and marinate for 4 hours, or refrigerate for up to 2 days, turning several times.

3. Take the lamb from the refrigerator about 2 hours before serving, and let it come to room temperature.

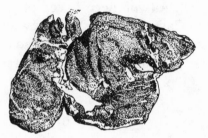

4. Preheat the broiler, and brush the grill with a little oil to keep the meat from sticking. Remove the meat from the marinade, and reserve the marinade. Scrape excess marinade off the surface of the meat (to keep the spices from burning). Broil the meat 2 inches away from the heat source—10 minutes on each side for medium, or 12 minutes if you prefer well-done). While it is broiling, brush the meat with the oil floating on top of the marinade. Place the meat on a carving board and let it rest briefly (about 5 minutes) before you slice it.

5. While the meat is resting, prepare the sauce.

FOR SAUCE:

Reserved marinade from meat
2 teaspoons all-purpose flour
1½ teaspoons sugar
1 teaspoon Kosher salt

¾ cup water
1 tablespoon minced fresh mint leaves or ½ teaspoon dry mint

(continued)

Mix all the ingredients for the sauce except the mint leaves in a small saucepan and cook, stirring constantly, until the sauce thickens. Turn off heat and stir in the mint.

6. Slice the meat in thin slices, across the grain. Place it on a warm serving platter. Serve accompanied by mint sauce in a warm bowl.

Accompany with either rice or bread. Good choices are Indian Fried Rice (p. 363), Emperor's Pilaf with Black Mushrooms (p. 375), or Patiala Pilaf (p. 366). Or a stuffed bread, such as Cauliflower Stuffed Bread (p. 405), Spinach Bread (p. 410), or Potato- and Herb-Stuffed Bread (p. 409). All you need to complete the meal is a cool yogurt salad such as Cucumber and Yogurt Salad (p. 343), or, for a sweeter touch, Sweet Banana and Yogurt Salad (p. 349). Or serve a relish such as Grated Cucumber Relish (p. 434) instead.

Royal Roast Leg of Lamb with Saffron Raisin Sauce

(Shahi Raan)

This slightly sweet pot roast of lamb laced with saffron and *Mughal garam masala* is probably the most beautifully flavored and stunning presentation in all of Moghul cooking. Originally cooked slowly in the leftover heat of the *tandoor, Shahi Raan* makes its own sauce and develops a unique tenderness.

Traditionally, the roast is broken into chunks and served on a large platter over a bed of rice, with the sauce poured over it, but I think that serving the roast separately with the sauce on the side is much more suitable to modern ways of eating. I also prepare the leg of lamb in a special way so that it fits into the pot snugly and is easier to carve (see description for preparing lamb on p. 153).

Shahi Raan has many lovely uses in addition to being served as a roast. It can be turned into a pilaf (see Lamb Pilaf with Leftover Roast Lamb on p. 188), or rolled sandwich-style between two layers of Indian bread *(roti)* with slices of raw tomato and onions, or sliced in strips and eaten as an appetizer *(kati kabab)*. The meat can also be minced and added to Savory Meat Pastries (p. 130) or Meat Cutlets (p. 197) with a little chopped fresh coriander.

For 10–12 persons

1 medium to large leg of lamb,
   about 7½ to 9 pounds

MARINADE:

1 tablespoon chopped garlic
2 tablespoons chopped fresh
   ginger root
1 teaspoon black cumin seeds
   or white cumin
1 teaspoon red pepper, or to
   taste
1½ teaspoons *Mughal garam
   masala* (p. 37)
4 teaspoons Kosher salt
¾ cup seedless raisins

½ cup raw pistachio nuts, or
   walnuts
4 tablespoons lemon juice
¼ cup light brown sugar
¾ cup plain yogurt
¼ cup sour cream

2 teaspoons saffron threads
2 tablespoons all-purpose flour
   or cornstarch, dissolved in
   3 tablespoons water

1. Bone, butterfly, and re-form the leg of lamb, following the instructions given for preparing the lamb for roasts on page 153. Or you can ask your butcher to prepare it for you.

2. Prick the top of the lamb with a fork or thin skewer, and place it in a large flameproof nonmetal (5-quart) casserole or Dutch oven that can hold the lamb snugly. Set aside.

3. Put all the ingredients of the marinade into the container of a food processor or electric blender, and process until the ingredients are reduced to a fine thick paste. If the machine begins to clog, add 2–3 tablespoons water.

4. Pour the marinade all over the lamb and spread to coat it thoroughly. Cover, and let it marinate in the refrigerator for 3 days. Take the casserole from the refrigerator about one hour before cooking (or 4 hours before serving), and let it come to room temperature.

(continued)

5. Preheat the oven to 350°F.

6. Put the saffron threads in a small bowl or saucer and, using your fingers, powder it as fine as possible. Add 2 tablespoons hot water, and let soak for 15 minutes. Sprinkle the saffron water over the lamb.

7. Place the casserole on the stove at medium-heat and bring the contents to a boil. Pour 1 cup of boiling water down the sides of the casserole. Place a piece of aluminum foil on top of the casserole and cover tightly with the lid.

8. Roast the lamb in the middle level of the oven for 1½ hours. Lower heat to 225°F, and continue roasting for an additional 45 minutes. Turn off heat and let the casserole remain in the oven, with the door shut, for another 45 minutes. The cooking process is now completed, but keep the casserole in the oven until you are ready to serve the lamb. The roast will remain warm for 45 minutes in the oven.

9. To serve, take the casserole from the oven, uncover and carefully place the lamb on a carving board. Cut off and discard the trussing strings. Heat the contents of the casserole to a gentle simmer over low heat on top of the stove, skimming off the fat floating on the surface. Add the flour-water mixture and cook, stirring rapidly, until the sauce is thickened (1–2 minutes). Check for salt. (The roast may be returned to the casserole and kept warm,

covered, over an electric warmer or in the 225°F oven.) Slice the meat in ⅛–¼-inch-thick slices and arrange them on a warm serving platter. Spoon some sauce over the slices and serve the rest of it in a heated bowl or gravy boat.

Since this roast has a unique moist tenderness, almost like a freshly baked fruitcake, the carving is little tricky, as the meat falls apart with a little pressure of the knife. A good sharp carving knife, serrated and preferably electric, works very well. It is not of course essential that the meat be carved into slices—you can break it into large chunks—but I personally think that slices look much more elegant and appealing.

Note: You can make ½ recipe of *Shahi Raan* by using ½ leg, weighing about 3–4 pounds, and reducing all the other ingredients by half. To cook the lamb, use a small 3-quart casserole and pour only ½ cup of boiling water down the sides of the casserole. Roast the lamb at 350°F for 45 minutes, lower heat to 225°F, and continue roasting for 20 minutes. Turn off heat and let the casserole remain in the oven for 15 minutes before serving. This will serve 4–6 persons.

For a perfect meal, precede this dish with an elegant appetizer or first course. My choice would be Crab Malabar (p. 101), Cauliflower Fritters (p. 115), Indian Cheese Fritters (p. 117), or Mulligatawny Soup (p. 143). This beautiful roast should be accompanied by a plain fragrant pilaf, such as Patiala Pilaf (p. 366), so that the sweet flavors of saffron and lamb may emerge and be enjoyed to the fullest. I always serve either Broccoli Smothered in Garlic Oil (p. 296) or Glazed Cauliflower with Ginger (p. 299) with this meal. For a more elaborate meal, I include a *dal* such as Buttered Black Beans (p. 337). Perfect desserts would be Almond and Rice Dessert (p. 461), or Cheese Dumplings in Pistachio-Laced Cream Sauce (p. 465).

Lamb Pilaf with Leftover Roast Lamb

(Gosht Pullao)

A wonderful way to serve leftover broiled or roast meat is to create a pilaf. For best results, this pilaf should not be made with leftover meat that has been frozen.

A word of advice: There is nothing worse than fatty meat, if it is lamb and if it is used in a pilaf. When cutting the pieces of meat for the pilaf, trim away all traces of fat.

For 4 persons

4 tablespoons *usli ghee* (p. 50), or light vegetable oil
1½ cups coarsely chopped onions
2 cups roast lamb, either from Royal Roast Leg of Lamb with Saffron Raisin Sauce (p. 184), or Mint-Scented Broiled Leg of Lamb (p. 182).

3 cups cooked rice, preferably *basmati* rice
⅓ cup sauce, either Saffron Raisin Sauce (p. 185) or Mint Sauce (p. 183)
Kosher salt
2–3 tablespoons finely chopped fresh coriander leaves (or substitute 1 tablespoon dried coriander leaves)

1. Heat the *ghee* in a large frying pan or a wide shallow saucepan, and add onions. Over medium heat, sauté the onions until they are wilted and begin to turn pink (about 5 minutes), stirring constantly to prevent burning.

2. Add meat, and sauté for two minutes. Add rice and sauce, and mix well. If the pilaf looks a little dry, add a few tablespoons of water. Lower heat, cover, and let the pilaf steam until thoroughly heated (about 3–5 minutes). Taste and add salt if necessary. Fold in the chopped coriander leaves and serve.

This pilaf makes a perfect light and simple lunch when accompanied by a few lentil wafers (p. 425) and a glass of chilled rosé. If you want to serve a vegetable, a good choice would be Buttered Smothered Cabbage (p. 298) or, for an interesting variation, Cauliflower Fritters (p. 115). To make the meal more elaborate, serve a substantial appetizer, such as Shrimp Fritters (p. 118) or Savory Pastries with Spicy Potato Filling (p. 125).

Lamb Pilaf

(Mughalai Pullao)

A pilaf made with lamb is one of the most festive and comforting of all dishes. Pilaf is generally made with the best of ingredients, the tenderest chunks of meat, the finest *Basmati* rice, the freshest spices, because there is no sauce or gravy to shield the inadequacies of any ingredient.

This pilaf recipe, a specialty of my mother-in-law, is truly one of the finest I have encountered—another glowing example of the refined art of Moghul pilaf-making. To keep the meat from turning dark and losing its flavor, the fried onions are folded in at the end instead of being added at the beginning of the cooking. Also, the spices are tied in a bag so that only their essences are released into the pilaf.

Even though this pilaf needs no accompaniment, an onion relish—especially Onion and Roasted Tomato Relish (p. 433)—is traditionally served.

For 8–10 persons

3 pounds loin lamb chops (about 8–12 chops)	2 tablespoons Kosher salt
2 cups *basmati* rice	3 tablespoons finely chopped garlic
14 tablespoons light vegetable oil	4 tablespoons finely chopped fresh ginger root
4 cups finely chopped onions	

(continued)

FOR THE SPICE BAG:

4 black and 6 green cardamom pods, or 14 green cardamom pods	½ teaspoon black peppercorns
	10 whole cloves
	1½ teaspoons each cumin and
1 stick cinnamon, 3 inches long, broken into 2–3 pieces	coriander seeds
	3 bay leaves, crumbled

1. Trim every trace of fat off the chops. The meat should be completely lean if possible (after trimming, the meat with bones should weigh about 2¼ pounds).

2. Place all the spices for the spice bag on a double layer of cheesecloth, about 6 inches square, and tie the corners of the cheesecloth to form a bag. Hit the bag lightly with a wooden mallet, rolling pin, or any heavy tool to crush the spices slightly, and set aside.

3. Pick over, clean, wash, and soak rice, following instructions given under Preparing Basmati Rice for Cooking on page 356.

4. Bring 3 quarts of water to a boil in a deep pot. Add the soaked rice, and stir immediately for ½ minute (this keeps the rice from settling), being careful not to break the fragile rice grains. Bring the water to a second boil (it will take about 3 minutes) and cook the rice for 2 minutes. Pour the entire contents of the pot into a large sieve held over the kitchen sink. Hold the sieve under the tap, and let cold water run through the rice and sieve at medium speed for 3–5 seconds. Shake sieve to drain the rice thoroughly. Return the rice to the pot, add a little oil (about 1 teaspoon), and mix gently but thoroughly to coat the rice grains evenly. Cover and set aside until needed.

5. Heat 6 tablespoons of the oil in a large heavy-bottomed ovenproof casserole, and add onions. Over medium-high heat, fry the onions until they turn caramel brown (about 30 minutes), stirring constantly to prevent burning. (See directions for Brown-frying Onions, p. 71.) Put the fried onions, along with ⅔ cup warm water and 1 tablespoon salt, into the container of an electric blender or food processor, and blend until finely pureed. Set aside until needed.

6. Add the remaining 8 tablespoons of oil to the casserole, and heat. Add garlic and ginger, and cook over medium heat until they turn light brown (about 5 minutes). Add lamb chops in one layer, and cook, turning frequently until the meat loses its pink color (about 4 minutes). The chops at this point will begin to give out their juices and to steam. Let the meat steam undisturbed, uncovered, until most of the moisture evaporates (about 5 minutes). Watch the chops carefully during this period, because as soon as the moisture evaporates, the browning begins almost instantly, and unless the meat is stirred immediately it will burn.

7. Add 4 cups boiling water along with the remaining tablespoon of salt and the spice bag. Reduce heat and simmer, covered, for 45 minutes, or until the meat is cooked through. Increase heat to medium and continue cooking, uncovered, until most of the moisture is absorbed and the meat is melting tender (about 30 minutes).

8. Preheat the oven to 300°F. Remove spice bag from the meat, squeeze hard to extract as much juice as possible, and discard. Add reserved onion puree, and cook for 2 minutes, stirring constantly to mix in the ingredients and flavors. (The meat, rice, and onion puree may all be prepared ahead and set aside, covered, for several hours, or refrigerated for up to 3 days. The meat and onions may be frozen, but not the rice. Defrost and bring to room temperature before proceeding with the recipe.)

9. Using a flat spatula, fold the cooked rice into the meat mixture. Place aluminum foil on top of the casserole and cover tightly with the lid. Bake the pilaf in the middle level of the oven for 30 minutes. Turn off the oven, and leave the casserole inside for an additional 10 minutes. The pilaf, left in the oven, will remain warm for an additional 30 minutes.

Note: The classic way of making pilaf is with bone-in meat, as described above. If, however, you prefer a boneless meat pilaf, do not use boneless chops for much of the flavor of the pilaf comes from the bones. Instead, remove the bones carefully when you remove the spice bag, or bone all the chops before cooking and make a stock (about 4 cups) by simmering the bones in water for 2 hours. Use this stock in place of the water for cooking the meat.

(continued)

Note: A freshly made and assembled pilaf will keep in the refrigerator for up to 5 days. In fact, the flavor mellows and improves with each day of keeping. To reheat, place the casserole, tightly covered with foil and lid, in the middle level of a preheated 300°F oven for 20–25 minutes.

This mellow and beautifully flavored pilaf requires no special side dishes or staple. For a light meal, serve it with the tomato relish and a glass of chilled rosé. If you want to expand the meal, serve any stir-fried vegetable or *dal*. Good choices are Stir-fried Okra (p. 309), Cauliflower and Scallions with Black Mustard Seeds (p. 301), Buttered Black Beans (p. 337), or Lucknow Sour Lentils (p. 335). For a subtle contrast in flavor, start off with Mulligatawny Soup (p. 143).

Emperor's Layered Meat and Fragrant Rice Casserole

(Shah Jahani Biriyani)

Biriyani, an elaborate pilaf with breathtaking garnishes and decorations, is another wondrous Moghul creation. It takes a little extra time and trouble to prepare, but once you make it, you will agree that the results are well worth the effort. *Biriyani* is prepared by layering partially cooked rice and partially or fully cooked meat in a casserole and adding different flavorings, such as saffron, *kewra* essence, and mint. The entire dish is then steamed by the *dum* process (see p. 76). Then the pilaf is arranged decoratively on a platter and garnished with fried onions and sautéed nuts. *Biriyani* is traditionally decorated with silver foil *(vark)*.

This particular *biriyani* is named after the Moghul emperor Shah Jahan, who built the magnificent Taj Mahal. This dish, like that architectural marvel, is stunningly beautiful.

Note: One good feature of this *biriyani* is that you can prepare the meat ahead and refrigerate it. On the day you plan to serve, all you need do is cook the rice and assemble the dish.

For 8–10 persons

All the ingredients for
  making Fragrant Rice
  (*Yakhni Chawal*, p. 361)
All the ingredients for
  making Royal Braised
  Lamb with Fragrant Spices
  (*Shahi Korma*, p. 174)
8 tablespoons light vegetable
  oil
¼ cup each slivered blanched
  almonds, raw cashew
  nuts, and seedless raisins
2 cups thinly sliced or
  shredded onions

¼ cup tightly packed fresh
  mint leaves (or substitute
  2 teaspoons dry mint)
2 green chilies, seeded and
  minced
½ cup milk
2 teaspoons saffron threads
4 tablespoons *usli ghee* (p. 50)
2–3 teaspoons screw-pine
  essence (*Ruh Kewra*—
  optional)
2 three-inch square pieces
  silver foil (*Vark*—optional)

1. Prepare *Yakhni Chawal* following instructions on page 361.
2. Prepare *Shahi Korma* following instructions on page 174.
3. Heat 2 tablespoons of the oil in a frying pan or *kadhai* over medium heat. Add almonds, and fry until they are light brown (about 2 minutes). Take them out with a slotted spoon, and drain on paper towels. Add cashew nuts to the oil, and brown and drain them similarly. Finally, add the raisins and fry them, turning and tossing rapidly, until they puff up (about 30 seconds). Drain them also on paper towels. Set nuts and raisins aside for garnish.
4. Add the remaining 6 tablespoons of oil to the pan along with the onions. Increase heat to high, and fry them until they turn dark brown (about 12 minutes), stirring constantly to prevent burning. Drain onions on paper towels, and set aside for garnish.
5. Mix mint and green chilies with ¼ cup of the milk in a small bowl. In another bowl put the saffron, and powder it with your fingers. Scald the remaining ¼ cup of milk, add to the saffron, and let soak for at least 15 minutes. (All this can be prepared several hours ahead and set aside until you are ready to serve. About an hour before you are going to serve, begin assembling the *biriyani*.)
6. Preheat the oven to 300°F.
7. Place a heavy-bottomed casserole (5-quart size) on the work

surface. Arrange all other ingredients for assembling the *biriyani* next to it. Pour 2 tablespoons of *ghee* into the casserole. Tilt the casserole gently, or use a pastry brush, to coat the bottom and sides thoroughly. Add ¼ of the rice to the casserole, and even it with a spatula. Sprinkle ½ the mint mixture evenly over the rice. Add ½ the lamb, making sure the meat pieces are in one layer. Add another ¼ of the rice, spreading it out evenly. Sprinkle the remaining mint mixture over it, and add the rest of the lamb in one layer. Cover the lamb with the remaining ½ of the rice. Press it gently to compact it slightly. Dribble the saffron and the remaining 2 tablespoons of *ghee* on top. Lastly, sprinkle the *Kewra* essence over it. Place aluminum foil on top of the casserole and cover tightly with the lid.

8. Bake the *biriyani* in the middle level of the oven for 30 minutes. Turn off the oven and leave the casserole inside for an additional 10 minutes.

9. Take the casserole from the oven and place it on the work surface. Gently scoop out as much of the top layer of rice as is possible without disturbing the lamb mixture, and put it in another bowl. Carefully mix the meat and rice that remains in the casserole. Mound the lamb-rice mixture on a large heated serving platter, and cover it with the reserved rice, enclosing the meat completely. Garnish with the toasted nuts, raisins, fried onion shreds, and silver foil *(Vark)*. Serve immediately.

Follow the serving suggestions given for Lamb Pilaf on page 189.

Meat-Stuffed Cabbage Rolls with Ginger Lemon Sauce

(Keema Bhare Bandh Gobhi)

This is an ideal dish to serve when you have a mixed group of vegetarians and meat-eaters. You can serve its vegetable counterpart, Spicy Potato-Stuffed Cabbage Rolls with Ginger Lemon Sauce (p. 263), to the vegetarians.

The wonderful thing about this dish is that it freezes superbly. I always make a batch and keep it ready for those occasions when company drops by unexpectedly or I am running short of time.

Stuffing vegetables with *keema* is a popular technique in North Indian cooking. It not only creates interesting flavors but stretches the meat to serve more people. Although just about any vegetable can be stuffed with *keema*, the most popular are cabbage, eggplant, and green pepper.

Unless you already have precooked *Sookha Keema* on hand, this recipe will take a little extra time, but the results will be very rewarding.

For 4–6 persons

All the ingredients for making Dry-cooked Spicy Ground Meat (*Sookha Keema*, p. 158)
1 small cabbage (about 1¾–2 pounds)
3 tablespoons light vegetable oil
1½ cups thinly sliced onions
1¼ cups chopped fresh ripe tomatoes, or 1 cup canned tomatoes with their juices, chopped

1 tablespoon shredded fresh ginger root
1 lemon, peeled, seeded, and thinly sliced
2½ teaspoons Kosher salt
¼ teaspoon black pepper

1. Prepare *Sookha Keema* following instructions on page 158.

2. Insert a sharp-pointed knife into the cabbage where the leaves join the stem. Slowly run the knife around the stem, in a conical circle, to disjoin it from the cabbage leaves. Discard the stem and the attached hard core.

3. Rinse the cabbage thoroughly, place it in a deep pot, and add enough cold water to cover the cabbage by at least 1 inch. Bring to a boil, add 1 tablespoon of salt, and cook for 5 minutes. Let the cabbage drain thoroughly in a colander placed in the kitchen sink. When cool enough to handle, separate the leaves of the cabbage

carefully, so as not to tear them. (If some should tear a little, don't worry—they can be sealed when you are rolling them.) Save 15–16 leaves, and finely shred the remainder (there should be approximately 1½–1¾ cups of shredded leaves). Set aside.

4. Heat the oil in a medium-sized saucepan, and add onions. Over medium heat, sauté the onions until they are wilted and begin to color (about 5 minutes). Add shredded cabbage, tomatoes, ginger, lemon slices, salt, pepper, and 1½ cups water, and bring the contents to a boil. Reduce heat and simmer, uncovered, for 2 minutes. Turn off heat, and set sauce aside. [The cabbage and the sauce can be prepared a day ahead and refrigerated until you are ready to assemble the dish.]

5. About 1¼ hours before you are ready to serve, begin assembling. Preheat the oven to 375°F.

6. Place one large cabbage leaf at a time on the workboard. If there is a large rip in a leaf, cover it with another small piece of cabbage leaf. Put about 2½ tablespoons of Dry-cooked Spicy Ground Meat filling in the center of the leaf, and fold the cabbage leaf over, jelly-roll fashion, tucking in the ends as you roll. There should be 12 cabbage rolls in all.

7. Add ⅓ of the pulpy tomato sauce to the bottom of a baking dish just large enough to hold all the cabbage rolls snugly in one layer (such as an 8-inch by 12-inch pan). Pour the remaining sauce over the rolls, distributing the shredded cabbage evenly. Cover and seal the dish tightly with a piece of aluminum foil.

8. Bake in the middle level of the oven for 50 minutes. Uncover the pan and continue baking for an additional 10 minutes. Serve immediately.

Note: This dish may be prepared a day ahead and refrigerated or frozen. Defrost thoroughly before reheating. To reheat, place the covered dish in the middle level of a preheated 350°F oven for 50 minutes.

These cabbage rolls are so mellow and subtly flavored that anything more than plain cooked rice (p. 357) would probably detract from the full enjoyment of them. Good vegetable choices are Turmeric Potatoes (p. 314), Turmeric Potatoes with Green Peppers

(p. 316), or Spicy Baby Eggplant (p. 303). Ideal *dals* are Lentils with Garlic Butter (p. 332) or Mung Beans Laced with Black Mustard Seeds (p. 333). To add to the meal, serve Hyderabad Lime Soup (p. 141) or Spinach and Mung Bean Dumplings (p. 120). For a lighter appetizer, serve Indian Fenugreek Crackers (p. 133), or Lentil Wafers (p. 425) with cocktails.

There is no need for an accompaniment, but Hot Lemon Pickle (p. 449) goes well with this meal. You may also serve lentil wafers, provided they have not been served with cocktails earlier.

Meat Cutlets

(*Gosht Tikka* or Mutton Cutlets)

One hundred and fifty years of British rule in India left its mark on every aspect of life. Food was no exception. These cutlets, Indian in taste and very Western in appearance, reflect the strong influence of that rule. They are marvelous served as an appetizer or as a side dish.

An important note: Since these cutlets are extremely fragile, handle them with utmost caution and use a wide flat spatula, such as a pancake turner, while frying.

For 8 persons (makes 16 cutlets)

All the ingredients for making Dry-cooked Spicy Ground Meat (*Sookha Keema*, p. 158)
4 tablespoons canned tomato sauce
2 tablespoons finely chopped fresh coriander leaves or mint leaves
8 medium-sized boiling potatoes (about 2 pounds altogether)

1 teaspoon Kosher salt
6 tablespoons all-purpose flour
4 tablespoons sweet butter
½ cup all-purpose flour for dusting
3 large eggs, slightly beaten
4 cups bread crumbs

Peanut or corn oil enough to fill a frying pan to a depth of 1 inch.

(continued)

1. Prepare *Sookha Keema* following instructions on page 158.

2. Mix dry-cooked meat with tomato sauce and chopped coriander or mint, and set aside.

3. Boil the potatoes in their jackets until soft. Plunge them in cold water while they are still warm, and peel. Mash the potatoes with a potato masher, or using your hands, until there are no lumps left. Add salt, 6 tablespoons of flour, and butter, and work in until well blended.

4. Divide the meat filling and the potatoes into 16 equal portions. Put the ½ cup flour, eggs, and bread crumbs on 3 separate plates and set them near the work surface.

5. Cut a piece of waxed paper 7 inches square, and place it on the workboard. Place 1 portion of potato in the center of the paper. Using your fingers or a spatula, spread it into a thin 5-inch square. Put 1 portion (about 2 tablespoons) of meat filling in the center, and spread it into a neat 4 by 2 inches, carefully, so as not to break the potato layer. Fold the potato layer, with the waxed paper, over the filling. Fold and pinch the narrow edges to enclose the meat completely in mashed potato. Pat this cutlet into a neat 4-inch by 2½-inch rectangle with smooth round edges. Peel off the waxed paper square. Sprinkle a large piece of waxed paper generously with the dusting flour, and put the cutlets on it as they are formed.

6. Place the dusting flour, the beaten eggs in a flat dish, and the plate of bread crumbs on the work surface. Sprinkle the cutlets generously with flour and pat it in. Using a pancake turner and your fingers, very carefully put a floured cutlet into the beaten egg, flip it gently to coat the other side, lift it out of the egg, and slip it into the plate of bread crumbs. Coat the cutlet generously with bread crumbs, pat gently, and place the breaded cutlet on the floured waxed paper. Continue with the remaining potatoes and meat mixture the same way. (The cutlets may be shaped several hours before frying and kept refrigerated until you are ready to serve them.)

7. When ready to fry, heat the oil in a frying pan. When the oil is hot (350°F), gently slip 4 cutlets, one at a time, into the oil. Fry the cutlets for 3 minutes, then carefully flip them over with a slotted spoon, and continue frying until they are golden brown on both

sides. Drain them on paper towels, put them on a serving dish, and keep warm till all the cutlets are done. Serve hot, accompanied by Sweet Tomato Relish (*Tamatar Chutney*, p. 440), or Mint Coriander Dip (*Dhania-Podina Chutney*, p. 437).

Note: The cutlets may be made ahead and refrigerated for up to 2 days. To reheat, place them uncovered in the middle level of a preheated 300°F oven for 15 minutes.

To fully complement the delicate taste of these cutlets, serve them with a simple pilaf such as Patiala Pilaf (p. 366), Fragrant Pilaf Banaras Style (p. 368), Indian Fried Rice (p. 363), or a simple plain cooked rice (p. 357). A good choice for a side dish would be a *dal*, such as Spice- and Herb-Laced Split Peas (p. 330), or Lucknow Sour Lentils (p. 335). For a more elaborate meal, serve a vegetable such as Buttered Smothered Cabbage (p. 298) or Stir-fried Okra (p. 309), accompanied by a relish such as Raw Onion Relish (p. 431), Grated Cucumber Relish (p. 434), or Hot Hyderabad Tomato Relish (p. 441). Serve an appetizer such as Spinach and Mung Bean Dumplings (p. 120) or Silky Bean Dumplings (p. 123).

Goanese Hot and Pungent Curry

(*Vendaloo*)

Vendaloo is the famous fiery-hot, mustard-laced dish from Goa, a state on the southwest coast of India. Traditionally, *vendaloo* is made with pork, but there are many variations prepared with beef, chicken, lamb, and even duck. Pork is rarely eaten in India, except by the Portuguese Christians in Goa. Even though some religious sects permit the eating of pork, it is not as highly prized a meat in India as lamb or chicken. Indians tend to regard the pig, who eats most anything from everywhere, with suspicion. Another reason for its lack of popularity is that the feed-corn needed to raise the best grade of pig for good pork is not grown in India on a wide enough scale to feed an animal population.

Vendaloo is made by first marinating the pork in a mixture of spices and seasonings. It is then cooked in the marinade along with such additional flavorings as fried onions and tamarind juice. The ingredient that imparts the authentic *vendaloo* flavor is mustard oil. Mustard oil in its raw form has a very strong smell that many people find unpleasant. Before Indians use it in cooking, it is put through a mellowing process. This is done by heating the oil to a very high temperature (the smoking point), which releases the pungent smell and vaporizes the oil. When cool, the mustard oil is ready for use.

For 4 persons

6 pork chops (about 1½ pounds)

FOR MARINADE:

1 teaspoon cumin seeds	2 tablespoons cider vinegar
1 teaspoon black mustard seeds	2 tablespoons light vegetable oil
1 medium-sized onion, peeled and quartered	½ teaspoon ground cinnamon
4 medium cloves garlic	¼ teaspoon ground clove
1 tablespoon chopped fresh ginger root	

FOR COOKING:

1-inch ball tamarind pulp	1½ cups thinly sliced onions
½ cup mustard oil, or substitute light vegetable oil	1½ teaspoons turmeric
	1½ teaspoons red pepper
	1½ teaspoons paprika
	2 teaspoons Kosher salt

1. Using a sharp boning knife, cut the meat off the bone. Reserve the bones. Trim all traces of fat from the meat and bones, and discard. Cut the meat into ¾-inch cubes, and set aside.

2. Heat a small frying pan over medium heat, and add cumin and mustard seeds. Roast the seeds, stirring constantly, until the cumin seeds turn dark and the mustard seeds gray (about 3 minutes). Transfer to a small bowl and let cool briefly. Then grind to a fine powder. Set aside.

3. Put onion, garlic, ginger, vinegar, and oil into the container of an electric blender or food processor, and run the machine until the contents are a fine pasty puree.

4. Place the pork, along with the bones, in a nonmetallic bowl. Add ground cumin and mustard seeds, pureed mixture, cinnamon, and clove. Mix thoroughly to distribute the spice paste over the meat pieces. Cover and marinate for 8 hours, or refrigerate for 48 hours.

5. Put the tamarind pulp in a bowl, add 1¼ cups boiling water, and let it soak for 15 minutes. Mash the pulp with the back of a spoon, or use your fingers. Strain the liquid, squeezing the pulp as much as possible, into another small bowl, and set aside. Discard the stringy fiber.

6. When ready to cook the meat, heat the mustard oil over high heat in a large enamel-coated pan. When the oil begins to smoke, turn off the heat, and let it cool completely. (Skip this step if you are using a vegetable oil other than mustard.)

7. Heat the oil again over medium-high heat, and add onions. Fry them until they turn caramel brown (about 12 minutes), stirring constantly to prevent burning. Reduce heat to medium, add turmeric, red pepper, and paprika. When the spices begin to sizzle and turn dark (about 15 seconds), add the meat and bones (reserve any marinade left in the bowl), and fry until the meat pieces are slightly seared and the oil begins to separate from the gravy (about 10 minutes). Add tamarind juice, salt, and any remaining marinade, and bring it to a boil. Lower heat and cook, partially covered, until meat is thoroughly done and very tender (about 30 minutes). Carefully pick out the bones, and discard. Check for salt, and serve.

(continued)

Note: This dish improves with keeping. It may be made ahead and refrigerated for up to 4 days, or frozen. Defrost thoroughly before reheating. To reheat, simmer gently over low heat until warmed through.

Vendaloo is traditionally eaten with rice, but I also like to serve it with bread, such as Whole Wheat Puffy Bread (p. 397), or Whole Wheat Flaky Bread (p. 402). For a vegetable, serve Green Beans with Coconut and Black Mustard Seeds (p. 307), Glazed Beets with Black Mustard Seeds (p. 295), or Cauliflower and Scallions with Black Mustard Seeds (p. 301). It is a good idea to serve a yogurt salad with this dish because it will offset the hot taste nicely and is the classic accompaniment to most southern Indian dishes. Good choices are Tomato and Yogurt Salad (p. 345) or Okra and Yogurt Salad (p. 347). For a first course, serve Mysore Spicy Lentil Broth (p. 138), or Cold Minted Potatoes (p. 103). For accompaniments serve Lentil Wafers (p. 425), and Shredded Carrot and Mustard Seed Relish (p. 435). A perfect choice of dessert would be Saffron Almond Pudding (p. 457). Or you might also try Coconut Wedding Pudding (p. 459), Mango Fool (p. 471), or Cream Pudding (p. 455).

Poultry and Eggs

(Murghi aur Anda)

POULTRY *(Murghi)*

Moghul Braised Chicken   *(Mughalai Korma)*
Chicken in Onion Tomato Gravy   *(Murgh Masala)*
Fragrant Yogurt-Braised Chicken   *(Dahi Murghi)*
Chicken in Creamed Coconut Sauce   *(Malai Murgh)*
Royal Chicken in Silky Almond Sauce   *(Shahi Murgh Badaami)*
Chicken Smothered in Aromatic Herbs and Almonds   *(Badaami Murgh)*
Chicken Kabuli   *(Murgh Kabuli)*
Tandoori (Indian Barbecued) Chicken   *(Tandoori Murghi)*
Velvet Butter Chicken   *(Makhani Murgh)*
Chicken Pilaf   *(Murgh Biriyani)*
Cornish Hens Braised in Fragrant Apricot Sauce   *(Murgh Khoobani)*

EGGS *(Anda)*

Scrambled Eggs with Cumin and Fragrant Herbs   *(Ande ki Bhorji)*
Whole Eggs in Spicy Tomato Sauce   *(Ande ki Kari)*

POULTRY

(Murghi)

In North India when a marriage is arranged between families, one of the things the bride's father says to the bridegroom's father is *"Khoob Badhia murghi khilayenge,"* meaning plenty of chicken will be served at the wedding reception. This line never fails to please the bridegroom's father and his family. If all other aspects of the arrangement are found satisfactory, the marriage contract is considered concluded.

This reaction to chicken in India is very similar to American reactions to Russian beluga caviar or truffle-laced Strasbourg *foie gras.* This is because chicken is still a very expensive meat in India, more than goat's meat or lamb. (Pork and beef, because of the religious restrictions of Moslems and Hindus, are seldom eaten, and therefore never served on social or religious occasions.) Another reason for this special attachment to chicken is that it is generally believed that while Moslems in India excel at lamb preparations, Hindus have had mastery of the art of cooking chicken. And among Hindus, it is the Punjabis who have always favored and relished chicken over any other fowl or meat. They are famous for their delicately flavored, exquisite chicken preparations. Some wonderful examples from their extensive repertoire are Velvet Butter Chicken (p. 225), Fragrant Yogurt-Braised Chicken (p. 211) and Chicken Smothered in Aromatic Herbs and Almonds (p. 217).

On restaurant menus in India, chicken preparations are often the most expensive dishes, just as lobster and filet mignon are here. In the home, chicken preparations are reserved for special joyous occasions.

Preparing chicken for cooking:

Except when it is roasted, the chicken in Indian cooking is cut into small serving pieces. The wing tips and neck bone are often removed and saved for the stockpot. In Indian cooking the chicken is always—and I mean always—skinned before being cooked. This is because, first, Indians believe the skin to be unclean and, along with feathers, beak, and other inedible parts, not to be eaten. Second—a more valid reason—the skin prevents the seasonings and flavorings from penetrating the meat, an essential process in Indian cooking.

Skinning a chicken is very simple. The only difficulty is that both the skin and the flesh are slippery, so that getting a good grip can be a problem. This can be solved by using a kitchen towel. To skin, hold the chicken firmly with one hand and, with the other, grip the skin near the neck and pull away to release the skin from the flesh. Slash and tear the skin with a sharp boning knife as you go along. Skinning, of course, is much easier if the chicken is cut up into quarters or eighths.

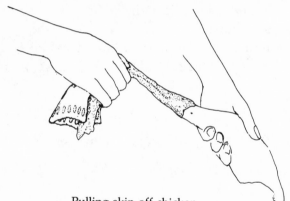

Pulling skin off chicken

TIPS ON COOKING CHICKEN:

Chicken is done two ways in Indian cooking: either in a sauce (braised or stewed) or dry (fried, roasted, or grilled). It is never poached, sautéed, or stir-fried, as in French or Chinese cooking, because the cooking time in those methods is too short for the flavorings to penetrate the meat. Also, Indians do not like their chicken to be slightly pink near the bones with the juices still running. According to the Indian standard, such chicken is still raw. The Indian way, therefore, is to cook the chicken until the juices have stopped running and the meat is moist and butter-tender, with solid firm flesh.

Since the fried, roasted, and grilled preparations take only a few minutes to cook, the chicken is usually marinated in a spice-laced yogurt marinade which, in addition to flavoring the chicken, tenderizes it. In the braised and stewed preparations, the chicken is usually browned separately before being added to other ingredients and cooked.

A few precautions are necessary while browning chicken: The chicken pieces should be thoroughly patted dry with a kitchen or paper towel before being cooked, or they will not brown. And a cover, such as the lid of the pan or a spatter screen, should be kept handy. This is because the chicken blood and other moisture is sometimes released from the joints and bones during frying. When this moisture comes in contact with the hot fat, it may explode and splatter in all directions.

In addition to chicken, the other birds used in Indian cooking, though very sparingly, are partridge, duck, goose, and peacock.

Moghul Braised Chicken

(Mughalai Korma)

This delectable and very finely flavored *korma* of chicken takes no time at all to prepare. Once you have sautéed the seasonings, spices, and yogurt, simply braise the chicken in the mixture. I prefer to use only the breast of chicken, because its light taste allows the intricate flavorings of bay leaves, cloves, and cardamom to be more noticeable. I also prefer to use whole rather than powdered spices, so the beautiful creamy color of the dish isn't destroyed.

This particular *korma* is delicious by itself, but it is often mixed with cooked rice to create the classic Chicken Pilaf (p. 228).

For 4 persons

1½ pounds skinned boneless chicken breast meat	24 whole cloves
¾ cup light vegetable oil	4 bay leaves
3 cups finely chopped onions	2 teaspoons ground coriander
1 tablespoon finely chopped garlic	¼–½ teaspoon red pepper
1½ tablespoons finely chopped fresh ginger root	1 cup plain yogurt
12 green cardamom pods, slightly crushed	2 teaspoons Kosher salt
	½ cup heavy cream

1. Place the chicken breasts on a cutting board, and using a sharp knife, slice them thinly into ¼-inch-thick medallions, as for scaloppine. Cut the medallions into 2½-inch by 1½-inch pieces, and set aside.

2. Heat the oil in a wide heavy-bottomed pan, preferably one with a non-stick surface, and add onions, garlic, and ginger. Over medium-high heat, cook them until they turn pale and begin to brown (about 10 minutes), stirring constantly to prevent burning. Add cardamom, cloves, and bay leaves, and cook, stirring rapidly, until cardamom pods and cloves are fried and puffed and the bay leaves turn brown (about 5 minutes). The onions should by now be light golden brown. Add coriander and red pepper, stir for 10–15 seconds, and add 2 tablespoons of the yogurt. Continue frying the mixture until the moisture from the yogurt evaporates. Then add two more tablespoons of yogurt, and fry. Keep adding yogurt and frying until the whole cup of yogurt is used up (about 5 minutes).

3. Add the chicken pieces, and sauté, turning and tossing until the meat loses its pink color (about 3–5 minutes). Add ½ cup boiling water with the salt, and mix. Reduce heat to medium-low and

simmer, covered, until the fillets are cooked and fork-tender (about 25 minutes). The oil will begin to separate from the gravy, which should be fairly thick by now, and to coat the chicken pieces. Stir in the cream, and turn off heat. Let the *korma* rest, covered, for an hour before serving. When ready to serve, heat thoroughly, check for salt, and serve.

Note: Mughalai Korma may be prepared ahead and refrigerated for up to 2 days. Since the dish is practically dry, with a thick and scanty gravy, it does not take well to freezing. To reheat, gently simmer the *korma* over low heat until bubbling hot. If the dish looks very dry (which usually happens with keeping), add a little water. Taste the dish, and add more salt if necessary before serving.

Either plain cooked rice (p. 357) or Saffron Rice with Peaches (p. 371) should accompany this *korma*. Baked Whole Wheat Bread (p. 393), or Baked Whole Wheat Puffy Bread (p. 397) are equally good. Appropriate side dishes are Lucknow Sour Lentils (p. 335) or Lentils with Garlic Butter (p. 332). You can serve any appetizer except kabobs and dumplings. Fresh Mint Relish (p. 436) goes extremely well with this meal.

Chicken in Onion Tomato Gravy

(Murgh Masala)

This is a classic dish from Punjab, a state in the North of India. Traditionally, the chicken is cut into small pieces and stewed in a tomato-rich fried-onion gravy. Chopped fresh coriander is folded in immediately before serving to lend herbal fragrance and to provide a nice color contrast to the reddish brown gravy. The special flavor of the dish comes from the garlic; ginger root and turmeric enrich the color and aroma. The whole spices (cinnamon and cardamom) in this dish are not eaten, but no harm will come to you if you bite into them.

For 8 persons

2 three-pound chickens cut
　　into 8–10 pieces each (or
　　use cut-up legs and
　　breasts in any
　　combination)
10 tablespoons light vegetable
　　oil
6 cups thinly sliced onions
2 tablespoons finely chopped
　　garlic
3 tablespoons finely chopped
　　fresh ginger root
2 cinnamon sticks, 3 inches
　　long
4 black (or 8 green) cardamom
　　pods

1 tablespoon turmeric
1 teaspoon red pepper
2½ cups pureed or finely
　　chopped fresh ripe
　　tomatoes, or 2 cups
　　drained canned tomatoes,
　　chopped
1 tablespoon Kosher salt
2 cups boiling water
1 tablespoon ground roasted
　　cumin seeds (p. 66)
3–4 tablespoons chopped fresh
　　coriander leaves (or
　　substitute 2 tablespoons
　　dried coriander leaves)

1. Cut off the wing tips, and pull the skin away from the chicken pieces, using a kitchen towel to get a better grip. (Reserve wing tips and skin for the stockpot).

2. Heat 2 tablespoons of the oil in a large (5-quart) heavy-bottomed pan, preferably one with a non-stick surface, over high heat. When the oil is very hot, add the chicken pieces, a few at a time, and sear them until they lose their pink color and get nicely browned on all sides (about 3–4 minutes). Remove them with a slotted spoon and reserve them in a bowl. Continue with the rest of the chicken pieces until all of them are seared.

3. Add the remaining 8 tablespoons of oil to the pan, along with the onions. Reduce heat to medium-high, and fry the onions until they turn light brown (about 30 minutes), stirring constantly to prevent burning. (See directions for Brown-frying Onions, p. 71.) Add garlic and ginger, and fry for an additional 5 minutes. Add cinnamon and cardamom, and continue frying until the spices are slightly puffed and begin to brown (about 2 minutes). Add turmeric and red pepper, and stir rapidly for 10–15 seconds. Add

pureed or chopped tomatoes, along with the chicken, salt, and two cups of boiling water. Stir to mix, reduce heat and simmer, covered, until chicken is cooked and very tender and the gravy has thickened (about 45 minutes). If the gravy has not thickened adequately, increase heat and boil rapidly, uncovered, until it thickens to the consistency of a beef stew. If, on the other hand, the evaporation is too fast, add a little water. Check frequently during cooking to ensure that the sauce is not burning. The finished dish should have plenty of thick pulpy gravy. Turn off heat, and let the dish rest, covered, for at least 1 hour, preferably 2, before serving. When ready to serve, heat thoroughly, fold in roasted cumin and chopped coriander, check for salt, and serve.

Note: This is a typical example of stewing meat. Like all stews it improves with keeping. It can be kept in the refrigerator for up to 2 days, or frozen. Defrost thoroughly before reheating. To reheat, gently simmer the chicken over low heat until warmed through. Taste, and if necessary add salt. To perk up the flavors, fold in a little ground roasted cumin and chopped coriander leaves before serving.

I like to serve this dish with Baked Whole Wheat Puffy Bread (p. 397) or Baked Whole Wheat Bread (p. 393), but Whole Wheat Flaky Bread (p. 402) or Chick-pea Flour Bread (p. 399) are attractive alternatives. You may also serve it with a plain cooked rice (p. 357) for a simple meal; or with a pilaf such as Patiala Pilaf (p. 366) or Fragrant Pilaf Banaras Style (p. 368) for more substantial dining. For a vegetable, serve Turmeric Potatoes (p. 314) or Turmeric Potatoes with Green Peppers (p. 316). A *raita,* such as Dumplings in Fragrant Yogurt (p. 348), may be included if you want another side dish. Serve an onion relish on the side, and if you like, Sweet Lemon Pickle with Cumin (p. 447) as well.

Fragrant Yogurt-Braised Chicken

(Dahi Murghi)

This is a simple everyday method of preparing chicken that is utterly delicious. The chicken pieces are called yogurt-braised, even though only a small amount of yogurt is used. The fragrance and flavor of yogurt is distinct, because only certain spices are added, and in very moderate amounts.

For 4–6 persons

1 3–3½-pound chicken cut into 8–10 pieces (or use cut-up legs and breasts in any combination)
4 tablespoons light vegetable oil
3 cups thinly sliced onions
1 tablespoon finely chopped garlic
1 tablespoon ground coriander
½ teaspoon red pepper, or to taste

1½ teaspoons *garam masala* (p. 38)
1 teaspoon ground roasted Indian poppy seeds (p. 66)
1 cup plain yogurt
¼ cup sour cream
4 tablespoons *usli ghee* (p. 50), or light vegetable oil
1 tablespoon Kosher salt

1. Cut off the wing tips, and pull the skin from the chicken pieces, using a kitchen towel to get a good grip. Set aside. (Reserve the wing tips and skin for the stockpot.)

2. Heat the oil in a large heavy-bottomed pan, and add onions. Over medium-high heat, fry the onions until they turn limp and pale golden and begin to brown (about 10 minutes), stirring constantly to ensure even browning. Add garlic, and cook for an additional 2 minutes. Add coriander, red pepper, *garam masala*, and poppy seeds, and stir rapidly for 1 minute. Add yogurt, sour cream, and ⅓ cup water, and bring to the boil. Reduce heat and simmer the mixture, covered, for 5 minutes. Turn off heat, and let

the mixture cool slightly. Finely puree it in either an electric blender or a food processor. Set aside until needed.

3. Put the *ghee* into the pan, and place it over medium heat. When the *ghee* is very hot, add chicken pieces and sauté, turning and tossing, until they lose their pink color (about 4 minutes). Add the pureed mixture and salt, and bring to a boil. Reduce heat and cook the chicken, covered, until very tender but not falling apart (about 45 minutes). Check often during cooking to ensure the sauce is not sticking to the bottom of the pan and burning. By this time the gravy should have thickened to a velvety smooth white sauce, and a glaze will be coating the chicken pieces. It is absolutely essential that the sauce be of the right consistency in this dish. If the sauce has not thickened enough, it will be thin and runny with no shine. To remedy, simply increase heat and boil rapidly, uncovered, to evaporate excess moisture, until the sauce reduces to the desired consistency and glaze. On the other hand, the sauce may be too thick and pasty, in which case a considerable amount of fat will separate and float on the surface. In this instance, add some water or milk, little by little, until the sauce is thinned to the desired consistency and the fat has been incorporated back into the sauce. Turn off heat and let the dish rest, covered, at least 1 hour before serving. When ready to serve, heat thoroughly, check for salt, and serve.

Note: This preparation tastes particularly good if made a day ahead, refrigerated, and heated just before serving. It can also be frozen successfully. Defrost thoroughly before reheating. To reheat, simmer over low heat until piping hot. As always, taste and if necessary add more salt before serving.

This dish can be accompanied by a simple pilaf, such as Patiala Pilaf (p. 366), Fragrant Pilaf Banaras Style (p. 368), plain cooked rice (p. 357), Okra Pilaf (p. 373), or Indian Fried Rice (p. 363). Any baked bread may also be served. For a side dish, serve Smoked Eggplant with Fresh Herbs (p. 305) if you are having bread; and Cauliflower and Scallions with Black Mustard Seeds (p. 301) if you are serving rice. Lucknow Sour Lentils (p. 335) make a nice additional side dish. A good hot relish to spice this meal is Hot

Hyderabad Tomato Relish (p. 441). Indian Cheese Fritters (p. 117) make an especially good appetizer.

Chicken in Creamed Coconut Sauce

(Malai Murgh)

In India it is commonly believed that if a dish contains coconut it must be from southern India. This dish proves otherwise. Even though the use of coconut is limited in the North, the dishes created with it are very special indeed. Coconut cream is called *malai* in the North. In this recipe the chicken is simmered in rich coconut milk and a blend of Moghul spices to produce a marvelously flavored and very satisfying dish.

An *important* note: the coconut milk must be fresh and sweet, or the dish will taste of rancid coconut oil. Unless you have a ready supply of coconut milk, allow an extra hour before the cooking time to prepare it from fresh unshelled coconut (see p. 46).

The cardamom, cloves, and cinnamon in this dish are not meant to be eaten, but no harm will come to you if by chance you swallow a clove or bite into the cinnamon stick.

For 4–6 persons

2¼–2½ pounds chicken breasts (2 whole chicken breasts, bone in)
½ cup light vegetable oil
½ cup finely chopped onions
4 teaspoons finely chopped garlic
4 teaspoons finely chopped fresh ginger root
8 green cardamom pods
12 whole cloves
1 cinnamon stick, 3 inches long

2 tablespoons blanched almonds, powdered
1½ cups coconut milk (p. 46)
¼ teaspoon turmeric
½ teaspoon red pepper, or more, to taste
2 teaspoons Kosher salt
¼ cup heavy cream
2 tablespoons finely chopped fresh coriander leaves

(continued)

1. Pull the skin off the chicken breasts and cut each into 4 pieces. You should have a total of 8 pieces of skinned chicken breasts with bone.

2. Heat the oil in a large heavy-bottomed pan, and add onions, garlic, and ginger. Over medium-high heat, cook them until onions are pale and limp (about 5 minutes). Add cardamom, cloves, and cinnamon, and cook until the spices are slightly puffed and begin to brown (about 5 minutes). Add almond powder and cook, stirring rapidly, for an additional 2 minutes. Reduce heat to medium, and add chicken pieces in one layer. Let cook undisturbed for 1 minute. Turn the chicken pieces and continue cooking just until they lose their pink color (about 2 minutes altogether). The chicken should remain as white as possible.

3. Add coconut milk, turmeric, red pepper, and salt, and bring to a boil. Reduce heat and simmer, covered, until the chicken pieces are thoroughly cooked and melting tender (about 30 minutes). Check often to ensure the sauce is not evaporating too fast and burning. Stir in the cream, and turn off heat. Let the dish rest, covered, for at least 1 hour before serving. When ready to serve, heat thoroughly, check for salt, and serve sprinkled with chopped coriander leaves.

Note: This dish definitely tastes better if made several hours ahead. It can be kept in the refrigerator for up to 2 days, or frozen. Defrost thoroughly before reheating. To reheat, gently simmer over low heat until warmed through. Taste, and add more salt if necessary. Serve sprinkled with chopped fresh coriander leaves.

Follow the menu suggestions given for Fragrant Yogurt-Braised Chicken on page 211.

Royal Chicken in Silky White Almond Sauce

(Shahi Murgh Badaami)

Almonds *(Badaam)* were a great favorite of the Moghuls; they used them as an occasion to create many sensational dishes. Of all the *Badaami* (meaning "in almond sauce") dishes, this is by far the most delicious. This recipe produces a very subtly flavored dish. If you want a hotter taste, add all eight pepper pods as suggested. In this recipe the word "silky" refers to the appearance of the sauce, not to its texture, which is indeed grainy.

For 6 persons

1 three-pound chicken cut into 8–10 pieces (or use cut-up legs and breasts in any combination)	4 tablespoons coriander seeds
10 tablespoons light vegetable oil	4 teaspoons green cardamom pods (about 50 pods)
4–4½ cups thinly sliced onions	4–8 hot red pepper pods, or 1–2 teaspoons red pepper
6 tablespoons slivered blanched almonds	2 cups plain yogurt
	2½ teaspoons Kosher salt

1. Cut off the wing tips, and pull the skin away from all the chicken pieces, using a paper towel to get a better grip. (Reserve wing tips and skin for the stockpot.)

2. Heat 2 tablespoons of the oil over medium heat in a wide, heavy-bottomed pan. When the oil is hot, add chicken pieces, a few at a time, and cook, turning constantly, until they lose their pink color and begin to sear. Do not allow them to brown or the sauce will turn dark. Take them out with a slotted spoon and reserve them in a bowl. Continue with the rest of the chicken pieces until all are seared and set aside.

(continued)

3. Add the remaining 8 tablespoons of oil to the pan, along with the onions. Fry the onions until they are wilted and pale golden (about 10 minutes), stirring constantly to keep them from coloring unevenly. Do not let the onions overbrown or the sauce will be dark. Add almonds, coriander, cardamom, and red pepper pods (if you are using red pepper powder, do not add it at this stage), and cook for an additional 3–5 minutes or until the almonds are lightly colored and cardamom pods are puffed up. If you are using red pepper powder, add it now, and stir. Turn off heat.

4. Put the entire mixture, along with 1 cup of water, into the container of an electric blender or food processor, and run the machine until the mixture is reduced to a fine smooth puree.

5. Return the puree to the pan, along with the chicken pieces, yogurt, and salt, and bring to a boil. Reduce heat and simmer, covered, until the chicken is melting-tender and the sauce has thickened nicely (about 45 minutes). At this point, the oil will begin to separate from the sauce, and a thin glaze will form over both sauce and chicken. Turn off heat and let the dish rest, covered, for ½ hour before serving. When ready to serve, reheat the dish until piping hot, check for salt, and serve.

Note: This dish tastes absolutely divine if made a day ahead and refrigerated. This prolonged resting allows the flavors to penetrate the meat of the chicken, and makes it taste even better. This dish may be kept in the refrigerator for up to 2 days, or frozen. Defrost thoroughly before reheating. To reheat, simmer gently until warmed through. Check for salt before serving.

For variation, you may substitute 2 or 3 Cornish hens (weighing about 3 pounds altogether), split in half. This looks more formal and elegant.

Present a fragrant pilaf with this elegant dish. Serve Sweet Saffron Pilaf (p. 369) or Saffron Pilaf with Peaches (p. 371) to introduce a subtle contrast of colors. Equally good are Fragrant Pilaf Banaras Style (p. 368) and Patiala Pilaf (p. 366). All baked breads go well with this dish. Good vegetable choices are Spicy Baby Eggplant (p. 303), Green Beans with Coconut and Black Mustard Seeds (p. 307), and Broccoli Smothered in Garlic Oil (p. 296). If you want the meal to be substantial, Kabob Patties Laced with Ginger and

Mint (p. 109), Cold Minted Potatoes (p. 103), and Cold Potato Appetizer (p. 105) are all ideal first courses.

Chicken Smothered in Aromatic Herbs and Almonds

(Badaami Murgh)

This is a classic North Indian dish. It is traditionally reserved for company and special festive occasions. The beautifully rich, thick, garnet-colored sauce that coats the chicken pieces is created from a blend of tomatoes, fried onions with spices, and almond butter. The chicken is then garnished with toasted almonds and chopped fresh coriander. For a smooth, creamy-textured sauce, it is essential to use almond butter and not almond powder, which is grainy.

The whole spices—cinnamon, cardamom, and clove, are not meant to be eaten. If you do bite into them, however, no harm will come to you.

For 4–6 persons

1 3–3½ pound chicken cut in 8–10 pieces (or use cut-up legs and breasts in any combination)
1½ teaspoons lemon juice
2 teaspoons Kosher salt
6 tablespoons light vegetable oil
3 tablespoons sliced or slivered blanched almonds
2 cups finely chopped onions
1 tablespoon finely chopped garlic
1 tablespoon finely chopped fresh ginger root
1 stick cinnamon, 3 inches long
4 black (or 8 green) cardamom pods

4 whole cloves
1 teaspoon ground cumin
1 teaspoon ground coriander
½ teaspoon turmeric
½ teaspoon red pepper, or to taste
1 cup finely chopped or pureed fresh ripe tomatoes (or ½ cup drained canned tomatoes, chopped)
2–3 tablespoons almond butter (see p. 163), or 4 tablespoons ground blanched almonds
1–2 tablespoons finely chopped fresh coriander leaves

(continued)

1. Cut off the wing tips and pull the skin off all the chicken pieces, using a kitchen towel to get a better grip. (Reserve the wing tips and skin for the stockpot.) Prick the chicken pieces all over with a fork or a thin skewer. Place them in a bowl and rub lemon juice and salt over them.

2. Cover and marinate for ½ hour, or refrigerate overnight. (If you are rushed, skip the marinating and simply proceed to the next step.)

3. Heat 1 tablespoon of the oil in a large heavy-bottomed pan, preferably with a non-stick surface. Add sliced or slivered almonds, and sauté over medium-low heat, turning and tossing until they turn light brown (about 3 minutes). Take them out immediately and drain on paper towels. Set them aside until needed for garnish.

4. Put the remaining 5 tablespoons of oil in the pan, and add onions. Over medium-high heat, fry the onions until they turn light brown (about 15 minutes), stirring constantly to prevent burning. Add garlic and ginger, and cook for an additional 2 minutes. Add cinnamon, cardamom, and cloves, and cook until the spices are slightly puffed and begin to brown (about 2 minutes).

5. Reduce heat to medium, add chicken pieces, and cook, turning and tossing until they lose their pink color and are lightly seared (about 5–7 minutes). Add cumin, coriander, turmeric, and red pepper. Stir rapidly for a couple of minutes to distribute the ground spices, and add tomatoes, almond butter or powder, along with half a cup of hot water. Bring to a boil. Reduce heat, and simmer the chicken, covered, for 50 minutes or until the chicken is fork-tender. Stir frequently during cooking to keep the sauce from sticking and burning. If the evaporation is too fast, add a few tablespoons of water. Turn off heat, and let the dish rest, covered, for at least 1 hour. When ready to serve, heat thoroughly, check for salt, and transfer to a warm serving platter. Serve sprinkled with chopped coriander and toasted almonds.

Note: This dish may be prepared up to two days in advance and kept refrigerated. (It does not freeze well.) In fact, the flavorings mellow and blend with keeping. If the chicken is to be refrigerated, do not add the garnish until you are ready to serve. To reheat, warm the dish gently over low heat until hot through. Taste, and if necessary add more salt before serving.

For a simple meal, serve this dish with a plain cooked rice (p. 357) or Whole Wheat Puffy Bread (p. 397). For a fancier meal, serve Emperor's Pilaf with Black Mushrooms (p. 375) and a yogurt salad, such as Cucumber and Yogurt Salad (p. 343) or Dumplings in Fragrant Yogurt (p. 348). Sweet Lemon Pickle with Cumin (p. 447) is a good accompaniment. Savory Pastries with Spicy Potato Filling (p. 125), Cauliflower Fritters (p. 115), and Shrimp Fritters (p. 118) are all fine choices for an appetizer.

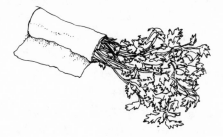

Chicken Kabuli

(Murgh Kabuli)

This recipe is an adaptation of a dish served at the Akbar India Restaurant in New York City. There it is prepared with lamb. I prefer to use the breast of chicken because it allows the spices to blend together more fully. Also, on a purely aesthetic level, the almond-colored sauce swathing the chunks of creamy-white chicken, with only specks of cracked pepper and deep green coriander for contrast, looks absolutely breathtaking.

(continued)

For 8 persons

4 large cloves garlic, peeled
3 tablespoons chopped fresh
  ginger root
3 medium-sized ripe tomatoes
  (about ¾ pound)
1 cup plain yogurt
¾ cup light vegetable oil
3 pounds skinned boneless
  chicken-breast meat
  (4 whole skinned, boneless
  chicken breasts), cut into
  1½-inch cubes
½ teaspoon mace
1 teaspoon nutmeg

2 tablespoons ground
  blanched almonds
1 teaspoon ground cardamom
1 teaspoon ground cumin
1 teaspoon ground coriander
½ teaspoon fennel seeds,
  powdered
1 tablespoon Kosher salt
½ cup heavy cream
2–3 teaspoons black
  peppercorns, coarsely
  ground
¼–⅓ cup finely chopped fresh
  coriander leaves

1. Put garlic, ginger, tomatoes, and yogurt into the container of an electric blender or food processor, and run the machine until the ingredients are reduced to a fine smooth puree.

2. Put oil and the pureed mixture in a large heavy-bottomed pan, preferably one with a non-stick surface. Place the pan over medium-high heat, and cook the puree until it reduces to a thick sauce and the fat begins to separate from it (about 15 minutes) stirring constantly to prevent the puree's sticking to the pan and burning. During the last few minutes of cooking, the sauce begins to splatter a little, so keep a lid or spatter screen handy.

3. Add chicken pieces and cook, stirring rapidly, until they lose their pink color and begin to sear slightly (about 5 minutes), but do not let them brown. Add mace, nutmeg, almond powder, cardamom, cumin, coriander, fennel, and salt, and mix well. Reduce heat, cover the pot, and let the chicken cook in its own juices for 15 minutes. Uncover, and continue cooking until the chicken is fully cooked and fork-tender and the sauce has almost dried (about 15 minutes). Stir in cream, black pepper, and coriander leaves, and turn off heat. Let the dish rest, covered, for at least 1

hour. When ready to serve, reheat thoroughly, check for salt, and serve.

Note: For best results, make this dish at least 4 hours, preferably a day, before you are going to serve it. This allows the flavors and sauce to penetrate the chicken, making it highly aromatic and juicy. Chicken Kabuli also freezes extremely well. Defrost thoroughly before reheating and serving. To reheat, simmer gently over low heat until warmed through. Taste, and if necessary add more salt and black pepper. Serve sprinkled with more chopped fresh coriander leaves.

You can serve this dish with any fried bread, such as Whole Wheat Flaky Bread (p. 402) or Deep-fried Puffy Bread (p. 413), or with a simple pilaf, such as Patiala Pilaf (p. 366) or Fragrant Pilaf Banaras Style (p. 368), and include a vegetable like Broccoli Smothered in Garlic Oil (p. 296). Or instead, combine the staple and side dish, and serve either a stuffed bread, such as Cauliflower-Stuffed Bread (p. 405) or Spinach Bread (p. 410), or a vegetable pilaf, such as Okra Pilaf (p. 373), Mint Pilaf (p. 377), Cumin and Turmeric Rice (p. 364), or Indian Fried Rice (p. 363). For an elegant meal, start with Mulligatawny Soup (p. 143), or Fragrant Stuffed Tomatoes (p. 106). Raw Onion Relish (p. 431) and Sweet Lemon Pickle with Cumin (p. 447) are wonderful accompaniments.

Tandoori (Indian Barbecued) Chicken

(Tandoori Murghi)

Of all the food cooked in a *tandoor*, the most popular and the best-tasting is chicken. The distinctive flavor, texture, and color of this dish are achieved by a particular yogurt marinade, by the use of tenderizers, a special *tandoori* coloring, and finally, by being cooked in the Indian clay oven. (For a full explanation of the *tandoor* and its origins in Indian cooking see p. 80.)

The recipe given here is designed for the conventional oven

and charcoal grill. (Household-model *tandoors* are not yet commercially available in the United States.) The results are very much to my satisfaction.

For 6 persons

3 very young broiling chickens (about 2–2¼ pounds each)	2½ teaspoons unseasoned natural meat tenderizer
	⅓ cup lemon juice

FOR MARINADE:

2 large cloves garlic
1 tablespoon chopped fresh
   ginger root
1 teaspoon ground roasted
   cumin seeds
½ teaspoon ground
   cardamom
½ teaspoon red pepper

1 teaspoon *tandoori* coloring,
   or 1 tablespoon paprika
⅓ cup plain yogurt

Usli ghee (p. 50), Indian vegetable shortening, or light vegetable oil for basting

1. Cut the wings off the chickens. Remove the neckbone carefully. Place the chickens on a cutting board and quarter them neatly. Then pull away the skin, using kitchen towels for a better grip if necessary. (Reserve the wings, neck, and skin for the stockpot.) Prick the chicken all over with fork or a thin skewer. Make diagonal slashes, ½-inch deep, 1 inch apart on the meat. Put the meat in a large bowl.

2. Add meat tenderizer and lemon juice to the chicken, and rub them into the slashes and all over for 2 minutes. Cover and marinate for ½ hour.

3. Put all the ingredients of the marinade into the container of an electric blender or food processor, and blend until reduced to a smooth sauce. (Alternatively, garlic and ginger may be crushed to a paste and blended with the remaining ingredients.)

4. Pour this marinade over the chicken pieces and mix, turning and tossing, to coat all the pieces well. (*A note of caution:* Since certain brands of *Tandoori* coloring tend to stain the fingers, it is

advisable either to use a fork to turn the chicken pieces in the marinade or use a pastry brush to spread it over the chicken.) Cover and marinate for 4 hours at room temperature, or refrigerate overnight, turning several times. Chicken should not remain in the marinade for more than 2 days, because the marinade contains a meat tenderizer which, with prolonged marinating, alters the texture of the chicken meat to very soft and doughy.

Rubbing lemon juice and tenderizer into slashes

Slashing pricked chicken

5. Take the chicken from the refrigerator at least 1 hour before cooking to bring it to room temperature. The chicken is now ready to be either roasted in the oven or broiled over an electric or charcoal grill.

TO ROAST IN THE OVEN:

Start heating the oven to 500°–550°F. Take the chickens out of the marinade. Brush them with *ghee*, and place them on an extra-large shallow roasting pan, preferably on a wire rack. Set the pan in the middle level of the oven, and roast for 25–30 minutes, or until the meat is cooked through. There is no need to baste while the chicken pieces are roasting, because the enclosed environment keeps the chickens from drying excessively.

(continued)

TO BROIL INDOORS:

Preheat the broiler. Brush the grill with a little oil to prevent the meat's sticking. Place the chicken pieces, slashed side up, on the grill, and brush the slashed side with *ghee*. Cook 2 to 3 inches away from the heat for 20 minutes. Turn and cook the other side for another 10 minutes, or until the chicken pieces are cooked through. Brush often with *ghee* during cooking.

TO GRILL OUTDOORS:

Fire the coal well in advance (about 1½ hours before you are ready to begin cooking), so that a white ash forms over the surface of the coal. This is when the coal is at its hottest. Place the grill at least 5 inches away from the heat, and rub generously with oil. Place the chicken pieces, slashed side up, over the grill and brush them with *ghee*. Let chicken cook without turning for 10 minutes. Turn, baste the other side, and cook for 10 minutes. Continue to cook, turning and basting the chicken every 10 minutes, until it is done. The cooking time for broiling and grilling usually varies widely. Much depends upon the intensity of the heat and its distance from the chicken. The point to remember is that the chicken pieces have been marinating in a very strong tenderizing solution for two days and therefore will cook much faster than standard broiled or barbecued chicken.

Serve the chicken immediately, lightly brushed with *ghee* or oil and accompanied by Roasted Onions (*Bhone Piaz*, p. 313).

Notes: 1. When the chicken is cooked in a *tandoor*, or outdoors, the question of pan drippings does not arise. When it is roasted in the oven, however, you will get pan juices. Traditionally it is not used, even for basting. I save it, however, and use it to moisten leftover chicken meat, which tends to taste dry when cold. I serve this as a snack, rolled like a taco or eggroll, in Indian bread with roasted onions.

2. The marinade remaining in the bowl, usually not added to the chicken before cooking, can be stirred into the sauce for Velvet Butter Chicken (see following receipe).

3. Since there are variations in commercial *tandoori* coloring, the cooked chicken will range from yellowish orange to deep reddish orange in color. If you use paprika instead, the chicken will have a redder tone. And if the chicken is grilled, especially over charcoal, the color will be more intense.

4. *Tandoori* chicken must be served immediately after cooking. Because of its dryish texture, it does not taste as good cold, especially after refrigeration and reheating. But if you are planning to make Velvet Butter Chicken with the leftovers, then refrigerating—even freezing—is acceptable. In fact, the dryness seems to prove an asset, enabling the chicken pieces to hold their shape while simmering. In addition, they absorb more of that wonderful creamy tomato sauce.

Both Sweet Saffron Pilaf (p. 369), and Saffron Pilaf with Peaches (p. 371) are excellent served with *tandoori* chicken. Since Roasted Onions traditionally accompany this dish, there is no need for another side dish. If you want to expand the meal, serve Buttered Black Beans (p. 337), and if you like, include a *raita* such as Sweet Banana and Yogurt Salad (p. 349). Precede the meal with a few tasty fritters, such as Cauliflower Fritters (p. 115) or Indian Cheese Fritters (p. 117), or with Savory Pastries with Spicy Potato Filling (p. 125). If you happen to be serving Mint Coriander Dip (p. 437) with the fritters, serve it with the meal as well, because the dip makes a good sauce for the chicken, particularly if it has become slightly dry or overdone in the cooking. *Ras Malai* (p. 465) is the perfect dessert to end this perfect meal.

Velvet Butter Chicken

(Makhani Murgh)

This chicken preparation is a classic example of the true flair and skill of Indian cooks. In this dish, *Makhani* (meaning "buttered," or "in butter") and *Murgh* (meaning chicken, and referring in this context to the leftover day-old *tandoori* chicken pieces) are combined. They are simmered in cumin-scented butter and a creamy rich tomato sauce and become a delicacy craved far more than *tandoori* chicken. An important element in the special flavor of this dish is the hefty amount of chopped fresh coriander leaves that are folded in prior to serving. If you have no leftover *tandoori* chicken, this dish will take some time to make, since you will first have to cook chicken *tandoori* style.

Note: If you omit the coriander, the *Makhani Murg* will still taste very good, but it won't be as fragrant and authentic.

For 8 persons

⅔ recipe Tandoori Chicken from preceding recipe (8 legs and breasts of chicken in any combination), or 2 *tandoori* chickens (about 2–2¼ pounds each) cooked by any recipe

3 cups canned tomatoes in puree, measured with puree (or substitute 4 cups chopped fresh ripe tomatoes)

4 green chilies, seeded (or substitute ½ teaspoon red pepper, or to taste)

2 tablespoons chopped fresh ginger root

10 tablespoons (1¼ sticks) sweet butter

4 teaspoons ground cumin

1 tablespoon paprika

2 teaspoons Kosher salt

1½ cups heavy cream

2 teaspoons *garam masala* (p. 38)

2 teaspoons ground roasted cumin seeds (p. 66, optional)

¼ cup firmly packed minced fresh coriander leaves

1. Cut the chicken pieces neatly into halves, so that you have 16 pieces of chicken.

2. Put tomatoes, green chilies, and ginger in the container of an electric blender or food processor, and blend to a fine puree.

3. Place 8 tablespoons (1 stick) of butter in large heavy-bottomed pan, preferably one with a non-stick surface, over medium heat. As the butter melts, tilt the pan in all direction to coat the bottom. When the foam begins to subside, add chicken pieces a

few at a time, and brown until they are nicely seared all over (about 2–3 minutes per batch). Remove them with a slotted spoon into a reserved bowl. Continue with the rest of the chicken pieces until all are browned.

4. Add cumin and paprika to the butter in the pan, and cook, stirring rapidly, for 10–15 seconds. Add tomato puree and cook, uncovered, until the sauce is thickened (about 5–8 minutes), stirring constantly to prevent sticking and burning.

5. Add salt, cream, and chicken pieces (with any juices that may have accumulated in the bowl). Gently stir the chicken to coat the pieces evenly and thoroughly with the sauce. Be careful not to break the fragile chicken pieces. Reduce heat to medium-low, and simmer, uncovered, until the fat begins to separate from the sauce and a thin glaze appears on the surface (about 10 minutes). Check and stir often (but only one or two stirs at a time) to ensure that the sauce is not burning. Stir in the remaining 2 tablespoons (¼ stick) of butter, *garam masala*, and roasted cumin if you are using it. Turn off heat, and let the dish stand, covered, for ½ hour before serving. When ready to serve, heat thoroughly, check for salt, and fold in chopped coriander leaves.

Note: This dish may be prepared and refrigerated for up to 2 days, or frozen. Defrost thoroughly before reheating. To reheat, simmer gently until heated through. Taste, and if necessary add salt. To perk up flavors, fold in a little *garam masala*, ground roasted cumin, and chopped coriander leaves before serving.

You can serve either a pilaf, such as Patiala Pilaf (p. 366) or Fragrant Pilaf Banaras Style (p. 368), or a fried bread, such as Whole Wheat Flaky Bread (p. 402) or Deep-fried Puffy Bread (p. 413). Buttered Smothered Cabbage (p. 298) or Fragrant Buttered Greens (p. 319) are good choices for vegetables, or you can serve a *dal* like Buttered Black Beans (p. 337). Any of the fritters, savory pastries, and kabobs are good before this meal, but I like Onion Fritters (p. 113) or Kabob Patties Laced with Ginger and Mint (p. 109) best.

Chicken Pilaf

(Murgh Biriyani)

Chicken pilaf is truly the most authentic of all North Indian pilafs—
a specialty of Hindus and Sikhs. (The Moslems, who excel in lamb
cooking, favor lamb pilafs such as *Shah Jahani Biriyani*, p. 192, and
Mughalai Pullao, p. 189.) Chicken pilaf is generally made in one of
two ways: Either all the ingredients are mixed and cooked together,
or the chicken and rice are cooked separately and mixed just before
serving. I prefer the latter procedure, because there is no danger of
the chicken remaining undercooked or the rice becoming overcooked, or of the rice grains falling apart with numerous stirrings.
This pilaf, made with a *korma* of chicken and cooked rice, takes no
time at all to prepare. It can be made with all parts of the chicken.

Note: Do not overfry the onions or the sauce will become too
dark. Also, it is good to use a slightly tart yogurt here; otherwise
the pilaf will taste slightly bland.

For 6 persons

All the ingredients for making Moghul Braised Chicken (*Mughalai Korma*, p. 206)	1 pound seedless grapes (optional)
2 cups *basmati* rice	1 tablespoon minced fresh coriander leaves (optional)

1. Prepare *Mughalai Korma* following instructions on page 206.
2. Pick over, clean, wash, and soak rice, following instructions
given under Preparing Basmati Rice for Cooking on page 356.
3. Preheat oven to 300°F.
4. Bring 3 quarts of water to a boil in a deep pot. Add the
soaked rice and stir immediately for half a minute (this prevents the
rice from settling) being careful not to break the fragile grains. Bring
the water to a second boil (it will take about 3 minutes) and cook the
rice for 2 minutes. Pour the entire contents of the pot into a large

sieve held over a kitchen sink. Hold the sieve under the tap and let the cold water run through the rice at medium speed for 3–5 seconds. Shake sieve to drain the rice thoroughly, and let it cool briefly.

5. Put the chicken with its gravy in a heavy oven-proof casserole with a tight-fitting lid. Add rice, and fold it in carefully. Place aluminum foil on top of the casserole and cover tightly with the lid.

6. Bake in the middle level of the oven for 30 minutes. Turn off the oven, leaving the casserole inside for an additional 10 minutes. The pilaf, left in the oven, will remain warm for an additional 30 minutes. Transfer the pilaf to a heated serving platter, and if desired, surround it with a ring of grapes and sprinkle with chopped coriander leaves.

Note: This pilaf, if made with *korma* which has not been refrigerated, will keep in the refrigerator for up to 4 days. In fact, it tastes best the second and third days. To reheat, place the covered casserole in the middle level of a preheated 300°F oven for 25 minutes.

This gorgeous pilaf is a complete meal in itself. Serve it simply with a glass of chilled white wine. But if you want additional side dishes, include a *raita*, such as Cucumber and Yogurt Salad (p. 343) or Sweet Banana and Yogurt Salad (p. 349). *Raitas* are especially good in the summer. For a more elaborate meal, include either a substantial vegetable preparation such as Cauliflower Fritters (p. 115), or any of the vegetable main dishes (pp. 255–287). Or serve a light meat preparation, such as Moghul Kabobs with Raisin Stuffing (p. 107). Sweet Lemon Pickle with Cumin (p. 447) goes well with this meal. So does Hot Hyderabad Tomato Relish (p. 441).

Cornish Hens Braised in Fragrant Apricot Sauce

(Murgh Khoobani)

Chicken blends well with fruits and fruit sauces. The sweet tartness of fruits is a perfect complement to the mellow flavor of chicken. In Moghul cooking, chicken is often cooked with peaches, plums, grapes, apples, and apricots (Khoobani).

This dish is traditionally made with chicken, but I use Cornish hens because they are most like the chickens used in India for Murgh Khoobani (the birds' small size permits the flavorings to penetrate thoroughly). Cornish hens are both more elegant and easier to serve. Murgh Khoobani is prepared just like any other braised dish: in a pot, on top of the stove. However, I prefer to cook the hens in the oven, arranged in one layer in a baking dish to ensure even cooking, and stove-to-table serving.

For 8 persons

4 Cornish hens weighing
   about 1½ pounds each
2 cups dried apricots (about
   ½ pound)
8 tablespoons *usli ghee* (p. 50),
   or light vegetable oil
2 cups finely chopped onions
2 tablespoons finely chopped
   fresh ginger root

2 teaspoons *Mughal garam
   masala* (p. 37)
2 cups finely chopped or
   pureed fresh ripe
   tomatoes, or 1½ cups
   chopped canned tomatoes
2½ teaspoons Kosher salt

1. Cut off the wing tips (reserve them for the stock pot), and neatly halve the Cornish hens. Pull the skin off, using a kitchen towel to get a better grip, and set the hens aside.

2. Put apricots in a bowl, and add enough boiling water to cover them by 1 inch. Soak for 2 hours, and drain. Coarsely chop them in a food processor or electric blender, or use a knife. Set aside.

3. Preheat the oven to 375°F.

4. Heat 2 tablespoons of the *ghee* or oil in a large frying pan over medium-high heat. Add hens, 3 or 4 halves at a time, and sear them until nicely browned on all sides (about 5–10 minutes per batch). Take them out with a slotted spoon, and place them meat side up in a large baking pan that can accommodate the eight halves snugly in one layer. Continue with the rest of the hens, adding them to the baking dish as they are browned. Add more *ghee* if necessary.

5. Add the rest of the *ghee* to the frying pan, along with the onions. Fry the onions until they turn light brown (about 15 minutes), stirring constantly to prevent burning. Add ginger, and cook for an additional 2 minutes. Add *Mughal garam masala*, and stir rapidly for 5 seconds. Then add tomatoes, salt, and apricots, along with 1½ cups water, and bring the mixture to a boil. Reduce heat and simmer at a gentle bubble, uncovered, until the sauce has reduced to a thick puree (about 15–20 minutes).

6. Pour the sauce over the hens. Pour ½ cup boiling water down the sides of the baking pan, and cover tightly with foil.

7. Bake in the middle level of the oven for 25 minutes. Reduce temperature to 325°F, and continue baking for an additional 25 minutes. Turn off the oven, leaving the dish inside until you are ready to serve. The Cornish hens will remain warm for ½ hour.

Note: This dish keeps well in the refrigerator for up to 2 days, or frozen. However, it must be defrosted thoroughly before reheating. To reheat, place the dish, still covered and sealed in foil, in the middle level of a 350°F preheated oven for 35 minutes.

Serve plain cooked rice (p. 357) or Rice Cooked in Fragrant Meat Broth (p. 361) for a simple meal. For a more substantial meal, present Sweet Saffron Pilaf (p. 369) or Royal Vegetable and Rice Casserole (p. 381). You do not need another side dish, but if you want one, Glazed Beets with Black Mustard Seeds (p. 295) or Broccoli Smothered in Garlic Oil (p. 296) are good choices. Serve Cold Minted Potatoes (p. 103), Cold Potato Appetizer (p. 105), or Spinach and Mung Bean Dumplings (p. 120) as a first course.

EGGS
(Anda)

Scrambled Eggs with Cumin and Fragrant Herbs
(Ande Ki Bhorji)

Most flights from New York to New Delhi arrive very early in the morning. By the time one gets through customs and security checks, out of the airport and home, it is breakfast time. In my mother-in-law's home it has become a tradition to serve *Ande ki Bhorji* with *Paratha* on such mornings. It is generally believed that after a long (approximately twenty-four-hour) tiring journey, one loses one's appetite for a while. Well, we just need a whiff of that Indian-style breakfast and our appetites are back on the double.

Bhorji means scramble. Indians scramble eggs somewhat differently from Americans. For one thing, they cook them in much the same way they cook meat and chicken, so that the eggs look and feel more like stir-fried vegetables that can be picked up with a piece of bread. Secondly, Indians add a lot of onions—enough to equal the quantity of the eggs. Finally, no Indian dish is complete without the addition of spices and herbs, so cumin, green chilies, and fresh chopped coriander are added at the end of the cooking to flavor the eggs properly.

For 4–6 persons

6 large eggs
1 teaspoon Kosher salt
2 tablespoons Indian vegetable shortening, or light vegetable oil
2 medium-sized onions, peeled and cut into ¾-inch pieces

½ teaspoon ground roasted cumin seeds (p. 66)
1 tablespoon finely chopped fresh coriander leaves
1–2 green chilies, seeded and sliced (optional)

1. Break the eggs into a small bowl, add salt, and beat slightly to mix. Do not overbeat, as eggs should not be foamy or frothy.

2. Heat the shortening or oil in a frying pan (9–10 inches in diameter), and add onions. Over medium-low heat, sauté onions until they are translucent but still firm and crisp (about 3–4 minutes).

3. Reduce heat to low, and add the beaten eggs. Let the eggs settle in the pan for 5 seconds. Then, using a fork, begin pushing the egg toward the center of the pan so that it cooks like a thick cake. When most of the egg has coagulated, turn it gently and cook the other side. (Do not worry if it breaks, as the finished dish will, in fact, look like little cakes of scrambled egg studded with onions.) Continue stirring and turning until the eggs are fully cooked (about 3 minutes). Do not let them brown. Turn off heat, and transfer to a warm serving platter. Serve sprinkled with roasted cumin, chopped coriander leaves, and green chilies.

This flavorful *Bhorji* is traditionally eaten with *Paratha* (p. 402), a classic northern breakfast combination usually accompanied by a pickle. A good choice is Sweet Lemon Pickle with Cumin (p. 447). Serve either a spiced tea (p. 486 or 487) or plain brewed breakfast tea. For a distinctly Indian touch, precede the breakfast with a chilled glass of yogurt drink (*Lassi* or *Mattha*, p. 488–489).

Whole Eggs in Spicy Tomato Sauce

(Ande ki Kari)

Indians take eggs very seriously. They consider them too refined a product of nature to be wasted as a cooking ingredient, so they pamper them the same way they do meat, and prepare and serve them with equal care.

Of all Indian egg preparations, *Ande ki Kari* is by far the most popular, especially with vegetarians who include eggs in their diet. This dish is made in two steps: First, the tomato and onion sauce is prepared. When the sauce is fully cooked, hard-boiled egg halves are carefully added. The contrast of the yellow-and-white of the eggs against the glazed reddish sauce is handsome indeed.

Two important points to keep in mind: the eggs should be as fresh as possible and boiled at the time you make the entire dish. (With keeping, the yolks begin to turn gray around the edges.) Secondly, after the egg halves have been added, the dish must be stirred with utmost caution or, if possible, not stirred at all, because the yolks have a tendency to slip out of the whites, scatter into the lovely red sauce, and look unappetizing.

Note: The cinnamon and cardamom in this dish are not meant to be eaten. But no harm will come to you if you bite into them.

For 8 persons

8 large eggs
10 tablespoons Indian vegetable shortening, or light vegetable oil
2 cups finely chopped onions
4 teaspoons finely chopped garlic
2 tablespoons finely chopped fresh ginger root
1 stick cinnamon, 3 inches long
4 black (or 8 green) cardamom pods

2 teaspoons ground coriander
1 teaspoon turmeric
¼ teaspoon each red and black pepper
2 cups finely chopped or pureed fresh ripe tomatoes
2 teaspoons Kosher salt
2 teaspoons *garam masala* (p.38)
3 tablespoons finely chopped fresh coriander leaves

1. Hard-boil the eggs, peel them, and put them in a bowl of cold water until needed.

2. Heat the shortening in a large heavy-bottomed pan, preferably one with a non-stick surface, and add onions. Over medium-high heat, fry the onions until they turn caramel brown (about 20 minutes), stirring constantly to ensure even browning. (See directions for Brown-frying Onions, p. 71.) Add garlic and ginger, and fry for an additional 2 minutes. Add cinnamon and cardamom, and fry until the spices are puffed and begin to brown (about 1 minute).

Add coriander, turmeric, red and black pepper. Stir rapidly for a moment or two, and immediately add tomatoes. Cook, uncovered, until the mixture turns into a thick pulpy sauce and the fat begins to separate from the gravy (about 10 minutes). Stir frequently to keep the sauce from sticking and burning. Add salt and 2½ cups boiling water, and stir to mix. Reduce heat to medium, and simmer the sauce, covered, for 20–25 minutes. At the end of the simmering, the sauce should be fairly thick, and a satiny glaze should develop to coat it. If it is too thin, uncover and boil briskly until the sauce reduces to the right consistency. Turn off heat, and let the sauce rest, covered, for at least ½ hour before serving. (The sauce may be prepared several hours ahead and kept, covered, at room temperature, or refrigerated for up to 4 days, or frozen. Defrost thoroughly before proceeding with the recipe.)

3. When ready to serve, drain the eggs and pat them dry on paper towels. Cut them neatly into halves lengthwise.

4. Simmer the sauce gently over low heat until piping hot, stir in *garam masala*, and check for salt. Carefully slip in the egg halves, and continue simmering until the eggs are heated through. Serve sprinkled with chopped coriander leaves.

For a complete meal plan, follow the menu suggestions given for Chicken in Onion Tomato Gravy on page 208.

Shellfish and Fish

(Machi)

Shrimp Laced with Mild Fragrant Spices   *(Masala Jheengari)*
Shrimp Poached in Coconut Milk with Fresh Herbs   *(Yerra Moolee)*
Velvet Creamed Shrimp   *(Jheenga Malai Khasa)*
Lobster in Fried Onion Sauce   *(Bara Jheenga Do-piaza)*
Panfried Fillet of Sole Laced with Carom   *(Bhoni Machi)*
Chick-pea Batter Fish   *(Tali Machi)*
Fish in Velvet Yogurt Sauce   *(Dahi Machi)*

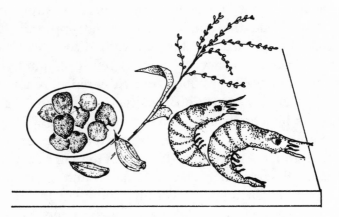

Looking at the menu in an Indian restaurant, one is often struck by the fact that there are hardly any seafood or fish selections offered. One may immediately conclude that either Indians are not fish eaters, probably because of limited varieties of fish available in India, or that their repertoire in the field of fish and shellfish cooking is simply too insignificant to be mentioned. All this is a gross misconception, for India has a coastline of over three thousand miles and the land itself is sculptured with rivers, streams, and lakes. These bodies of water support a variety of marine life so large that it would take an entire volume to enumerate all the dishes native to the various regions. For the people living along these waters, fish and seafood have always been part of their daily diet and livelihood.

Then why is there so little mention of the fish and shellfish cooking of India? The reasons are twofold.

First, Indian restaurants have traditionally served North Indian food (often known by the classic name, "Moghul" food). This style of cooking is noted for its meat and poultry preparations. Its repertoire has always been restricted, due to the limited availability—or in many cases, outright lack—of fish and shellfish. Therefore, the few seafood preparations served in these restaurants originated in Bengal (specially East Bengal), where fish and seafood are plentiful. Since the Moghul influence was strong in this region, the dishes had the familiar flavors and appearance. Most other seafood dishes are adaptations to seafood cooking of popular North Indian meat-cooking techniques. A few restaurants have recently broken the age-old tradition and gathered up enough courage to begin serving such regional specialties as Fish Goa and Lobster Kerala, which are being received enthusiastically.

Second, the fish found in Indian waters are very different from those found in American waters. Even the same species of fish have different flavors when cooked. The United States does not have anything similar to the sweet and succulent Indian giant prawns (*bagda jheengari*), each weighing as much as one and a half pounds.

Or the lovely fatty fish *eleesh,* found in the Hoogli river, whose flesh is so delicate and aromatic that it is often simply steamed, smothered with mustard paste, in a dish called *bhapa eleesh* or baked with cinnamon and clove in *dum eleesh.* We also don't see an equivalent to *vekti, topshe,* or *roi,* sold in *Bag Bazaar,* the famous marketplace in Calcutta. One of the most divine-tasting fish in the world is *pomfret,* found along the Bombay coast. Its size and bone structure is similar to our flounder. Its fine texture and delicate flavor is unsurpassed. The only other flatfish that comes anywhere close is the Dover sole caught in the English Channel. A good quality sole, however, is a reasonably good substitute. The large shrimps we get in U.S. markets are similar to the Indian *chotoo jheengari.* Also, our lobster (*golda jheengari*) and crab (*kekada*) here are very good. Lately we have also started getting excellent Alaska King Crab meat, fresh, or all precooked and instantly frozen to maximize freshness and natural flavors.

About fish and shellfish cooking: When my husband and I were up in Newfoundland a few years ago on our vacation, one of our favorite snacks used to be fried cod fillets which were nothing but large chunks of codfish caught a few hours before cooking, dusted generously with cracked black pepper and flour, and fried. On returning, I went to my fish shop and bought myself a couple of pounds of cod fillets that looked and smelled extremely fresh. I cooked them exactly the same way, but they never tasted quite the same. What I found missing was the sweet creamy flavor of freshly caught cod from Newfoundland waters. What I realized then was that some of the best fish preparations around the world have one thing in common: a simple, uncomplicated manner of cooking that enhances and accentuates the flavor of the fish itself. The enjoyment lies in relishing the sweet taste, delicate texture, and other fine qualities of the fish.

All the regions along the Indian coast, particularly Bengal in the East and Malabar and Goa to the West, are known for their wonderful fish and seafood preparations. Many of their cooking techniques have been developed around a particular variety of fish or shellfish, to complement and further enhance the flavor. Thus a prerequisite for reproducing many such preparations is the right kind of fish. Equally important is its freshness. Keeping that in mind, I have particularly chosen those recipes which are easily adaptable.

The shrimps available here are exceptionally good. Therefore I have given several regional recipes for cooking them, such as in fresh coconut and herb sauce from the Malabar coast, and in cream sauce or fragrant spice-laced gravy from Bengal. Also included is a recipe for preparing lobster in the classic onion sauce, an example of the adaptation of Moghul techniques to shellfish cooking. Sole and flounder are excellent fish that naturally lend themselves to Indian cooking, so an interesting yet easy recipe for frying them is included. What you will find unique is the batter made with chickpea flour. Also given is a mouth-watering recipe for a crumb-coated fish that is utterly simple to make. And finally, a recipe for poaching fish in fragrant yogurt sauce, a classic from Bengal, to give you a glimpse of the simplicity and unsophisticated cooking of the East Coast.

Shrimp Laced with Mild Spices

(Masala Jheengari)

Of all the wonderful shellfish dishes in India, *Masala Jheengari* or *Masala Jheenga*, is the most widely eaten. Originally prepared by the Moslems in Bengal, this dish today is as common and popular throughout North India as *Murgh Masala* (p. 208), or *Masala Gosht* (p. 172). Large shrimps, also known as prawns, are folded into a luscious brownish maroon sauce of fried onions and spices, which is then velvetized with cream. An interesting ingredient here is poppy seeds, which are roasted and ground before being added to the sauce. The poppy seeds, besides thickening and enriching the sauce, give it a special nutty aroma.

For 6 persons

2 pounds shrimps, preferably
    large to medium (about
    28–32 per pound)
½ teaspoon turmeric
½ cup light vegetable oil, or a
    mixture of oil and *usli
    ghee* (p. 50)
1½ cups finely chopped onions
2 teaspoons finely chopped
    garlic
1½ teaspoons ground roasted
    white poppy seeds
    (p. 66)

1 teaspoon ground cumin
2 teaspoons ground
    coriander
1½ teaspoons paprika
¼ cup plain yogurt
1½ teaspoons Kosher salt
2 green chilies, seeded and
    minced (or substitute
    ½ teaspoon red pepper)
¼–⅓ cup heavy cream
2 tablespoons finely chopped
    fresh coriander leaves

1. Shell and devein shrimps (see p. 118), and wash them
thoroughly.

2. Bring 1 quart of water to a boil on high heat. Add turmeric
and shrimps, and cook for 4 minutes (reduce the cooking time if
you are using smaller shrimps). Immediately drain the shrimps,
reserving the water, and set aside.

3. Heat oil in a large heavy-bottomed pan, preferably one with
a non-stick surface, and add onions. Over high heat, fry the onions
until they turn golden brown (about 8 minutes), stirring constantly
to prevent burning. Add garlic, and cook for an additional
½ minute. Reduce heat, and add ground poppy seeds, cumin,
coriander, and paprika. Stir rapidly for 5 seconds, and add half the
reserved liquid in which the shrimps were cooked. Increase heat to
high and boil rapidly, uncovered, for 10 minutes. Add the remaining liquid, and continue boiling, uncovered, until the sauce reduces
to a thick pulpy gravy (about 20 minutes). Stir occasionally to
ensure that the sauce does not stick to the pan. Add yogurt, salt,
and chilies or red pepper, and continue cooking for an additional
2–3 minutes, stirring constantly. Add cooked shrimps, and stir to
mix. Reduce heat and gently simmer, covered, for a couple of
minutes, or until the shrimps are heated through and absorb some

of the luscious gravy. Turn off heat, and stir in cream. Let the dish rest at least 1 hour. When ready to serve, gently simmer until heated through. Check for salt, stir in the chopped coriander leaves, and serve sprinkled with a few more chopped leaves.

Note: This dish improves with keeping. For best results, prepare it the day before you are going to serve it, and refrigerate. It also freezes rather well. Defrost thoroughly before reheating. Taste, and if necessary add salt, cream, and chopped coriander before serving.

Serve this subtly flavored *masala* shrimp with Okra Pilaf (p. 373), Emperor's Pilaf with Black Mushrooms (p. 375), or Mint Pilaf (p. 377). A vegetable side dish goes best with this. Good choices are: Glazed Cauliflower with Ginger (p. 299), Cauliflower and Scallions with Black Mustard Seeds (p. 301), or Broccoli Smothered in Garlic Oil (p. 296). For an additional side dish choose a *dal* such as Buttered Black Beans (p. 337). If you want a light appetizer, serve Lentil Wafers (p. 425) or Snow Flakes (p. 428). For a more substantial first course, serve Kabob Patties Laced with Ginger and Mint (p. 109), Savory Meat Pastries (p. 130), or Indian Cheese Fritters (p. 117). You do not need any accompaniments with this meal, but Hot Hyderabad Tomato Relish (p. 441) and Grated Cucumber Relish (p. 434) go especially well. Any dessert complements this dish; I like to serve Saffron Almond Pudding (p. 457) or Mangoes with Cream (p. 470).

Shrimp Poached in Coconut Milk with Fresh Herbs

(Yerra Moolee)

No matter what food is cooked in it or what spices are added, coconut milk never loses its distinct sweet flavor. Instead, it enriches all the other flavorings. In this dish from Kerala, a state on the southwestern coast of India, fresh juicy shrimps are gently poached in herb-laced coconut milk. The spicing here is intentionally kept very subtle, so that the natural flavors of the shrimp and the coconut milk can be relished to their fullest. *Yerra Moolee*, with its shimmering ivory-white sauce, can be made to taste much hotter than this recipe by increasing the quantity of green chilies.

For 6 persons

2 pounds shrimps, preferably large to medium (about 28–32 per pound)

7 tablespoons light vegetable oil

2 cups finely chopped onions

2 teaspoons minced garlic

1½ tablespoons ground or crushed fresh ginger root

2 green chilies, or more, to taste, seeded and minced

¼ teaspoon turmeric

2 tablespoons ground coriander

3 cups coconut milk (see p. 46)

1½ teaspoons Kosher salt

2 tablespoons minced fresh coriander leaves (or substitute 1 tablespoon dry coriander leaves)

1. Shell and devein shrimps (see p. 118). Wash them thoroughly, and set aside.

2. Heat the oil in a large heavy-bottomed pan, and add onions. Over high heat, fry the onions until they turn golden brown (about 10 minutes), stirring constantly to prevent burning. Reduce heat to medium, add garlic, ginger, and chilies, and fry for an additional 2 minutes. Add turmeric and coriander, stir rapidly for 15 seconds, and add coconut milk and salt. Cook the sauce, uncovered, until it

thickens (about 10 minutes). Stir frequently to ensure that the sauce does not stick and burn.

3. Add shrimps, mix, reduce heat to medium-low, and simmer, covered, for 5–7 minutes, or until the shrimps are cooked through. Do not overcook the shrimps, or they will become tough and chewy. Check for salt, stir in minced coriander leaves, and serve.

Note: This dish may be prepared a day ahead, refrigerated, and reheated just before serving. The coconut sauce does not take to freezing well. The cream of the fresh coconut separates during freezing. As a result, when the dish is defrosted the sauce becomes thin and runny, lacking in body. There is also considerable loss in flavor.

This dish has a lot of gravy and must be served with rice. Best, of course, is plain cooked rice (p. 357); then all the flavors can be enjoyed without any interference from the pilaf spices. Green Beans with Coconut and Black Mustard Seeds (p. 307), Cauliflower and Scallions with Black Mustard Seeds (p. 301), or Glazed Beets with Black Mustard Seeds (p. 295), are excellent vegetable choices. Accompany this lovely meal with Shredded Carrot and Mustard Seed Relish (p. 435), Puffy Lentil Wafers (p. 427), and if you like, Quick Mango and Shredded Ginger Pickle (p. 450). If you want an appetizer, Onion Fritters (p. 113) or Silky Bean Dumplings (p. 123) are good choices. For a contrast in flavor and color and an all-seafood dinner, serve Crab Malabar (p. 101) as a first course. Coconut Wedding Pudding (p. 459) and Saffron Almond Pudding (p. 457) blend harmoniously with this meal, since both come from the same area. For those who prefer a balanced contrast, serve Carrot Pudding with Cardamom and Pistachio (p. 456) or Semolina and Raisin Pudding (p. 460).

Velvet Creamed Shrimp

(Jheenga Malai Khasa)

Malai means cream—not only milk cream but also coconut cream. This dish, a popular preparation from Bengal, is also made with coconut. The flavor, color, and texture of the dish, however, are distinctly different from the coconut shrimp of Kerala (see preceding recipe), because in this recipe, dry coconut, known as *khopra*, is used. It is roasted and ground and added to the sauce to lend it a spicy, nutty flavor. Dry coconut flakes, used widely in baking and available in supermarket chains, should be fresh smelling, or else the dish will taste of rancid coconut oil. The whole spices in this dish—cinnamon, cloves, and cardamom—are not meant to be eaten, but if you bite into one, no harm will come to you.

Note: "Velvet" in this recipe refers to the appearance of the dish, not to the texture, which is coarse and grainy.

For 6 persons

1 cup dry flaked unsweetened coconut (supermarket variety)
¾ cup plain yogurt
2 teaspoons finely chopped garlic
1 tablespoon finely chopped fresh ginger root
2 green chilies, seeded
2 pounds shrimps, preferably large to medium (about 28–32 per pound)

½ cup light vegetable oil
1 stick cinnamon, 3 inches long
8 whole cloves
8 green cardamom pods
⅔ cup finely chopped onions
3 tablespoons ground blanched almonds
1½ teaspoons Kosher salt
2 tablespoons finely chopped fresh coriander leaves

1. Place a frying pan over medium heat. When it is hot, add flaked coconut, and toast, stirring and tossing, until it turns dark caramel brown (about 5–8 minutes). Transfer the toasted coconut to

the container of an electric blender or food processor. Add yogurt, garlic, ginger, and green chilies, and run the machine until the mixture is finely pureed. Set aside.

2. Shell and devein shrimps (see p. 118). Wash them thoroughly, and set aside.

3. Heat the oil in a shallow non-stick pan over medium heat. When the oil is hot, add cinnamon, cloves, and cardamom. When the spices get slightly puffed and begin to brown (about ½ minute), add onions. Increase the heat to high, and fry onions until they turn caramel brown (about 10 minutes), stirring constantly to prevent burning. (See directions for Brown-frying Onions, p. 71.) Add ground almonds, stir rapidly for ½ minute, and add coconut puree. Cook the mixture, uncovered, until the oil begins to separate from the sauce (about 3 minutes).

4. Add 1½ cups boiling water and salt. Reduce heat and simmer, covered, for 5 minutes. Add shrimps, and stir well to distribute them evenly into the sauce. Continue cooking, covered, for an additional 5–7 minutes, or until they are cooked through but still tender. Do not overcook the shrimps, or they will turn hard and chewy. Check for salt, and serve sprinkled with chopped coriander leaves.

Note: This dish may be prepared ahead, refrigerated for up to 2 days, and reheated just before serving. Because of the large amount of coconut in the sauce, it does not freeze well.

This lovely shrimp dish should be served with a plain fragrant pilaf, such as Patiala Pilaf (p. 366), Fragrant Pilaf Banaras Style (p. 368), or any one of the saffron pilafs. Serve Smoked Eggplant with Fresh Herbs (p. 305), Buttered Smothered Cabbage (p. 298), or Turmeric Potatoes with Green Peppers (p. 316). Lentil Wafers (p. 425) and Sweet Lemon Pickle with Cumin (p. 447) go particularly well with this meal. Fragrant Stuffed Tomatoes (p. 106) or Crab Malabar (p. 101) are lovely first courses with which to precede the meal.

Lobster in Fried Onion Sauce

(Bara Jheenga Do-piaza)

Lobster is not commonly eaten in India, but the Bengalis in the East have many interesting techniques for preparing it. My favorite is the *Do-piaza* of Lobster, an adaptation of the popular Moghul *Do-piaza* for meat (see page 166). In the classic *Do-piaza*, onions are added at the beginning and cooked with the other ingredients (including the meat) to form the basic sauce. The second quantity of onions is fried to a dark brown color and then folded in just before serving time, giving the dish its characteristic flavor. In this Lobster *Do-piaza* the only difference is that lobster is substituted for the meat.

For 6 persons

½ cup light vegetable oil
2 medium-sized onions, peeled and sliced into thin shreds
1½ cups finely chopped onions
2 teaspoons finely chopped garlic
1 tablespoon finely chopped fresh ginger root
1 tablespoon ground coriander
½ teaspoon turmeric
¼ teaspoon fennel seeds, crushed

½ teaspoon red pepper, or to taste
1½ teaspoons paprika
1½ cups chopped fresh ripe tomatoes (or substitute 1 cup drained canned tomatoes, chopped)
1½ teaspoons Kosher salt
1½ pounds cooked lobster meat, diced into large pieces
¼ cup heavy cream
2 tablespoons finely chopped fresh coriander leaves

1. Heat the oil in a large shallow pan, preferably one with a non-stick surface, over high heat. When the oil is very hot, add the onion shreds, and fry, stirring them until they turn dark brown (about 9 minutes). Take them out with a slotted spoon and spread on paper towels to drain.

(continued)

2. Add the 1½ cups chopped onions to the same oil, and fry them until they turn caramel brown (about 15 minutes), stirring constantly. (See directions for Brown-frying Onions, p. 71.) Add garlic and ginger, and fry for an additional 2 minutes. Reduce heat to medium, and add coriander, turmeric, fennel, red pepper, and paprika. Stir rapidly for 5 seconds, and then add tomatoes. Cook the mixture, uncovered, until it reduces to a thick pulpy sauce and the oil begins to separate from it (about 4 minutes). Add 2 cups boiling water and salt. Reduce heat and simmer, covered, for 15 minutes or until the water evaporates and the sauce reduces to a thick gravy. If the sauce looks thin and runny, increase heat and boil rapidly, uncovered, until it reduces to the desired consistency. (The sauce may be prepared several hours ahead and kept, covered, at room temperature, or refrigerated for up to 4 days, or frozen. Defrost thoroughly and reheat before proceeding with the recipe.)

3. Add lobster meat, and simmer until heated through. Stir in cream and chopped coriander leaves. Check for salt, and transfer to a serving platter. Serve garnished with fried onion shreds and, if desired, more chopped coriander leaves.

Follow the menu suggestions given for Shrimp Laced with Mild Spices (page 240).

Panfried Fillet of Sole Laced with Carom

(Bhoni Machi)

Breading fish fillets and shallow-frying them is a relatively new technique in Indian cooking. Since it is Western, it is more popular with urban Indians and in better-quality restaurants.

The fish fillets are first marinated in lemon juice, which has an effect not unlike pickling. Consequently, when they are fried they cook in no time at all; they also stay creamy and tender, insulated by the crisp cooking. The delicate fragrance of the fried fish is lent by the garlic and carom seeds in the lemon juice marinade. The taste of this marinade is so wonderful, I have often simply broiled the marinated fish and served it.

Fish, as we all know, takes only a few minutes to cook. Therefore, take care while frying not to overcook it. If it isn't cooked just right, it will taste dry and chewy. To test for doneness, pierce a fillet at one end. The knife should go in without any resistance, like cutting softened butter.

For 6 persons

6 whole skinless, boneless sole
    fillets, weighing about 6–8
    ounces each

FOR MARINADE:

1 teaspoon Kosher salt
2 tablespoons lemon juice
1 tablespoon minced garlic

½ teaspoon carom seeds,
    crushed

FOR SPICY CRUMB COATING:

¼ cup all-purpose flour
2 large eggs
2½ cups bread crumbs
½ teaspoon Kosher salt
½ teaspoon black pepper

Peanut or corn oil enough
    to fill a frying pan to a
    depth of ¾ inch.

1. Rinse fish fillets in cold water, and pat them dry on paper towels.

2. Put the fish in a large shallow bowl. Add all the ingredients for the marinade, and rub it over the fillets, turning and tossing them. Cover and marinate in the refrigerator for 24 hours (the fish may be in the marinade for up to 48 hours).

3. When ready to serve the fillets, place three shallow bowls on the work board. Add flour to one bowl, beat the 2 eggs slightly in the second, and into the third bowl put the bread crumbs, salt, and pepper, and mix well.

(continued)

4. Take the fish fillets from the refrigerator. One at a time, roll fillets in the flour, then in the beaten egg, and finally in breadcrumbs (make sure the fillets are thoroughly breaded), and place them on waxed paper. Continue till all fillets are coated.

5. Heat the oil in a frying pan until very hot (350°–375°F), and slip 2–3 fillets in the oil. (Do not overcrowd the pan, or the oil will cool causing the fillets to brown unevenly.) Fry the fillets on one side for 3 minutes, then carefully flip them over with a wide spatula, and continue frying until they are light golden on both sides. Drain them briefly on paper towels, and place them on a serving dish in a preheated 275°F oven to keep warm while you cook the remaining fillets. Serve hot.

Serve this elegant and delicious fish with just a Sweet Tomato Relish (p. 440) and a glass of chilled white wine to make a perfect light meal or the first course of a more elaborate meal. For a vegetable, you may serve Potatoes Smothered with Shallots (p. 317). Or omit the vegetable and serve a vegetable rice dish, such as Indian Fried Rice (p. 363), Royal Vegetable and Rice Casserole (p. 381), or Vegetable and Rice Casserole with Herbs (p. 379). To start with, serve Indian Fenugreek Crackers (p. 133), or wafers (p. 423 to 428) if you are planning a light meal. Or for more elaborate dining, try Cold Minted Potatoes (p. 103), provided you are not serving potatoes for the vegetable side dish, or Kabob Patties Laced with Ginger and Mint (p. 109). Mango Fool (p. 471) and Mangoes with Cream (p. 470) are good choices for dessert.

Chick-pea Batter Fish

(Tali Machi)

Tali means deep-fried. In this dish the fish filets are coated with a spicy batter and deep-fried. They come out golden and spongy and delicious. The unique flavor comes from a batter made with chick-pea flour and cumin. The same fish, cut into thin strips and fried in the same batter, is called a fish fritter and is popular as an appetizer or a snack.

Note: For a crispier coating, eliminate the baking powder from the batter. For variation in the flavor, substitute ⅓ teaspoon carom seeds for the cumin.

The batter left over after coating the fish fillets may be used to make vegetable fritters, especially potato and onion fritters. Simply dip thin slices of onion and potato in the batter, and deep fry. They are excellent with the fried fish.

For 6 persons

FOR THE BATTER:

1½ cups unsifted chick-pea flour
  (*besan*)
2 teaspoons garlic, ground to
  a paste
2 tablespoons light vegetable oil
1¼ cups warm water (90°–100°F)
2 teaspoons ground cumin
½ teaspoon black pepper
½ teaspoon turmeric
¾ teaspoon baking powder
  (optional)

1½ teaspoons Kosher salt
6 whole skinless, boneless sole
  fillets, or any other non-
  oily, firm-fleshed fish
  fillets, weighing about
  6–8 ounces each
Peanut or corn oil enough to
  fill a *kadhai*, French fryer,
  or deep saucepan to a
  depth of 3 inches.

1. Put all the ingredients for the batter in a bowl, and beat with a beater, wire whisk, or fork until thoroughly blended and free of

lumps. (Alternatively, the batter may be mixed in an electric blend-er or food processor.) Cover, and let the batter rest for ½ hour.

2. Rinse the fillets under running cold water, and pat them dry with paper towels. Cut each fillet in half lengthwise along the central line.

3. When ready to fry the fish, heat the oil in a *kadhai*, French fryer, or any deep saucepan until very hot (375°F). Dip a fillet into the batter to coat it. Hold the fillet briefly over the bowl to let excess batter drip off, and then drop it into the hot oil. Fry only 3–4 fillets at a time, so that there is ample room for them to float easily in the oil. Fry the fillets for 3 minutes. Then flip them over with a slotted spoon, and continue frying until they are light golden on both sides. Drain the fillets on paper towels, put them on a serving dish, and keep them warm in a preheated 275°F oven. Serve hot, accompanied by Sweet Tomato Relish (*Tamatar Chutney*, p. 440), or Fresh Mint Relish (*Podina Chutney*, p. 436).

This lovely fried fish needs no further accompaniment than a glass of chilled Chablis to make a light meal. If you're really hungry, serve a pilaf—a simple one such as Patiala Pilaf (p. 366) for a mellow blending of fragrances, or for a balanced contrast, Sweet Saffron Pilaf (p. 369). Serve a *dal* such as Spice- and Herb-Laced Split Peas (p. 330) for a side dish. Indian Cheese Fritters (p. 117) or Spinach and Mung Bean Dumplings (p. 120) are good choices for appetizers.

Fish in Velvet Yogurt Sauce

(Dahi Machi)

This Bengali preparation of fish fillets poached in a mild onion-rich yogurt sauce is eaten every day by the local people.

Note: There is only one thing to keep in mind when making this dish: do not overcook the fillets. Not only will they become chewy, but they will also flake and scatter into the delicate sauce, changing its texture. The cooked fillets are extremely fragile and will flake at the slightest touch. Handle them gently. (Many cooks use unboned fish to make cooking easier. I don't like to use unboned fish in any gravy-based dish, because it is so complicated and messy to eat— you have to concentrate on the bones instead of on the food and its lovely flavor.)

For 4 persons

1 pound skinless, boneless haddock fillets	¾ teaspoon Kosher salt
8 tablespoons light vegetable oil	Small pinch each ground cinnamon and clove
¼ cup all-purpose flour	¾ cup plain yogurt
2 cups finely chopped onions	2 tablespoons finely chopped fresh coriander leaves
1½ tablespoons finely chopped fresh ginger root	2–4 green chilies, seeded and minced
⅛ teaspoon turmeric	

1. Rinse the fillets in cold water, pat dry with paper towels, and cut them neatly into 1-inch by 2-inch pieces. Set aside.

2. Heat 3 or 4 tablespoons of the oil in a large shallow non-stick pan over medium-high heat. Dust the fish fillets lightly with flour, and add them to the pan in one layer. (Add no more pieces than may be accommodated comfortably without overlapping.) Fry until they are lightly browned (about 1 minute). Flip them with a

spatula, and continue frying for another ½ minute or until they are seared on both sides. As each batch is seared, remove the pieces to a platter, and continue with the remainder the same way, adding more oil to the pan as necessary. Set aside.

3. Add the remaining oil to the pan along with the onions. Fry the onions until they turn butterscotch brown (about 15 minutes), stirring constantly so they do not burn. Add ginger, and continue frying for an additional minute. Add turmeric, salt, cinnamon, and clove, stir rapidly for 15 seconds, and add yogurt. Turn off heat.

4. Pour the onion mixture into the container of an electric blender or food processor, and blend until finely pureed to a smooth sauce. Return sauce to the pan. Over low heat, simmer gently until hot and bubbling. Slip the fried pieces of fish carefully into the sauce, along with any oil and juices that may have collected in the platter. Make sure the fish pieces are evenly distributed in the sauce. Simmer covered, until the fish is cooked through (not more than 3–4 minutes). Do not overcook the fish, or it will become chewy and tasteless. Check for salt, and serve sprinkled with chopped coriander and chopped green chilies.

To enjoy the mellow flavor of this dish to the fullest, serve a plain cooked rice (p. 357). Green Beans with Coconut and Black Mustard Seeds (p. 307), Cauliflower and Scallions with Black Mustard Seeds (p. 301), or Spicy Baby Eggplant (p. 303) are all fine vegetable choices. For accompaniments, serve Lentil Wafers (p. 425) and Hot Lemon Pickle (p. 449). Contrast this subtly flavored meal with a spicy appetizer. Good choices are Onion Fritters (p. 113), Fragrant Stuffed Tomatoes (p. 106), or Cold Potato Appetizer (p. 105).

Vegetables, Cheese, and Legumes

(Sabzi, Paneer, aur Dal)

VEGETABLES *(Sabzi)* and **CHEESE** *(Paneer)*

Cauliflower, Green Peas, and Potatoes in Spicy Herb Sauce *(Gobhi Matar Rasedar)*
Whole Potatoes in Spicy Yogurt Gravy *(Dum Aloo)*
Potatoes in Fragrant Gravy *(Tari Aloo)*
Spicy Potato-Stuffed Cabbage Rolls with Ginger Lemon Sauce *(Aloo Bhare Bandh Gobhi)*
Round Gourd in Fragrant Gravy *(Tari-wale Tinde)*
Green Peas and Indian Cheese in Fragrant Tomato Sauce *(Matar Paneer)*
Royal Braised Vegetables in Cardamom Nut Sauce *(Shahi Sabz Korma)*

LEGUMES *(Dal)*

Chick-peas in Tangy Tamarind Sauce *(Khatte Channe)*
Chick-peas in Ginger Sauce *(Safaid Channe)*
Spicy Brussels Sprouts, Green Beans, and Lentil Stew *(Chaunk Gobhi aur Sem Sambaar)*
Mung Bean and Cauliflower Stew *(Gobhi Moong)*
Mixed Lentils and Vegetable Stew *(Gujrati Dal)*
Dumplings in Fragrant Herb Gravy *(Mungaude ki Bhaji)*
Chick-pea Dumplings in Yogurt Sauce *(Kadhi)*
Buttered Black Beans *(Kali Dal)* See p. 337

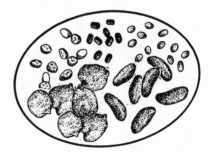

VEGETABLES AND CHEESE

(Sabzi aur Paneer)

Cauliflower, Green Peas, and Potatoes in Spicy Herb Sauce

(Gobhi Matar Rasedar)

This dish, with its bright contrasting colors and lovely bouquet of fresh herbs, is a spectacular entree. For the cauliflower, peas, and potatoes, you may substitute green peppers, green beans, zucchini, and/or mushrooms. The consistency of the dish should be like thin vegetable soup, with the vegetables cooked until soft. Stir carefully so that fragile pieces of cauliflower and potato do not break.

Note: A specialty of the Brahmins of Kanuj, a city in the state of Uttar Pradesh, this preparation is a typical example of their onion- and garlic-free cooking. It is traditionally served at wedding banquets accompanied by special stuffed bread, *kachauri* (p. 416).

For 6–8 persons

1 small head cauliflower (about 1–1¼ pounds)

2 medium-sized potatoes (about ½ pound)

½ cup *usli ghee* (p. 50), or light vegetable oil

2 teaspoons cumin seeds

1 teaspoon ground cumin

2 tablespoons ground coriander

1 teaspoon turmeric

½–1 teaspoon red pepper

1½ cups shelled fresh green peas, or 1 ten-ounce package frozen peas, defrosted

1½ cups pureed or finely chopped fresh ripe tomatoes, or ¾ cup canned tomato puree

4 teaspoons Kosher salt

3 tablespoons finely chopped fresh coriander leaves (or substitute 1½ tablespoons dry coriander leaves)

1. Wash cauliflower in running cold water. Break or cut it into about 1½–inch flowerets. Peel the central stem, and cut into ¼-inch thin slices.

2. Peel the potatoes, and cut each into 6 pieces.

3. Measure out all spices and place them, and all the vegetables, right next to the stove.

4. Heat the *ghee* over medium-high heat in a deep heavy-bottomed pan. When the fat is hot, add cumin seeds, and fry until they turn dark brown (about 20 seconds). Add cumin powder, coriander, turmeric, and red pepper, all at once, stir for a moment, and immediately add cauliflower, potatoes, and fresh green peas (if you are using frozen peas, do not add them yet). Fry, stirring constantly, until the vegetables begin to sear a bit (about 5 minutes). Add tomato puree, and continue frying until the puree thickens and the fat begins to separate from the sauce (about 3 minutes). Add 3 cups boiling water along with the salt. Reduce heat and simmer the vegetables, covered, until they are tender and cooked through (about 15 minutes). If you are using frozen peas, add them now, and continue cooking for an additional 5 minutes. Turn off heat. Check for salt, and serve sprinkled with chopped coriander leaves.

Note: This dish must be served in small bowls, such as *katoori*, since its consistency is much like a minestrone with the vegetables cut into large chunks. Traditionally, a little vegetable shortening or *ghee* (about 2–3 tablespoons) is poured over the dish before sprinkling coriander leaves. This, in addition to enhancing and enriching the flavors, makes the dish taste mellow and subtle. It may be prepared ahead and refrigerated for up to 4 days. It also freezes well. Defrost thoroughly before reheating. To reheat, gently simmer over low heat until it comes to a boil. Taste, and if necessary add salt. To perk up flavors, add a little ground roasted cumin seed and chopped coriander leaves before serving.

Traditionally, this dish should be accompanied by Deep-fried Bread with Spicy Stuffing (p. 416), but Baked Whole Wheat Puffy Bread (p. 397) and Deep-fried Puffy Bread (p. 413) are equally good. For a side dish, good choices are Spice- and Herb-Laced Split Peas (p. 330) or Mung Beans Laced with Black Mustard Seeds (p. 333), or try a cool yogurt salad, such as Spinach and Yogurt Salad (p. 344) or Sweet Banana and Yogurt Salad (p. 349). A vegetarian meal should traditionally be accompanied by relishes and pickles. Fresh Mint Relish (p. 436) and Sweet Lemon Pickle with Cumin (p. 447) are good choices. Precede the meal with Spinach and Mung Bean Dumplings (p. 120), Cold Potato Appetizer (p. 105), or Indian Cheese Fritters (p. 117), if you want to keep the entire meal vegetarian. Otherwise, serve Kabob Patties Laced with Ginger and Mint (p. 109) or Shrimp Fritters (p. 118).

Whole Potatoes in Spicy Yogurt Gravy

(Dum Aloo)

Indians love potatoes, not because they are inexpensive and available year-round, but because they have a mellow, almost neutral taste that allows them to absorb deeply the flavors of spices. Here, whole potatoes are first peeled and pricked (so that the seasonings will penetrate fully), sautéed, and then simmered in spice-laced yogurt sauce. *Dum Aloo*, a popular dish throughout North India, is cooked by the *dum* process (see page 76).

These potatoes are so good that I always make a few extra and set them aside to be served in place of hashbrowns for breakfast.

For 6–8 persons

12 even-sized small boiling potatoes, such as red wax potatoes (about 2 pounds altogether)

7 tablespoons Indian vegetable shortening, or light vegetable oil

1½ cups finely chopped onions

1 tablespoon finely chopped fresh ginger root

2 teaspoons ground cumin

4 teaspoons ground coriander

1 teaspoon turmeric

½–1 teaspoon red pepper

1 teaspoon *Mughal garam masala* (p. 37)

2 cups chopped or pureed fresh tomatoes, or 1 cup canned tomato sauce

⅔ cup plain yogurt

4 teaspoons Kosher salt

⅔ cup heavy heavy cream

1. Peel potatoes, and prick them with a thin skewer or knife in 4 or 5 places. Put them in a bowl of cold water until you are ready to cook them.

2. Heat 5 tablespoons of the shortening in a large non-stick pan that can hold all the potatoes in one layer (such as a 5-quart casserole) over medium-high heat. When the shortening is very hot, drain the potatoes, pat them dry on paper towels, and add. Fry them until they acquire several tiny browned spots and a crust (about 8–10 minutes), turning and tossing them to ensure even browning. (This is an essential step, as the browning prevents the potatoes' falling apart during prolonged cooking.) With a slotted spoon, transfer them to a bowl.

3. Add the rest of the shortening to the pan along with the onions. Fry until the onions turn caramel brown (about 15 minutes), stirring constantly so that they do not burn. Add ginger, and fry for an additional ½ minute. Add cumin, coriander, turmeric, red pepper, and *Mughal garam masala* all at once, and stir rapidly for 15 seconds. Add tomatoes, yogurt, salt, and the fried potatoes (in one layer), and bring to a boil. Reduce heat and simmer very gently, covered, for 35 minutes or until the potatoes are fully cooked.

(continued)

Check during cooking to make sure the gravy is not sticking and burning. The gravy should be thick enough to coat the potatoes. If it looks thin and runny, increase heat and boil rapidly, uncovered, until it reduces to the desired consistency. If, on the other hand, the gravy is too thick, add a few tablespoons of water.

4. Add cream, stir, and simmer until heated through. If you want the dish to taste milder and subtler, stir in a little more shortening or oil (about 2 tablespoons). Check for salt, and serve.

Note: This dish improves with keeping. For best results make it at least a few hours before you are going to serve it. It can be refrigerated for up to 4 days without loss of flavor.

This dish is traditionally served with either staple. I prefer a rice pilaf, such as Fragrant Pilaf Banaras Style (p. 368) or Emperor's Pilaf with Black Mushrooms (p. 375). A flavorful *dal* on the side is a good idea. Lentils with Garlic Butter (p. 332) and Mung Beans Laced with Black Mustard Seed (p. 333) are both good choices. If you want to serve a vegetable instead, try Buttered Smothered Cabbage (p. 298) or Stir-fried Okra (p. 309).

Potatoes in Fragrant Gravy

(Tari Aloo)

You don't have to be a vegetarian to like this spicy golden yellow dish. Like most southern Indian dishes, this one begins with sizzling black mustard seeds. But perhaps because it is such a simple entree, it has become known in all of India. Note here that the onions are used as a vegetable rather than as a seasoning. Traditionally it is served with *poori* for a Sunday brunch, accompanied by tea in North India and coffee in the South, but it is perfectly suitable as a light luncheon entree. The lack of garlic makes this dish a truly Indian vegetarian dish.

For 8 persons

½ cup light vegetable oil

1 teaspoon black mustard
  seeds

2 teaspoons yellow split peas
  (channa dal) (optional)

2 tablespoons fresh ginger
  root, chopped into tiny
  cubes

1–2 green chilies, seeded and
  sliced, or ¼ to ½ teaspoon
  red pepper

1 tablespoon ground coriander

1 teaspoon turmeric

½ teaspoon paprika

6 medium-sized potatoes
  (about 1½ pounds)

4 medium-sized onions (about
  1 pound), roughly
  chopped

3½ teaspoons Kosher salt

2 teaspoons lemon juice

3–4 tablespoons chopped fresh
  coriander leaves (or
  substitute 2 tablespoons
  dry coriander leaves)

1. Boil potatoes in their jackets, in water to cover, until fully cooked (a skewer or cake tester will pierce right through the potato without resistance). Drain, plunge them in cold water, peel, and cut into roughly ½-inch pieces.

2. Measure out all the spices and place them and the prepared vegetables right next to the stove.

3. Heat the oil over high heat in a deep saucepan. When the oil is very hot, carefully add the mustard seeds. Keep a saucepan lid or spatter screen handy, since the seeds may splatter and sputter when added.

4. When the mustard seeds start to turn gray and the spluttering begins to subside, add yellow split peas, if you are using them. Fry until the peas turn light brown (about ½ to 1 minute), stirring constantly to ensure even browning, and lifting the pan away from the heat if it is too hot.

5. Reduce heat to medium, add ginger and chilies, and cook for 2 minutes or until they begin to brown (if you are using red pepper, add it with the dry spices). Add coriander powder, turmeric, and paprika, stir for a moment, and add potatoes and

onions. Sauté the vegetables for 10 minutes or until they are lightly browned, stirring frequently.

6. Add 4 cups hot water along with the salt, and bring to a boil. Reduce heat and simmer, covered, for 15 minutes or until the potatoes are very tender. With the back of the spoon, mash a few pieces of potato; this will thicken the gravy to a nice consistency. Serve piping hot in individual bowls (*katoori*) or a tureen, sprinkled with the lemon juice, chopped coriander, and if desired, a little paprika or red pepper.

Note: This dish may be prepared ahead and kept refrigerated for up to 2 days, or frozen. Defrost thoroughly before reheating. The potatoes in *Tari Aloo* are usually very soft and broken up, and the gravy is more like a broth used for dipping bread. The dish thickens with keeping, as the starch from the mashed pieces of potato mixes with the gravy. If the gravy thickens too much, simply add a little water to thin it. To reheat, simmer gently over low heat until warmed through. Check again for salt and, if desired, sprinkle on a few more chopped coriander leaves and a little red pepper before serving.

Serve *Tari Aloo* with Deep-fried Puffy Bread (p. 413) or Whole Wheat Flaky Bread (p. 402). The classic combination of this dish with bread is called *Aloo-Poori*. It could be served for a Sunday brunch, accompanied by a flavorful tea such as Spiced Tea (p. 486), or Cardamom Tea (p. 487). Also, Sweet Lemon Pickle with Cumin (p. 447) goes beautifully with this perfect meal. Precede the brunch, if you want, with a cool glass of yogurt drink such as *Mattha* or *Lassi* (p. 488 and 489).

Spicy Potato-Stuffed Cabbage Rolls with Ginger Lemon Sauce

(Aloo Bhare Bandh Gobhi)

These cabbage rolls are the vegetarian version of Meat-Stuffed Cabbage Rolls with Ginger Lemon Sauce. A specialty of Uttar Pradesh, they can have a variety of stuffings ranging from mixed vegetables to *paneer* or mashed cooked lentils. The potato-stuffed version is by far the most popular. Since potatoes absorb spices, they have a mellowing effect on flavorings. Therefore additional spices and herbs are added to perk up the flavors.

For 4–6 persons

1 small cabbage (about 1¾–2 pounds)
3 tablespoons light vegetable oil
1½ cups thinly sliced onions
1¼ cups chopped fresh ripe tomatoes, or 1 cup canned tomatoes with their juices, chopped
1 tablespoon shredded fresh ginger root
1 lemon, peeled, seeded, and thinly sliced

2½ teaspoons Kosher salt
¼ teaspoon black pepper
1 recipe Spicy Potato Filling from Savory Pastries with Spicy Potato Filling (*Aloo Samosa*, p. 125)
2 tablespoons chopped fresh coriander leaves
2 green chilies, seeded and sliced
½ teaspoon paprika

To make Spicy Potato-Stuffed Cabbage Rolls with Ginger Lemon Sauce, follow the directions given for Meat-Stuffed Cabbage Rolls with Ginger Lemon Sauce (*Keema Bhare Bandh Gobhi*, p. 194) substituting potato filling for meat filling. Also, before serving, sprinkle with chopped coriander leaves, green chilies, and paprika.

(continued)

When serving the cabbage rolls, follow the menu suggestions given for Meat-Stuffed Cabbage Rolls with Ginger Lemon Sauce on page 194. Any additional dishes containing potatoes should be avoided if possible.

Round Gourd in Fragrant Gravy

(Tari-wale Tinde)

Tinda belongs to the gourd or melon family, which includes such vegetables as ivy gourd (known popularly as pumpkin), ash gourd (known as Chinese winter melon), and squash gourd (known simply as squash). *Tinda* is a small round light-green vegetable, about one to two inches in diameter, resembling a green tomato from the outside. Its texture inside is like zucchini, but firmer. The tender young *tindas*, like tender cucumbers or zucchini, have practically no seeds, whereas the larger, more mature ones do. Both are edible.

In India, *tinda* is considered a delicacy and cooked in many wonderful ways—stir-fried with spices, stuffed and baked, or cooked in spicy gravy. The recipe here has a spicy gravy, and is a specialty of Uttar Pradesh.

Fresh *tinda* is not yet available in the United States, so the recipe here is perforce for the canned variety. When you buy it, you'll have a chance to see all the exotic Indian vegetables available in cans.

For 6 persons

2 14½-ounce cans round gourd
   (Tinda)
6 tablespoons *usli ghee,* (p. 50)
   or light vegetable oil
¾ teaspoon cumin seeds
½ cup thinly sliced onions
1½ teaspoons ground cumin
2 teaspoons ground coriander

¼ teaspoon turmeric
¼ teaspoon red pepper, or to
   taste
⅓ cup canned tomato puree, or
   ½ cup chopped or pureed
   fresh tomatoes
2 teaspoons Kosher salt
2 tablespoons minced fresh
   coriander leaves

1. Drain the *tinda* pieces, pressing them gently to squeeze out excess water. (Do not press them too hard, or they will break.) Cut large pieces in half, so that all the pieces are of approximately the same size.

2. Heat the *ghee* in a deep heavy-bottomed pan over medium-high heat. When the *ghee* is very hot, add the cumin seeds. When the cumin turns dark (about 20 seconds), add onions, and fry until they turn dark brown (about 4 minutes), stirring constantly to prevent burning. Add ground cumin, coriander, turmeric, and red pepper. Stir rapidly for 5 seconds, and add tomato puree. Cook the puree until it thickens and the fat begins to separate from it (about 3 minutes).

3. Add 2½ cups boiling water and salt. Reduce heat and simmer the sauce, covered, for 10 minutes. Add drained *tinda* pieces, and continue simmering for an additional 5 minutes. Turn off heat. To make the dish taste mellow and more flavorful, stir in a couple of tablespoons of *ghee* or oil. Check for salt, and serve sprinkled with minced coriander leaves. *Tari-wale Tinde* has the consistency of a clear vegetable soup, so it is essential that it be served in small individual bowls (*katoori*).

Note: This dish may be made ahead and refrigerated for up to 4 days. Fold in a few fresh chopped coriander leaves before serving.

(continued)

This simple and light dish should be served with a bread, such as Whole Wheat Puffy Bread (p. 397) or Baked Whole Wheat Bread (p. 393), or a simple plain pilaf. A serving of *dal*, such as Buttered Black Beans (p. 337), or Spice- and Herb-Laced Split Peas (p. 330) is a good side dish. For an additional side dish, serve a yogurt salad, either Dumplings in Fragrant Yogurt (p. 348) or Spinach and Yogurt Salad (p. 344). Relishes go very nicely with this meal. I like Onion Vegetable Relish (p. 432) or Raw Onion Relish (p. 431), and Mint Coriander Dip (p. 437) or Sour Mango Relish (p. 439).

Green Peas and Indian Cheese in Fragrant Tomato Sauce

(Matar Paneer)

Indian cheese, known as *paneer* or *chenna*, is a delicacy that all Indians—particularly northerners—love. Its use in the preparation of savory dishes is limited, but the few dishes created with it are absolute masterpieces. The most popular, without doubt, is *Matar Paneer*—moist pieces of sautéed cheese with sweet green peas wrapped in a luscious red sauce bursting with the fragrance of spices and fresh coriander leaves. *Matar Paneer*, a classic North Indian dish, is popular with vegetarians and nonvegetarians alike.

The flavor and texture of the *paneer* are of prime importance here. The cheese should be sweet and fresh-smelling; it should feel firm to the touch but not hard; it should be moist but not wet; and finally, its texture should be close and compact, not porous. (If the *paneer* is dry and too solid, the cheese pieces will taste hard and rubbery, and the sauce will not penetrate the *paneer*, leaving it with a bland taste. If the *paneer* is too wet and loose-textured, it will not hold its shape, but will fall apart while it is being fried, disintegrating into the oil.)

For 6 persons

Indian Cheese *(paneer)*
made with 8 cups milk
(p. 52) and cut into
½ by ½ by 1½-inch pieces
12 tablespoons *usli ghee*
(p. 50), or Indian
vegetable shortening, or
light vegetable oil
2 cups finely chopped onions
1 teaspoon finely chopped
garlic
2 tablespoons finely chopped
fresh ginger root
2 teaspoons ground
coriander
1 teaspoon turmeric
¼–½ teaspoon each red and
black pepper

1 teaspoon paprika
2 cups finely chopped or
pureed fresh ripe
tomatoes, or 1½ cups
canned tomatoes with
their juice, chopped
1½ cups shelled fresh green
peas, or 1 ten-ounce
package frozen peas,
defrosted
2 teaspoons Kosher salt
2 teaspoons *garam masala*
(p. 38)
4 tablespoons finely chopped
fresh coriander leaves (or
substitute 2 tablespoons
dry coriander leaves)

1. Spread the *paneer* pieces on a piece of waxed paper and leave them to dry slightly for ½ hour.

2. Heat 3 tablespoons of the *ghee* over medium heat in a large heavy-bottomed pan, preferably one with a non-stick interior. When the *ghee* is hot, add cheese pieces. Keep a saucepan lid or spatter screen handy, since the moisture from the cheese may be released explosively, causing tiny particles of cheese to fly all over. Dusting the *paneer* pieces with a little flour prevents splattering. Fry the cheese, turning and tossing often to prevent sticking and burning, until lightly seared (about 5 minutes). Transfer the pieces to a bowl. (The *paneer* should be fried in batches so that there is ample room in the pan for turning them without fear of their breaking.)

3. Add the remaining *ghee* to the pan, and increase the heat to high. Add onions, and fry until they turn light brown (about 5 minutes), stirring constantly so that they do not burn. Add garlic and ginger, and fry for an additional 2 minutes. Add coriander,

turmeric, red and black pepper, and paprika, all at once. Stir rapidly for a moment, and immediately add tomatoes. Cook until the mixture thickens to a pulpy sauce and the fat begins to separate (about 10 minutes), stirring often.

4. Add 2½ cups hot water, and bring the sauce to a boil. Reduce heat to medium, and cook the sauce, covered, for 20 minutes. Cool the sauce briefly. Then puree it in an electric blender or food processor, leaving the sauce a little coarse so that it has a certain texture.

5. Return the sauce to the pan. Add peas, salt, and the fried cheese, along with ½ cup hot water, and bring the sauce to a boil. Reduce heat to medium and simmer, covered, until the peas are cooked through (about 15 minutes for fresh peas and 5 for frozen). Turn off heat and let the dish rest, covered, for an hour before serving. When ready to serve, heat thoroughly. Fold in *garam masala* and chopped coriander leaves. Check for salt, and serve.

Note: This dish tastes best if made a couple of hours before serving. The resting allows the flavors of the different ingredients to blend and mellow. It may be refrigerated for up to 3 days without loss of flavor. To reheat, gently simmer over low heat until warmed through.

Serve this beautifully colored and exquisitely flavored dish with a fragrant pilaf such as Patiala Pilaf (p. 366), Fragrant Pilaf Banaras Style (p. 368), or Emperor's Pilaf with Black Mushrooms (p. 375). It goes beautifully with all plain baked or fried breads. For a side dish, serve Smoked Eggplant with Fresh Herbs (p. 305), Stuffed Okra with Fragrant Spices (p. 311), or Spicy Baby Eggplant (p. 303). To add to the meal, include a *dal* such as Lucknow Sour Lentils (p. 335) or Lentils with Garlic Butter (p. 332), or a cool *raita* such as Cucumber and Yogurt Salad (p. 343) or Dumplings in Fragrant Yogurt (p. 348). There is no need for any accompaniments, but Lentil Wafers (p. 425), and Sweet Lemon Pickle with Cumin (p. 447) go well. Precede the meal with a mild appetizer, such as Spinach and Mung Bean Dumplings (p. 120), Silky Bean Dumplings (p. 123), or Cold Minted Potatoes (p. 103), for a complete vegetarian meal. For a nonvegetarian appetizer, serve Shrimp Fritters (p. 118) or Savory Meat Pastries (p. 130).

Royal Braised Vegetables in Cardamom Nut Sauce

(Shahi Sabz Korma)

This ivory-white dish with its shimmering glaze is indeed, as the name suggests, a royal entree. The vegetables are carefully chosen so that they will go perfectly with the flavorings. Except for carrots, only light-colored vegetables are chosen, to blend harmoniously with the almond-yogurt sauce. The vegetables are carefully cut to a uniform size to make them look attractive. If you are running short of time, you may substitute for the *paneer* 1 additional medium-sized potato, cut like the others.

This *korma* is one of the most elegant vegetarian entrees you can serve. It can also be folded into plain cooked rice and transformed into another mouthwatering delicacy, Royal Vegetable and Rice Casserole (p. 381).

For 6–8 persons

2 medium-sized potatoes (about ½ pound altogether)

2 medium-sized turnips (about ½ pound altogether)

1 carrot, 6 inches long (about ¼ pound)

12 tablespoons Indian vegetable shortening or light vegetable oil

Indian Cheese (*paneer*) made with 4 cups of milk (p. 52), and cut into ¼ by ¼ by 1½-inch pieces

2 cups finely chopped onions

1 tablespoon finely chopped garlic

1½ tablespoons finely chopped fresh ginger root

2 green chilies, seeded and minced

12 green cardamom pods

1 stick cinnamon, 3 inches long

24 whole cloves

5 tablespoons ground blanched almonds

1 cup plain yogurt

¼ cup shelled fresh green peas, or frozen peas, defrosted

1 tablespoon Kosher salt

¼ cup heavy cream

(continued)

1. Peel potatoes, turnips, and carrot, and cut them into uniform ¼ by ¼ by 1½-inch pieces. Put them in a bowl of cold water to prevent discoloring, and set aside.

2. Heat 3 tablespoons of the shortening over medium heat in a large heavy-bottomed pan, preferably one with a non-stick interior. When the fat is hot, add the cheese pieces very carefully. Keep a saucepan lid or spatter screen handy, since the moisture in the cheese may be released and cause tiny particles of cheese to fly all over. Dusting the *paneer* pieces with a little flour will prevent splattering. Fry the cheese until lightly colored on both sides (about 5 minutes), turning and tossing often to prevent sticking and burning. Transfer the cheese to a bowl, and set aside.

3. Add the remaining shortening to the pan along with the onions, garlic, ginger, and chilies. Increase heat to high, and fry the seasonings until they turn light brown (about 10 minutes), stirring constantly to prevent uneven browning or burning. Add cardamom, cinnamon, and cloves, and continue frying for an additional 5 minutes. Add almond powder, stirring rapidly, and fry for 2 more minutes.

4. Add 2 tablespoons of the yogurt and fry the mixture. When the moisture from the yogurt evaporates, add 2 more tablespoons of yogurt. Continue adding yogurt and frying until the entire cup is used up (about 5 minutes). Stir constantly while frying, making sure that the sauce does not stick to the bottom of the pan and burn.

5. Drain and add the vegetables. Add the fresh green peas (if you are using frozen peas do not add them now), salt, and 1½ cups hot water to the sauce. Bring to a boil, reduce heat to medium-low, and cook the vegetables, covered, until tender but still firm (about 30 minutes). Add fried cheese pieces, heavy cream, and frozen peas (if you are using them). Cook, uncovered, for 10 minutes. The sauce should be thick in this *korma*. If the sauce is not thick enough, increase heat to medium and simmer until the sauce thickens to the desired consistency. If, on the other hand, the sauce is too thick, add a few tablespoons of milk or water. Check for salt, and serve.

Note: This dish definitely tastes better if prepared a day ahead, refrigerated, and reheated before serving. It keeps in the refrigerator for up to 3 days. It also freezes well. Defrost thoroughly before reheating. The freezing process sometimes produces a thick and grainy texture. If this happens, add enough milk or water to bind the sauce while it is simmering. Taste, and if necessary add salt. To perk up flavors add ½ teaspoon *Mughal garam masala*.

This gorgeous dish may be served with either bread or rice. Deep-fried Puffy Bread (p. 413), Whole Wheat Flaky Bread (p. 402), Sweet Saffron Pilaf (p. 369), Fragrant Pilaf Banaras Style (p. 368), or Saffron Pilaf with Peaches (p. 371) are all good choices. A side dish of Buttered Black Beans (p. 337) goes perfectly with this meal. Fresh Mint Relish (p. 436), Hot Hyderabad Tomato Relish (p. 441), and Onion Relish (p. 431) all go well. Sweet Lemon Pickle with Cumin (p. 447) is nice if you want to add a pickle. Precede the meal with spicy fritters such as Cauliflower Fritters (p. 115) or Onion Fritters (p. 113), or serve Fragrant Stuffed Tomatoes (p. 106). Mulligatawny Soup (p. 143) also makes a lovely first course.

LEGUMES

(Dal)

Chick-peas in Tangy Tamarind Sauce

(Khatte Channe)

Channa, or chick-peas, can be a true delicacy, a gourmet's delight, if they are properly cooked and appropriately flavored. No one knows this art better than the people of Punjab, particularly the Sikhs, who cook them in unbelievably fabulous ways. The three most popular dishes are *Khatte Channe*, in which the peas are cooked in a tangy tamarind or pomegranate sauce; *Safaid Channe*, peas cooked in a light ginger sauce; and *Kale Channe*, peas cooked with *garam masala* and mango powder. Often, brown fried onions and coloring are added to darken the sauce.

The consistency of the dish ranges anywhere from that of a very thick pea soup to very dry. The following recipe produces a fairly thick souplike dish with the whole chick-peas intact. The tamarind gives it its characteristic tangy taste and brownish-black color, which is deepened by the addition of brown fried onions.

Khatte Channe, traditionally accompanied by a deep-fried bread, *Bhatoore*, makes a complete meal in itself. This classic combination, *Channe-Bhatoore*, is popular throughout India.

For 6–8 persons

2 twenty-ounce cans chick-peas, or 4 cups cooked chick-peas with 1 cup liquid
1 one-and-a-half-inch ball tamarind pulp
½ cup light vegetable oil
1½ cups thinly sliced onions
2 teaspoons minced garlic
½ teaspoon turmeric

½ teaspoon red pepper
1 cup fresh or canned chopped tomatoes
1 tablespoon grated fresh ginger root
1¼ teaspoons *garam masala* (p. 38)
1¼ teaspoons ground roasted cumin seeds (p. 66)

FOR GARNISH:

1 medium-sized onion, peeled and thinly sliced

1–2 green chilies, seeded and shredded

1. Drain chick-peas, reserving the liquid.

2. Put the tamarind pulp in a small bowl, add 1½ cups boiling water, and let soak for 15 minutes. Mash the pulp with the back of a spoon, or use your fingers. Strain the liquid into another small bowl, squeezing the pulp as much as possible, and set aside. Discard the fibrous residue.

3. Heat the oil in a large heavy-bottomed pan over medium-high heat. Add onions, and fry until they turn caramel brown

(about 20 minutes), stirring constantly so that they do not burn. (See directions for Brown-frying Onions p. 71.) Add garlic, and cook for an additional 2 minutes. Add turmeric and red pepper, stir rapidly for a moment, and add tomato puree along with ginger shreds. Reduce heat to medium, and cook until the fat begins to separate from the gravy (about 5 minutes).

4. Add tamarind juice and the reserved chick-pea liquid. Cover, and simmer the mixture over low heat for 15 minutes.

5. Add drained chick-peas, *garam masala*, and roasted cumin, and continue cooking for an additional 10 minutes. Check for salt, and transfer to a heated serving dish. Serve, garnished with sliced onions and shredded chilies.

Note: This dish may be prepared ahead and refrigerated for up to 3 days. It also freezes very well. Defrost thoroughly before reheating. To reheat, simmer over low heat until warmed through.

Although *Khatte Channe* is usually served with a *Bhatoora*, it is quite common to serve it with Deep-fried Puffy Bread (*Poori*, p. 413). *Bhatoora* and *Poori* are both deep-fried. The only difference is that *Bhatoora* is leavened and therefore richer. This combination is perfect for lunch. Generally, vegetables are not served with this meal. The meal may, however, include a yogurt salad: Cucumber and Yogurt Salad (p. 343), or Tomato and Yogurt Salad (p. 345), and is best accompanied by a cool yogurt drink (pp. 488 and 489), a fruit punch, or a fruity cocktail like Sangria. For dessert the best choices are Mangoes with Cream (p. 470) or Mango Fool (p. 471).

Chick-peas in Ginger Sauce

(Safaid Channe)

This chick-pea dish has a thinner, lighter, more fragrant sauce than the preceding *Khatte Channe*. It is also more mildly flavored, and so is perfect served as an entree for a Sunday brunch. *Safaid Channe* is traditionally served with *Poori* (p. 413) and plenty of tea.

For 6–8 persons

2 twenty-ounce cans chick-peas with their liquid, or 4 cups cooked chick-peas, with 1 cup liquid

¼ cup light vegetable oil

2 cups finely chopped onions

2 teaspoons finely chopped garlic

2 tablespoons finely shredded fresh ginger root

2 teaspoons ground coriander

⅓ teaspoon ground cardamom

½ teaspoon mango powder, or 1½ teaspoons lemon juice

¼ teaspoon each red and black pepper

1 medium-sized tomato, finely chopped (or ½ cup canned tomatoes, chopped)

1 teaspoon Kosher salt, or to taste

FOR GARNISH:

1 medium-sized onion, peeled and thinly sliced

1 green chili, shredded

1. Drain chick-peas, reserving the liquid.

2. Heat the oil in a large pan over medium-high heat. Add onions, and fry for about 5 minutes or until they turn light brown, stirring constantly to prevent burning.

3. Add garlic and ginger, reduce heat to medium, and fry for an additional 2 minutes. Add coriander powder, cardamom, mango powder and red and black pepper. Mix well, and fry for a moment or two. Add chopped tomatoes, and cook until the oil begins to separate from the tomato-spice mixture (about 6 minutes).

4. Add the reserved chick-pea liquid, the lemon juice if you are using it, salt, and ½ cup water. Cover and simmer over low heat for 10 minutes or until the mixture is reduced to a pulpy gravy. Add the drained chick-peas, and continue cooking, covered, for an additional 10 minutes. Turn off heat. Check for salt, and transfer to a serving bowl. Serve garnished with onion slices and shredded chilies.

Note: This dish may be made ahead and kept refrigerated for up to 3 days, or frozen. Defrost thoroughly before reheating. To reheat, simmer gently over low heat until warmed through. To perk up flavors, sprinkle with a little *garam masala* (p. 38), and serve.

Serve this dish for a lively Indian brunch accompanied by Deep-fried Puffy Bread (p. 413) or Whole Wheat Flaky Bread (p. 402). There is generally no vegetable served with this combination at brunch; however, serving a yogurt salad containing vegetables is not uncommon. Spinach and Yogurt Salad (p. 344) is a particularly good choice. Accompany this very wholesome and satisfying meal with a flavorful tea such as Spiced Tea (p. 486). You may also, if you like, precede the meal with a cool and refreshing yogurt drink (see recipes on p. 488 and 489), and conclude it with a simple dessert such as Mangoes with Cream (p. 470).

Spicy Brussels Sprouts, Green Beans, and Lentil Stew

(Chaunk Gobhi aur Sem Sambaar)

An interesting way of making a *dal* is to add many different vegetables and spices. Cooking them in combination gives the vegetables a chance to exchange flavors and enhance the savor of the dish. Mixed vegetable *dal* stews are common throughout India, but it is the people of the South who create the most intriguing flavors, most hypnotizing aromas, and the most popular *dal* stews in all of India. Of the many different varieties, the *sambaar*, or vegetable and yellow lentil stew, is the most widely eaten. *Sambaar* is usually made with a spice blend called *Sambaar podi* (powder). The dish is very spicy, but when mixed with its classic accompaniments, *ghee* and glazed rice, it mellows to become one of the most satisfying of all vegetarian dishes.

For 4–6 persons

1 cup yellow lentils *(toovar dal)* or yellow split peas (supermarket variety)	3 tablespoons light sesame oil or light vegetable oil
⅓ teaspoon turmeric	¾ teaspoon black mustard seeds
1 pound Brussels sprouts	¼ teaspoon fenugreek seeds
¼ pound fresh green beans, trimmed and cut into 1-inch pieces, or use ½ cup frozen cut green beans	2 teaspoons chopped garlic
	1 tablespoon *sambaar* powder (p. 38)
1 one-inch ball tamarind pulp (or substitute one large tomato + 1 teaspoon lemon juice)	2½ teaspoons Kosher salt
	6–8 kari leaves (fresh or dry), or 2 tablespoons chopped fresh coriander leaves

1. Pick over, clean, and wash lentils following directions for cleaning legumes on page 327.

2. Put the lentils in a deep 3-quart pot with turmeric and 4

cups cold water and bring to a boil. Reduce heat to medium-low and cook, partially covered, until the lentils are tender and cooked through (about 30 minutes). Add another ¾ cup water, and simmer, covered, over very low heat for an additional 30 minutes or until the lentils are very soft and reduced to a fine puree. Stir often during these 30 minutes to prevent burning. Turn off heat. Beat the puree vigorously, using a wire whisk or a spoon, for 1 minute and set aside.

3. While the lentils are cooking, wash the vegetables in cold water and pat dry on paper towels. Trim off the hard stem of each Brussels sprout, and using a sharp knife, slash the base, making a cross about ¼ inch deep (this will ensure even cooking of the Brussels sprouts).

4. Put tamarind pulp in a small bowl, add ½ cup boiling water, and let it soak for 15 minutes. Mash the pulp with the back of a spoon, or use your fingers. Strain the liquid into another small bowl, squeezing the pulp as much as possible, and set aside. Discard the fibrous residue. If you are using tomato instead, puree it with its skin or chop it finely, and stir in the lemon juice.

5. Place all the ingredients right next to the stove. Heat the oil over high heat in a deep saucepan. When the oil is very hot, carefully add the mustard seeds. Keep a pot lid or spatter screen handy, since the seeds may splatter and splutter when added. When the seeds turn gray (about 15 seconds), add fenugreek seeds. When the fenugreek seeds turn dark, add garlic, and *sambaar* powder. Stir for a moment, and add Brussels sprouts and beans. Fry the vegetables, turning and tossing them, for 2–3 minutes. Add tamarind juice (or tomato puree), salt, and ¼ cup of warm water. Reduce heat slightly, and cook the vegetables, covered, for 20 minutes or until they are partially cooked.

6. Add lentil puree, stir to mix, and continue cooking until the vegetables are tender and cooked through (about 10–15 minutes). Turn off heat and stir in kari leaves or chopped coriander leaves. Check for salt, and serve.

Note: This stew may be made ahead and refrigerated for a day. Reheat thoroughly before serving. (The keeping time depends upon the vegetables used in the stew. Some keep longer than others. For example, a stew made with potatoes, onions, and shallots will keep for up to 3 days whereas zucchini, Brussels sprouts, scallions, and cabbage are at their best for up to 24 hours after cooking.

This delicious stew is traditionally served with plain cooked rice (p. 357). Accompany it with ½ cup *usli ghee* (p. 50) on the side in a bowl, to be poured, about two or three teaspoons to each serving of *sambaar*, over either the *sambaar*, or the rice, or both. The contents are then mixed together before eating.

For a side dish, serve Cauliflower and Scallions with Black Mustard Seeds (p. 301), Green Beans with Coconut and Black Mustard Seeds (p. 307), or Glazed Beets with Black Mustard Seeds (p. 295). Since the *sambaar* is a fairly spicy dish, the meal is always accompanied with plain yogurt (about ½ cup per person) but I prefer to serve a yogurt salad, such as Tomato and Yogurt Salad (p. 345), or Okra and Yogurt Salad (p. 347), because they are more flavorful. The accompaniments to this meal may be wafers (especially *Puppadam*, p. 427), Shredded Carrot and Mustard Seed Relish (p. 435), and Hot Lemon Pickle (p. 449) or Quick Mango and Shredded Ginger Pickle (p. 450). Ideally, this meal should be preceded by Silky Bean Dumplings (p. 123), accompanied by Coconut Relish (p. 438), and concluded with Saffron Almond Pudding (p. 457) or Coconut Wedding Pudding (p. 459).

Mung Bean and Cauliflower Stew

(Gobhi Moong)

This dish is indeed for mung-bean lovers. The flavorings here are purposely kept subtle so that the delicate taste of the cauliflower and mung beans can be enjoyed to their fullest. In place of the cauliflower, other vegetables, such as cucumber, broccoli, squash, spinach, or kohlrabi, may be substituted. But remember to adjust the cooking time to suit your choice of vegetable.

For 6–8 persons

1 cup yellow split mung beans
  (*moong dal*)
⅔ cup finely chopped onions
1 tablespoon grated fresh
  ginger root
2 teaspoons minced garlic
⅓ teaspoon turmeric

3 medium-sized potatoes
  (about ¾ pound), peeled
  and quartered
⅓ small cauliflower cut into
  1½-inch flowerets (about
  2½–3 cups)
1 tablespoon Kosher salt

FOR TADKA:

12 tablespoons *usli ghee* (p. 50),
   or light vegetable oil
1 teaspoon cumin seeds
2–4 green chilies, seeded
   and shredded, or
   ¼–½ teaspoon red pepper

2 teaspoons lemon juice
2–3 tablespoons chopped fresh
   coriander leaves (or
   substitute 1–2 tablespoons
   dried coriander leaves)

1. Pick over, clean, and wash mung beans following directions for cleaning *dal* on page 327.

2. Put the mung beans in a deep pot, along with chopped onions, ginger, garlic, and 3 cups water. Add turmeric, and bring to a boil. Reduce heat and simmer, partially covered, for 15 minutes or until the mung beans are cooked but are still very firm.

3. Add potatoes, cauliflower, salt, and 2 more cups of water, and cook for an additional 15 minutes or until the vegetables are tender and the beans are thoroughly cooked. (This dish may be cooked up to this point and kept refrigerated for up to 2 days. Reheat thoroughly before proceeding with the recipe. These beans usually thicken with keeping. In addition, the vegetables, especially the potatoes, have a tendency to absorb a great deal of moisture from the stew. Therefore, always check the consistency of the stew before serving. If necessary add water [about ½ cup] to thin it to the desired consistency.)

4. *To make the* tadka: Heat the *ghee* over high heat in a frying pan. When it is very hot, add cumin seeds, and fry until they turn dark brown (about 15 seconds). Add green chilies or red pepper,

stir for a moment, and immediately pour the contents of the frying pan into the stew. Add lemon juice and chopped coriander leaves. Stir well to mix. Check for salt, transfer the stew to a heated serving dish, and serve.

This simple yet very satisfying vegetarian dish is a fine single luncheon entree when accompanied by plain cooked rice (p. 357). It can also be served with plain breads, such as Baked Whole Wheat Bread (p. 393) or Baked Whole Wheat Puffy Bread (p. 397). For a more substantial meal, include a stir-fried vegetable, such as Spicy Baby Eggplant (p. 303), Stir-fried Okra (p. 309), or Stuffed Okra with Fragrant Spices (p. 311). Accompany the meal with Lentil Wafers (p. 425), Fresh Mint Relish (p. 436) or Hot Hyderabad Tomato Relish (p. 441), and Hot Lemon Pickle (p. 449).

Mixed Lentils and Vegetable Stew

(Gujrati Dal)

This stew offers just a glimpse of the wonderful cuisine from the state of Gujrat. The food of the Gujratis especially the Gujrati Jains, flavored with a unique blend of northern and southern spices, reflects a warm merger. The technique for cooking this stew is very similar to making *sambaar*, except that here the *dal* is cooked with several ingredients before being added to the vegetable, instead of being cooked plain. This is the characteristic feature of Gujrati cooking. The stew, flavored with cumin as well as black mustard seeds, makes a very satisfying entree, especially for lunch, if simply accompanied by plain cooked rice. Like other Gujrati Jain food, this stew contains no garlic, but I often add a few cloves of it, partly because I happen to like garlic and mainly because I think it does wonders for the stew.

For 4–6 persons

1 cup *dal*—use a mixture of
yellow lentils *(toovar dal);*
pink lentils *(masar dal);*
yellow split peas *(channa
dal);* and yellow split
mung beans *(moong dal)*

3 medium-sized tomatoes
(about ¾ pound)

1 small eggplant (about
¾ pound)

1 medium summer squash or
zucchini (about 6–7 inches
long)

½ teaspoon turmeric

1 tablespoon finely chopped
fresh ginger root

1 teaspoon chopped garlic
(optional)

2 green chilies, seeded and
minced, or ⅓ teaspoon red
pepper

4 tablespoons *usli ghee* (p. 50)

¾ teaspoon black mustard
seeds

¾ teaspoon cumin seeds

⅓ teaspoon ground asafetida

2½ teaspoons Kosher salt

8 kari leaves (fresh or dry), or
2 tablespoons chopped
fresh coriander

1. Pick over and wash *dal* following the directions on page 327.

2. Put the legumes in a bowl, and add water to cover to a depth of 2 inches. Let soak for 2 hours. Drain and set aside.

3. Blanch and peel tomatoes, and cut into 1-inch wedges. Cut eggplant and squash or zucchini into thick 1½-inch sticks, like short French fries.

4. Put the soaked legumes in a deep pot with turmeric, ginger, garlic, chilies, and 3 cups of cold water, and bring to a boil. Reduce heat and cook, partially covered, for 45 minutes or until the lentils are fully cooked and tender. Turn off heat. When slightly cool, puree the mixture and measure. There should be 4 cups of lentil puree. If not, add enough water to bring it up to that quantity. (The lentil puree can be made ahead and refrigerated for up to 4 days. It can also be frozen successfully. Defrost and heat thoroughly before proceeding with the recipe.)

5. Place all the spices and vegetables right next to the stove. Heat the *ghee* over high heat in a deep saucepan. When the *ghee* is very hot, carefully add the mustard seeds. Keep the lid of a pan or a

spatter screen handy, since the seeds may splatter and splutter when added. When spluttering stops and the seeds turn gray (about 5 seconds), add cumin seeds. When cumin turns dark (about 5–10 seconds), add asafetida, stir for a second or two, and add the tomatoes. Cook, stirring rapidly but carefully so as not to mash up the tomato pieces, for 3–4 minutes. Add eggplant and squash and continue cooking for an additional 3 minutes.

6. Add lentil puree and salt, and bring to a boil. Reduce heat and cook the vegetables, covered, for 20 minutes or until the vegetables are cooked and very tender. Add kari leaves and serve.

Note: The stew may be made ahead and refrigerated for up to 2 days. The stew takes well to freezing only as far as flavor is concerned. The texture is another matter. The vegetables, particularly summer squash and zucchini, disintegrate while defrosting. As a result, the stew looks more like a thick hearty soup with tiny fragments of vegetables floating in it. If you are not particular about the texture, the freezing is recommended. Defrost thoroughly before reheating. To reheat, simmer over low heat until warmed through. Check for salt before serving.

To serve this lovely stew, follow the menu suggestions given for Mung Bean and Cauliflower Stew on page 278.

Dumplings in Fragrant Herb Gravy

(Mungaude ki Bhaji)

Although this recipe requires a little time and effort, since it involves making the dumplings first, you will be well rewarded by the results.

For 6 persons

1 recipe Spinach and Mung Bean Dumplings (p. 120)	1¼ cups chopped fresh ripe tomatoes (about 2 medium tomatoes), or use 1 cup canned tomatoes with their juice
½ cup Indian vegetable shortening or light vegetable oil	
4 teaspoons finely chopped garlic	1½ teaspoons Kosher salt
2 tablespoons finely chopped fresh ginger root	1 teaspoon ground roasted cumin seeds (p. 66)
2 cups thinly sliced onions	1 teaspoon ground roasted coriander seeds (p. 66)
1 teaspoon turmeric	¼–½ teaspoon black pepper
¼–½ teaspoon red pepper	2–3 tablespoons finely chopped coriander leaves

1. Place dumplings in a bowl, add cold water to cover, and soak them for 1 minute. Drain, squeezing them slightly to extract excess water, but being careful not to break the fragile dumplings. Set aside.

2. Heat the shortening or oil in a large heavy-bottomed pan, preferably one with a non-stick surface, and add garlic. Over medium-high heat, sauté garlic until pale and cooked (about 15 seconds). Add ginger, and cook for an additional 1 minute. Add onions, and fry until they turn caramel brown (about 20 minutes). Stir constantly while frying all these ingredients to prevent burning. (See directions for Brown-frying Onions p. 71.)

3. Add turmeric and red pepper, stir for a moment or two, and

add tomatoes. Cook until the tomatoes turn to a thick pulpy sauce and the fat begins to separate from it (about 10 minutes). If the gravy begins to stick to the bottom of the pan, reduce heat and add a few tablespoons of water to slow the cooking. Add 3½ cups of hot water and the salt, and bring to a boil.

4. Add the reserved dumplings, and simmer, uncovered, over medium heat until the sauce is reduced by half (about 8–10 minutes). Reduce heat to low and continue simmering, partially covered, for an additional 15 minutes. Turn off heat. Stir in cumin, coriander, black pepper, and chopped coriander leaves. Check for salt, and serve.

Note: This dish may be prepared ahead and refrigerated for up to a day. However, a little more cumin, coriander, and chopped coriander leaves should be added before serving, since they lose most of their flavor when kept.

For a light meal, accompany this fragrant dish with a plain cooked rice (p. 357), or a simple baked bread such as Baked Whole Wheat Puffy Bread (p. 397) or Chick-pea Flour Bread (p. 399). Vegetable side dishes such as Fragrant Buttered Greens (p. 319), Stir-fried Okra (p. 309), or Buttered Smothered Cabbage (p. 298) are all good choices. For a more elaborate meal, include a yogurt salad, especially Cucumber and Yogurt Salad (p. 343). The meal may be accompanied by Onion Vegetable Relish (p. 432) or Raw Onion Relish (p. 431), and Lentil Wafers (p. 425).

Chick-pea Dumplings in Yogurt Sauce

(Kadhi)

This is yet another way of preparing *dal*. *Kadhi* is made with ground *channa dal*, or hulled and split black chick-peas (see more on page 327), commonly known as *besan* or chick-pea flour. The *besan* is mixed with yogurt to make a thick batter which is then dropped by tablespoonfuls into hot oil and fried into dumplings. The dumplings are then simmered in a yogurt sauce until they puff up and become light and airy, soft and spongy. The prolonged uncovered simmering also thickens the sauce. Its consistency is like a smooth, creamy, and slightly foamy custard sauce. This North Indian specialty is usually served with plain cooked rice for Sunday lunch. There are many ways to make *kadhi*. This is the way it is prepared in my mother's home, except for one variation: I add chopped vegetables along with the dumplings, a practice followed by my sister Roopa, who in turn learned it from her in-laws.

Note: The yogurt should be of medium sourness—if it is too tart the dish will taste too sharp and tangy; if it is too sweet the *Kadhi* will taste bland and flavorless. Be sure to simmer the dumplings in the yogurt sauce over a very low heat or they will not become soft. The sauce has a tendency to stick to the pan and burn, so be sure to stir often.

The *kadhi* batter is generally prepared by hand, which requires long hard beating that is both tiring and time-consuming. I have developed a way of preparing it in the food processor which takes only a fraction of the time taken by the traditional method. The results are as good, if not better!

For 6–8 persons

FOR DUMPLINGS:

2 cups chick-pea flour *(besan),* measured unsifted

2 teaspoons ground coriander

⅛ teaspoon red pepper

1 teaspoon Kosher salt

¼ cup plain yogurt

½ cup warm water (90–100°F)

Pinch of baking soda

Peanut or corn oil enough to fill a frying pan to a depth of 1½ inches

(continued)

FOR SAUCE:

2 cups plain yogurt

6 cups cold water

⅔ cup chick-pea flour
  (besan), measured
  unsifted

½ teaspoon turmeric

½ teaspoon red pepper

1 tablespoon Kosher salt

¼ cup Indian vegetable
  shortening or light
  vegetable oil

½ teaspoon black mustard
  seeds

1 teaspoon cumin seeds

2 teaspoons ground
  coriander

1 medium onion, peeled
  and cut into 8 wedges

1 medium-sized potato,
  peeled and cut into
  8 pieces

¼ cup Indian vegetable
  shortening or *usli ghee*
  (p. 50)

1. *To make batter by hand:* Sift flour into a large bowl. Add all the other ingredients for dumplings except the pinch of baking soda, and beat vigorously, using a whisk or spoon, until pale, light, and fluffy (about 15 minutes). The batter will be very thick. Cover and let the batter rest for at least 2 hours in a warm place. This will ferment the batter, making it even lighter and fluffier. (To test if the batter has risen enough, drop about ½ teaspoon of batter into a bowl of cold water. If it rises to the top, the batter is ready. If it sinks to the bottom of the cup, the batter is too thick and dense and needs further beating.)

To make batter in a food processor: Mix the yogurt, water, and baking soda in a measuring cup. Attach the steel cutting blade to the food processor. Put the flour, coriander, red pepper, and salt in the container, cover, and process for 10 seconds to mix the ingredients. With the machine running, pour the yogurt mixture through the feed tube. The contents of the container will reduce to a thick paste. To beat the batter, continue processing for 4 minutes, turning the machine off and on every 15–20 seconds. The batter should be light and slightly fluffy, like cake batter. (To test if the batter has been beaten enough, use the test described above.)

2. Heat the oil for deep frying in a *kadhai,* chicken fryer, or

frying pan until hot but not very hot (325°F). Put about 6 cups of cold water in a large bowl and place it close by.

3. When ready to fry the dumplings, stir the baking soda into the batter, and mix well. Take a heaping teaspoonful of batter and, using another spoon to push the batter, drop it into the hot oil. Do not worry if the dumplings have odd shapes—they will. Fry 16 dumplings at a time, making sure not to overcrowd the pan. Fry until they turn light golden (about 4–5 minutes), watching carefully that they do not burn. Take them out with a slotted spoon, and drop them into the bowl of water. Add another 16 dumplings to the hot oil. While the second batch of dumplings is frying, take the soaking dumplings out of the water, and shake them gently to extract excess water. Put them in another bowl. Continue until all the dumplings are fried and soaked this way, and set aside. You will fry 3 batches altogether.

4. Make the sauce: Mix yogurt, water, chick-pea flour, turmeric, red pepper, and salt in a bowl until thoroughly blended. (Alternatively, you may put all these ingredients into the container of a blender or food processor, and blend. Remember to do it in 2 batches, since the volume is large.)

5. Heat the ¼ cup of shortening or oil in a deep enamel 5-quart saucepan. When the oil is very hot, carefully add the mustard seeds. Keep a pot lid or spatter screen handy, since the seeds may splatter and splutter when added. When the seeds turn gray (in a moment or two), reduce the heat slightly and add cumin seeds. When cumin turns brown (about 10 seconds), add coriander powder. Stir rapidly, and immediately add the onion and potato. Fry them for 5 minutes, turning and tossing them to brown evenly.

6. Add the yogurt mixture, and bring to a boil. Stir constantly to prevent the yogurt from separating and lumping.

7. Add the reserved dumplings, and stir to mix. Lower heat to medium-low and cook at a gentle bubble, uncovered, for 45 minutes. Check and stir often to keep the sauce from sticking and burning. Check for salt, and transfer to a warm serving bowl. Add shortening or *ghee*, and stir just once (the butter should streak the sauce). Serve immediately.

(continued)

Note: This dish may be made ahead and refrigerated for up to 3 days. In this case, the shortening or *ghee* should be added just before serving.

This gorgeous luncheon entree should be served with either plain cooked rice (p. 357) or Baked Whole Wheat Puffy Bread (p. 397), accompanied by a fruit punch (alcoholic or nonalcoholic) or a yogurt drink (see recipes on p. 488 and 489).

Side Dishes

Vegetables

(Sabzi)

VEGETABLES *(Sabzi)*

Glazed Beets with Black Mustard Seeds   *(Chukandar ki Sabzi)*
Broccoli Smothered in Garlic Oil   *(Hare Gobhi ki Sabzi)*
Buttered Smothered Cabbage   *(Bandh Gobhi ki Sabzi)*
Glazed Cauliflower with Ginger   *(Gobhi Sabzi)*
Cauliflower and Scallions with Black Mustard Seeds   *(Gobhi Kari)*
Spicy Baby Eggplant   *(Baigan Masaledar)*
Smoked Eggplant with Fresh Herbs   *(Bharta)*
Green Beans with Coconut and Black Mustard Seeds   *(Beans Kari)*
Stir-fried Okra   *(Bhindi Sabzi)*
Crisp Fried Okra   *(Bhoni Bhindi)*
Stuffed Okra with Fragrant Spices   *(Bhindi Bharva)*
Roasted Onions   *(Bhone Piaz)*
Turmeric Potatoes   *(Peele Aloo)*
Turmeric Potatoes with Green Peppers   *(Aloo Mirch)*
Potatoes Smothered with Shallots   *(Aloo Piaza)*
Cooked Spinach   *(Obla Saag)*
Fragrant Buttered Greens   *(Saag)*

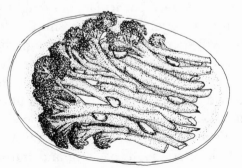

It is almost impossible to imagine India without vegetables, for it is well known that India has the largest number of vegetarians in the world. For centuries whole segments of the population have been living on a meatless diet. Some cannot eat meat because it is beyond their means (meat costs seven to eight times as much as vegetables); others prefer not to eat meat for health reasons. But most do not eat meat because of religious dietary restrictions. Women in general, particularly unmarried ones and widows, are not allowed meat. Most people reaching old age give up meat as a gesture of preparation for encountering God, with the anticipation of being sent to heaven (in Hindu mythology one scores points toward heaven by practicing *A-himsa*, meaning "no killing," or nonviolence). When you add all this up, and set it against the 675 million Indians, the number of vegetarians runs into the hundreds of millions.

It is therefore natural that India grows the finest assortment of vegetables in the world, unsurpassed in quality and variety. The cooking of these vegetables is an art, so refined, sophisticated, and intricately varied from region to region that it is often referred to as a separate classic cuisine, holding its own esteemed place in the culinary world.

In India there are no such things as canned, frozen, or even freeze-dried vegetables for general consumption. This is partly because the techniques used for cooking vegetables, like those of Chinese cooking, require fresh produce. But the main reason is that Indians are very particular, one might almost say fussy, about the quality of vegetables. They simply don't settle for second-best. They will spend hours going through the mounds of green beans or okra at the vegetable shop, picking the tender ones. As a result, fresh flavorful young vegetables of exceedingly good quality are still widely available year-round in all parts of India. They are, of course, seasonal, just as they are here.

Vegetables are usually grown in farms around the city. Due to the lack of adequate packing and transportation facilities, most of the produce is consumed locally. The vegetables are still sold in sunlit open-air markets called *Sabzi bazaar*, as they have been for centuries. The farmers bring their produce every morning early in bullock carts, and arrange them in an enticing array in stalls called *Sabzi ki ducan*. Walking through the narrow walkways lined with rows of these stalls is an experience one seldom forgets. The air is filled with the gentle lingering aroma of freshly picked vegetables, the earthy scent of the moist soil clinging to their roots, and the freshly cut stem-ends still dripping juices. You can see the morning dew as yet undisturbed on their surfaces. This is where vegetables are sold as vegetables, and not as we often see them here in supermarkets—plasticized and sanitized, depriving us of the simplest, most basic pleasures of life.

In Indian cooking, the place of vegetables is not restricted to side dishes. Vegetables are turned into appetizers, snacks, soups, main dishes, relishes, pickles, conserves, desserts, sweetmeats, breads, and beverages. Just about any vegetable can be cooked in all these forms, using different ingredients and techniques. Let us take carrots as an example. They are sliced and cooked with turmeric and mace, grated and turned into delicious dumplings, or cooked in sauce and served as kaftas. They are shredded and perfumed with black mustard seeds in Carrot Relish (p. 435), folded in yogurt and served as salad, or cooked with saffron and rice in Carrot Pilaf. For people with a sweet tooth, they are grated and cooked with milk, raisins, and sugar to become the delicate silky dessert Carrot Pudding (p. 456), or mixed and cooked with almonds and cardamom to make *halwa*, or fried with milk fudge into carrot fudge. And that is not all, for they are also simmered in cardamom-laced syrup for a conserve, or pickled in red-pepper-flecked mustard-seed water. The water from the pickle is served as a beverage, especially during the summer.

Vegetables served as side dishes with an Indian meal are cooked in just about every way conceivable to man. The most popular and commonly used technique, however, is *bhojia*, a process which can be described as twice stir-fried—for that is exactly what it is. The process is quick and utterly simple, some vegetables taking as little as ten minutes for total cooking.

In this process, the spices are first fried in hot oil; then the vegetables are added and quickly stir-fried until lightly seared. Some spices, such as turmeric, red pepper, ginger powder, and mango powder are often added with or after the vegetables, because they burn so easily. All this is done over high heat. The heat is then reduced and the vegetables are cooked in their own moisture and vapor. (If the vegetables look dry, a little water is sprinkled on.) Finally the heat is increased and the vegetables go through a second stir-frying, to get nicely browned and develop a beautiful shiny glaze. Sometimes a little oil or fat is added to the vegetables at the end, to increase the glaze. Vegetables cooked thus have a roasted flavor and very soft texture, though the pieces hold their shape.

Some vegetables, such as potatoes, yams, plaintain (green banana), and red beets are often cooked prior to stir-frying. This is done to preserve the full robust aroma of fried spices, as these vegetables require a lot of water and time to cook, and prolonged moist cooking robs the spices of much of their fried flavor.

One last note: Take a little time and care to choose vegetables that are fresh and in season. Avoid the wilted, rotting, and sad-looking. Remember, in all vegetable dishes the natural taste of the vegetables is as important as the herbs and spices flavoring them.

These recipes for preparing vegetable side dishes have been particularly selected to introduce you to some of the important and interesting cooking techniques and flavoring principles of different regions. And the vegetables used are easily available in super-market chains and produce markets.

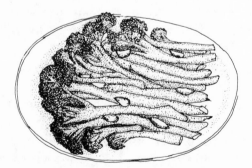

Glazed Beets with Black Mustard Seeds

(Chukandar Ki Sabzi)

In Indian cooking, red beets are seldom used in gravy dishes because they tint the whole dish. They are usually stir-fried with only a few spices so that their distinct sweet flavor may be savored to the fullest. In the North, the beet greens are often cooked with the beets to give this dish a leafy fragrance.

This delicate recipe comes from southwestern India, where dishes begin with mustard seeds sizzled in oil. The beets, cooked in turmeric water, are then folded into the spicy, fragrant oil.

For 4–6 persons

6 medium fresh beets (about 1½ pounds or 2 bunches)	½ teaspoon black mustard seeds
½ teaspoon turmeric	1 teaspoon Kosher salt
2 tablespoons light vegetable oil	1 teaspoon sugar

1. Cut off the stems and leaves from the beet root bunch. (Save them for cooking with potatoes (*Saag*, p. 319).

2. Wash beets in running cold water, and pat dry with kitchen towels. Cut them into ⅛-inch to ¼-inch thin sticks.

3. Put the cut beets and turmeric into a deep pan, add enough water to barely cover the beets, and bring to a boil. Cook the beets, uncovered, in briskly boiling water for 5–10 minutes or until they are fully cooked but still firm and hold their shape. (The cooking time will vary depending upon the freshness and quality of the beets and on the thickness of the sticks.) Drain, and set aside.

4. Heat the oil over high heat in a large frying pan. When the oil is very hot, carefully add the mustard seeds. Keep a pan lid or spatter screen handy, since the mustard seeds may splatter and splutter when added. When the spluttering stops and the mustard seeds turn gray (about 5 seconds), add the drained cooked beets, and cook for a minute, turning and tossing to coat the beets with

mustard-seed-flavored oil. Sprinkle salt and sugar, and cook for an additional minute. Turn off heat. Check for salt and serve hot, at room temperature, or chilled.

Note: These beets keep well in the refrigerator for up to 4 days.

Glazed beets are excellent served cold as a relish or salad. They are ideal with dishes that have a southern flavor or contain mustard seeds or coconut, such as Goanese Hot and Pungent Curry (p. 199), Shrimp Poached in Coconut Milk with Fresh Herbs (p. 243), Spicy Brussels Sprouts, Green Beans, and Lentil Stew (p. 276), or Mixed Lentils and Vegetable Stew (p. 280). Rice generally accompanies any meal with beets.

Broccoli Smothered in Garlic Oil

(Hare Gobhi Ki Sabzi)

Broccoli, known as green cauliflower, is not an Indian vegetable, although it lends itself amazingly well to Indian spices and flavorings. This is an utterly simple and quick recipe that yields an elegant-looking and exquisite-tasting dish. The technique finds its roots in the classic cooking of the North, where green vegetables are briefly stir-fried with spices in oil before being cooked in their own moisture. The vegetables are stir-fried again, to coat them with that wonderful shiny glaze characteristic of many North Indian vegetable dishes. For best results, choose the freshest broccoli and cut and peel it carefully, so that the pieces will cook uniformly.

For 4–6 persons

One bunch broccoli (about 1½ pounds)	8–10 garlic cloves, peeled
3 tablespoons light vegetable oil	⅓ teaspoon turmeric
	1 teaspoon Kosher salt

1. Cut broccoli into spears, leaving long stems attached to the flowerets. Peel the stems carefully—they break easily. Rinse the spears under running cold water. Leave them for 5 minutes to drain.

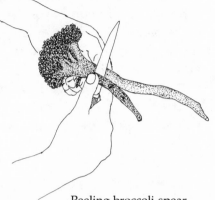

Peeling broccoli spear

2. Heat the oil over medium-high heat in a frying pan large enough to accommodate the broccoli in a single layer. When the oil is hot, add garlic, and sauté, turning and tossing until it turns golden (about 1–2 minutes). Add turmeric and immediately follow it with the broccoli. Spread the broccoli so that it lies in one layer. Let it sizzle undisturbed for 1 minute; then sprinkle on the salt. Turn the broccoli carefully with a flat spatula or a pair of tongs, and sauté for an additional minute.

3. Reduce heat and cook, covered, until the broccoli is cooked but still crisp and dark green (about 8–10 minutes). Uncover, and continue cooking until all the moisture evaporates and the broccoli spears are glazed with garlic oil (about 3–5 minutes). Check for salt, and serve immediately.

This garlic-scented broccoli dish goes especially well with mildly flavored lamb dishes, such as Royal Roast Leg of Lamb with Saffron Raisin Sauce (p. 184), Royal Braised Lamb with Fragrant Spices (p. 174), Lamb Pilaf (p. 189), or Lamb Fillets Braised in Yogurt Cardamom Sauce (p. 168).

Buttered Smothered Cabbage

(Bandh Gobhi Ki Sabzi)

Cabbage, known as *Bandh* (closed) or *Patta* (leaf) *Gobhi*, is a popular vegetable with Indians. They cook it in many wonderful ways. The best method of all is a slow sautéeing in butter until the cabbage releases its natural sweetness. Generally a little turmeric is added to enhance the flavor and color. This technique is common throughout India, although flavorings change from state to state. Here the cabbage is flavored with cumin and ginger root and cooked in asafetida-laced oil, to produce a warm and refreshing taste.

For 6–8 persons

1 small cabbage (about 1¾–2 pounds)

2 tablespoons *usli ghee* (p. 50), or light vegetable oil

1½ teaspoons cumin seeds

¼ teaspoon ground asafetida (optional)

¼ teaspoon turmeric

1 tablespoon finely chopped fresh ginger root

1 cup chopped fresh ripe tomato (1 large one)

2 green chilies, seeded and minced, or ¼ teaspoon red pepper

2 teaspoons Kosher salt

1–2 tablespoons coarsely chopped fresh coriander leaves (or substitute 1 tablespoon dried coriander leaves)

1. Cut the cabbage into quarters, and core out the stem from each quarter. Shred the cabbage into ¼-inch-thick shreds. Heat the *ghee* over medium-high heat in a large heavy-bottomed pan, preferably one with a non-stick surface. When the *ghee* is hot, add cumin. When cumin turns dark brown (about 10–15 seconds), add ground asafetida, if you are using it, and immediately add the shredded cabbage. Sprinkle turmeric over the cabbage, and sauté,

turning and tossing rapidly until the cabbage is wilted (about 5 minutes).

3. Add ginger, tomato, and chilies or red pepper, and continue cooking for an additional 5 minutes. Add salt and 1 cup of hot water. Reduce heat to medium-low and cook the cabbage, covered, until it is tender and the water is absorbed into the vegetables (about 20 minutes). Check and stir often while it is cooking to prevent burning. Fold in chopped coriander leaves, check for salt, and serve.

Note: This vegetable preparation may be made several hours ahead and reheated just before serving.

These buttery shreds of cabbage are good enough to be served as a first course. They are moist and juicy, hence ideal with bread. They are particularly good with Meat Cutlets (p. 197), Mint-Scented Broiled Leg of Lamb (p. 182), Tandoori Chicken (p. 221), Panfried Fillet of Sole Laced with Carom (p. 248), or Chick-pea Batter Fish (p. 251).

Glazed Cauliflower with Ginger

(Gobhi Sabzi)

Indians love cauliflower—they never seem to get enough of it. This particular fondness has resulted in the creation of cooking techniques that do justice to this very special vegetable. Indians never boil cauliflower (if it is cooked in a liquid, the broth becomes part of the dish) because it might become mushy and lose its flavor. Instead, they stir-fry it and cook it in its own moisture. This dish, a classic from the states of Punjab and Uttar Pradesh, is flavored with turmeric, cumin, and fresh ginger root shreds.

For a variation: Substitute potatoes or green peas, or both, for a part of the cauliflower. If you use potatoes, increase the cooking time by 5 to 10 minutes, depending on how large the pieces of potato are.

(continued)

For 4–6 persons

1 small head cauliflower
  (about 1¼ pounds)
4 tablespoons light vegetable
  oil
1 teaspoon coriander seeds, or
  ½ teaspoon cumin
1½ tablespoons shredded fresh
  ginger root

1–2 green chilies, seeded and
  chopped (optional)
½ teaspoon turmeric
¾ teaspoon Kosher salt
1 teaspoon lemon juice
2 tablespoons chopped fresh
  coriander leaves

1. Separate the cauliflower into small flowerets (about 1–1½ inch pieces), cutting them with a knife if necessary. Wash them under running cold water, and drain. On a surface next to the stove, place all the spices, the drained cauliflower, and ¼ cup hot water.

2. Heat 3 tablespoons of the oil over medium-high heat in a *kadhai*, large frying pan, or skillet. When the oil is very hot, add coriander or cumin, and fry until the seeds turn dark brown (about 10 seconds). Add ginger and chilies, if using them, and stir for a couple of seconds. Immediately add turmeric and salt, and follow at once with the cauliflower. Stir rapidly to distribute the spices and to prevent burning. Add the hot water, reduce heat and cook, covered, until the cauliflower is fully cooked to crispy tenderness (about 20–25 minutes). Stir once or twice during cooking. (The cauliflower may be cooked up to this stage and set aside, covered, for several hours.)

3. Increase heat to medium, and stir-fry to evaporate any moisture remaining in the pan and to lightly brown the cauliflower (about 5–10 minutes). Stir carefully, as cooked cauliflower is usually very fragile and breaks easily. If the vegetable looks a little dry, stir in the remaining oil. Add lemon juice and chopped coriander leaves, and toss gently. Check for salt, and serve immediately.

This dish goes wonderfuly well with cardamom-laced dishes. Also, cream and yogurt sauce dishes look subtly elegant against its sparkling yellow color. Good choices are Lamb in Fragrant Garlic

Cream Sauce (p. 176), Royal Chicken in Silky White Almond Sauce (p. 215), Moghul Braised Chicken (p. 206), Chicken Pilaf (p. 228), and Royal Braised Vegetables in Cardamom Nut Sauce (p. 269). For a lighter meal, serve this as an entree accompanied by a fried bread, such as Deep-fried Puffy Bread (p. 413) or Whole Wheat Flaky Bread (p. 402), and if desired, a cool yogurt salad, such as Spinach and Yogurt Salad (p. 344) or Cucumber and Yogurt Salad (p. 343).

Cauliflower and Scallions with Black Mustard Seeds

(Gobhi Kari)

Americans use scallions mostly to season dishes. Indians treat them as a vegetable in their own right, or mix them with another vegetable—in this case, cauliflower. *Gobhi Kari* is a specialty of the southern and southwestern regions. It is flavored with black mustard seeds and turmeric. The turmeric-laced golden-yellow cauliflower pieces look dazzling against the green scallions and black mustard seeds.

Urad dal (p. 24), although not an essential ingredient, does lend a spicy aroma and an interesting texture to the dish.

For 4–6 persons

1 small head cauliflower (about 1¼ pounds)	1 teaspoon white split gram beans (*Urad dal*, optional)
2 bunches scallions (about 12–15 sprigs)	½ teaspoon turmeric
4 tablespoons light vegetable oil	1–2 green chilies, chopped, or ¼ teaspoon red pepper
½ teaspoon black mustard seeds	1½ teaspoons Kosher salt
	6–8 fresh or dry kari leaves, slightly crushed (optional)

(continued)

1. Separate cauliflower into very small flowerets (about ½–¾-inch pieces), cutting them with a knife if necessary. Wash them in running cold water, and drain.

2. Trim the root ends of the scallions, and chop them (including the green part) into ¼–⅓-inch pieces.

3. Measure out the spices and place them, the vegetables, and ⅓ cup hot water right next to the stove.

4. Heat 3 tablespoons of the oil over high heat in a *kadhai*, large frying pan, or skillet. When the oil is very hot, carefully add the mustard seeds. Keep a pot lid or spatter screen handy, since the seeds may splatter and splutter when added. When the seeds are spluttering, add gram beans. When the beans turn light brown and the mustard seeds gray, add turmeric, chilies, salt, and scallions, stirring rapidly. Sauté briefly (about 15 seconds), and add cauliflower. Stir to distribute the spices and scallions, and add the hot water. Reduce heat to medium-low and cook, covered, until the cauliflower is cooked to crispy tenderness (about 15–20 minutes). Uncover, increase heat to medium, and stir-fry to evaporate any moisture remaining in the pan and to lightly brown the cauliflower (about 5–10 minutes). Stir in the remaining tablespoon of oil during browning. Add kari leaves, if you are using them. Stir to mix. Check for salt, and serve immediately.

To serve this fragrant vegetable dish, follow the menu suggestions given for Glazed Beets with Black Mustard Seeds on page 295.

Spicy Baby Eggplant

(Baigan Masaledar)

This recipe calls for tiny eggplants—as small as two to three inches and weighing about two ounces, available in both white and purple colors. In India they are a highly prized delicacy and are prepared in many different ways: simmered with lentils in *sambaar*, cooked with spices and coconut, braised in tamarind juice, or stuffed with spices and stir-fried. Stuffed eggplant is the most popular method, and the stuffings will inevitably vary from state to state. This particular recipe reflects the typical flavoring of the Rajasthanis, and is very spicy.

For 2–4 persons

8–10 tiny eggplants (about 1 pound)

THE STUFFING:

2 teaspoons ground
  coriander
1 teaspoon ground cumin
¼–½ teaspoon red pepper
½ teaspoon mango powder,
  or 1½ teaspoons lemon
  juice

½ teaspoon *garam masala*
  (p. 38)
1 teaspoon Kosher salt

2 tablespoons light vegetable
  oil
½ teaspoon cumin seeds
⅛ teaspoon ground asafetida

1. Cut off the stem from the eggplant, being careful not to cut the green skirtlike top. Quarter the eggplants from the stem end, cutting through the green part, to within ¾ inch of the bottom. Put the eggplants in a bowl, and add enough cold water to cover. Soak them for 15 minutes. (This will make the eggplants open up slightly like flower buds. Do not oversoak, or they will open up too much.) Drain and pat dry the outsides with kitchen towels.

2. Mix all the spices for the stuffing, and stuff the eggplants,

making sure to distribute the mixture evenly. Press gently to reshape the eggplants. Do not worry if some of the spice stuffing falls out. Just be sure to reserve it.

3. Heat the oil over medium-high heat in a large frying pan (about 10 inches in diameter). When the oil is very hot, add the cumin seeds. When the cumin turns dark brown (about 10 seconds), add asafetida and immediately follow with the eggplants. Stir for 10–15 seconds, then reduce heat to low. Sprinkle on any reserved stuffing mixture, and fry, turning and tossing for 3–5 minutes or until the oil coats the eggplants all over. Increase heat to medium, and fry the eggplants until they are lightly browned (about 5 minutes). Sprinkle 2–3 tablespoons of water over the eggplants, reduce heat to very low, and cook, covered, until they are tender (about 20 minutes). Watch constantly to prevent burning, and stir a few times, being very careful not to break the eggplants as they become extremely fragile when cooked. Uncover, increase heat to medium-low, and continue cooking the eggplants until all the remaining moisture evaporates and the eggplants look fried and glazed (about 5–10 minutes). Check for salt, and serve.

Note: This dish may be prepared a couple of hours before you are ready to serve. Reheat gently but thoroughly before serving.

These eggplants offer a perfect contrast to mildly seasoned dishes. Serve them with Lamb Braised in Yogurt Cardamom Sauce (p. 168) or Royal Chicken in Silky White Almond Sauce (p. 215). For a lighter meal, fold the eggplants into plain cooked rice (p. 357) and serve it as spicy pilaf with a chilled Chablis or a cool yogurt drink (see p. 488 or 489). Or you might serve them with Whole Wheat Flaky Bread (p. 402) or Deep Fried Puffy Bread (p. 413). You can include a *dal,* such as Lentils with Garlic Butter (p. 332), or a cool yogurt salad, such as Tomato and Yogurt Salad (p. 345).

Smoked Eggplant with Fresh Herbs

(Bharta)

The pear-shaped eggplant with its deep purple color and shiny skin is a sheer joy to look at and even more a joy to eat. It is a most versatile vegetable and Indians, with characteristic resourcefulness, cook it in many ways to create mouth-watering delicacies. Of the many preparations, this classic North Indian one is the most popular and the most subtle-tasting.

The eggplants are first roasted over a flame; this process gives *Bharta* its special smoky flavor. The eggplant is then pureed, mixed with fragrant herbs and seasonings, and cooked. The more subtle and prolonged the roasting process, the more flavorful the *Bharta* becomes. For this reason, the eggplant is traditionally roasted over the ashes of a burnt-down wood fire for 2 to 2½ hours. *Bharta* cannot be cooked on a hot plate or electric stove. For the sake of convenience, I have outlined a method of roasting it in a gas oven, even though the eggplant will not develop a smoked flavor this way. (Use this method for days when you cannot give the necessary 20 to 30 minutes of undivided attention.) But remember, for an authentic *Bharta* you *need* that smoke flavor.

For 6 persons

2 medium eggplants (about 1 pound each)	1½ cups finely chopped fresh ripe tomatoes (or 1 cup canned tomatoes, drained and chopped)
½ cup shelled peas, fresh or frozen	
9 tablespoons light vegetable oil	2 green chilies, seeded and minced (optional)
1 teaspoon minced garlic	2 teaspoons Kosher salt
1 tablespoon grated fresh ginger root	2–3 tablespoons finely chopped coriander leaves
1¼ cups finely chopped onions	

(continued)

1. Wash eggplant under running cold water, and wipe dry with kitchen towels.

2. First, roast the eggplants. To roast, stand one eggplant on a burner of a gas stove, stem side uppermost, over a low flame, until the bottom of the eggplant is thoroughly charred (about 5 minutes). Now lay the eggplant on its side, and roast, turning it every minute with a pair of tongs until it is fully charred and very soft (about 15–20 minutes). When fully cooked, the eggplant will be quite limp, the skin blistered, and the juices beginning to ooze out. The eggplant may be roasted on a high or medium flame as well. The time taken for roasting will vary, of course, depending upon the heat. Or the eggplants may be roasted on a baking sheet in the middle level of a preheated 500°F oven for 20 minutes.

3. Let the eggplants cool briefly. Then carefully scrape the charred skin off. Rinse quickly under running cold water to wash away any skin that may still cling to the eggplant. Place the eggplants in a small bowl. With paper towels, pat dry all the juices oozing out, pressing the eggplant slightly. (The juices carry the bitterness often found in eggplant. Therefore it is essential you dry them thoroughly.) Then chop the pulp coarsely with a knife. If there are any large hard lumps, chop them fine. Put the pulp in a small bowl, and beat with a fork for a minute. Set aside.

4. Cook the fresh peas in a little water to cover, for 5 minutes or until tender. (If you are using frozen peas, cook them following directions on the package). Drain, and set aside.

5. Heat the oil over medium-high heat in a shallow pan, preferably one with a non-stick surface. When the oil is hot add garlic and ginger, and cook, stirring, for a minute. Add onions, and fry until they are light golden—do not let them brown—(about 8 minutes), stirring constantly to prevent burning. Reduce heat to medium, add eggplant puree, and cook for an additional 8 minutes, stirring often.

6. Add tomatoes and chilies, if you are using them, and continue cooking until the eggplant and tomatoes are fried (about 10 minutes). Add peas, and cook until a glaze forms on the puree and the fat begins to separate (about 5 minutes). Turn off heat, and

stir in salt. Just before serving, check for salt, and fold in chopped coriander leaves.

Note: This dish may be made ahead and kept refrigerated for up to 3 days. It also freezes well. Defrost thoroughly before reheating. Taste and add more salt, if necessary, and a little chopped coriander.

This velvety eggplant puree, bursting with the fragrance of ginger root, coriander leaves, and most important of all, smoked eggplant, is best accompanied by only North Indian dishes, such as Beef in Fragrant Spinach Sauce (p. 179), Meat Smothered with Onions (p. 166), Royal Chicken in Silky White Almond Sauce (p. 215), Velvet Butter Chicken (p. 225), or Chicken in Onion Tomato Gravy (p. 208). For a simpler meal, serve the *Bharta* with a kabob, such as Moghul Kabobs with Raisin Stuffing (p. 107), accompanied by Baked Whole Wheat Puffy Bread (p. 397).

Green Beans with Coconut and Black Mustard Seeds

(Beans Kari)

Kari is the popular southern Indian technique for preparing fresh vegetables. The dish prepared in this way is also called a *kari*. Coconut and mustard seeds are its primary ingredients.

In this *kari* of beans, freshly grated coconut is folded in during the last few minutes of cooking, so that its sweet fragrance and snow-white color will not be overpowered. The contrast of green beans against the white coconut specked with black mustard seeds makes for a most attractive dish.

(continued)

For 4 persons

1 pound fresh green beans

⅓ teaspoon turmeric

¾ teaspoon Kosher salt

2 tablespoons light sesame oil, or light vegetable oil

½ teaspoon black mustard seeds

1 teaspoon white split gram beans (*urad dal*, optional)

⅓ cup firmly packed grated coconut (p. 46)

1–2 green chilies, seeded and minced, or ¼ teaspoon red pepper

1 tablespoon finely chopped fresh coriander leaves

1. Snap off the ends of the green beans, and cut beans into 1-inch-long pieces.

2. Put the beans, along with turmeric, salt, and 2 cups of water in a saucepan, and bring to a boil. Cook over medium heat, covered, until the beans are tender but still crisp (about 15–20 minutes). Drain, and set aside.

3. Heat the oil over high heat in a large frying pan. When the oil is very hot, add the mustard seeds. Keep a pot lid or spatter screen handy, since the seeds may splutter and splatter when added. When the seeds begin to splutter, add gram beans, and cook until they turn light brown.

4. Add grated coconut and green chilies or red pepper, and stir for a minute or two. Add the cooked beans, and stir-fry for 5 minutes. Turn off heat, add chopped coriander leaves and mix thoroughly. Check for salt, and serve immediately.

To serve, follow the menu suggestion plan given for Glazed Beets with Black Mustard Seeds (p. 295).

Stir-fried Okra

(Bhindi Sabzi)

If there is one vegetable that is grossly misunderstood and underrated it is okra. It can be truly delicious if properly cooked. In my intermediate-level cooking classes, I always include an okra preparation. This inevitably elicits dismay and not a little disgust from the students. They picture the overcooked, bland stewed okra in a slimy sauce that they have tasted so often. Sliminess results when cut okra comes in contact with water. In Indian cooking, particularly North Indian, okra is never cooked with water. The North Indian technique, which is just about perfect, calls for stir-frying okra in oil. After this explanation and a little persuasion, my students reluctantly give in, probably just to satisfy their curiosity. But when the dish is finally made and sampled, they are de-lightfully surprised and sorry to have missed out on such a delicacy all these years.

Note: When buying okra, select deep-green unblemished ones that snap easily at the end when bent. Always remember two things when cooking okra: Dry the washed okra thoroughly before cutting it. Salt it only *after* it is fully cooked, as salt will cause the okra to sweat.

For 4 persons

1 pound fresh okra	3 tablespoons light vegetable oil
2 green chilies (optional)	½ teaspoon Kosher salt

1. Wash okra under running cold water, and wipe dry with kitchen towels. Trim both ends, and slice the okra into ¼-inch-thick rounds. Slit and seed the chilies, and slice them also into ¼-inch-thick rounds.

2. Heat the oil over high heat in a large frying pan. When it is very hot, add the okra and chilies. Spread them into an even layer.

(continued)

Let the okra sizzle undisturbed for a minute, then reduce heat to medium. Cook the okra, uncovered, for 20 minutes, stirring frequently to ensure even cooking. Increase heat to high, and now fry the okra, stirring rapidly, for 5 minutes, or until it is lightly browned (the browning will be uneven). Turn off heat, sprinkle with salt, and toss the fried okra well to coat all pieces evenly.

Note: Fried okra may be prepared a day ahead and refrigerated. To reheat, place the okra in a frying pan over low heat until heated through, stirring frequently. If it looks a little dry, add a teaspoon of oil while heating.

Tasty stir-fried okra go well with just about any main dish. I often serve them with a *dal,* such as Spice- and Herb-Laced Split Peas (p. 330), accompanied by plain cooked rice (p. 357) for a lovely light meal.

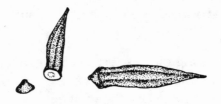

Crisp Fried Okra

(Bhoni Bhindi)

These okra are shallow-fried in oil until they turn crisp and brown. They are then drained and used in various dishes, including Okra Pilaf (p. 373) and Okra and Yogurt Salad (p. 347). They are delicious folded into Dry Cooked Spicy Ground Meat (p. 158).

Makes ¾ cup

1 pound fresh okra   6 tablespoons light vegetable oil

1. Wash okra under running cold water, and wipe dry with kitchen towels. Trim both ends, and slice the okra into very thin (about ⅛ inch) rounds.

2. Heat the oil over high heat in a large frying pan. When it is very hot, add the okra in one even layer. Let the okra sizzle undisturbed for a minute; then reduce heat to medium-high. Fry the okra, turning and tossing until cooked and crispy brown (about 20–25 minutes). Remove with a slotted spoon, and spread over paper towels to drain and cool.

Note: The crisp fried okra can be made several hours ahead and set aside, uncovered, until needed.

Stuffed Okra with Fragrant Spices

(Bhindi Bharva)

Stuffing and stir-frying okra is a common technique popular in Uttar Pradesh, particularly with vegetarians. The young tender pods of the okra are slit, filled with fennel, cumin, coriander, and dry mango powder, and fried until cooked. These irresistible stuffed okra are often served just with Whole Wheat Flaky Bread (p. 402) for a light meal.

For 4–6 persons

1 pound fresh okra, preferably even-sized pods (3–4 inches long)
2 teaspoons fennel seeds, crushed
1 tablespoon ground cumin
1 tablespoon ground coriander

¼ teaspoon red or black pepper
¾ teaspoon mango powder, or 2 teaspoons lemon juice
2–3 tablespoons light vegetable oil
1¼ teaspoons Kosher salt

(continued)

1. Wash okra, and wipe dry. Cut off the head from the okra. Working with one pod at a time, make a slit along the length of each with a small pointed knife, such as a paring knife. Leave about ¼ inch unslit at either end. Slit all the okra pods this way, and set aside.

2. Mix fennel, cumin, coriander, red or black pepper, and mango powder (if you are using lemon juice, do not add it yet) in a small bowl.

3. Hold one okra pod in your left hand (if you are right-handed) so that the slit is facing up. Insert your left thumb into the slit to open it slightly. With your right hand, take about ¼–½ teaspoon of the spice mixture with a small spoon (such as a ¼-teaspoon measuring spoon) or a butter spreader, and insert it evenly into the slit. Press the okra by closing your palm to cover the slit; this will make the spices adhere to the inside of the pod, thus preventing their falling out. Continue with the rest of the slit okra pods the same way, until all are stuffed and all the spice mixture is used up. (The okra can be stuffed and set aside for several hours until you are ready to cook.)

4. When you are ready to cook, heat the oil over high heat in a large frying pan 10 inches or more in diameter. When the oil is very hot, add the okra, preferably in one layer. Let it sizzle undisturbed for 1 minute. Reduce heat to medium. Then carefully turn the okra with a flat spatula, making sure the slits do not open. Fry for 5 minutes, turning now and then to prevent burning.

5. Reduce heat to low, cover the pan, and cook for 10 minutes. Uncover, and continue cooking until all the moisture evaporates and the okra is fried brown (about 15 minutes), stirring frequently and regulating heat from low to medium-low.

6. Turn off heat, and sprinkle with salt. If you are using lemon juice in place of mango powder, stir it in now. Serve immediately.

Note: Stuffed okra can be made several hours ahead and reheated just before serving. In such a case, do not add salt and lemon juice until you reheat and are ready to serve the dish.

These are excellent accompaniments to North Indian main dishes such as Chicken in Onion Tomato Gravy (p. 208), Meat-Stuffed Cabbage Rolls with Ginger Lemon Sauce (p. 194), Meat Curry (p. 170), Beef in Spicy Tomato Gravy (p. 172), and Lobster in Fried Onion Sauce (p. 247).

Roasted Onions

(Bhone Piaz)

Here is a simple and delicious way to prepare onions—and it takes only a few minutes! The onions are thickly sliced and placed in a smoking-hot greased pan. They sizzle, roast, and become coated with a shimmering glaze. Although you can use regular super-market-variety onions, I prefer the large Spanish kind because they tend to be sweeter. They also look more elegant.

(continued)

For 6 persons

1 large Spanish onion (about
    1 pound)
1 tablespoon light vegetable oil

2 tablespoons coarsely chopped
    coriander leaves (optional)

1. Peel onion, cut in half, and slice into ¼-inch-thick slices. Separate the slices into shreds.

2. Heat a large iron skillet or a heavy-bottomed frying pan over high heat. When the skillet is very hot, add the oil, tilting the pan to coat it thoroughly. When the oil is smoking hot, add the onions. Do not stir, but let the onions sizzle and roast undisturbed for ½ minute. Now stir, and keep roasting, tossing and turning, until the onions are translucent and slightly browned (about 2 minutes). The roasted onions should be crisp, not limp, and sweet to the taste. Fold in coriander leaves and transfer to a serving platter.

Note: Almost essential to preparing roasted onions is a good heavyweight skillet or frying pan that holds heat uniformly. Otherwise, the onions will burn instead of roasting.

These roasted onions traditionally accompany Tandoori Chicken (p. 221). They are also served with Kabob Patties Laced with Ginger and Mint (p. 109).

Turmeric Potatoes

(Peele Aloo)

Here is a refreshingly different way to prepare potatoes. The potatoes are first boiled and cut into cubes. They are then laced with turmeric and stir-fried in oil. This technique, common throughout India, produces potatoes that are buttery inside and crisp on the outside. For best results, the boiled potatoes should be thoroughly cooled before being fried. I usually boil them a day ahead and then refrigerate them. That way, I can peel them just before frying.

For 6–8 persons

8 medium potatoes	3–4 tablespoons light vegetable oil
2½ teaspoons Kosher salt	1–2 green chilies, seeded and
1¼ teaspoons turmeric	sliced (optional)

1. Boil potatoes in their jackets until cooked but still firm. Plunge them in cold water for a minute, and peel. Cut them into 1-inch pieces and put them in a bowl. Sprinkle salt and turmeric over them and toss to coat all the pieces evenly.

2. Heat the oil over medium-high heat in a large frying pan. When the oil is very hot, add the potatoes and fry, turning and tossing, for 5 minutes. Sprinkle the sliced chilies and 2–3 tablespoons of water over the potatoes, and stir carefully. Cover the pan, and let the potatoes steam over low heat for 10 minutes or until they are tender. Uncover and continue frying, turning the pieces regularly, until any moisture remaining in the pan has evaporated and the potatoes are lightly browned. (The potatoes will develop a crunchy outer crust. This may take anything from 3 to 10 minutes, depending upon the moisture contained in the potatoes and the heat used. Check for salt, and serve.

Except that you should avoid a main dish that contains potatoes, you can serve this with practically any dish. For a simple vegetarian meal, serve it as an entree with a *dal*—Lentils with Garlic Butter (p. 332) or Mung Beans Laced with Black Mustard Seeds (p. 333)—and plain cooked rice (p. 357). Or accompany it with Cucumber and Yogurt Salad (p. 343) and any of the plain baked breads, such as Baked Whole Wheat Puffy Bread (p. 397).

Turmeric Potatoes with Green Peppers

(Aloo Mirch)

Here is another popular dish from the North. Potatoes have a marvelous ability to enhance the flavor of any food cooked with them. For this reason, green vegetables are often cooked with a few pieces of potato. You can also make this lovely dish with cabbage, cauliflower, or green peas in place of the green pepper.

For 8 persons

8 medium-sized boiling potatoes (about 2 pounds)	3–4 tablespoons light vegetable oil
4 medium-sized green peppers (about 1 pound)	1½ teaspoons turmeric
	1 tablespoon Kosher salt

1. Boil potatoes in their jackets until cooked but still firm. Plunge them in cold water for a minute, and peel. Cut them into 1-inch pieces. Cut green peppers into quarters, and core out the stem and seeds from each quarter. Cut them into 1-inch pieces.

2. Heat the oil over medium-high heat in a large frying pan. When the oil is very hot, add turmeric, and immediately add the potatoes and green peppers. Sprinkle with salt, and fry, turning and tossing for 3–4 minutes. Sprinkle 2–3 tablespoons of water over the vegetables, reduce heat, and cook, covered, until the green peppers are cooked but still very crisp and bright green (about 5–10 minutes).

3. Uncover, and stir-fry the vegetables to evaporate any excess moisture remaining in the pan and to brown the vegetables (about 5 minutes). Check for salt, and serve.

To serve, follow the menu suggestions given for Turmeric Potatoes on p. 314.

Potatoes Smothered with Shallots

(Aloo Piaza)

In the United States, shallots are treated as a precious seasoning. In India they are used as a vegetable in place of onions, since they are considered to be superior. They are almost always cooked with a vegetable—most commonly with potatoes. The only ingredients here are potatoes and shallots. The gentle frying releases and mixes their flavors and makes this dish utterly delicious. *Aloo Piaza* is popular in the South, where shallots are commonly found, and is usually much hotter than my adaptation. If you like, add a few chopped green chilies.

For 4 persons

4 medium baking potatoes (1½ pounds)	½ cup finely chopped shallots
4 tablespoons *usli ghee* (p. 50), or light vegetable oil	1¼ teaspoons Kosher salt
	Generous pinch of white or black pepper

1. Peel the potatoes and cut them into thick ½-inch strips like old-fashioned thick French fries. Put them in a bowl, add cold water to cover, and set aside.

2. Heat the *ghee* in a large heavy-bottomed frying pan or skillet that can accommodate the potatoes in one layer. Add potatoes, and fry over medium-high heat, turning and tossing to lightly brown them (5 minutes). Remove them with a slotted spoon, and reserve them in a bowl.

3. Add chopped shallots to the pan, and cook for 5 minutes or until nicely browned. Stir constantly to prevent burning. Return the potatoes to the pan, and sprinkle the salt evenly over them. Sprinkle about 3 tablespoons of water over the potatoes, and immediately cover the pan. Reduce heat and let the potatoes cook in buttery steam for 20–25 minutes or until fork-tender. Check during cooking to make sure the potatoes have not dried out and that there is enough steam in the pan to cook them. Add more

water if necessary. Do not, however, add too much water, as the potatoes are supposed to be pan-roasted, not boiled.

4. Uncover, and increase heat to evaporate any moisture that may remain in the pan and to brown the potatoes. Stir frequently while browning. Turn off heat, and sprinkle with pepper. Check for salt, and serve.

Follow the menu suggestions given for Turmeric Potatoes on p. 314. In addition, these potatoes are wonderful with Panfried Fillet of Sole Laced with Carom (p. 248). For a quick, simple fried rice that is delicious, fold these potatoes into plain cooked rice (p. 357), and serve with roasted or fried food. For a simple, light vegetarian meal, serve them as an entree accompanied by Tomato and Yogurt Salad (p. 345) or Okra and Yogurt Salad (p. 347).

Cooked Spinach

(Obla Saag)

This is a basic recipe for making cooked spinach. It is used in Beef in Fragrant Spinach Sauce (p. 179), Cream of Spinach Soup (p. 145), Spinach and Yogurt Salad (p. 344), and Spinach Bread (p. 410).

Makes 3 cups

3 pounds fresh spinach, or
  3 ten-ounce packages frozen
    leaf spinach
	2 tablespoons Kosher salt

1. Snip the stems from the tender leaves of spinach. For the more mature leaves, fold the leaf vertically along the stem, and with one hand pull away the stem, including that portion of it attached to the leaf's underside. Pick out and discard all rotting, wilting, or yellow leaves.

2. Wash the spinach thoroughly by swishing it around in several changes of cold water until all sand is washed away.

3. Bring about 8 quarts of water mixed with the salt to a boil in a deep pot. Drop the spinach leaves into the rapidly boiling water. When the water comes to the boil again, reduce heat to medium, and let the spinach boil, uncovered, for 5 minutes. (If you are using frozen leaf spinach, defrost thoroughly, and separate the leaves. Cut off the stems, and discard. Cook the spinach, if you are using it in salad, in the boiling water, to which salt has been added, for 3 minutes.)

4. Pour the entire contents of the pot immediately into a colander or a sieve held firmly over the kitchen sink. Let cold water run through for a minute to refresh the spinach—this will preserve its bright green color and also prevent any further cooking.

5. Squeeze as much water out of the spinach as possible by pressing it with the back of a spoon, or use your hand.

6. Place the spinach on a chopping board, and chop it as coarse or fine as called for in a recipe.

Note: The chopped spinach may be kept covered for several hours, or refrigerated for up to one day, or frozen. Defrost thoroughly before using it in any recipe.

Fragrant Buttered Greens

(Saag)

For an Indian, it is not enough that any food be good for him—*it must also taste good.* Indians eat a lot of greens for this reason. Greens have a distinct, subtle, natural flavor which needs to be released and enhanced before they can be enjoyed. This is achieved by slow stir-frying in a gentle spice-laced *ghee* or oil—a common technique in India. If the spicing tends to be too overpowering, potatoes are added to right the balance. This wonderful-tasting dish can be made with a variety of different greens—as long as half of them are spinach.

(continued)

Serves 6–8 people

1 pound fresh spinach, or 1 ten-ounce package frozen chopped spinach	5 tablespoons *usli ghee* or light vegetable oil
1 pound fresh mustard, kale, or collard greens (or substitute 1 ten-ounce package of frozen greens), or 1 pound fresh beet greens (p. 295)	1 teaspoon cumin seeds
	1 teaspoon finely chopped garlic
	2 green chilies, seeded and minced, or ¼ teaspoon red pepper (optional)
8 small or 4 medium-sized boiling potatoes (about 1 pound)	½ teaspoon ginger powder
	1½ teaspoons Kosher salt
	¾ teaspoon *garam masala* (p. 38)

1. Pick over and discard all rotting, wilted, and yellow leaves. Wash the greens by dunking them into several changes of cold water until all the sand is washed away. Drain, pat the greens dry with paper towels, and place them on a chopping board. Chop the greens (leaves and stem) coarsely. If you are using frozen chopped greens, defrost thoroughly, and squeeze out the excess water by pressing with the back of a spoon, or use your hand. Set aside.

2. Peel the potatoes, and cut small ones in half and medium ones in quarters.

3. Heat the *ghee* over medium-high heat in a large frying pan or any shallow pan, preferably one with a non-stick surface. When it is very hot, add cumin seeds. When the cumin turns dark (about 10 seconds), add garlic and chili or red pepper if you are using them. Stir rapidly for a moment or two, and add potatoes. Reduce heat to medium and fry the potatoes, turning and tossing them until they are lightly browned all over (about 5–8 minutes). Add about 1 cup of the chopped greens and stir it in. When the greens get limp (about ½ minute) add another cup of greens. Continue until all greens are incorporated. Sprinkle with ginger powder and salt. Stir well to mix. Add 1¼ cups boiling water, reduce heat and cook, covered, until the potatoes are tender (20–25 minutes). Uncover, and continue cooking until the excess moisture evapor-

ates (about 15 minutes). The vegetables must be stirred very carefully at this stage, as the potatoes break easily. Increase heat to medium and continue frying, stirring the vegetables gently until the potatoes and greens look almost dry and the butter begins to coat and glaze the vegetables (about 5 minutes). Stir in *garam masala*, and turn off heat. Check for salt, and serve.

Note: This vegetable dish may be prepared several hours before you are ready to serve. It also keeps well in the refrigerator for up to 4 days.

This vegetable preparation represents the authentic peasant-style cooking in both its ingredients and its flavor. It is best served with robust dishes such as Beef in Spicy Tomato Gravy (p. 172) or Whole Eggs in Spicy Tomato Sauce (p. 233).

Legumes—Lentils and Dried Peas and Beans
(Dal)

Spice- and Herb-Laced Split Peas   *(Masala Dal)*
Lentils with Garlic Butter   *(Masar Dal)*
Mung Beans Laced with Black Mustard Seeds   *(Moong Dal)*
Lucknow Sour Lentils   *(Lakhnawi Khatti Dal)*
Buttered Black Beans   *(Kali Dal)*

Yellow lentils
Toor dal

Chick-peas
Channa

Black gram beans
Sabat urad dal

Yellow split peas
Channa dal

Red kidney beans
Badi rajma

Yellow mung beans
Moong dal

We are all familiar with yellow and green split peas, brown lentils, and several varieties of beans, such as kidney, pinto, navy, and cranberry, which we see on supermarket shelves. They are just a few varieties of the edible leguminous seeds known as legumes or pulse, and in India as *dal*. There are many kinds of legumes in the world, and due to the composition of soil and local climate, even the same species of legume may vary widely in different parts of the globe.

Glancing through cookbooks by well-known authors, I am constantly surprised and disappointed when I come to the section on legumes. They mention German split pea soup, French *cassoulet*, Egyptian *hummus*, Mexican refried beans, Cuban black bean soup. They even talk about the soybean and its use in Chinese cooking. But there is no mention of legumes in Indian cooking. Indians knew the versatility of legumes long before many civilizations even heard of them. At the *shradha*, a Vedic Indian ritual paying homage to a dead relative, a feast consisting of several courses, all containing legumes, is still prepared in its full tradition today. The legumes cultivated in India are many and varied, and Indians cook them in different lovely ways. Legumes are an important source of rich, inexpensive protein for Indians, particularly the vegetarians, and throughout India, meals, especially meatless ones, always contain a legume dish.

The use of legumes in Indian cooking is so widespread that it would be impossible to include all the pertinent information in this book. I will, however, give you an idea of the most common and important uses. There are three basic and popular ways of preparing legumes: One, they are simply boiled in water, with or without herbs and seasonings, and mashed to a velvety smooth golden puree, which is then flavored and enriched with spice-perfumed butter (*Tadka*, p. 73). The puree is usually used for dipping bread, or it is poured over rice and mixed. Two, they are briefly soaked in water and steamed with spice-laced butter, so that the legumes emerge with each grain separate and intact. Three, they are cooked with other ingredients, such as vegetables, meat, fish, poultry, nuts, and even rice, and turned into hearty stews (see pp. 276–280). Such preparations are generally served as main dishes.

In addition to these three methods, legumes are also used in soups, stuffing for breads, turnovers, dumplings, puddings, and desserts. Legumes are ground to a flour and used to make batter for fritters and dough for wafers, as well as candies, fudge, and other sweetmeats. They are soaked, ground into paste, and used for making dumplings which are either served as appetizers (see page 120), simmered in various sauces and served as main dishes (p. 283), or dressed with yogurt and served as a cold side dish (page 348). Mixed with herbs and seasonings, legumes are cooked into crepes, pancakes, buns, and breads.

Classification of Legumes

Legumes can be grouped into three broad categories; lentils, beans, and peas. Of all the varieties, the most widely used in Indian cooking are two kinds of lentil: yellow lentils *(toovar dal)* and pink lentils *(masar dal)*; two kinds of beans: mung beans *(moong dal)* and black gram bean *(urad dal)*; and yellow split peas *(channa dal)*. All are available in Indian grocery stores. The wonderful characteristic of these legumes is that they are virtually indestructible, and thus can be stored indefinitely.

Lentils are thin lens-shaped seeds ranging in color from yellow to walnut brown. They are the most commonly consumed legumes in India. As a matter of fact, half the world's production and consumption of lentils is concentrated in India. They are among the easiest to digest legumes.

The yellow lentil *(toovar dal,* also known as *toor dal* or *arhar dal)* is the seed of the plant *Cajanus cajan.* The seeds are hulled and split to yield golden yellow lentils. These yellow lentils should not be confused with the common supermarket variety, an altogether different species that, since they are sold unhulled, with the thin brown skin on, turn into a dirty brown puree when cooked instead of a golden yellow one.

The pink lentil (*Masar dal*, also known as *Masoor dal*) is the seed of the plant *Lens culinaris*. The tiny brown seeds are hulled to yield lens-shaped salmon-colored lentils. The red Egyptian lentils available in Middle Eastern stores make a good substitute. These pink lentils when cooked turn pale yellow. The pink lentils are similar to yellow lentils (in most recipes they can be used interchangeably) except that the puree is not as thick and creamy. Pink lentil puree is much lighter and thinner. It also cooks faster, in about half the time taken by yellow lentils.

Beans are the next most common legumes consumed in India. They are cooked whole, as well as hulled and split. The tiny cylindrical seeds are rectangular in shape when split.

Mung bean (*moong dal*), technically known as green gram bean, is the seed of the plant *Phaseolus aureus*. The name *moong dal* usually refers to the hulled and split bean, yellow in color. This is the form most widely used in Indian cooking. In this form it is the most easily digestible legume, and is therefore cooked with rice to make a porridge called *khichari*, served to ailing people. (The boiled rice-and-fish preparation known as "kedgeree" is not an Indian dish, for a proper *khichari* must contain *dal* and does not contain fish. Kedgeree, very popular in British countries, was originally concocted by the British stationed in India to suit the Western palate.) The whole seed, dark green in color, is called *sabat* (whole) *moong*, and is more popular in the northern and western regions of India.

Black gram bean (*urad dal*, also known as *dhooli* [washed] *urad*) is the seed of the plant *Phaseolus mungo*. The name *urad dal* usually refers to the hulled and split seed, ivory white in color. This is the form most widely used. The whole seed, black in color, is called *sabat* (whole) *urad*, *maan*, or *kali* (black) *dal*. This bean is popular in the North, especially in Punjab where it is cooked with onions, ginger, herbs, and butter, and turned into a rich creamy puree called *Kali Dal* (p. 337). In better quality restaurants this dish is often called "special *dal*."

Peas, if properly cooked with aromatic herbs and spices, can be a true delicacy. The northerners, particularly the people of Punjab, have a natural knack for turning these hard-to-flavor legumes into ravishing main dishes. They are cooked either whole or hulled and split. The most popular and commonly used pea throughout India is the yellow-colored split pea *(channa dal)* from the pod of the plant *Cicer arietinum.* The name *channa dal* usually refers to the hulled split peas. The yellow split peas commonly available in supermarket chains may be substituted in the event that Indian ones are unavailable, but they are not really the same. The American split peas taste like a cross between Indian yellow lentils and yellow split peas.

The whole peas known as chick-peas, *ceci,* or *garbanzos* are called *kabuli channa* or *safaid channa* in Indian. Chick-peas are widely available in supermarket chains in dry form or as cooked and canned, either of which is suitable in Indian cooking. In India, another variety of chick-pea called black chick peas *(kala* [black] *channa)* is also available; it is the *channa dal* chick-pea before hulling. These are particularly savored by the people of Delhi. They cook these peas, as well as the white ones, in a tangy pomegranate or tamarind sauce and serve them with the famous leavened potato bread, *bhatoora.* This combination, called *Channa* or *Cholle bhatoore,* is today popular throughout India and is served in restaurants specializing in North Indian food.

In addition to the above-mentioned legumes, red kidney beans *(badi rajma),* pink beans *(choti rajma)* and black-eyed peas *(lobhia)* are all easy to find in supermarket chains in dry, canned, and frozen form, and are quite suitable to Indian cooking.

Preparing Legumes *(Dal)* for Cooking

Cleaning: All varieties of legumes *(dal)* imported from India and sold in Indian grocery stores need to be cleaned, because they often contain such foreign matter as pieces of stone, sticks, and mud.

To clean, put the *dal* on a large plate, such as a *paraath* (see page 387 for description), or a serving platter, or simply put them on the kitchen or dining table. Spread a small portion so that the seeds are all separated and the dirt pieces are clearly visible. Pick out and discard all such foreign objects, and push the cleaned *dal* to one side. Spread more of the *dal* the same way, and continue until the entire amount is cleaned.

Washing: Put the *dal* in a large fine-mesh sieve. Hold the sieve under the tap in the kitchen sink and let the cold water run through at medium speed for about 30 seconds, or until the water runs clear and the *dal* is thoroughly washed. Shake the sieve now and then to ensure proper cleaning.

How Much *Dal* to Prepare per Person

There is no hard and fast rule about the size of a serving of *dal* with an Indian meal. Much depends upon one's taste, appetite, and the composition of the meal—how elaborate or light it is. In my family we like an extra bowl of *dal* to sip after eating the rest of the dishes, so that we can relish its delicate flavor and leave it lingering in our mouths and minds. But as a general rule, 6–9 ounces of *dal* per person will make a generous serving as a side dish and 9–12 ounces as a main dish.

How to Serve and Eat *Dal*

Except for certain dry preparations, most *dal* dishes in India are in the form of puree, ranging from very thin to medium thick. (*Kali dal* is an exception. See page 337). *Dal* is best served in small bowls, ideally the Indian bowls called *katoori* (see description on page 90). A good substitute is a small custard cup or fruit bowl. It is a good idea to place a small spoon alongside. The *dal* may either be served directly in these bowls or poured into a deep dish or soup tureen and brought to the table for self-service.

Eating *dal* can be very satisfying, and a lot of fun, if you know the right way. A prerequisite is to choose the right staple to go with it. While dry *dal* preparations can be eaten with either rice or bread, the pureed *dals* are best accompanied only by rice. To eat *dal* with bread, tear off a piece of the bread and use it as a scoop. To eat *dal* with rice, spoon out, or simply lift the small bowl and pour a few tablespoons of *dal* over the rice on your plate, and mix before eating. You may also, from time to time, sip or eat the *dal* by itself.

Important Facts About *Dal*

After eating *dal* some people experience stuffiness, heaviness, and even gaseousness in the stomach—a feeling that the food, even several hours after the meal, is still sitting inside undigested. This feeling is of course intensified if you take a nap immediately following a meal of *dal*.

Dal is naturally rich in protein nitrogen compounds, important for muscle-building and body growth, and abundant in meat, poultry, fish, eggs, milk, and other dairy products. The proteins present in *dal*, however, are very different from those in meat, fish, milk, cheese, and eggs. The latter are much easier and quicker to digest. Vegetable proteins, particularly those present in certain types of unhulled beans and peas, such as the black gram bean, kidney bean, and chick-pea, require more time and effort to digest. They are ideal for people who work out-of-doors, especially doing heavy physical labor. That's why people around the world who work in fields and forests or on rivers are able to consume great quantities of *dal* day after day without any problem. When we transplant them to our sedentary urban setting, our digestive systems rebel. So it is imperative that you make certain adjustments when cooking with them. One is to serve them in moderate portions, no more than four to eight ounces of *dal* per person. And always increase the quantity of digestive spices, such as asafetida, and fresh ginger root, that you add to the dish.

Spice- and Herb-Laced Split Peas

(Masala Dal)

This is a lovely *dal* recipe that you can make with supermarket variety yellow split peas. Since the peas cook like Indian split peas (*Channa dal*) but taste like lentils (*Arhar* or *Toovar dal*), I have slightly modified the recipe to suit its particular flavor and texture. The *dal* is flavored with onions and cumin, a technique popular in Uttar Pradesh and Punjab, and it is divine.

In Indian cooking, split peas are traditionally accompanied by bread, and lentils by rice. The unique flavor and texture of this *dal* make it suitable for serving with either staple.

For 4–6 persons

1½ cups yellow split peas
   (supermarket variety)

⅓ teaspoon turmeric
2 teaspoons Kosher salt

FOR TADKA:

½ cup Indian vegetable
   shortening or light
   vegetable oil
1 teaspoon cumin seeds
1½ cups finely chopped onions

¼ teaspoon red pepper
   (optional)
2 tablespoons finely chopped
   coriander leaves

1. Wash the peas following directions on page 327. Put the peas in a bowl, and add enough hot water to cover by 1 inch. Let soak for 1 hour. Drain.

2. Put the peas in a deep pot along with the turmeric and 4½ cups of water. Bring to a boil, stirring well to keep the peas from lumping. Reduce heat to medium-low and simmer, partially covered, for 45 minutes or until the peas are thoroughly cooked and tender when pressed between your fingers. Stir now and then to ensure that they do not stick to the bottom of the pan. Turn off

heat, and beat the split peas with a wire whisk or wooden spoon for a minute or until finely pureed. Measure the puree. There should be about 5 cups; if not, add enough water to complete the measurement. Stir in salt, and set aside. (The split pea puree may be prepared and kept refrigerated for up to 4 days. It also freezes extremely well. Defrost thoroughly before proceeding with the recipe.)

3. When ready to serve, simmer the puree over low heat until piping hot. Check the consistency of the puree if you have made it ahead of time: keeping often thickens it considerably and you may need to add water. Transfer the puree to a warm serving bowl, and make the spiced butter (*tadka*).

4. Heat shortening or oil over medium-high heat in a frying pan. When it is very hot, add cumin seeds, and fry until they turn dark brown (about 10 seconds). Add onions, and fry until they turn dark brown (about 20 minutes), stirring constantly to prevent burning. (See directions for Brown-Frying Onions, p. 71.) Stir in red pepper if you are using it, and immediately pour this perfumed butter with its spices and onions over the split pea puree. Garnish with chopped coriander, and serve immediately in small bowls (*katoori*).

This *dal* is particularly good accompanied by main dishes served with rice, such as Meat-Stuffed Cabbage Rolls with Ginger Lemon Sauce (p. 194), Meat Cutlets (p. 197), Panfried Fillet of Sole with Carom (p. 248), Chick-pea Batter Fish (p. 251), Whole Potatoes in Spicy Yogurt Gravy (p. 258), or Spicy Potato-Stuffed Cabbage Rolls with Ginger Lemon Sauce (p. 263).

Lentils with Garlic Butter

(Masar Dal)

This is my favorite everyday *dal*—a smooth and silky golden puree of pink lentils known as *masar dal*. It is laced with lightly sautéed garlic slivers, a typical example of how Punjabis prepare and flavor the *masar dal*. For a variation, you can add a teaspoon of cumin seeds to the oil and brown them before adding the garlic.

For 4–6 persons

1½ cups pink lentils *(Masar dal)* or yellow lentils *(Toovar dal)*	¾ teaspoon turmeric 2 teaspoons Kosher salt

FOR TADKA:

5 tablespoons Indian vegetable shortening, or light vegetable oil	5–6 large garlic cloves, peeled and sliced lengthwise

1. Pick over, clean, and wash lentils following the directions on page 327.
2. Put the lentils in a deep pot along with the turmeric and 5 cups of water, and bring to a boil, stirring often, as the lentils have a tendency to lump together at this stage. Reduce heat to medium-low and simmer, partially covered, for 25–30 minutes (40–45 minutes for yellow lentils) or until the lentils are thoroughly cooked and tender when pressed between your fingers. Stir now and then to prevent sticking. Turn off the heat, and beat the lentils with a wire whisk or wooden spoon for a minute to smooth the puree. Measure. There should be 5–5½ cups of lentil puree. If you have less, add sufficient water to make 5 cups. Stir in the salt. (The lentil puree may be prepared ahead and refrigerated for up to 3 days. It also freezes well. Defrost thoroughly before proceeding with the recipe.)

3. When ready to serve, simmer the puree in the pot over low heat until piping hot. The puree thickens with keeping; therefore check the consistency and add water if necessary. It should be like a moderately thick cream soup. Keep the puree warm while you make the garlic butter (*tadka*).

4. Heat the shortening or oil over medium heat in a small frying pan. When it is hot, add the garlic slices, and fry just until they turn light brown and are still soft (about 1–2 minutes). Turn off heat and immediately pour this perfumed garlic butter with the slivers over the lentil puree. Stir to mix, and serve in small bowls (*katoori*).

Follow the menu suggestions given for Spice- and Herb-Laced Split Peas on page 330.

Mung Beans Laced with Black Mustard Seeds

(Moong Dal)

This *dal* is very light and has a refreshing taste lent by the chopped fresh coriander and lemon juice. A classic from the state of Maharashtra, it reflects the garlic-free cooking of the Maharashtrian Brahmins, known as Poona Brahmins.

(continued)

For 4 persons

1 cup yellow split mung beans (*Moong dal*)	1 teaspoon Kosher salt
¼ teaspoon turmeric	2 teaspoons lemon juice
½ teaspoon grated fresh ginger root	

FOR TADKA:

3 tablespoons *usli ghee*, (p. 50), or light vegetable oil	1–2 green chilies, seeded and shredded (or ¼–½ teaspoon black pepper)
½ teaspoon black mustard seeds	2 tablespoons chopped coriander leaves

1. Pick clean and wash mung beans following directions on page 327.

2. Put the beans along with the turmeric and ginger root in a deep heavy-bottomed saucepan. Add 4 cups of water, and bring to the boil, stirring often, as the beans have a tendency to lump together at this stage. Reduce heat to medium and simmer, partially covered, for 30 minutes or until the beans are fully cooked and soft when pressed between your fingers. Stir now and then to prevent sticking. Turn off heat, and when slightly cool, beat the puree with a wire whisk or wooden spoon for a few seconds to thicken the puree. There should be 4 cups of puree; if not, add enough water to increase it to that level. (The puree may be prepared ahead and refrigerated up to 2 days.)

3. Simmer the bean puree gently until piping hot. Stir in the salt and lemon juice. Keep the puree hot while you make the perfumed butter (*tadka*).

4. Heat the *ghee* over high heat in a small frying pan. When it is very hot, carefully add black mustard seeds. Keep a pot lid or spatter screen handy, since the seeds may splatter and splutter. When the seeds stop sputtering and turn gray, add the shredded chilies or black pepper. Stir rapidly for a moment, and turn off heat. Pour the *ghee* with its seasonings over the bean puree. Fold in the

chopped coriander. Check for salt, and serve immediately in small bowls *(katoori)*.

To serve, follow the menu suggestions given for Spice- and Herb-Laced Split Peas on page 330. This dish is excellent with almost any vegetarian vegetable and cheese main dish.

Lucknow Sour Lentils

(Lakhnawi Khatti Dal)

Khatti Dal, a classic from the city of Lucknow in the state of Uttar Pradesh, is indeed a superbly flavored lentil dish. It is fragrant with garlic and fresh ginger root and laced with black cumin-seed-flavored oil. The characteristic feature of this *dal* is the tamarind juice added to perk up the flavors and provide a tang.

For 6 persons

1½ cups pink lentils
1 tablespoon finely chopped
    fresh ginger root
½ teaspoon turmeric
1 one-inch ball tamarind
    pulp, or 1 teaspoon
    mango powder, or 1
    tablespoon lemon juice

1 cup boiling water
2 teaspoons Kosher salt

FOR TADKA:

5 tablespoons Indian
    vegetable shortening, or
    light vegetable oil
1 teaspoon black cumin
    seeds, or ½ teaspoon
    white cumin seeds

1 tablespoon mashed or
    minced garlic
¼–½ teaspoon red pepper

(continued)

1. Pick clean and wash lentils following directions on page 327.

2. Put the lentils in a deep saucepan along with the turmeric, ginger, and 5 cups of water, and bring to the boil, stirring often, as the lentils have a tendency to settle at the bottom of the pan. Reduce heat to medium-low and simmer, partially covered, for 25 minutes, stirring now and then.

3. While the lentils are cooking, put the tamarind pulp in a small bowl, add 1 cup of boiling water, and let soak for 15 minutes. Mash the pulp with the back of a spoon or using your fingers. Strain the liquid into another bowl, squeezing out as much juice as possible from the pulp. Discard the stringy fibrous residue.

4. Add the tamarind juice to the cooked lentils, and continue cooking for an additional 15 minutes (if you are using mango powder or lemon juice in place of tamarind, do not add yet). Turn off the heat, and beat the lentils with a wire whisk or wooden spoon for 1 minute to smooth the puree. Measure the puree and, if necessary, add enough water to make 6 cups. If you are using mango powder or lemon juice, stir it in now with the salt. (The lentil puree may be prepared ahead and refrigerated for up to 3 days. It also freezes well. Defrost thoroughly before proceeding with the recipe.)

5. When ready to serve, simmer the puree over low heat until piping hot. The lentil puree thickens with keeping, so check the consistency again. You may need to add ½ cup water to bring the puree to the right consistency. Check for salt and transfer to a serving bowl while you make the spice-perfumed butter (*tadka*).

6. Heat the shortening over medium-high heat in a small frying pan. When it is very hot, add cumin seeds, and fry for a moment or two (white cumin seeds will take about 10 seconds). Remove the pan from the heat, add red pepper and the mashed garlic, and stir rapidly for 10 seconds or until the garlic loses its raw smell and begins to color—do *not* let it brown. Pour the butter with its seasonings over the lentil puree. Stir once or twice—just enough to lace the puree with ribbons of perfumed butter. Serve immediately in small bowls (*katoori*).

To serve, follow the menu suggestions given for Spice- and Herb-Laced Split Peas on page 330.

Buttered Black Beans

(Kali Dal)

This is the most exquisite of all *dal* preparations, completely different both in texture and in flavoring. *Kali dal*, popularly known as Butter *dal* or Special *dal*, is a Moghul classic. It is made with black whole gram beans, known as *sabat urad* or *maan dal*. The beans are traditionally cooked in the leftover oven heat of the *tandoor*. Its consistency, which resembles a thick chili con carne, comes from the slow, prolonged cooking of beans with yogurt, tomatoes, and onions. The important ingredients that give the *dal* its velvet-smooth texture and satiny sheen are sweet butter and cream. In India, *Kali dal* is not an everyday dish. Partly because it tastes rich and mainly because it contains such expensive ingredients, *Kali dal* is usually reserved for special company. A favorite with Indians, this *dal* is a standard feature in better-quality restaurants that serve North Indian specialities, particularly *tandoori* food.

Note: It is important to cook the beans over a very slow fire so that they can expand and become plump without breaking. *Kali dal* takes 5 hours to cook, although most of the cooking requires little or no supervision, rather like simmering stock, and the results will more than compensate for the time.

For 8 persons

1 cup (½ pound) black whole gram beans (*Sabat urad dal* or *Kali dal*)

2 tablespoons red kidney beans

(continued)

FOR COOKING BEANS:

1 cup finely chopped onions
2 tablespoons finely chopped
   fresh ginger root
¾ cup chopped fresh tomatoes,
   or ½ cup canned drained
   tomatoes, or ⅓ cup
   canned tomato puree
1 cup plain yogurt

½ teaspoon ground cardamom
1 tablespoon ground coriander
½ teaspoon red pepper
2 teaspoons Kosher salt
8 tablespoons (1 stick) sweet
   butter, or 6 tablespoons
   usli ghee (p. 50)

FOR TADKA:

4 tablespoons *usli ghee*, or light
   vegetable oil
1½ teaspoons cumin seeds
1 cup minced or finely
   chopped onions

½ cup heavy cream
¼ cup firmly packed chopped
   fresh coriander leaves

1. Pick clean and wash gram beans following directions on page 327.

2. Put the gram beans and the kidney beans in a deep saucepan. Add 4 cups water, and bring to a boil. Turn off heat, and let the beans soak, covered, for 2 hours. *Do not drain,* as the beans will cook in the water they are soaking in.

3. Add all the ingredients for cooking the beans, and stir to mix. Bring to a boil. Reduce heat and simmer, partially covered, for 4½–5 hours. Stir the beans very carefully every ½ hour during cooking. (The heat should be as low as possible so that the beans barely simmer during the entire 5 hours of cooking. *At no point should they ever boil rapidly, or the beans will crack and become slimy.)*

5. Take out about 2–3 cups of the cooked beans from the pan, and finely puree them in a blender or food processor. Return the puree to the pan. Or mash about a third of the cooked beans in the pan itself, with the back of a spoon. (This will give the bean mixture a smoother, creamier consistency.) Keep the *dal* on a low simmer while you make the perfumed butter (*tadka*).

6. Heat the *ghee* or oil over medium-high heat in a frying pan.

When it is hot, add the cumin seeds. When the seeds turn dark brown (about 10 seconds), add the onions, and cook until they turn light brown (about 10 minutes), stirring constantly so they do not burn. Pour the entire contents of the frying pan over the simmering bean mixture. Add the heavy cream and chopped coriander leaves, and stir well to mix thoroughly. Simmer until heated through. Check for salt, and serve.

Note: This dish can be made several hours before you are ready to serve it. It also keeps in the refrigerator for up to 4 days, and freezes extremely well. Defrost thoroughly before reheating. To reheat, simmer over low heat until warmed through, stirring often but very carefully. Check for salt. Fold in a little ground roasted cumin seeds and fresh chopped coriander leaves to perk up the flavors.

Red kidney beans
(*Badi rajma*)

Black gram beans
(*Kali dal*)

This *dal* traditionally accompanies all *tandoori* food. Because of its unique consistency, *Kali Dal* is served with bread as well as rice. Its rich wholesome quality makes it an ideal vegetarian main dish for those days when you are planning a light meal. It is excellent with Lamb Pilaf with Leftover Roast Lamb (p. 188), Lamb Pilaf (p. 189), Emperor's Layered Meat and Fragrant Rice Casserole (p. 192), Chicken Pilaf (p. 228), or Royal Vegetable and Rice Casserole (p. 381). It can be served as an entree accompanied by a simple stir-fried vegetable and a plain fried bread or plain cooked rice.

Yogurt Salads

(Raita)

Cucumber and Yogurt Salad   *(Kheere ka Raita)*
Spinach and Yogurt Salad   *(Palak Raita)*
Tomato and Yogurt Salad   *(Tamato Pachadi)*
Okra and Yogurt Salad   *(Bhindi Pachadi)*
Dumplings in Fragrant Yogurt   *(Dahi Bhalle)*
Sweet Banana and Yogurt Salad   *(Keela Raita)*

An Indian meal, especially a vegetarian meal, is never considered complete without a dish containing yogurt, a primary source of protein. And there is no better way to serve yogurt than in a salad with all its nutrients intact. Yogurt salad should not be confused with the recently popularized yogurt dressing, a thin tasteless sauce. In yogurt salads, yogurt is an ingredient; therefore its rich flavor and texture are of prime importance. Indian yogurt is thick, creamy, and sweet, almost like cheese. This is because it is made from buffalo's milk, which has a high fat content, and also because it is sometimes poured into several layers of cheesecloth and hung for a few minutes to drain off the moisture—a process which makes it even creamier. When you make *raita*, you should use homemade yogurt made with whole milk. The commercially available plain yogurt, with some minor modifications, makes a satisfactory substitute: You should first taste the commercial yogurt to be sure it doesn't taste too tangy. Then add a little cream (preferably sour or heavy) to enrich its flavor and texture.

Yogurt salads, though more popular in the summer, are eaten all year round in all parts of India. The spices naturally vary from region to region. However all *raitas* can be grouped under three broad categories:

1. *Raitas* made with raw vegetables, the easiest and fastest to make. Raw vegetables are peeled, grated, or chopped, and then folded into seasoned yogurt, as in Tomato and Yogurt Salad (p. 345).

2. *Raitas* made with cooked vegetables. The vegetables are cooked separately and folded into the seasoned yogurt just before serving, as in Spinach and Yogurt Salad (p. 344).

3. *Raitas* made with dumplings, fruits, nuts, and such. These salads are often a little sweet. Since they require either special preparation or expensive ingredients, they are usually reserved for weddings, formal dinners, and other special occasions. A classic example is Sweet Banana and Yogurt Salad (p. 349).

Many of these yogurt salads, especially those made with

cooked vegetables and dumplings, make charming and delicious little meals in their own right when served with stuffed breads or special pilafs.

To make your own yogurt, follow the directions on p. 49.

Cucumber and Yogurt Salad

(Kheere ka Raita)

This cool refreshing yogurt salad is both easy and quick to put together. For best results, use only young tender cucumbers. You may have experienced the bitterness that many cucumbers have. To get rid of this bitterness, cut off the top of the cucumber and rub the two parts against each other in a circular motion for a minute. A white froth will collect around the edges. This is what sometimes gives cucumbers a bitter flavor. Cut another thin slice, removing the froth with it, and discard. The cucumber is now ready for use.

For 4–6 persons

2 medium-sized cucumbers
   (about 1½ pounds)
1 medium-sized ripe tomato
1 green chili, seeded and
   sliced (optional)
1½ cups plain yogurt
½ cup sour cream

½ teaspoon ground roasted
   cumin seeds (p. 66)
2 tablespoons finely chopped
   fresh mint, or coriander
   leaves, or 2 teaspoons dry
   mint leaves (optional)
½ teaspoon Kosher salt

1. Peel the cucumbers and cut them in half. If the seeds look hard and mature, scrape them out with a spoon, and discard. Using the coarse blade of the grater or a food processor, grate the cucumbers into a bowl.

2. Wash the tomato and wipe dry. Cut it in quarters and using a spoon, scrape out the pulp with the seeds (reserve them for some other use). Slice the tomato into thin shreds, and add them to the bowl.

(continued)

3. Slit and seed the chili, cut it into thin shreds, and add.

4. Put the yogurt, sour cream, cumin, and mint or coriander leaves in another bowl, and mix thoroughly. (The vegetables and the yogurt mixture can be prepared several hours ahead and refrigerated separately until needed. If dry mint leaves are used, the refrigeration is essential to allow the yogurt to absorb the full flavor of mint.)

5. When ready to serve, stir the salt and prepared vegetables into the yogurt mixture. Check for salt, and transfer to a serving bowl. Sprinkle with additional cumin, if desired.

On a hot summer day, the addition of a cool yogurt salad to the regular meal is essential. When you serve yogurt salad, try to avoid serving a main dish that contains a lot of yogurt, such as Chick Pea Dumplings in Yogurt Sauce or Fragrant Yogurt-Braised Chicken. Also, the main dish should not contain an excessive amount of the vegetable that is in the yogurt salad. For a refreshingly light lunch or supper or an unusual Sunday brunch, serve yogurt salad with just a stuffed bread, such as Cauliflower Stuffed Bread (p. 405), Spinach Bread (p. 410), or Potato- and Herb-Stuffed Bread (p. 409), accompanied by a fragrant cup of tea, perhaps Cardamom Tea (p. 487).

Spinach and Yogurt Salad

(Palak Raita)

This is a simple yet very tasty yogurt salad made with cooked spinach. All you need to do is mix the cooked spinach with the spices and yogurt. You can substitute cooked potatoes, peas, mixed vegetables or smoked eggplant pulp for the spinach.

For 4–6 persons

1 cup cooked spinach (p. 318)
1½ cups plain yogurt
½ cup sour cream
1 teaspoon ground roasted
　cumin seeds (p. 66)
1 teaspoon ground roasted
　coriander seeds (p. 66)

¼ teaspoon each black and red
　pepper
½ teaspoon Kosher salt
　paprika (optional)

1. Coarsely chop the spinach in a food processor, or on a chopping board, using a knife.

2. Put the yogurt, sour cream, cumin, coriander, and black and red pepper in a bowl, and mix thoroughly. (Both these items can be prepared several hours ahead and refrigerated.)

3. When ready to serve, stir the salt and the spinach into the seasoned yogurt, and transfer to a serving bowl. If desired, sprinkle with additional cumin, coriander, and a little sweet paprika.

To serve, follow the menu suggestions given for Cucumber and Yogurt Salad (p. 343).

Tomato and Yogurt Salad

(Tamato Pachadi)

This very simple yogurt salad is a universal favorite—red ripe tomatoes chopped and folded into thick creamy yogurt, streaked with mustard-seed-flavored oil. For this salad you need fully ripe sweet tomatoes with firm flesh; otherwise the tomato pulp will scatter into the yogurt, making the salad look unappealing.

(continued)

For 4–6 persons

4 medium-sized red ripe
  tomatoes (1 pound)
1½ cups plain yogurt
½ cup sour cream
½ teaspoon Kosher salt
2 tablespoons light sesame oil,
  or light vegetable oil

⅓ teaspoon black mustard
  seeds
1 green chili, seeded and
  shredded (optional)

1. Wash tomatoes and wipe dry. Dice them into neat ½-inch pieces.

2. Mix yogurt, sour cream, and salt in a serving bowl. Add tomatoes but do not stir. Cover and refrigerate until needed. (This may be prepared several hours ahead and kept refrigerated until you are ready to serve the dish.)

3. Heat the oil over high heat in a small frying pan. When the oil is very hot, add the mustard seeds. Keep a pot lid or spatter screen handy, since the seeds may splatter and splutter. When the mustard seeds stop sputtering and turn gray, add the chili, if you are using it. Stir rapidly for a moment, and pour the entire contents of the pan over the vegetable-yogurt mixture. Stir the salad carefully to mix the ingredients. Do not overstir; the salad must remain a little lumpy. Serve immediately.

To serve, follow the menu suggestions given for Cucumber and Yogurt Salad on page 343, except try to serve southern and southwestern specialties with it, such as Goanese Hot and Pungent Curry (p. 199), Spicy Brussels Sprouts, Green Beans, and Lentil Stew (p. 276), or Mixed Lentils and Vegetable Stew (p. 280).

Okra and Yogurt Salad

(Bhindi Pachadi)

Whether or not you like okra, you will love this yogurt salad made with crisp crunchy pieces of okra. The only thing to remember is that you should fold the okra into the yogurt just prior to serving, because fried okra loses its wonderful crisp texture and becomes limp if it sits too long in yogurt, and also turns the snowy-white yogurt brown and unpleasant-looking.

For 4–6 persons

1½ cups plain yogurt
½ cup sour cream
½ teaspoon Kosher salt
1 tablespoon oil, preferably
   light sesame oil

⅓ teaspoon black mustard
   seeds
1 green chili, seeded and
   shredded
¾ cup crisp fried okra (p. 310)

1. Put the yogurt, sour cream, and salt in a bowl, mix thoroughly, and set aside.

2. Heat the oil over high heat in a small frying pan. When the oil is very hot, carefully add the mustard seeds. Keep a pot lid or spatter screen handy, since the seeds may splatter and splutter. When the seeds stop sputtering and turn gray, add the shredded chili. Stir rapidly for a moment, and pour the entire contents of the pan over the yogurt. Add the fried okra, folding all the ingredients into the yogurt. Do not overmix. The salad should be a little lumpy. Serve immediately.

Follow the menu suggestions given for Cucumber and Yogurt Salad on page 343. In addition, serve this salad with dishes flavored with mustard seeds, such as Spicy Brussels Sprouts, Green Beans, and Lentil Stew (p. 276), Goanese Hot and Pungent Curry (p. 199), or Mixed Lentils and Vegetable Stew (p. 280).

Dumplings in Fragrant Yogurt

(Dahi Bhalle)

This is the classic recipe for making *Dahi Bhalle*, even though the flavorings may vary slightly from state to state. This recipe is from the state of Punjab, where the salad is flavored with cumin, coriander, and fresh ginger root, and wrapped in the fragrance of fresh coriander leaves. The dish takes a little time to make, since you first have to make the bean dumplings, but the results will reward you.

For 8–12 persons

24 silky bean dumplings (*Bade*, p. 123)	¼ teaspoon black pepper
3½ cups plain yogurt	¼ teaspoon red pepper
½ cup sour cream	¾ teaspoon Kosher salt
½ cup cold water	2 green chilies, finely chopped
1¼ teaspoon ground roasted cumin seeds (p. 66)	2 tablespoons chopped fresh coriander leaves

1. Put the bean dumplings in a bowl, and cover with hot water. Let them soak for 15 minutes, and drain. Pick up one dumpling at a time, and press very gently between your palms to squeeze out as much water as possible. Do not overpress, or the dumpling will fall apart. Repeat the same process with the rest of the dumplings. Set aside.

2. Blend the yogurt, sour cream, and water in a bowl, beating with a fork for 1 minute or until the ingredients are thoroughly mixed. Add 1 teaspoon of the cumin, ⅛ teaspoon each of the black and red pepper, and salt. Mix again.

3. Dip the dumplings, one at a time, in the seasoned yogurt, and lay them in a shallow serving dish big enough to hold the dumplings in one slightly overlapping layer. Pour the remaining yogurt over the dumplings, distributing it evenly, and cover. Chill

for at least 4 hours. (During this period the dumplings will soak up the yogurt sauce.)

4. When ready to serve, uncover, sprinkle with the remaining cumin and black and red pepper. Scatter the chopped chilies and coriander over all and serve accompanied by Sweet and Sour Tamarind Relish (*mli Chutney*, p. 442), if desired.

Since this yogurt salad is made with bean dumplings, avoid serving any other *dal* in the main dish—unless you want a very substantial meal. *Dahi Bhalle* is fairly filling; therefore, for a light meal, serve it as an entree accompanied by a stuffed bread such as Cauliflower Bread (p. 405), Potato- and Herb-Stuffed Bread (p. 409), or Spinach Bread (p. 410), or by a plain fried bread such as Whole Wheat Flaky Bread (p. 402) or Deep-fried Puffy Bread (p. 413), accompanied by a pickle like Sweet Lemon Pickle with Cumin (p. 447).

Sweet Banana and Yogurt Salad

(Keela Raita)

This is a luscious salad traditionally reserved for special occasions in India. Usually bananas are used, but you can substitute pineapple, peaches, apricots, or grapes. Just remember to adjust for sweetness, as all these fruits are more tart than bananas.

For 4–6 persons

2 tablespoons slivered blanched almonds	3–4 tablespoons honey or sugar
2 tablespoons seedless raisins	⅛ teaspoon ground cardamom or grated nutmeg
1 cup plain yogurt	1 medium-sized ripe banana, peeled and thinly sliced
1 cup sour cream	

(continued)

1. Put almonds and raisins in a small bowl, and add about ½ cup boiling water. Soak for 15 minutes, and drain.

2. Mix the drained almonds and raisins with the yogurt, sour cream, honey or sugar, and cardamom or nutmeg in a serving bowl. Add the banana slices and gently fold them into the yogurt mixture. Cover, and chill thoroughly before serving. If desired, sprinkle with additional cardamom or nutmeg.

This yogurt salad with its sweet nutty overtone is ideal with such pilafs as Emperor's Layered Meat and Rice Casserole (p. 192), Chicken Pilaf (p. 228), Sweet Saffron Pilaf (p. 369), and Saffron Pilaf with Peaches (p. 371).

Accompanying Staples

Rice

(Chawal)

Rice Cooked in Fragrant Meat Broth   *(Yakhni Chawal)*
Indian Fried Rice   *(Ghee Chawal)*
Cumin and Turmeric Rice   *(Peele Chawal)*
Patiala Pilaf   *(Patiala Pullao)*
Fragrant Pilaf Banaras Style   *(Banarasi Pullao)*
Sweet Saffron Pilaf   *(Zarda)*
Saffron Pilaf with Peaches   *(Zaffrani Pullao)*
Okra Pilaf   *(Bhindi Pullao)*
The Emperor's Pilaf with Black Mushrooms   *(Badshahi Pullao* or
      Gochian Pullao)
Mint Pilaf   *(Hari Chutney ka Pullao)*
Vegetable and Rice Casserole with Herbs   *(Tahari)*
Royal Vegetable and Rice Casserole   *(Shahi Sabz Biriyani)*

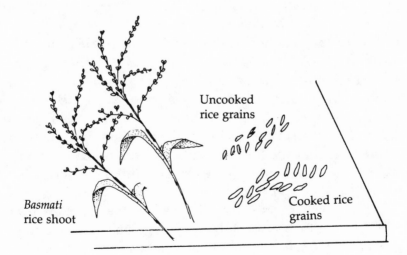

Uncooked
rice grains

*Basmati
rice shoot*

Cooked rice
grains

Rice is one of the oldest grains known to mankind. In India it has been cultivated for some six thousand years. Today it is the staple of more than two thirds of the country's population. This long and close association with rice has resulted in a classic Indian cuisine that makes full use of it. Rice is the occasion for hundreds of ingenious and delectable Indian dishes.

To begin with, Indians cook the rice itself to perfection—in a way that is unbeatable anywhere in the world.

It is ground and turned into flour or roasted into flakes, and in one or the other of these forms, is used in making pancakes, crepes, fritters, buns, cakes, dumplings, wafers, savories, desserts, puddings, and sweetmeats. Rice flour dissolved in water is considered holy and is used as a paint for decoration during religious festivals and on other special occasions. Raw rice grains are thrown on newly married couples as a symbol of fertility; this ancient Hindu custom is observed in many cultures around the world.

Even though there are thousands of different varieties of rice grains in the world, they basically fall into two categories—long grain rice and short grain rice. (Sometimes a third category, medium grain rice, is added.) The short grain variety with fat oval grains is popular in southern European countries and parts of eastern China. When cooked, these starchy grains become plump and creamy, and adhere to each other. They are used in such Italian dishes as *risotto* and in the Spanish *paella*. Short grain rice is particularly suited for making puddings and cakes.

The long grain variety is more popular and is eaten widely around the world. This rice cooks to light fluffy grains that are nonsticky. In India several varieties of long grain rice, known as *arwa chawal*, are cultivated in the southern and eastern regions, where they grow abundantly. There the staple is rice, and it is usually served plain—steamed or boiled.

The Northerners eat much less rice than Indians from other regions since their staple is bread. But no one in the world pampers rice and cooks it with such meticulous care as they do. Their techniques of rice cooking are so refined and their rice dishes so exquisite and elaborate that they even surpass their main and side dishes. The rice is often cooked with fragrant spices, such as cinnamon, cardamom, and saffron, and includes vegetables and meat. The famous *pullao* and *biriyani* which owe their origin to Moghul cooking, come from this region.

There is one particular variety of long grain rice grown in limited quantity along the foothills of the Himalayas in the North and this is considered the best rice in the world. Its generic name is *basmati*. Cooked *basmati* has long thin grains, is tender and spongy to the touch, and exudes a special nutty-milky aroma. As a result, even plain cooked *basmati* has the aroma, flavor, and appeal of an exquisite pilaf. That is why it is essential to use *basmati* to make authentic-tasting *pullao*, *biriyani*, and other Indian rice preparations. The two most commonly available varieties of *basmati* are *Patna basmati* from the state of Bihar, and *Dehradun basmati* from the state of Uttar Pradesh. *Dehradun basmati* is considered to be superior. All *basmati* rice is processed and then graded by the percentage of whole, unbroken grains in each batch. The number one grade contains no broken grains. The *basmati* is then aged for several years in *godowns;* this process enhances its aroma and flavor. The best quality *basmati* commercially available in India today is well-aged *Dehradun basmati*. It is this variety that is generally recommended for making pilafs. Presently there is no shortage of *basmati* in India, especially in New Delhi and other big cities in the North. However, the supply of the best grade is limited to the *Dehradun* region.

Another point of interest: A small town called Ran Bir Singh Pura, in the state of Jammu, is believed to produce a rare variety of *basmati*, which is reputed to be the best of all *basmatis*. Unfortunately, most of the fertile land lies right at the border of Pakistan and cannot be irrigated, thus limiting the supply of this rice to a bare minimum. Since this area is off limits for defense reasons, the only way to obtain this exquisite *basmati* is via army personnel returning from a tour of duty there.

The very best grade of the *Dehradun basmati* is not yet available in the United States. But you can still buy many fine grades of it in the stores.

Because of its high grade and limited cultivation, *basmati* costs a few cents more than the American long-grain variety, but it is not difficult to find. It is sold in Indian grocery stores, in bags weighing from two to ten pounds and under three labels: Indian *Basmati;* Pakistani *Basmati* (from Pakistan); and Dehradun *Basmati.* The first two are very similar in cost and quality. The third, which costs more because it is of a higher grade, is worth the price. *Basmati* is available in all Indian, Middle-eastern, and specialty food stores. Recently, several major department stores have started carrying it in their gourmet food sections.

Basmati requires no special skills to cook. It is like any other long-grain rice, requiring twice as much water as short grain and about twenty-five minutes to cook. There is, however, one major difference between regular long grain rice cooking and *basmati* cooking: *basmati* is always soaked in cold water prior to being cooked. Also there are a few special techniques that ensure fluffy tender rice grains that come out looking like lace.

Preparing *Basmati* Rice for Cooking:

Cleaning: Often when you buy *basmati* rice you may notice that it contains a few unhulled rice grains, pieces of stones, and sticks. These should be removed. Put the rice in a large plate such as a *paraath* (p. 387) or a serving platter, or simply spread it on the kitchen or dining table. Gather a small portion aside so that the grains are all separated and the foreign objects clearly visible. Pick out and discard all the dirt pieces, and push the cleaned rice to one side. Spread more of the rice the same way, and continue cleaning until the entire amount is clear of foreign particles. (There is no need to remove the husk and bran pieces, since they will disappear when the rice is washed.)

Washing: No matter which quality *basmati* you use, as long as it is *basmati,* and cooked the Indian way, *it must be washed.* Washing removes light foreign objects, which will float. It also removes the starch clinging to the rice grains, which could make the cooked rice sticky and gummy.

To wash the rice, put it in a large bowl, and fill with cold water. The water will grow milky, and several pieces of bran, husk, and other objects will float to the top. Let the rice settle to the bottom for 2–3 seconds. Then tilt the bowl and pour off the water. Repeat this process 8 or 9 times, until the water runs clean and clear.

Soaking: This is an essential step, unique to *basmati* rice cooking. The only other rice in the world that is soaked before being cooked is the Persian rice called *Domsia*. But *Domsia* requires a much longer soaking, usually overnight. In the soaking process, the rice grains absorb moisture and thereby "relax" prior to being cooked. As a result, they expand to long thin grains that will not crack or break when water is added during cooking.

To soak the rice, add twice the amount of cold water as there is raw rice (2 cups water to 1 cup rice, and so on). Let the rice soak exactly ½ hour, and drain, reserving the water. (In Indian cooking, unless otherwise specified, the rice is always cooked in the water in which it is soaked.) The soaked rice will be chalk-white in color and very fragile. Therefore be careful when you handle it.

Cooking *Basmati* Rice

The *basmati* rice can be cooked plain in one of three ways; steamed, boiled, or baked, all referred to as *sada chawal* or *obla chawal*. All three methods produce excellent results. It can be cooked with fat or oil, spices, herbs, vegetables, and all types of meat and cheese. When it is cooked with other ingredients the dish is called *pullao*, *biriyani*, or *tahari*. No matter what rice dish you are preparing, each is created from one of these three basic techniques.

Basic Technique for Cooking Plain Steamed *Basmati* Rice

In this process the rice is simmered, in the same water it has been soaking in, until it is almost tender and the water is absorbed. It is then steamed gently over very low heat until the rice grains are all separated and become tender, springy, and fluffy.

1. Put the reserved water into a large heavy-bottomed pan with a tight-fitting lid, and bring to a boil. Add the soaked rice, and stir carefully with a narrow stirring implement such as a fork or knife (so that the rice grains are not crushed) until the water comes to a second boil. (Stirring will keep the rice from settling or lumping.)

2. Reduce heat to low and simmer, partially covered, until most of the water is absorbed and the surface of the rice is full of steamy holes (about 10–15 minutes). There is no need to stir the rice but if you wish to do so, use a fork or knife.

3. Cover the pan tightly, reduce heat further to the lowest possible level, and raise the pan about an inch away from the source of the heat. (This can be achieved by placing a pair of tongs or a Chinese wok ring over the burner and resting the pot on it.) Let the rice steam for 10 minutes.

Basic Technique for Cooking Plain Boiled *Basmati* Rice

Here the rice is boiled briskly for a short time in a large quantity of water until almost tender. Then it is drained and rinsed, and returned to the pot. The pot is then placed over the lowest possible heat. The rice is steamed until it is fluffy and tender, and the grains are all separated. The water for soaking the rice is not used for cooking.

1. Bring a large quantity of water (about 6–7 times the quantity of rice) to a boil in a deep pot. Add the soaked rice, and stir immediately for ½ minute (this prevents the rice from settling) being careful not to break the fragile rice grains. Bring the water to a second boil (it will take about 3 minutes), and cook the rice for 2 minutes.

2. Pour the entire contents into a large sieve held over the kitchen sink. Hold the sieve under the tap, and let cold water run through the rice at medium speed for 3–5 seconds. Shake the sieve to drain the rice thoroughly.

3. Return the rice to the pot, and cover it tightly. Place the pot over the lowest possible heat, raised above the burner with a pair of tongs, or a Chinese wok ring. Let the rice steam for 10 minutes.

Basic Technique for Cooking Plain Baked *Basmati* Rice

In this process the rice is first boiled quickly until almost tender, then drained, and baked in the oven to finish the cooking. A little butter or oil is folded into the rice before baking it. Rice cooked in this way expands fully and the grains become long and a little dry.

1. Preheat the oven to 300°F.

2. Bring a large quantity of water (about 6–7 times the quantity of rice) to a boil in a deep pot. Add the soaked rice, and stir immediately for ½ minute (this will prevent the rice from settling), being careful not to break the fragile grains. Bring the water to a second boil, and cook the rice for 2 minutes.

3. Pour the entire contents into a large sieve held over the kitchen sink, and drain the rice thoroughly.

4. Return the rice to a heavy oven-proof casserole with a tight-fitting lid. Add a little fat or oil, and mix carefully but thoroughly to coat all the grains. Put a piece of foil on top of the casserole, and cover tightly with the lid.

5. Bake the rice in the middle level of the oven for 25 minutes.

Resting the Cooked *Basmati* Rice

No matter which of the three basic cooking techniques is followed for the *basmati* rice, it must rest undisturbed, covered, on top of the stove or in the turned-off oven for a short period (about 5 minutes) before being handled. During this time the pan should not be opened and the contents never stirred. This is an essential step that causes the firm, springy separate grains to retain their shape, even with repeated handling. This is because freshly cooked rice, just like a fresh roast, is moist, steamy, and very fragile; when handled it becomes sticky and mushy. Just before serving, the rice should be fluffed with a fork or knife. Cooked rice generally remains warm for up to 25 minutes, covered.

Preparing Rice Dishes Ahead of Time

Except for *biriyani* and certain *pullao*, most rice preparations should be made just before serving, because the fragrance of such spices as cinnamon, cloves, and cumin is much more pronounced in a freshly made pilaf. Storing, especially refrigeration, makes these dishes lose much of their delicate aroma and flavor. It is possible to reheat rice dishes, however, especially if you have some left over. They can be reheated either on top of the stove or in the oven.

To heat in the oven: Place the rice in a large sheet of heavy-duty aluminum foil, sprinkling a little cold water over the rice if it looks somewhat dry. Cover, wrap, and seal tightly. Bake in the middle level of a preheated 300°F oven for 25–30 minutes or until heated through.

To heat on top of the stove: Place the rice in a heavy-bottomed pan. Add a few tablespoons of cold water. Heat the pan over medium heat, stirring and tossing the rice constantly until enough steam builds up. Cover the pan tightly, reduce heat, and let the rice steam until heated through (about 10–15 minutes).

How Much Rice to Cook per Person with an Indian Meal

In America, and in the West in general, much less rice is eaten than in India. In India, easterners and southerners consume more rice per serving than the northerners. Preference for rice is not just cultural, but a matter of taste. Many like the taste of rice itself. Others like it but do not indulge themselves fully, as they consider it simply starch. Therefore, I would advise you to use your own judgment in determining the quantity of rice to cook. Remember that leftover rice can always be heated and served the next day, mixed and stir-fried with cooked meat or vegetables, at breakfast in place of hashed brown potatoes, or as a light lunch or supper.

But just as a general rule, two cups of raw rice will make six generous servings or eight fairly large servings.

About Substitutions

There is no substitute for *basmati* rice, not even the Persian *domsia* rice, for that does not have the *basmati* aroma or flavor. Therefore, if you want to cook *basmati* rice, you have to use *basmati* rice. In the event you are unable to get *basmati*, or your supply has run out, you may substitute the regular long grain rice (supermarket variety) but remember it will taste, smell, and look quite different. When substituting regular long grain rice for *basmati*, the following modifications have to be made in the recipe:

1. There is no need to clean the rice, since regular rice is thoroughly cleaned before being packaged.

2. The washing and soaking steps can be omitted, as the regular long grain rice no longer contains a starch coating.

3. The cooking process is practically the same, except that regular long grain rice takes a little longer to cook (partly because the *basmati* grains are much thinner, but mainly because they have been soaked, which is comparable to a partial cooking.)

Rice Cooked in Fragrant Meat Broth

(*Yakhni Chawal*)

This is a quick and easy recipe for making a very fragrant batch of rice. A rich meat broth (*yakhni*) is all you need to prepare it. The rice is cooked in the broth instead of in water. *Yakhni Chawal* is traditionally used for making *Shah Jahani Biriyani*, the famous Emperor's Layered Meat and Fragrant Rice Casserole (p. 192), but it is equally good with all Moghul lamb or beef preparations.

(continued)

For 8–10 persons

3 cups *basmati* rice	5¼ cups homemade meat broth
4 tablespoons *usli ghee*, (p. 50)	(*Yakhni*, p. 43)
or light vegetable oil	2 teaspoons Kosher salt

1. Wash *basmati* rice following directions on page 356.

2. Place rice in a bowl, and add enough cold water to cover the rice by 1 inch. Let it soak for exactly ½ hour. (The rice grains will turn opaque and chalk-white in color.) Drain the rice, and set aside. Discard the water in which the rice was soaking.

3. Heat the *ghee* over medium heat in a heavy-bottomed pan. When it is hot, add the drained rice, and fry, stirring with a spatula for 3 minutes or until the rice turns translucent again. Add broth and salt, and stir carefully to keep the rice from lumping. Bring to a boil.

4. Reduce heat to low and simmer, partially covered, until the water is almost absorbed and the surface of the rice is full of steamy holes (about 12–15 minutes).

5. Cover the pan tightly and reduce heat to the lowest possible level. If possible, also raise the pan about an inch from the source of heat by placing a pair of tongs or a Chinese wok ring over the burner. Let rice steam for 10 minutes. Turn off the heat, and let the rice rest undisturbed, covered, for 5 minutes before serving. The rice should not be stirred during this final steaming and resting, as the grains of rice are sticky and very fragile, and will break easily if handled. The resting process firms and separates them; as a result they retain their shape no matter how often they are handled. The rice will remain warm for 20 minutes, covered. Uncover, and if desired, fluff the rice, and serve.

Indian Fried Rice

(Ghee Chawal)

This delicious fried rice takes only a few minutes to prepare. The onions and cauliflower are cooked first, and then the rice is folded in. *Ghee Chawal* is a southern specialty; it can also be made with a combination of peas, green pepper, scallions, shallots, and potatoes.

For 8 persons

3 tablespoons light vegetable oil
1 cup coarsely chopped onions
1 small head cauliflower (about 1 pound), cut into ¾-inch pieces
2 cups leftover plain cooked rice (*basmati*, regular long grain, or converted)

2 teaspoons ground roasted cumin seeds (p. 66)
1 teaspoon ground roasted coriander seeds (p. 66)
1¼ teaspoons Kosher salt
2–3 tablespoons finely chopped fresh coriander leaves

1. Heat the oil over medium-low heat in a large frying pan, or any large shallow pan, and add the onions and cauliflower. Fry the vegetables until they are lightly browned (about 5 minutes), stirring constantly to prevent burning. Add ⅓ cup cold water, cover, and cook for 15 minutes or until the vegetables are cooked but still crisp and there is *some water* left in the pan.

2. Add the cooked rice, mix well, replace the cover, and continue cooking for an additional 2 minutes or until the rice is heated through.

3. Uncover, sprinkle in the cumin, coriander, salt, and chopped coriander leaves, and mix thoroughly to distribute the herbs and spices.

(continued)

You can serve this rice by itself for a light lunch, accompanied by a cool yogurt drink (see pp. 488 and 489) or a yogurt salad. You can expand the meal and serve it with other fried foods, such as Chick-pea Batter Fish (p. 251), Panfried Fillet of Sole with Carom (p. 248), Meat Cutlets (p. 197) or Shrimp Fritters (p. 118).

Cumin and Turmeric Rice

(Peele Chawal)

The Punjabis don't like to color their rice dishes; they prefer to display the pearly white grains. This hearty, peasant-style northern specialty is the one exception. The beautiful golden yellow color is lent by the turmeric.

For 4–6 persons

2 medium-sized potatoes	1 teaspoon cumin seeds
1½ cups *basmati* rice or regular long grain rice	¾ teaspoon turmeric
4 tablepoons Indian vegetable shortening, or light vegetable oil	2 teaspoons Kosher salt, or to taste

1. Peel the potatoes, and dice them into neat ½-inch pieces. Put them in a bowl, cover with cold water, and set aside.

2. Wash *basmati* rice following directions on page 356.

3. Place the rice in a bowl, add 3 cups of cold water, let soak for half an hour, and drain, reserving the water. (Omit this step if you are using regular long grain rice).

4. Heat the shortening or oil over medium-high heat in a heavy-bottomed pan. When it is very hot, add the cumin seeds. When the cumin turns dark brown (about 10 seconds), add the potatoes and turmeric, and fry until potatoes are slightly browned (about 3 minutes). Add the rice, and continue cooking until the rice is slightly fried (about 2 minutes), stirring constantly to prevent burning. Add the reserved water (or 3 cups of cold water if you are using regular long grain rice) and salt. Stir for a moment to mix all the ingredients, and bring to a boil. Reduce heat to medium-low and simmer, covered, for 10 minutes (15 minutes for regular long grain rice), or until most of the water is absorbed and the surface of the rice is full of steamy holes. There is no need to stir the rice, but if you wish to do so, use a fork or a knife and be very careful not to break the fragile rice grains.

5. Reduce the heat to the lowest point, and raise the pan about an inch away from the source of heat. (This can be done by placing a pair of tongs or a Chinese wok ring on the burner and resting the pan on it.) Let the rice steam for 10 minutes. Turn off heat, and let the rice rest undisturbed, covered, for 5 minutes before serving. Do not stir the rice during these last 15 minutes, as the grains are moist, steamy, and very fragile, breaking easily when handled. The resting process firms and separates the grains; as a result they retain their shape no matter how often they are handled. The rice remains warm for 20 minutes, if left covered. Uncover, and if desired, fluff the rice with a fork, and serve.

Peele Chawal is usually served as a light luncheon dish, along with a cool yogurt salad, such as Cucumber and Yogurt Salad (p. 343), or Dumplings in Fragrant Yogurt (p. 348). For a more substantial meal, serve it with Chick-pea Batter Fish (p. 251) or Moghul Kabobs with Raisin Stuffing (p. 107).

Patiala Pilaf

(Patiala Pullao)

Although pilaf is made throughout North India, it is the Punjabis who excel in creating this Moghul delicacy to perfection. So it is not surprising that the basic, the most exquisitely flavored pilaf of all is called *Patiala* (a city in the state of Punjab) or *Punjabi Pullao*.

Made with the finest quality *basmati* grown in the North, and the best quality spices, this pilaf is indeed sensational. Its wonderful fragrance and delicate flavor linger on in one's memory long after the pilaf has been devoured.

The Punjabis use only whole spices in their pilafs, to flavor them without changing the color of the rice. This pilaf is traditionally served with all the whole spices left in, because it makes the dish look attractive. Except for the cumin, the spices are not eaten, although no harm will come to you if you bite into the cardamom pods, chew a bay leaf, or swallow a few cloves.

For 6–8 persons

3 medium-sized onions
2 cups *basmati* rice
6 tablespoons light vegetable oil
1 teaspoon black (or white) cumin seeds
2 teaspoons finely chopped garlic

3 black (or 6 green) cardamom pods
1 cinnamon stick, 3 inches long
8 whole cloves
2 bay leaves
2 teaspoons Kosher salt

1. Peel onions, and finely chop one of them. Slice the remaining two into paper-thin shreds, and set aside.

2. Wash *basmati* rice following the directions on page 356.

3. Place the rice in a bowl, add 4 cups cold water, and let soak for ½ hour. Drain the rice, reserving the water, and set aside.

4. Heat the oil in a heavy-bottomed pan, and add the 2 shredded onions. Over medium-high heat, fry the onions, stirring

constantly, until they turn dark brown (about 20 minutes). Take the onions out with a slotted spoon, and drain them on paper towels. When cool, these fried onion shreds will become crackling crisp. (See Crispy Fried Onions, p. 74.) Set them aside for the garnish.

5. Turn the heat to medium high. If you are using white cumin, add the seeds now, and fry until they turn dark brown (about 10 seconds). Then add the 1 chopped onion, and fry until light brown (about 4 minutes), stirring constantly to prevent burning. Do not let the onion brown too much, or the pilaf will turn brown. Add the garlic, and fry for an additional minute. Add all the spices, and continue frying for ½ minute or so, or until the spices are slightly puffed and browned. Add rice, and fry until the rice becomes translucent again and begins to brown (about 2–3 minutes). Add the reserved water and salt, and bring to a boil, stirring frequently to keep the rice from settling.

6. Reduce heat and simmer, partially covered, until the water is almost absorbed and the surface of the rice is covered with several tiny steam holes (about 10–12 minutes). There is no need to stir the rice, but if you wish to do so, use a fork or a knife so that you don't crush the rice grains.

7. Cover the pan tightly, reduce the heat to the lowest possible level, and raise the pan about an inch away from the source of heat (this can be done by placing a pair of tongs or a Chinese wok ring over the burner and resting the pan on it.) Let rice steam for 10 minutes. Turn off heat, and let the rice rest undisturbed, covered, for another five minutes. Do not stir the rice during these last 15 minutes, as the grains are very moist and fragile, breaking easily with every touch. The rice will remain warm for 20 minutes, if left covered. Uncover, fluff the rice with a fork, and transfer to a warm serving platter. Spread the fried onion shreds over it and serve immediately.

This elegant pilaf goes with practically all North Indian and Moghul dishes. It is particularly good with cream-braised dishes, such as Lamb Braised in Aromatic Cream Sauce (p. 164), Lamb Fillets Braised in Yogurt Cardamom Sauce (p. 168), Royal Braised Lamb with Fragrant Spices (p. 174) or Lamb in Fragrant Garlic Cream Sauce (p. 176). It also melds well with seafood preparations, particularly those with a North Indian or Moghul flavor, such as Lobster in Fried Onion Sauce (p. 247) or Shrimp Laced with Mild Fragrant Spices (p. 240).

Fragrant Pilaf Banaras Style

(Banarasi Pullao)

Located along the river Ganges, Banaras is the holy city of the Hindus. The people here adhere strictly to Hindu dietary principles, which means, among other things, no onions or garlic in the food. Banaras pilaf gets its fragrance, therefore, from a variety of spices and fresh ginger root. The flavor, although different from Patiala Pilaf, is extremely good.

As in Patiala Pilaf, the whole spices are left in the rice, though they are not eaten. But biting into one will do you no harm.

For 6–8 persons

2 cups *basmati* rice	1 bay leaf
3 tablespoons Indian vegetable shortening, or light vegetable oil	1 stick cinnamon, 3 inches long
	24 black peppercorns (optional)
	2 teaspoons grated fresh ginger root
4 black (or 8 green) cardamom pods	2 teaspoons Kosher salt
10 whole cloves	

1. Wash *basmati* rice following directions on page 356.

2. Place the rice in a bowl, add 4 cups cold water, and let soak exactly ½ hour (the rice grains will turn opaque and chalk-white in color). Drain the rice, reserving the water, and set aside.

3. Heat the shortening over medium heat in a heavy-bottomed pan, and add all the spices except the ginger. Fry until the spices are slightly brown and puffed (about 2 minutes). Add rice, and

continue frying until the rice turns translucent and begins to brown (about 3 minutes), stirring constantly to prevent burning.

4. Add the reserved water, ginger, and salt, stir well to keep the rice from settling, and bring to a boil. Reduce heat and simmer, partially covered, for 10 minutes or until the water is almost totally absorbed and the surface of the rice is covered with several steamy holes. There is no need to stir the rice, but if you wish to do so, use a fork or knife, being very careful not to break the rice grains.

5. Cover the pan tightly, reduce heat to the lowest point, and if possible, raise the pan about an inch away from the source of heat (this can be done by placing a pair of tongs or a Chinese wok ring on the burner and resting the pan on it). Let the rice steam for 10 minutes. Turn off the heat and let the rice rest undisturbed, covered, for 5 minutes. Do not stir the rice during the last 15 minutes of steaming and resting; the grains are very moist and fragile, thus breaking easily. The rice remains warm for 20 minutes, if left covered. Uncover, and fluff the rice with a fork before serving.

To serve, follow the menu suggestions given for Patiala Pilaf on p. 366.

Sweet Saffron Pilaf

(Zarda)

Zarda is traditionally prepared by the Moslems in India for their religious festival Muharram. Many cooks substitute a yellow vegetable coloring known as Zarda coloring for a part of the saffron, mainly to economize, and thus produce a less fragrant zarda. To enjoy this gorgeous rice preparation to its fullest, you must use only the pure thing and no substitutes.

This pilaf is slightly sweet. The whole spices are not meant to be eaten, but if you do bite into one, no harm will come to you.

(continued)

For 6–8 persons

2 cups *basmati* rice
1 teaspoon saffron threads
4 tablespoons *usli ghee*, (p. 50)
    or light vegetable oil
10 whole cloves
8 green cardamom pods

1 stick cinnamon, 3 inches
    long
¼ cup seedless raisins
¼ cup sugar
1¼ teaspoons Kosher salt

1. Wash *basmati* rice following the directions on page 356.

2. Place the rice in a bowl, add 4 cups cold water, and let soak for ½ hour. Drain the rice, reserving the water, and set aside.

3. Place the saffron threads in a small plate, and using the back of a spoon or your fingertips, powder it. Add 2 tablespoons of water, and continue mashing until thoroughly dissolved. Set aside.

4. Heat the *ghee* over medium heat in a heavy-bottomed pan. When it is hot, add the cloves, cardamom, and cinnamon, and fry until they are lightly browned and puffed (about 1 minute). Add rice, and fry until the rice is thoroughly coated with the *ghee* and begins to brown (about 3 minutes), stirring constantly to prevent burning.

5. Add reserved water, saffron water, raisins, sugar, and salt, and stir well to keep the rice from settling. Bring to a boil. Reduce heat, and simmer partially covered for 10 minutes or until most of the liquid is absorbed and the surface of the rice is filled with steamy holes. There is no need to stir, but if you wish to do so, use a fork or knife so that the rice grains are not crushed.

6. Cover the pan tightly, reduce heat to the lowest possible point and, if possible, raise the pan an inch away from the source of heat by resting the pan on a pair of tongs or a Chinese wok ring placed over the burner. Let the rice steam for 10 minutes, and turn off the heat. Now let it rest undisturbed, covered, for 5 minutes. Do not stir the rice during these final 15 minutes of steaming and resting, as the grains are still very moist and fragile at this stage. The rice remains warm for 20 minutes if left covered. Uncover, and fluff the rice with a fork before serving.

This saffron-perfumed pilaf is ideally served with such *Tandoori* foods as Tandoori Chicken (p. 221), and with Moghul braised dishes such as Royal Braised Lamb with Fragrant Spices (p. 174), Lamb in Fragrant Garlic Cream Sauce (p. 176), and Lamb Fillets Braised in Yogurt Cardamom Sauce (p. 168). For an interesting contrast in flavor, serve Panfried Fillet of Sole Laced with Carom (p. 248) or Chick-pea Batter Fish (p. 251).

Saffron Pilaf with Peaches

(Zaffrani Pullao)

Saffron Pilaf, a Moghul classic, is without question the most gorgeous of all pilafs. The beautiful orange-yellow rice is studded with raisins, almonds, and pistachios, and is served enclosed in a ring of shimmering butter-glazed peaches. Its sweet flavor is imparted by the sweet spices: cinnamon, cardamom, and of course, saffron. The cinnamon stick is included only for aroma and is not meant to be eaten.

For 6–8 persons

2 cups *basmati* rice	½ cup finely chopped onions
3–4 fresh ripe peaches (about 1 pound), or 1 sixteen-ounce can peach slices in syrup	1 stick cinnamon, 3 inches long
6 tablespoons *usli ghee* (p. 50), or light vegetable oil	½ teaspoon ground cardamom
	1 teaspoon saffron threads, powdered
2 tablespoons slivered blanched almonds	1½ teaspoons Kosher salt
2 tablespoons unsalted blanched pistachios	¼ cup seedless raisins
	1 cup milk

(continued)

1. Wash the *basmati* rice following the instructions on page 356.

2. Put the rice in a bowl, add 3 cups of cold water, and let soak for ½ hour. Drain the rice, reserving the water, and set aside.

3. Drop fresh peaches in rapidly boiling water, and blanch for ½ minute. Take the peaches out, and immediately put them into a bowl of cold water (this will loosen the skin and make peeling easier). Peel the peaches, and cut them lengthwise into ½-inch-thick slices. If you are using canned peach slices, soak them in cold salted water (1 teaspoon salt for each quart of water) for ½ hour. This will remove the excess sweetness. Drain, pat dry with paper towels, and set aside.

4. Heat the *ghee* over medium heat in a heavy-bottomed pan. When it is hot, add the peach slices, and sauté until they are lightly browned on both sides (about 2–3 minutes). Remove them with a slotted spoon, and put them in a bowl.

5. Add slivered almonds to the same *ghee*, and sauté, turning and tossing until lightly browned (about 1–2 minutes). Transfer them to paper towels to drain. Repeat with the pistachios the same way. Set nuts aside for the garnish.

6. Increase heat to medium-high, and add onions to the *ghee*. Fry until they turn pale and limp (about 2 minutes), stirring constantly to prevent burning. Add cinnamon, and fry for an additional minute or until the cinnamon is fried and puffed. Add drained rice, and continue frying until the rice is thoroughly coated with butter and begins to brown (about 2 minutes). Add cardamom, saffron, salt, raisins, reserved water, and milk, and bring to the boil, stirring rapidly to keep the rice from settling. Reduce heat and simmer, partially covered, for 10 minutes or until most of the liquid is absorbed and the surface of the rice is filled with steamy holes. There is no need to stir, but if you wish to do so, use a fork or knife so that the rice grains are not crushed.

7. Cover the pan tightly, reduce heat to the lowest point and, if possible, raise the pan an inch away from the source of heat by resting the pan on a pair of tongs or a Chinese wok ring placed over the burner. Let the rice steam gently for 10 minutes. Turn off the heat, and let the rice rest undisturbed, covered, for 5 minutes. Do not stir the rice during these last 15 minutes of cooking, as the rice

grains are very moist and fragile, and will break easily when handled. The rice remains warm for 20 minutes, if left covered. Uncover, and transfer to a heated serving platter. Surround the rice with a ring of peach slices, sprinkle almonds and pistachios on top, and serve.

To serve, follow the menu suggestions given for Sweet Saffron Pilaf on page 369.

Okra Pilaf

(Bhindi Pullao)

This is a simple, unusual, and very tasty pilaf made with crisp fried okra. The rice is first cooked separately with all the spices. Then the crisp fried okra is folded into it. Or the crisp fried okra may be arranged in a ring circling the rice. Except for the cumin, the spices are not to be eaten, but no harm will come to you if you bite into a cardomom pod, chew a bay leaf, or swallow a few cloves.

For 6–8 persons

2 cups *basmati* rice
3 tablespoons light vegetable oil
¾ cup finely chopped onion
1½ teaspoons finely chopped garlic
1½ teaspoons finely chopped fresh ginger root
1 teaspoon black (or white) cumin seeds

3 black (or 6 green) cardamom pods
1 cinnamon stick, 3 inches long
6 whole cloves
2 bay leaves
12 black peppercorns (optional)
2 teaspoons Kosher salt
¾ cup Crisp Fried Okra (p. 310)

(continued)

1. Wash the *basmati* rice following directions on page 356.

2. Place the rice in a bowl, add 4 cups cold water, and soak for ½ hour. Drain, reserving the water, and set aside.

3. Measure out the onions, garlic, ginger root, and spices and place them right next to the stove.

4. Heat the oil over medium-high heat in a heavy-bottomed pan. If you are using white cumin seeds, add them now, and fry until they turn dark brown (about 10 seconds). Add onion, garlic, and ginger. Fry until the onions are light brown, stirring constantly so they do not burn (about 5–8 minutes). Do not let them turn dark, or the pilaf will turn dark. Add cumin, cardamom, cinnamon, cloves, bay leaves, and peppercorns, and fry for an additional 2 minutes or until the spices are slightly puffed. Add drained rice, and continue frying until the rice grains are thoroughly coated with oil and begin to brown (about 2–3 minutes). Add the reserved water and salt. Stir rapidly to prevent the rice from settling, and bring to a boil.

5. Reduce heat and simmer, partially covered, until the water is almost absorbed and the surface of the rice is covered with steamy holes (about 10–12 minutes). There is no need to stir the rice at this point, but if you wish to, use a fork or a knife so that you don't crush the rice grains.

6. Cover the pan tightly, reduce heat to the lowest possible level, and if possible, raise the pan at least an inch away from the source of heat by resting the pan on a pair of tongs or a Chinese wok ring placed over the burner. Let the rice steam for 10 minutes. Turn off the heat, and let the rice rest undisturbed, covered, for 5 minutes. Do not stir the rice during these last 15 minutes of steaming and resting, as the grains are very moist and fragile, breaking easily with every touch. The rice will remain warm for 20 minutes, if left covered. Uncover, and fluff the rice. Mound the rice on a heated serving platter, surround it with a ring of Crisp Fried Okra, and serve immediately.

You can make a meal with this pilaf alone. For a light lunch, serve it with a cool yogurt salad, such as Dumplings in Fragrant Yogurt (p. 348) or Spinach and Yogurt Salad (p. 344), accompanied by a chilled glass of punch or wine. This pilaf is also good with dishes that have reddish brown gravies, such as Beef in Spicy Tomato Gravy (p. 172), Lobster in Fried Onion Sauce (p. 247), or Shrimp Laced with Mild Spices (p. 240).

The Emperor's Pilaf with Black Mushrooms

(Badshahi Pullao or Gochian Pullao)

When people in the West think of India, mushrooms are probably the last thing that comes to mind. Yet India produces the finest, the most delicate-tasting beehive-shaped mushrooms known as morels (*Gochian*). *Gochians* grow in the Kashmir region and are very expensive. They are understandably reserved for special company, parties, and wedding banquets. Morels are widely available in specialty food stores and gourmet food sections of department stores. Although Indian morels are less flavorful than the French morels, the difference is insignificant in Indian cooking.

Except for the cumin, whole spices in pilaf are not eaten, but no harm will come to you if you bite into them.

For 6–8 persons

24 dry morels (*Gochian*, about ¾ ounce), or dried Polish mushrooms, or ½ pound fresh mushrooms (*champignons*)

4 medium-sized onions

2 cups *basmati* rice, or regular long grain rice

8 tablespoons Indian vegetable shortening or light vegetable oil

1½ teaspoons black (or white) cumin seeds

1½ teaspoons minced garlic

3 black (or 6 green) cardamom pods

6 whole cloves

1 stick cinnamon, 3 inches long

1 bay leaf

2 teaspoons Kosher salt

(continued)

1. Put the dry mushrooms in a bowl, add enough boiling water to cover, and let soak for 1 hour (15 minutes if you are using Polish mushrooms). Drain, and wash the mushrooms thoroughly in several changes of water. Cut the large mushrooms in half. If you are using fresh mushrooms, wipe them with a clean moist towel, and cut them into thick slices (about ⅛-inch). Set aside.

2. Peel onions, and finely chop 2 of them. Slice the remaining 2 into paper-thin shreds, and set aside.

3. Wash the *basmati* rice following instructions on page 356.

4. Place the rice in a bowl, add 4 cups of cold water, let soak for ½ hour. Drain the rice, reserving the water, and set aside. (Omit this step if you are using regular long grain rice.)

5. Heat the shortening in a heavy-bottomed pan, and add the 2 shredded onions. Over medium high heat, fry until the onions turn dark brown (about 20 minutes), stirring constantly to ensure even browning. Take the onions out with a slotted spoon, and drain them on paper towels. (See Crispy Fried Onions, p. 74.) When cool, these fried onion shreds will become crackling crisp. Set them aside for the garnish.

6. Turn the heat to medium-high, add the cumin seeds, and stir for a moment or two (if you are using white cumin seeds, fry until they turn brown—this may take about 10 seconds). Add the two chopped onions, and fry until they turn caramel brown (about 15–20 minutes), stirring constantly to prevent burning. Add garlic, and cook for an additional ½ minute. Add mushrooms and sauté for 3 minutes or until lightly fried. (Fresh mushrooms take a little longer, because they emit a lot of water in the beginning which has to evaporate before they can be fried.) Add cardamom, cloves, cinnamon, and bay leaf, and continue frying until the spices are slightly fried and puffed.

7. Add the drained rice, and as soon as it is thoroughly coated with the fat and begins to brown, add the reserved water (or 4 cups cold water if you are using regular long grain rice) and salt. Stir rapidly to prevent the rice from settling, and bring to a boil. Reduce heat and simmer, partially covered, for 10 minutes (15 minutes for regular long grain rice) or until most of the water is absorbed and the surface is covered with steamy holes. There is no need to stir,

but if you wish to do so, use a fork or a knife so that the fragile rice grains do not break.

8. Cover the pan tightly, reduce heat to the lowest possible level, and if possible raise the pan an inch away from the source of heat by resting the pan on a pair of tongs or a Chinese wok ring placed over the burner. Let the rice steam for 10 minutes, and turn off the heat. Now let it rest undisturbed, covered, for 5 minutes. Do not stir the rice during these last 15 minutes, as the grains are extremely fragile, breaking easily with every touch. Resting firms and separates the grains, making them easier to handle. The rice remains warm for half an hour, if left covered. Uncover, and fluff the rice. Transfer to a heated serving platter, cover the rice with the fried onion shreds, and serve immediately.

Follow the menu suggestions given for Okra Pilaf on page 373.

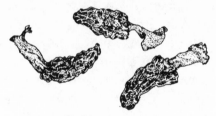

Gochian

Mint Pilaf

(Hari Chutney ka Pullao)

This delicious pilaf with its appealing pale green color is a specialty of Hyderabad, a city in the southern state of Andra Pradesh. It is made with freshly grated coconut and green chilies, and flavored in the Moghul tradition—with cinnamon, cloves, and mint. This unusual combination of southern ingredients and Moghul spicing reflects the mixed heritage of Hyderabad.

This recipe was given to me by my sister Reena. She prepared it on one of my visits to her family in New Delhi.

(continued)

For 6–8 persons

2 medium-sized potatoes
2 cups *basmati* rice, or converted
   rice
⅓ cup water
½ cup firmly packed fresh
   grated coconut (p. 46)
¾ cup loosely packed fresh mint
   leaves

2 green chilies
⅓ teaspoon ground cloves
½ teaspoon ground cinnamon
8 tablespoons *usli ghee*, (p. 50)
   or light vegetable oil
1 tablespoon Kosher salt

1. Peel the potatoes, and dice them into ½-inch pieces. Put them in a bowl, add water to cover, and set aside.

2. Wash *basmati* rice following directions on page 356.

3. Place the rice in a bowl, add 4 cups of cold water, and let soak for ½ hour. Drain the rice, reserving the water, and set aside. (Omit this step if you are using converted rice.)

4. While the rice is soaking, put ⅓ cup water, coconut, mint, chilies, cloves and cinnamon into the container of an electric blender or food processor, and puree finely.

5. Heat the *ghee* over medium-high heat in a heavy-bottomed pan, preferably one with a non-stick surface. Drain the potatoes, pat them dry, and add them to the pan. Fry the potatoes, turning and tossing until golden brown (about 7–10 minutes), stirring constantly to ensure even browning. Remove them to a bowl.

6. To the same pan, add coconut-mint puree, and cook until it is slightly fried and the fat begins to separate (about 8–10 minutes). Add the rice, and continue frying until the grains are thoroughly coated with the herb puree (about 3 minutes), stirring constantly to prevent the rice from sticking to the bottom of the pan and burning. Add the reserved water (or 4½ cups of cold water if you are using converted rice), salt, and fried potatoes. Stir for a moment to prevent the rice from settling, and bring to the boil.

7. Reduce heat and simmer, partially covered, for 10 minutes (20 minutes for converted rice) or until most of the water is absorbed by the rice and its surface is covered with steamy holes. There is no need to stir the rice, but if you wish to do so, use a fork or knife so that you don't break the rice grains.

8. Cover the pan tightly, reduce heat to the lowest possible level, and raise the pan an inch away from the source of heat by resting the pan over a pair of tongs or a Chinese wok ring placed over the burner. Let the rice steam for 10 minutes, and turn off heat. Let it rest undisturbed, covered, for an additional 5 minutes. Do not stir the rice during these last 15 minutes, as there is a danger of breaking the moist and fragile rice grains and potato pieces. The rice remains warm for 20 minutes, if left covered. Uncover, fluff the rice with a fork, and serve.

This pilaf, like most Hyderabad food, is on the hot side. Therefore, always serve it with a cool salad, such as Tomato and Yogurt Salad (p. 345) or Okra and Yogurt Salad (p. 347). For the most authentic flavor, include Hot Hyderabad Tomato Relish (p. 441). Or you may simply serve Hot Lemon Pickle (p. 449). These combinations make perfect light meals accompanied by a glass of chilled Chablis.

Vegetable and Rice Casserole with Herbs

(Tahari)

Tahari, a specialty of Uttar Pradesh, is a spicy, bright yellow, and very fragrant casserole made with rice, potatoes, and peas. It is like a pilaf, but much spicier because of the addition of cumin, garam masala, green chilies, and fresh coriander leaves. Its distinguishing feature is the yellow color, which the turmeric imparts.

This is a favorite dish among Indian vegetarians, who traditionally serve it for a Sunday lunch, sometimes accompanied by a cool yogurt salad such as Cucumber and Yogurt Salad (p. 343).

(continued)

For 4–6 persons

1 cup *basmati* rice, or regular long grain rice	½ teaspoon turmeric
2 tablespoons Indian vegetable shortening or light vegetable oil	¾ teaspoon *garam masala* (p. 38)
¾ teaspoon white cumin seeds	⅛–¼ teaspoon red pepper
1 medium potato, peeled and diced into ½-inch pieces	1¾ teaspoons Kosher salt
1 cup fresh or frozen green peas	2 tablespoons chopped fresh coriander leaves
	1 green chili, seeded and sliced (optional)

1. Wash *basmati* rice following directions on page 356.

2. Place the rice in a bowl, add 2¼ cups of cold water, and let soak for ½ hour. Drain the rice, reserving the water, and set aside. (Omit this step if you are using regular long grain rice).

3. Heat the shortening or oil over medium-high heat in a heavy-bottomed pan. When the oil is very hot, add the cumin seeds. When the seeds turn dark brown (about 10 seconds) add the potatoes and peas, and fry for 3 minutes, stirring rapidly. Add rice, and fry for an additional minute or until the rice grains are thoroughly coated with the fat. Add turmeric, *garam masala*, red pepper, salt, and reserved water (or 2¼ cups cold water if you are using regular long grain rice). Stir for a moment to prevent the rice from settling, and bring to a boil. Reduce heat to medium and simmer, covered, for 10 minutes (15 minutes for regular long grain rice) or until most of the water is absorbed by the rice and the surface is filled with steamy holes. There is no need to stir the rice, but if you wish to, use a fork or a knife so that you don't break the fragile rice grains.

4. Reduce the heat to the lowest point, and raise the pan about an inch away from the source of heat by resting the pan on a pair of tongs or a Chinese wok ring placed over the burner. Let the rice steam for 10 minutes, and turn off heat. Let it rest undisturbed, covered, for 5 minutes. Do not stir the rice during these last 15

minutes, as the grains are very moist and fragile, breaking easily if stirred. The rice will remain warm for half an hour, covered. Uncover, and fluff the rice with a fork. Transfer it to a warm serving platter, and serve sprinkled with the chopped coriander leaves and sliced chili.

Royal Vegetable and Rice Casserole

(Shahi Sabz Biriyani)

This is the most elegant entree of all vegetarian dishes—and it is very simple to prepare. All you have to do is prepare a vegetable *korma* and mix it with cooked rice. Another wonderful feature of this recipe: the *korma* can be prepared earlier and frozen, so that when you want to serve the *biriyani*, you have only to mix the *korma* with the cooked rice.

For 6–8 persons

All the ingredients for
    making Royal Braised
    Vegetables in Cardamom
    Nut Sauce (p. 269)
2 cups *basmati* rice, or regular
    long grain rice

2–3 tablespoons finely chopped
    mixed nuts (such as
    almonds, pistachios,
    cashew nuts, and walnuts)

1. Prepare Royal Braised Vegetables according to the recipe on page 269.
2. Preheat the oven to 300°F.
3. Wash the *basmati* rice following directions on page 356.
4. Place the rice in a bowl, add enough cold water to cover by an inch, and let soak for ½ hour. Drain the rice, and set aside. Discard the water the rice was soaking in. (Omit this step if you are using regular long grain rice.)
5. Bring about 3 quarts of water to boil in a deep pot. Add the

rice, and stir immediately for ½ minute to keep the rice from settling. Bring to a second boil, and cook the rice for 2 minutes (10 minutes for regular long grain rice).

6. Pour the entire contents of the pot into a large sieve held over the kitchen sink. Hold the sieve directly under the tap, and let the cold water run at medium speed through the rice for 5 seconds, to wash away the excess starch clinging to the rice grains.

7. Put the rice in an oven-proof casserole. Add the braised vegetables, and mix gently but thoroughly. Put a piece of foil on top of the casserole, and cover tightly with the lid.

8. Bake in the middle level of the oven for 30 minutes or until heated through and the rice grains fully cooked but still firm. Turn off the oven, and let the casserole remain inside with the door shut for an additional 10 minutes. The rice will remain warm for ½ hour if left undisturbed in the oven. (This pilaf, if made with fresh *korma* that has not been refrigerated or frozen, will keep in the refrigerator up to 4 days. In fact, it tastes better the second and third day. To reheat, place the casserole, tightly covered, in a 300°F preheated oven for 25 minutes.)

9. To serve, transfer to a warm serving platter, and sprinkle with the chopped nuts.

Biriyanis are generally complete meals in themselves. Just add a chilled glass of Chablis. For a more substantial meal, serve a *dal* such as Buttered Black Beans (p. 337), and a kabob such as Kabob Patties Laced with Ginger and Mint (p. 109).

Breads
(Roti)

Baked Whole Wheat Bread   *(Chapati* or *Roti)*
Baked Whole Wheat Puffy Bread   *(Phulka)*
Chick-pea Flour Bread   *(Besan ki Roti)*
Whole Wheat Flaky Bread   *(Paratha)*
Cauliflower-Stuffed Bread   *(Phool Gobhi Paratha)*
Potato- and Herb-Stuffed Bread   *(Aloo Paratha)*
Spinach Bread   *(Palak Paratha)*
Deep-fried Puffy Bread   *(Poori)*
Deep-fried Bread with Spicy Stuffing   *(Kachauri)*

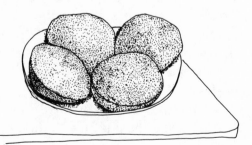

There is nothing more enticing than the well-made, wholesome-tasting breads of India. The honesty of ingredients and the utter simplicity of the cooking techniques make these natural breads the best in the world. And baking them can be the most satisfying experience of one's life.

Indian breads can be put into two categories: commercial and homemade.

Commercial, or bakery breads are those made in a *tandoor*, the Indian clay oven. These are the breads most popular in Indian restaurants. They are particularly suited for mass production, since they are cooked in large ovens in which several can be baked simultaneously. Also they are not rolled but are formed by patting, folding, and stretching with the hands. This is a quick process, developed for turning out large quantities of bread. The bakery or commercial Indian breads include *nan, kulcha, tandoori roti, tandoori paratha,* and *roomali roti*.

Homemade breads are in a category by themselves. Once you try them, you will become an instant addict. These breads are lighter and more flavorful and nutritious than bakery breads. There is an incredible variety of homemade breads, and listing all of them is not possible. But they all have one thing in common: they are uncomplicated, and therefore quick and easy to make.

Most of the breads eaten every day in Indian homes are made with unleavened stone-ground whole-grain flour. Leavened breads are cooked on special occasions. Breads, as a general rule, accompany dishes that are substantially dry, roasted, fried, or those whose thick gravies can be scooped up with a piece of bread. There is no hard and fast rule as to which bread accompanies which main dish. Much depends upon one's taste and how rich and elaborate the meal is.

This chapter on breads deals mainly with the homemade varieties—making them is an art, and not much light has been shed upon the process. Most of these breads cannot be found on the menus of Indian restaurants. When they are, they are often so poorly made that they bear no resemblance to the authentic classic home varieties.

Homemade breads can be classified in three general categories: griddle-baked breads, griddle-fried breads, and deep-fried breads.

Griddle-baked Breads

These breads are by far the most popular and widely eaten in India. They are made with whole-grain flour, such as whole wheat, corn (or maize), chick-pea, and millet. Only water is incorporated into the flour to make the dough. The bread is then baked on the griddle or over an open flame. These breads are traditionally made with the rest of the meal and served while still warm and filled with the aroma of cooked dough. This category includes *Chapati* or *Roti* (p. 393), *Phulka* (p. 397), and *Besan ki Roti* (p. 399).

Griddle-fried Breads

These breads are made with whole wheat flour. The dough is usually enriched with a little fat and salt. They are often referred to as "flaky" or "layered" breads, because they are brushed with fat or oil and folded several times before being rolled and panfried. This bread is called *Paratha* (p. 402). They are also stuffed with a variety of ingredients, such as herbs, spices, cooked vegetables, chopped greens, lentils, and meat. The stuffing is either used as a filling or mixed with the dough before it is rolled and fried. These breads are called *bhara* (stuffed) *paratha* (flaky bread) in general. Examples include *Aloo Paratha* (p. 409), *Phool Gobhi Paratha* (p. 405) and *Palak Paratha* (p. 410).

Deep-fried Breads

Indian deep-fried breads are known for their stunning appearance and wonderfully delicate taste. They are popular items on the menus of Indian restaurants. The dough for these breads is similar to the dough made for griddle-fried breads. The only difference is that instead of being fried on the griddle, these are deep-fried in hot oil, where they puff up like balloons.

In addition to their beautiful shape, aroma, and taste, they are uniquely nonperishable. They stay fresh and moist for several days at room temperature. These breads are often called "travel breads" in India, and are carried by people on long journeys because they survive prolonged exposure to heat without spoiling or any change in taste. Deep-fried breads are traditionally served at wedding banquets and other festive occasions. This category of breads includes *Poori* (p. 413), and *Kachauri* (p. 416).

FLOUR

The flour used in most Indian homemade breads is whole wheat. The Indian whole wheat flour is different from the kind available either in supermarket chains or health food stores. In Indian whole wheat flour, the entire kernel of wheat is ground to a very fine powder. The flour is thus an even buff color and does not adhere together. Indians usually sift it through a fine sieve (*chalni*, see p. 60) to remove the few remaining coarse bran flakes. The resulting flour is like a very fine powder loaded with ground bran and germ. This flour is called *aata* and is widely available in Indian grocery stores under the label "*chapati* flour." The dough made with it has a silky smooth texture and little resistance to kneading and rolling.

To get good results with baking, however, it is not essential to have this flour. The whole wheat flour available in supermarket chains, although too coarse-textured to be used straight, can give exceedingly good results with slight modifications. You will, however, need to do one of two things:

1, Sift the flour through a fine sieve to remove the bran flakes. (If it shocks and distresses you to see all that bran thrown away, then this method is not for you.) Or 2, substitute all-purpose flour, preferably unbleached, for a portion of the whole wheat flour. This will reduce the proportion of bran in the flour, thus decreasing the coarseness. The amount of all-purpose flour to be added depends on the quality of the whole wheat flour. Generally, 2 cups of whole wheat mixed with 1 cup of all-purpose should give very good results.

Because whole wheat flour contains bran and germ, which have natural oils, it will become musty and turn rancid if stored in a warm place, such as on a kitchen counter, or in any part of a home without air-conditioning in the summer. To keep your flour smelling sweet and fresh, store it in airtight containers in the refrigerator. However, remember to bring the flour to room temperature before using it in a recipe.

EQUIPMENT

I cannot think of more humble and unpretentious equipment than that used in Indian bread making. Since there are no cooking surfaces in an Indian kitchen, utensils are designed and selected for their versatility. The *paraath*, for instance, is a broad metal platter with a high rim that makes it a shallow bowl for mixing ingredients, and a large flat surface suitable for kneading the dough. *Paraaths* come in a variety of metals and sizes, but the best suited are those made of stainless steel, 18 to 24 inches in diameter. The *paraath* is available in stores that carry Indian utensils. A good substitute for the *paraath* is a round basin (the kind used for hand laundry) made of plastic or enamel-coated steel. It is not essential to have either of these, of course, as long as you have a medium-sized mixing bowl to mix the dough and a marble or wooden surface for kneading.

A good wooden rolling pin with handles, and preferably with a 9-inch ball-bearing pin, is absolutely essential for rolling the bread. This type of rolling pin is widely available where kitchenware is sold.

In India, bread dough is rolled on wooden or marble rolling boards, 9 inches in diameter. This equipment is not essential; any flat clean surface will do.

Griddle-fried breads are cooked on the Indian cast-iron griddle called *tava*. The American cast-iron griddle with a smooth cooking surface is an excellent substitute. Do not buy the rough-surfaced griddle, hoping that with use it will become smooth. It is not suitable for preparing Indian breads. A good substitute for a griddle is a heavy-bottomed 9-inch-diameter frying pan, which I find gives results just as good.

For deep frying, the ideal utensil is the *kadhai* (see page 62). A skillet, chicken fryer, or any large pan that can hold enough oil for deep frying bread makes a good substitute. The *kadhai* will require the least oil to do the job.

A pair of tongs is another essential item for baking the breads. It is used to lift, turn, and cook the breads over a flame. The Indian tongs specially designed for this purpose consist of two thin flat steel pieces that are highly elastic and have smooth curved edges joined together at one end. Their ingenious design allows you to pick up a fully puffed bread without breaking it. The commonly available unserrated 9-inch tongs make a fine substitute.

For deep frying and draining breads, you will need a slotted spoon. Any commercially available slotted spoon with a wide flat surface works beautifully.

PREPARING THE DOUGH

The dough for all homemade breads, whether griddle-cooked or deep-fried, is prepared in the same way. The technique is exclusively Indian. It is important to understand and follow it carefully; otherwise the bread will not come out right.

There are three steps in this process: mixing the dough, kneading the dough, and resting the dough.

Mixing the Dough

This is the most important of all the steps in the process of preparing the dough. Unlike European breads, to which the liquid is added without fine precision (since the dough is finally firmed and dried with flour), when making Indian breads the water added is exactly the amount specified—or a little less. This does not mean the water is measured to an exact amount and then added; but rather that the amount added is precisely what will form a firm, kneadable dough. This is important, because once too much water is added, the dough becomes sticky and impossible to knead. Another reason for caution is that instead of incorporating a little extra flour during kneading, you will be kneading a little extra water into this Indian dough. If, on the other hand, you are overcautious and add too little water, you will end up with a very firm dough that is too hard and rubbery to knead. No matter how much water is later sprinkled over it, it will not become properly soft and pliable.

Therefore, while mixing, pay careful attention to the way the dough feels to the touch.

The process: Place the flour in a bowl. With your left hand if you are right handed, add the water in a stream, pouring it fast at first. Simultaneously mix the flour with the fingers of your right hand, in a rotating motion, to moisten it enough so that it gathers into a mass. As the flour begins to lump up, add water more and more slowly until all the flour forms a mass, and the dough is firm but soft enough to be kneaded. In most instances you will need only the amount of water suggested in the recipe. But if you find that for any reason the dough looks and feels a little dry, simply add a few extra spoonfuls of water. Do not, however, add more water than necessary, as you will be using water not flour, to knead the dough. Also, the dough will be allowed to rest before being rolled, which further softens and moistens it. Gather the dough into a rough ball, place it on the work surface, and wash your hands clean.

(continued)

Kneading the Dough

The Indian method of kneading dough is completely different from any other method used elsewhere in the world. It is mostly wrist work. Also, instead of being dusted with flour and folded, the dough is sprinkled with water and kneaded.

The process: First put about ¼ cup of water in a small shallow bowl, and place it close to the work surface where the dough is to be kneaded. Clench your right hand into a fist (if you are right handed), and dip your knuckles into the water. Knead by pressing your knuckles repeatedly into the dough, as though punching it, while simultaneously pushing and spreading it away from you, to form an approximately 9-inch round. Lift one edge of the round, and fold the dough over. Continue kneading, punching, and spreading the same way, dipping your knuckles in water from time to time, until you have a very soft, pliable dough. This will take about 10 to 15 minutes. (You will have incorporated about 1 tablespoon of water into the dough.) Press your index finger lightly and quickly about ¼ inch into the kneaded dough. If the dough springs back, it is fully kneaded. Put it back in the bowl.

Notes:

1. Instead of dipping your knuckles in the water, you can sprinkle water directly over the dough. However, this should be done after spreading the dough into a round.

2. You can use the heel of your palm instead of your knuckles to knead the dough.

3. The dough can be kneaded in an electric mixer, with the dough hook attachment in place, for 3–4 minutes at medium speed. *Caution:* most mixers will not knead dough made with less than 3 cups of flour: therefore, if you are making bread with less than that amount, you may not be able to use the machine.

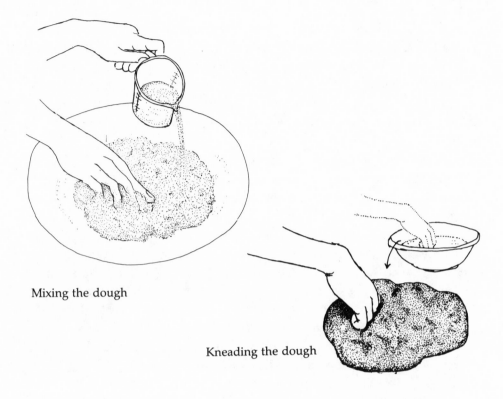

Mixing the dough

Kneading the dough

Mixing and Kneading in the Food Processor

My use of a food processor for both mixing and kneading dough came about quite literally by accident.

A couple of years ago during one of my cooking classes, I sprained my wrist by lifting a very heavy pot with one hand. The wrist took almost a year to heal, but during that time the making of the breads had to go on, since my desire to eat these wonderful breads did not diminish with the diminished strength of my wrist. One day, out of sheer desperation, I threw all the ingredients for the dough into the container of the processor and let the machine run. What I saw forming to my delight, was a lump of dough that upon close examination, though a little lumpy and dry, was quite good. That was the beginning. Since then I have learned that the liquid should not be added all at once with the dry ingredients, and the fats and oils should be added before the liquid. Also it takes 40 to 50 seconds of processing to knead the mixed dough to a satiny smooth texture. Finally, no further liquid need be added while kneading the dough. All in all, the results are so good, the process so simple and quick and clean, that I recommend this procedure as an excellent alternative.

The process: To mix the dough, attach the metal cutting blade, and put the flour (or combination of flours), seasonings, and spices if you are using them, into the container. Cover. Run the machine until all the ingredients are blended well (about 10 seconds). Add fat or oil, and greens or herbs as the recipe suggests, and process for another 10 seconds to mix. Now, with the machine running, start to add the water. Add about half the suggested amount in a steady stream. Be careful not to run the machine too long at one stretch. Turn it off and on every 5 to 10 seconds, and add water only while the machine is running. As the flour begins to adhere into a mass, slow the speed of water to dribbles. Process the dough between additions of water, and stop adding water as soon as a ball of dough forms on the blades.

To knead the dough, turn on the processor and continue processing for 40–50 seconds, turning the machine on and off every 5 to 10 seconds. If your processor overheats or shows signs of strain, divide the ball of dough and knead half at a time. The dough is kneaded when it looks smooth and shiny and feels soft and pliable to the touch. With your hands, carefully take the dough from the container and place it in a bowl.

Resting the Dough

The final step in the preparation of the dough is letting it rest before it is rolled. This is a very important step because it relaxes the dough, thus making it less resistant to stretching and rolling. Also, the temperature in kitchens in India generally ranges between 100°

and 120°F, which even though quite unbearable for human beings, is ideal for the dough. The warm temperature ferments it and causes it to rise, thus making the dough light, airy, and spongy, as though it had been leavened slightly. The cooked bread is thus moist and soft.

The process: To rest the dough, cover the bowl with a moist towel or a sheet of plastic wrap and let it rest, preferably in a warm place, for at least ½ hour. The dough can be made a day ahead and refrigerated, tightly covered and sealed in foil. Remove it from the refrigerator about 30 minutes before you are ready to roll.

Baking Indian breads is an art that you learn and perfect, with practice and patience, in time. The preparation of dough described earlier and the rolling techniques for each different bread are special skills that need to be developed. To do this you need to learn the techniques first and then practice until you are fully familiar and comfortable with them. As I mentioned earlier, the process itself is utterly simple; all you need is the confidence that automatically comes with practice.

Baked Whole Wheat Bread

(Chapati or Roti)

This is the basic bread of India—it is made every day in North Indian homes. Its smooth, soft, and very pliable texture comes from the finely ground whole wheat flour. Only water is added to make the dough. It is then rolled into thin rounds ranging in size from four to eight inches (the size varies from state to state) and baked on a griddle. It takes a bit of practice to learn to roll the dough properly. Don't worry if your first few batches are not perfectly round, or if they don't roll out to the full size indicated. With practice you will soon master this technique. In the meantime, the bread will still taste good, even if it doesn't look perfect.

(continued)

Makes 24 seven-inch chapati
For 6–8 persons

3 cups *chapati* flour (or 2 cups
    whole wheat flour mixed
    with 1 cup all-purpose
    flour), measured by
    scooping the flour with a
    measuring cup and
    leveling off with a
    spatula or knife

1 cup warm water
    (90°–100°F)
½–¾ cup *chapati* flour, or all-
    purpose flour, for
    dusting

1. Place *chapati* flour (or whole wheat mixed with all-purpose flour) in a bowl. Add water, pouring it fast at first, to moisten the flour enough that it adheres into a mass; then slowly, little by little, until the dough is formed and can be kneaded. (See Mixing and Kneading the Dough, pp. 389–390.)

2. Place the dough on the work surface and knead for 10–15 minutes, or mix and knead the dough in the food processor (see page 391). This will be a very soft and pliable dough, quite sticky to the touch. Put the dough back in the bowl, cover with a moist towel or a sheet of plastic, and let it rest, preferably in a warm place, for at least ½ hour. (The dough may be made a day ahead and refrigerated, tightly sealed in foil. Remove from the refrigerator about 30 minutes before you are ready to roll it.)

ROLLING THE BREAD:

3. Put the flour for dusting in a plate or a shallow bowl and keep it close to the work surface where you are rolling the dough. Knead the dough again for a minute, and divide it into 2 equal portions. Using your hands, roll each into a rope, cut into 12 equal parts, and roll the small pieces into smooth balls (or pinch off small pieces of dough from the rope, and roll them into 1-inch balls). Dust the balls lightly with flour to prevent their sticking to each other, and put them back in the bowl. Keep the bowl covered loosely with a damp towel or a sheet of plastic wrap to prevent the dough's drying out.

4. Start heating the griddle or frying pan over medium heat. Working one at a time, pick up a ball and place it on the dusting flour. Press the ball lightly but firmly, both to flatten it into a round pillow and simultaneously to coat the underside with flour. Turn and repeat, to coat the other side with flour. Pick up the patty with your fingers, shake it gently to release any excess flour, and place it on the work surface.

5. Roll the patty into a very thin 8–9-inch circle, pressing and stretching with the rolling pin with a brisk back-and-forth motion, going from edge to edge to keep it circular. Dust the dough from time to time to prevent its sticking to the work surface or rolling pin. Those of you familiar with Mexican or Chinese cooking techniques will notice that the rolling of this bread is very similar to the rolling of the Mexican wheat flour tortilla or the Chinese pancakes that traditionally accompany Roast Peking Duck or 'Moo Shu' dishes. (Bear in mind that this method of rolling is altogether different from the familiar technique used for pies, tarts, and quiches. There you position the rolling pin in the center and roll the dough away or toward you, thus spreading and not stretching the dough.)

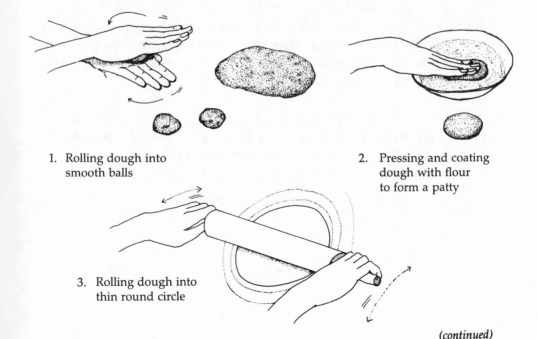

1. Rolling dough into
   smooth balls

2. Pressing and coating
   dough with flour
   to form a patty

3. Rolling dough into
   thin round circle

(continued)

BAKING THE BREAD:

6. Lift the bread gently, place it on the hot griddle, and bake until the side in contact with the griddle is cooked and several tiny brown spots appear. Flip the bread, using a pair of unserrated tongs, and bake the other side the same way. (Generally, when the griddle temperature is right, the first side of the bread will take about 20–30 seconds and the second side 8–10 seconds. But if it is too hot, the bread will brown too fast and burn before cooking; if it is not hot enough, it will take too long to brown, by which time the bread will become dry, tough, and leathery. Therefore it is essential to check and keep the griddle at the right temperature at all times.) Take the bread out, and if desired, brush with clarified butter or shortening. Place it in a covered dish, preferably lined with a kitchen towel. Repeat with the rest of the dough the same way. As the breads are baked, pile them one on top of the other in the dish. (The dish is lined because as more and more breads are piled in the dish, the steam from the breads begins to condense and accumulate at the bottom, which could cause the bottom few breads to be soft. The towel absorbs the moisture, preventing such a disaster.)

Note: If the breads are to be served immediately, simply stack them up as they are baked on a thick napkin placed in a small round bread basket. Keep the napkin folded on top, enclosing the bread fully, to keep it warm. (The *chapati* can be made a couple of hours ahead and warmed up, wrapped and sealed in foil, in a preheated 300°F oven for 12 minutes.)

Chapati goes well with just about all dishes. It is usually served when a light meal is intended. It is also a good choice when the main dish is rich with butter, cream, and nuts. Since there is no fat or oil in the bread, it provides the needed balance against rich dishes.

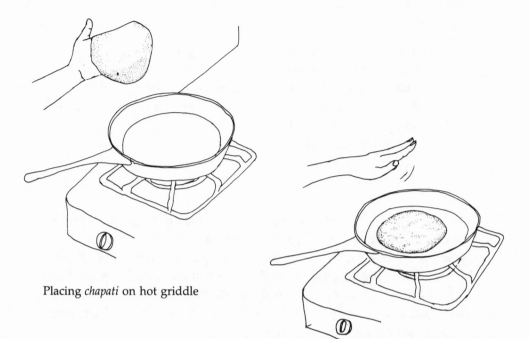

Placing *chapati* on hot griddle

Baked Whole Wheat Puffy Bread

(Phulka)

Phulka dough is similar to *chapati* dough. The texture and taste are also very similar, except *phulka* is baked for a second time over flame, after it has been griddle-baked. This method is generally used for breads made with a dense flour, such as chick-pea or millet. Since these breads are also rolled thicker than *chapati*, the griddle-baking process is usually not sufficient to cook them thoroughly. So they are held over the flame for a few seconds and baked until completely cooked. Don't be afraid to do this. The bread will not burn, it will puff up like a balloon (hence the name *phulka*, meaning puffed) and freckle all over. *Phulka* looks so beautiful and has such an aromatic taste that many cooks make whole wheat bread this way.

(continued)

Makes 24 six-inch phulka
For 6–8 persons

3 cups *chapati* flour (or 2 cups whole wheat flour mixed with 1 cup all-purpose flour), measured by scooping the flour with measuring cup and leveling off with a spatula or knife

1 cup warm water (90°–100°F)
½–¾ cup *chapati* flour or all-purpose flour for dusting

1. Follow the preceding recipe's instructions for making *chapati*, from Step 1 to Step 6, except that instead of storing the *chapati* after baking them on the griddle, place them directly on a burner with a high flame on, and bake until the bread is puffed and several brown spots appear on the underside (about 5–10 seconds). Turn and bake the other side until the bread is puffed up like a balloon and covered with brown spots.

Note: The *phulka* should be rolled thicker than *chapati*, only to a 6-inch round. Also the bread should be handled very carefully during the rolling and baking processes, as any crack or tear in the bread will prevent it from puffing up.

To enjoy the full aroma and taste of these puffy breads, they must be eaten soon after they are baked. They also make an attractive and dramatic entrance when brought to the table puffed up and filling the room with their whole wheat aroma. This, however, is not always possible. Often all the breads are made and gently deflated before being placed in a covered dish or napkin-lined basket and served immediately. The bread can be made a couple of hours ahead, brushed with *usli ghee* or shortening and kept wrapped and sealed in foil. To reheat, place the sealed foil package in a 300°F preheated oven for 12 minutes.

Follow the menu suggestions given for the preceding recipe, Baked Whole Wheat Bread, on page 393.

Putting *phulka* directly over flame

Puffed bread: *phulka*

Chick-pea Flour Bread

(Besan ki Roti)

Chick-pea flour bread is generally very fragrant and pleasantly spicy. Like all breads made with a dense flour, it is first griddle-baked and then cooked over a flame. Chick-pea flour by itself is too rich and heavy to digest. Therefore it is mixed with whole wheat flour before baking.

(continued)

Makes 24 six-inch roti
For 8–12 persons

2 cups whole wheat flour
1 cup all-purpose flour
⅓ cup chick-pea flour *(besan)*
   (All flours measured by
   scooping flour with
   measuring cups and
   leveling off with a
   spatula or knife)

¼–½ teaspoon red pepper
   (optional)
½ teaspoon Kosher salt
1¼ cups (or more) warm water
   (90–100°F)
½ cup all-purpose flour for
   dusting

1. Place the whole wheat flour, one cup of all-purpose flour, and chick-pea flour in a bowl. Mix in red pepper if you are using it, and salt. Add water, pouring it fast at first, to moisten the flour enough that it adheres into a mass; then slowly, little by little, until the dough is firm and can be kneaded. (See Mixing and Kneading the Dough, pp. 389–390.)

2. Place the dough on the work surface and knead for 10–15 minutes (or mix and knead in the food processor, see p. 391). This will be a soft, pliable dough, slightly sticky to the touch. Cover and let it rest for ½ hour. (The dough can be made a day ahead and refrigerated, tightly sealed in foil. Remove from refrigerator about 30 minutes before you are ready to roll.)

3. Put the flour for dusting in a plate or a shallow bowl, and keep it close to the work surface where you are rolling dough.

4. Knead the dough again for a minute, and divide into 2 portions. Using your hands, roll each portion into a rope, and cut into 12 equal portions. Roll the small pieces into smooth balls, dust them lightly with flour to prevent their sticking together, and keep them loosely covered with a sheet of plastic wrap or a moist towel.

5. Start heating a griddle or frying pan over medium heat. You will need another burner next to it to puff the bread, so make sure the burner is free. Working one at a time and dusting generously with flour, place 1 ball on the work surface, and roll it into a 6-inch round. Dust the dough from time to time to prevent its sticking to the work surface or rolling pin.

6. Lift the bread gently, place it on the hot griddle, and bake until the bottom is cooked and a few brown spots appear (about ½ minute). Flip the bread, and cook the other side about 15–20 seconds.

7. Lift the bread, using a pair of unserrated tongs, and place the bread flat on the other burner with the high flame on. Cook the bread for 10 seconds, then turn it and cook the other side for an additional 10 seconds. (Because of the dense chick-pea flour this bread does not puff up as much as whole wheat bread. The reason for cooking the bread over the flame is not so much to puff the bread as to give it the characteristic flame-baked look and taste, and also to cook it thoroughly, since it is rolled much thicker than whole wheat bread.)

These breads are generally served brushed with *usli ghee* or shortening. They taste best hot off the burner, still warm and full of chick-pea aroma. They can, however, be served after all the breads are baked. When serving them this way, place the breads as they are baked on the work surface, and press each gently to deflate. Brush them generously with *ghee* or shortening, and stack them in a covered dish or napkin-lined basket.

This bread does not take well to reheating, principally because the breads are cooked over direct flame, which dries them somewhat; further heating only makes them crisp and leathery.

These breads are lovely to nibble on by themselves. They are particularly good accompaniments to such dry meat preparations as kabobs and roasts. For a light vegetarian meal, serve them with a stir-fried vegetable side dish, such as Stuffed Okra with Fragrant Spices (p. 311), Spicy Baby Eggplant (p. 303), Fragrant Buttered Greens (p. 319), Glazed Cauliflower with Ginger (p. 299), or Turmeric Potatoes with Green Peppers (p. 316), and a cool yogurt salad such as Cucumber and Yogurt Salad (p. 343).

Whole Wheat Flaky Bread

(Paratha)

This bread is known for its exquisite flakiness. Since it is folded three times, and oiled with each fold, the layers separate and flake while they fry. Also, the dough itself is enriched with oil, which causes the bread to taste crisp and rich. It is almost a simple version of the more complicated puff pastry.

Makes 16 seven-inch paratha
For 6–8 persons

2 cups *chapati* flour or whole wheat flour
1 cup all-purpose flour (both flours measured by scooping flour with measuring cups and leveling off with a spatula or knife)
1 teaspoon Kosher salt
¼ teaspoon carom seeds (optional)

3 tablespoons Indian vegetable shortening or light vegetable oil
1 cup warm water (90°–100°F)
½ cup flour for dusting
½ cup melted Indian vegetable shortening or oil for brushing

1. Combine *chapati* flour or whole wheat flour with 1 cup all-purpose flour, salt, and carom seeds in a bowl. Save about 1 teaspoon of shortening, and rub the remainder into the flour, following instructions on pp. 125–126. Add water, fast at first, to moisten the flour enough that it adheres into a mass; then slowly, little by little, until the dough is formed and can be kneaded. See Mixing and Kneading the Dough, pp. 389–390.

2. Brush the work surface and your fingers with the reserved teaspoon of shortening. Place the dough on the greased surface, and knead for 10–15 minutes. (Or mix and knead the dough in the food processor, see p. 391.) This will be a very soft and pliable dough. Put the dough back in the bowl, cover with a moist towel or a sheet of plastic wrap, and let it rest, preferably in a warm place,

for at least ½ hour. (The dough can be made a day ahead and refrigerated, tightly sealed in foil. Remove from refrigerator about 30 minutes before you are ready to roll it.)

3. Put the shortening for brushing in a shallow bowl and the flour for dusting in a plate or another bowl, and keep them close to the work surface where the dough is to be rolled.

4. Knead the dough again for a minute, and divide it into 2 equal portions. Using your hands, roll each portion into a rope, and cut each rope into 8 equal parts. Roll the small pieces into smooth balls, dust them lightly with flour, and put them back in the bowl. Keep them loosely covered with a damp towel or a sheet of plastic wrap to prevent a crust's forming.

5. Working one at a time, take a ball from the bowl and place it on the dusting flour. Press lightly but firmly, both to flatten it into a pillow and simultaneously to coat the underside with flour. Turn and repeat, to coat the other side with flour. Pick up the patty, shake off excess flour, place it on the work surface, and roll it into a 5-inch circle. Brush the top with melted shortening, using a pastry brush or your fingers, and fold the circle in half. Brush the top of the semicircle with fat and fold in half again. You will now have a triangle of dough. Pick up this folded dough, and place it on the dusting flour. Press lightly with your fingers so that the flour sticks to the underside of the dough. Turn and press again to flour the other side. Return the floured dough to the work surface, and roll it out to a 6-inch or 7-inch triangle. Keep dusting with flour from time to time, to prevent sticking. (These breads can be rolled out about an hour ahead of time, as long as they are kept covered with a sheet of plastic wrap or a damp towel to keep the dough from drying out. Don't stack them, or they will stick together and be impossible to separate. They may be kept slightly overlapping, provided the surfaces in contact are generously dusted with flour and separated by a sheet of plastic.)

6. When ready to fry, heat the griddle or frying pan over medium heat for 2 minutes or until hot. Put one bread at a time on the griddle. Cook for 2 minutes or until the side in contact with the griddle is baked and brown spots appear. Flip the bread upside down with a broad spatula, such as a pancake turner, and bake the other side for a short period (10–15 seconds).

(continued)

7. Meanwhile brush the baked side lightly but thoroughly with fat, and flip the bread again. Now the baked side in contact with the griddle is frying. Cook for ½ minute, then brush the other baked side with fat, and flip the bread to fry the second side for ½ minute. Take it off the griddle, and keep it warm in a covered dish or tightly wrapped with foil. Repeat with the remaining triangles of bread. Serve hot.

Note: Paratha can be made several hours ahead and reheated, loosely covered with foil, in a preheated 300°F oven for 10–12 minutes.

Paratha goes particularly well with dishes containing reddish brown sauces, such as Beef in Fragrant Spinach Sauce (p. 179), Beef in Spicy Tomato Gravy (p. 172), and Chicken in Onion Tomato Gravy (p. 208). *Paratha* generally accompanies Scrambled Eggs with Cumin and Fragrant Herbs (p. 232), a traditional combination served at breakfast. A pickle such as Sweet Lemon Pickle with Cumin (p. 447) should be served with it. For a light meal, brighten a vegetarian main dish or a vegetable side dish with *paratha*.

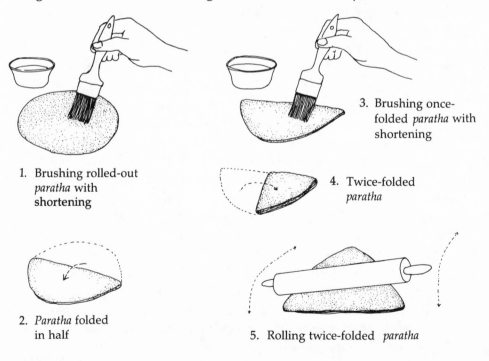

1. Brushing rolled-out *paratha* with shortening

2. *Paratha* folded in half

3. Brushing once-folded *paratha* with shortening

4. Twice-folded *paratha*

5. Rolling twice-folded *paratha*

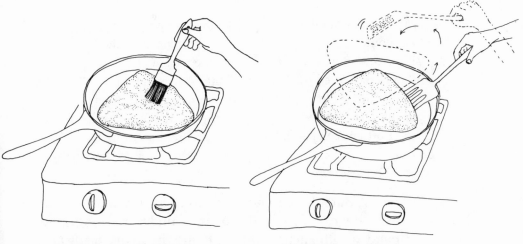

Brushing cooked side of
paratha with shortening

Flipping the *paratha*
to fry the cooked side

Cauliflower-Stuffed Bread

(Phool Gobhi Paratha)

This is the classic recipe for making stuffed bread, in which the dough is stuffed with the filling before being rolled into flat circles and griddle-baked. The bread is stuffed with sautéed cauliflower and ginger shreds. And it is delicious beyond words.

Makes 12 seven-inch stuffed paratha
For 6 persons

FOR CAULIFLOWER STUFFING:

1 small head cauliflower
  (about 1–1¼ pounds)
3 tablespoons Indian vegetable
  shortening, or light
  vegetable oil

1 tablespoon finely chopped or
  grated fresh ginger root
  (optional)
½ teaspoon red pepper
1¼ teaspoons Kosher salt

(continued)

FOR BREAD:

2 cups *chapati* flour or whole
wheat flour

1 cup all-purpose flour
(both flours measured by
scooping flour with
measuring cup and
leveling off with a spatula
or knife)

1 teaspoon Kosher salt

3 tablespoons Indian vegetable
shortening, or light
vegetable oil

1 cup warm water (90°–100°F)

½ cup flour for dusting

½ cup melted Indian vegetable
shortening, or light
vegetable oil for brushing

1. Cut off the outer leaves and stems from the cauliflower, and discard. Wash the cauliflower thoroughly under running cold water, and pat dry with kitchen towels. Using the coarse blade of a grater, or a food processor, grate the cauliflower into a bowl.

2. Heat the shortening over medium heat in a large frying pan for 2 minutes or until very hot. Add the grated cauliflower, and cook until most of its moisture is evaporated and it begins to look limp and fried (about 5 minutes). Turn off heat. Add the remaining stuffing ingredients. Mix well and set aside. (This filling can be made ahead and refrigerated for a day. There is no need to warm the stuffing before filling the breads.)

3. Combine *chapati* flour or whole wheat flour with 1 cup of all-purpose flour and salt in a bowl. Reserve about 1 teaspoon of shortening, and rub the remainder into the flour, following the instructions on pp. 125–126. Add water, initially fast, to moisten the flour enough that it adheres into a mass; then slowly, little by little, until the dough is formed and can be kneaded. (See Mixing and Kneading the Dough, pp. 389–390.)

4. Brush the work surface and your hands with the reserved teaspoon of fat. Place the dough on the greased surface, and knead for 10–15 minutes. (Or mix and knead the dough in the food processor, see p. 391.) This will be a very soft pliable dough. Put the dough back in the bowl, cover with a moist towel or a sheet of plastic wrap and let it rest, preferably in a warm place, for at least ½ hour. (The dough can be made a day ahead and refrigerated, tightly sealed in foil. Remove from refrigerator about 30 minutes before you are ready to roll.)

5. Put the shortening for brushing the bread in a shallow bowl and the flour for dusting in a plate or another bowl. Keep them, and the filling, close to the work surface where the dough is to be rolled.

6. Divide both *paratha* dough and filling into 12 equal portions. Take 1 piece of dough, and flatten it into a round 4-inch pillow with your hand. Depress the center slightly, and place a portion of the filling into the depression. Bring the sides of the dough over the filling and enclose it completely. Press lightly but firmly to flatten it into a pillow, either between your hands or on the workboard. With the fingers, pinch the edges slightly, so that the filling is in the center and not near the edge where it could break through the dough. Repeat with the rest of the patties the same way, and keep them covered with a sheet of plastic wrap or a moist towel to prevent their drying out.

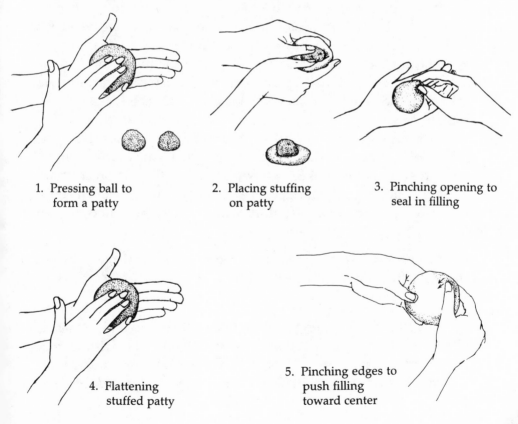

1. Pressing ball to form a patty

2. Placing stuffing on patty

3. Pinching opening to seal in filling

4. Flattening stuffed patty

5. Pinching edges to push filling toward center

(continued)

7. Pick up a filled patty, and place it on the dusting flour. Press lightly with fingers so that some flour sticks to the underside of the patty. Turn and repeat to dust the other side with flour. Return the patty to the work surface.

8. Hold the handles of the rolling pin firmly, and smack or pat the filled patty all over. (This will make the filling adhere to the inside of the bread, so that the filling spreads evenly with the bread when rolled). Roll the patty into a 6-inch circle. Keep dusting with flour from time to time to prevent sticking. (These stuffed breads can be rolled out an hour ahead of time and kept covered with a sheet of plastic wrap or a moist towel to prevent the dough's drying out. Be careful not to stack them one on top of the other, as they will stick together and be impossible to separate. They may be kept slightly overlapping, provided the surfaces in contact are dusted generously with flour.)

9. When ready to fry, heat the griddle or frying pan over medium heat for a couple of minutes or until hot. Put one bread at a time onto the griddle. Cook for 2 minutes or until the side in contact with the griddle is baked and brown spots begin to appear. Flip the bread over with a broad spatula, such as a pancake turner, and bake the other side for a short period (about 30 seconds).

10. Meanwhile brush the baked side, lightly but thoroughly, with melted shortening or oil, and flip the bread again. Now the baked side in contact with the griddle is frying. Cook for ½ minute, then brush the other baked side with fat, and flip the bread to fry the other side for ½ minute. Take it off the griddle, and keep it warm in a covered dish or tightly wrapped with foil. Repeat with the remaining stuffed breads.

Note: These stuffed breads can be made several hours ahead and reheated, loosely covered with foil in a 300°F preheated oven for 10–12 minutes.

These breads are wonderful cut into small pieces and munched with cocktails. Accompanied by a Sweet Lemon Pickle with Cumin (p. 447) or Hot Hyderabad Tomato Relish (p. 441), they make a very satisfying and warm breakfast. Include a yogurt salad such as

Dumplings in Fragrant Yogurt (p. 348) and you have a lovely light lunch. For a more substantial meal, add a few kabobs or a light meat or chicken dish.

Potato- and Herb-Stuffed Bread

(Aloo Paratha)

Aloo Paratha is similar to the Cauliflower-Stuffed Bread on page 405, except that here the *paratha* is filled with mashed potatoes.

Makes 12 seven-inch stuffed paratha
For 6 persons

FOR POTATO AND HERB STUFFING:

4 medium-sized potatoes
½ teaspoon red pepper
1 teaspoon ground cumin
1 teaspoon ground coriander

1¼ teaspoons Kosher salt
3 tablespoons chopped fresh
    coriander leaves

FOR BREAD:

2 cups *chapati* flour or whole
    wheat flour
1 cup all-purpose flour
    (both flours measured by
    scooping flour with
    measuring cup and
    leveling off with a spatula
    or knife)
3 tablespoons Indian vegetable
    shortening or light
    vegetable oil

1 teaspoon Kosher salt
1 cup warm water (90°–100°F)
½ cup flour for dusting
½ cup melted Indian vegetable
    shortening, or light
    vegetable oil for brushing

(continued)

1. Boil the potatoes in their jackets until very soft. Peel, and mash them thoroughly. Add the remaining stuffing ingredients. Mix well and set aside. (This filling can be prepared ahead and refrigerated for a day. There is no need to warm the stuffing before filling the bread.)

2. To prepare the dough and make the bread, follow all the instructions, from step 3 on, given for making stuffed breads in the preceding recipe.

Follow the menu suggestions given for Cauliflower-Stuffed Bread on page 405, except for the choices of yogurt salad. Spinach and Yogurt Salad (p. 344) or Cucumber and Yogurt Salad (p. 343) are better with this bread.

Spinach Bread

(Palak Paratha)

This is another technique for making stuffed bread. Here the filling is mixed in with the dough before the bread is rolled. Since the bread is also oiled and folded several times, it is flakier than the conventional stuffed bread.

Makes 8 paratha

1½ cups all-purpose flour
¾ cup whole wheat flour
(both flours measured by
scooping flour with
measuring cups and
leveling off with a spatula
or knife)
½ teaspoon cumin seeds,
slightly crushed
1 teaspoon Kosher salt

3 tablespoons Indian vegetable
shortening or light
vegetable oil
1 cup cooked spinach (p. 318)
¼ cup warm water (90°–100°F)
½ cup flour for dusting
½ cup melted Indian vegetable
shortening, light vegetable
oil, for brushing

1. Finely chop the spinach in a food processor or on a chopping board, using a knife. (Skip this step if you are making the dough in a food processor.)

2. Combine 1½ cups of all-purpose flour, whole wheat flour, cumin, and salt in a bowl. Rub 2 tablespoons of the oil or shortening into it, following the instructions on pp. 125–126. Add spinach, and mix thoroughly. Add water, little by little, until the dough can be gathered into a firm ball and kneaded (it will be very sticky, so do not try to knead it yet). Clean your hands thoroughly, and dip your fingers and knuckles in the remaining oil to grease them (this will prevent the dough from sticking to your hands while you knead it). Apply a little oil to the work surface. Lift the dough, and place it on the oiled surface. Knead the dough for 10 minutes, coating your fingers with more oil from time to time. Make sure to work all the remaining oil into the dough. Place the dough in a bowl.

In the food processor: To make the dough in a food processor, first attach the steel cutting blade. Put both flours, cumin, and salt in the container, cover, and process for 10 seconds to mix the ingredients. Add 2 tablespoons of the oil, and spinach, and process for another 20 seconds, turning the machine on and off every 5 seconds, until the spinach is thoroughly mixed with the flour. Add the water, little by little (about 1 tablespoon at a time), through the feed tube. As soon as the flour begins to adhere into a mass, stop adding water. Very soon a ball will form on the blades. (Be careful not to run the machine too long at a stretch, which causes the machine to heat up.)

To knead the dough, turn on the processor and continue processing for 40–50 seconds, turning the machine on and off every 5–10 seconds. Add the remaining tablespoon of oil through the feed tube, little by little, during kneading. The dough is kneaded when it looks smooth and shiny and feels very soft and silky to the touch. This is an extremely soft and pliable dough. Carefully remove the dough from the container and place it in a bowl.

3. Cover the bowl with a sheet of plastic wrap or a moist towel, and let it rest for ½ hour. (The dough may be made a day ahead and

refrigerated, tightly covered. Remove from refrigerator about 30 minutes before you are ready to roll.)

4. Put the oil for brushing in a shallow bowl, and flour for dusting in a plate, and keep them close to the work surface where the dough is to be rolled.

5. Knead the dough for another minute, and divide into 8 equal portions.

6. Working one at a time, place 1 ball, generously dusted with flour, on the work surface, and roll it (or spread it with your fingers) into a 6-inch circle, dusting from time to time to prevent sticking. Brush the top with oil (about 1 teaspoon), using a pastry brush or your fingers.

7. Make a cut from the center to the edge of the circle (1). Then roll it from one edge of the cut, all the way around into a cone (2). Stand the cone up vertically (3), with its apex at the top, and gently press down on the tip to compress the cone into a patty. Dust the patty generously with flour, and roll it into a 7-inch disc. (The bread can be rolled out an hour ahead of time, and kept covered with a sheet of plastic wrap or a moist towel to keep the dough from drying out. Be careful not to stack the patties one atop another, as they will stick together and be impossible to separate.)

8. When ready to fry, heat the griddle or frying pan over

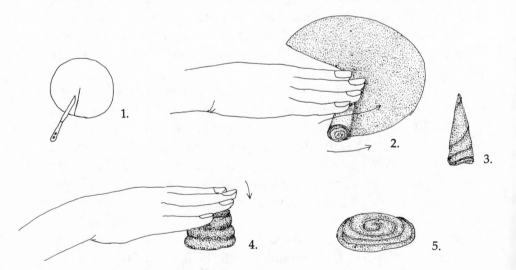

Making spinach bread

medium heat for 2 minutes or until hot. Put one bread on the griddle. Cook for 2 minutes or until the side in contact with the griddle is baked and brown spots appear. Flip the bread over with a broad spatula, such as a pancake turner, and bake the other side for a short period (about 10–15 seconds).

9. Meanwhile, brush the baked side lightly but thoroughly with oil, and flip the bread again. Now the baked side in contact with the griddle is frying. Cook for ½ minute, then brush the other side with oil, and flip the bread for the final time, to fry the second side for ½ minute. Take it off the griddle, and keep it warm in a covered dish or tightly wrapped in foil. Repeat with the remaining breads the same way. Serve hot.

Note: Palak Paratha can be made several hours ahead and reheated, loosely wrapped in foil, in a 300°F preheated oven for 10–12 minutes.

Follow the menu suggestions given for Cauliflower-Stuffed Bread on page 405.

Deep-fried Puffy Bread

(Poori)

In appearance, *poori* looks very much like *phulka*, the puffy bread baked over flame, except that *poori* has a beautiful sheen and is flakier because it is deep-fried and then cooked. Its ravishing appearance is matched only by its exquisite flavor. This is why *poori* is generally served at parties, special dinners, wedding banquets, and most festive occasions.

A word of caution: If you are planning to serve *poori* in a puffed-up state, you have to be sure to plan your menu carefully so that no other dish requires last-minute preparation, because *poori* will take about twenty to thirty minutes to roll and fry. Once fried, it *must* be served immediately.

(continued)

Makes 16 five-inch poori
For 6–8 persons

1 cup *chapati* flour plus ½ cup all-purpose flour; or ¾ cup whole wheat flour plus ¾ cup all-purpose flour (all measured by scooping flour with measuring cups and leveling off with a spatula or knife

¼ teaspoon Kosher salt
2 tablespoons, plus 1 teaspoon light vegetable oil
½ cup warm water (90°–100° F)
½ cup flour for dusting
   Peanut or corn oil enough to fill a fryer to a depth of 3 inches

1. Combine *chapati* flour and all-purpose flour (or whole wheat and all purpose flour) with salt in a bowl. Rub 2 tablespoons of oil into it, following instructions on pp. 125–126. Add water, fast at first, to moisten the flour so that it adheres into a mass; then slowly, little by little, until the dough is formed and can be kneaded. (See Mixing and Kneading the Dough, pp. 389–390.)

2. Place the dough on the work surface, brush your fingers and knuckles with the remaining teaspoon of oil (this will prevent the dough from sticking to your hand), and knead for 10 minutes or until you have a soft and pliable dough that is smooth and silky in appearance. (Or mix and knead the dough in the food processor, see p. 391.)

3. Cover the bowl with a sheet of plastic wrap or a moist towel, and let it rest for ½ hour. (The dough may be made a day ahead and refrigerated, tightly covered. Remove from refrigerator about 30 minutes before you are ready to roll.)

4. Put the flour for dusting in a plate, and keep it close to the work surface where the dough is to be rolled.

5. Knead the dough again for a minute, and divide into 2 equal portions. With your hands, roll each portion into a rope, and cut each rope into 8 equal portions (or pinch off small pieces of dough and roll them into 1-inch balls). Roll the small pieces into smooth balls, dust them lightly with flour to prevent their sticking to each other, and put them back in the bowl. Keep the balls covered loosely with a damp towel or a sheet of plastic wrap to prevent their drying out.

6. Working one at a time, place a ball, generously dusted with flour, on the work surface, and roll it into a 5-inch circle, pressing and stretching it with the rolling pin. Dust the dough from time to time to keep it from sticking to the work surface or rolling pin. (All the breads may be rolled ahead of time and kept covered with a sheet of plastic wrap or a moist towel until you are ready to fry them.)

7. While the last few breads are being rolled, start heating the oil in a *kadhai*, chicken fryer, or a deep saucepan that can be used as a fryer. When the oil is very hot and begins to smoke (400°F), drop one bread at a time into the oil. The bread will sink to the bottom. Immediately hold a slotted spoon flat over the bread, as though keeping it from rising, but not quite touching the bread. As the bread begins to sizzle and rise to the surface (about 3–5 seconds), press the bread very gently, as though patting it, for 2–3 seconds. This will puff the bread. Once the bread begins to puff up, be careful not to press the puffed part too hard, or the bread will break and oil will seep in. Let the bread cook until it stops sizzling and the underside is slightly brown. The entire process of puffing and cooking the first side should take about 15 seconds. Gently flip the bread, and let the other side cook about 15 seconds. Take it out, and

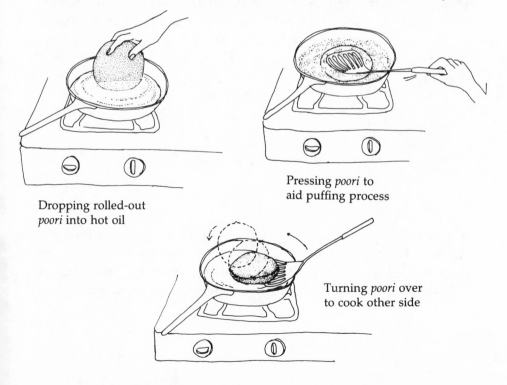

Dropping rolled-out *poori* into hot oil

Pressing *poori* to aid puffing process

Turning *poori* over to cook other side

drain it briefly on kitchen towels. Repeat with the rest of the rolled bread the same way. Serve immediately; or deflate them by placing them on the work surface and pressing gently, and put them in a covered dish or wrap in foil. Just before serving, warm them in a 300°F preheated oven for 15–20 minutes.

Plate of cooked *poori*

Poori can be served with practically all vegetarian main dishes, all side dishes, and those meat and chicken dishes that have reddish-brown sauces. *Poori* is traditionally served with *Tari Aloo* (p. 260) in *Aloo-Poori*, or with *Keema Matar* (p. 162) in *Keema-Poori*, a combination generally served for Sunday brunch. You can also serve these combinations at picnics and barbecue parties for an unusual yet delicious flavor. For such occasions, make the *pooris* ahead, deflate, and wrap them lightly in foil. Just before serving, place them, still wrapped in foil, near the charcoal grill or barbecue pit to heat them slightly.

Deep-fried Bread with Spicy Stuffing

(Kachauri)

This bread is similar to *poori*, except it is filled with a spicy bean stuffing. It is traditionally served with *poori* at the wedding banquets of the Hindu Brahmins of North India. It is also stuffed with different ingredients, such as spices, potatoes, and other vegetables. When it has a stuffing other than the one in this recipe, it is referred to not as *Kachauri*, but as *Masala-poori*, meaning Spicy Deep-fried Puffy Bread.

Makes 16 five-inch kachauri

For 8 persons

FOR SPICY STUFFING:

½ cup white split gram beans
    (*Urad dal*)
4 teaspoons *usli ghee* (p. 50), or
    light vegetable oil
⅛ teaspoon ground asafetida

¼ teaspoon red pepper
¼ teaspoon cumin seeds,
    slightly crushed
1 teaspoon Kosher salt

FOR BREAD:

¾ cup whole wheat flour
¾ cup all-purpose flour
    (both flours measured by
    scooping flour with
    measuring cups and
    leveling off with a spatula
    or knife)

2 tablespoons + 1 teaspoon
    light vegetable oil
½ cup warm water (90°–100°F)
½ cup flour for dusting
    Peanut or corn oil enough to
    fill a fryer to a depth of
    3 inches

1. Pick over, clean, and wash beans following directions on page 327.

2. Put the beans in a bowl, add enough water to cover the beans by 1 inch, and let soak for 24 hours. Drain, discard the water, and set aside.

3. Put the beans in the container of an electric blender or food processor, and grind them to a fine paste. (Use a little water if necessary. However, be careful not to add too much water. The bean paste should be fairly thick, like soft dough.)

4. Heat the *ghee* in a frying pan over medium heat. When it is hot, add asafetida, stir for a moment or two, and immediately add the bean paste. Reduce heat to medium-low, and fry until the paste

begins to look a little dry (about 3–5 minutes). Add the remaining ingredients, and mix well. Turn off heat, and set aside.

5. Combine the whole wheat and all-purpose flours in a bowl. Rub the 2 tablespoons of oil into it. Add water, initially fast, to moisten the dough so that it adheres in a mass; then slowly, little by little, until the dough is formed and can be kneaded. (See Mixing and Kneading the Dough, pp. 389–390.)

6. Place the dough on the work surface, brush your fingers and knuckles with the remaining teaspoon of oil to keep the dough from sticking to your hands, and knead for 10 minutes or until you have a soft and pliable dough that is smooth and silky in appearance. (Or the dough may be mixed and kneaded in the food processor, see p. 391.)

7. Cover the bowl with a sheet of plastic wrap or a moist towel, and let it rest for half an hour. (The dough may be made a day ahead and refrigerated, tightly covered. Remove from refrigerator about 30 minutes before you are ready to roll.)

8. Put the flour for dusting in a plate, and keep it close to the work surface where the dough is to be rolled.

9. Knead the dough again, and divide it into 2 equal portions. With your hands, roll each portion into a rope, and cut each rope into 8 equal portions (or pinch off small pieces of dough and roll them into 1-inch balls). Roll the small pieces into smooth balls, dust them lightly with flour to prevent their sticking to each other, and return them to the bowl. Keep the balls covered loosely with a damp towel or a sheet of plastic wrap to prevent drying out.

10. Divide the spicy stuffing into 16 equal portions. Working one at a time, place a ball, generously dusted with flour, on the work surface, and roll it into a 4-inch circle, or flatten it into a 4-inch pillow with your hand. Depress the center slightly, and place a portion of the filling into the depression. Bring the sides of the dough over the filling to enclose it completely. With your fingers, slightly pinch the edges so that the filling is in the center and not near the edge where it could break through the dough. Repeat with the rest of the balls the same way, and keep them covered with plastic wrap or a moist towel.

11. Place a filled patty on the dusting flour. Press it lightly with

your fingers so that some flour sticks to the underside. Turn and repeat, to dust the other side with flour. Return the patty to the work surface, and roll into a 4- to 4½-inch circle. Keep dusting with flour from time to time to prevent sticking. (These breads can be rolled out an hour ahead of time and kept covered with a sheet of plastic wrap or a moist towel to prevent the dough's drying out. Be careful not to stack them one atop another, as they may stick together. They may, however, be overlapped slightly, provided the surfaces in contact are generously dusted with flour.)

12. When ready to fry, heat the oil in a *kadhai*, chicken fryer, or deep saucepan that can be used as a fryer. When the oil is very hot and begins to smoke (400°F), drop 1 bread into the oil. It will sink to the bottom of the pan. Immediately hold the slotted spoon flat over the bread, as though to keep it from rising to the top. As the bread begins to sizzle and rise to the surface (about 5–8 seconds), press the bread gently for 3–5 seconds. This will make it puff slightly. Let the bread cook for ½ minute. Gently flip the bread, and let the other side cook for an additional ½ minute or until nicely browned. Take it out, and drain briefly on paper towels. Repeat with the rest of the rolled breads the same way. Serve immediately; or deflate them by pressing gently, and place in a covered dish or wrap in foil. Just before serving, warm them, wrapped in foil, in a 300°F preheated oven for 15–20 minutes.

Kachauri is delicious by itself. It ideally should accompany a vegetable main dish such as Cauliflower, Green Peas, and Potatoes in Spicy Herb Sauce (p. 256), Round Gourd in Fragrant Gravy (p. 264), or Whole Potatoes in Spicy Yogurt Gravy (p. 258), or a vegetable side dish such as Buttered Smothered Cabbage (p. 298), Spicy Baby Eggplant (p. 303), or Stuffed Okra with Fragrant Spices (p. 311). For a particularly light meal, serve this bread with any of the yogurt salads.

Traditional Accompaniments
to an Indian Meal

An Indian meal, whether formal or just for the family, always has accompaniments. The significance of serving them has been grossly misunderstood by people around the world. Many think accompaniments are garnishes, and serve grated coconut, chopped nuts, cardamom pods, chopped onions, and herbs—something never ever done in Indian homes. The accompaniments are generally served to provide extra pep to the dishes and to enhance their flavor. This could mean adding an extra tang, a bitter, sweet, or peppery taste, or crackling textures against smooth silky sauces. They are definitely not an essential part of a meal, but for an Indian who grew up on these crisp wafers, refreshingly fragrant relishes, and delicious pickles, meals taste quite incomplete without them— somewhat like eating pastrami on rye without mustard, or Peking duck without hoisin sauce.

Wafers

(Papad aur Phool Badi)

Lentil Wafers   *(Papad* or *Appalam)*
Puffy Lentil Wafers   *(Puppadam)*
Snowflakes or Tapioca Wafers   *(Phool Badi)*

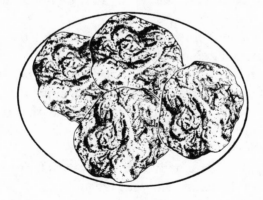

These ravishing crackling wafers are a delight by themselves. They generally accompany a meal to add contrasting flavor and texture. Since they are so easy to cook and easy to serve, they are often served as hors d'œuvres with cocktails. All the varieties of wafer mentioned here are available in Indian grocery stores. Some department stores and specialty food shops also carry them.

The most popular of all wafers is *papad*, especially those made with beans. They are popularly known as lentil wafers, although that is an inaccurate description. The wafers are made with tapioca, potatoes, and rice, as well as with beans. All have two things in common: One, they take laboriously long hours to make, and two, they cook in no time at all—about 2 or 3 seconds. Since they are so time consuming, the responsibility for wafer making, which was a household art a generation ago, has been left to the rural cooperatives who expertly mass-produce them.

The wafers are made by grinding the soaked beans to a paste and then beating the paste to a smooth, elastic dough that can be kneaded and rolled. Various flavorings are added to the dough, which is then rolled into paper-thin discs, and left to dry in the shade for several days, or weeks. The dried discs, still very flexible to the touch, are called *papad*, and will keep indefinitely if properly sealed in airtight containers.

The most commonly served wafer around the country is the one made with white split gram beans *(urad dal)*. The northerners season their wafers fiercely, to provide contrast to the mildly spiced, subtle food, with cracked black pepper, red pepper flakes, garlic flakes, cumin seeds, and carom. The southerners, on the other hand, prefer plain wafers to lend a mellow accent to their highly spiced food.

The *puppadam*, originally from Malabar along the west coast, are very different from *papad*, yet they are wafers all the same. The *papad* is a large wafer, usually 7 to 10 inches in diameter, as compared to the tiny *puppadam*, 2½ to 3½ inches in diameter. *Papad* contains a moderate amount of baking soda and a generous amount of salt whereas *puppadam* contains a large portion of soda and just a tiny pinch of salt. It is the baking soda that gives the *puppadam* its characteristic flavor and light porous texture. The dough for *papad* is rolled paper-thin, while *puppadam's* comparative thickness enables the wafers to puff up, giving them their resemblance to the Deep Fried Puffy Bread (*Poori*, p. 413). That is why many people confuse these wafers with bread and serve them as just that—a gross error. *Poori* is a soft bread eaten as part of the meal, to scoop up meat and vegetables. *Puppadam*, on the other hand, is a crunchy crisp wafer, to be munched on the side, with the meal, for contrasting texture and flavor.

The *Phool badi* is made by cooking tapioca and rice flour into a very thick custard. A little salt and a few chopped green chilies are folded into the custard—or paste—before it is spread into thin discs on a large sheet of cloth. They are then left to dry in the sun for several days. The dried discs, or *phool badi*, are crisp and fragile, breaking easily if roughly handled. These wafers also keep indefinitely if stored in airtight containers. The tapioca wafers are sold in the United States under the name "Sago Wafers" and the rice wafers as *Phool Badi*.

Lentil Wafers

(*Papad* or *Appalam*)

For 8 persons

8 lentil wafers (*Papad* or *Appalam*)	Peanut or corn oil enough to fill a frying pan to a depth of 1½ inches

1. Heat the oil in a *kadhai*, chicken fryer, or frying pan. When the oil is hot (350°–375°F), hold one wafer at a time with a pair of tongs, lower it into the oil, and gently release it. Push the wafer down and swirl it around, using the tips of the tongs, pressing it

gently to keep it submerged at all times during cooking. The wafer will expand to double its original size. The entire cooking takes about 3–5 seconds. Lift the wafer out, holding it at one end to prevent its curling, and give it a gentle shake over the pan to remove excess oil clinging to the wafer. Drain the wafer on a cookie sheet lined with several layers of paper towels. Continue with the rest of the wafers the same way.

This is the traditional method of draining fried wafers in Indian cooking. Wafers fried this way have a little oil, even though not visible, clinging to them, thus making them slightly richer and heavier. I have therefore devised a method for degreasing the wafers.

DEGREASING WAFERS:

1. While the oil is heating, make preparations for draining the wafers. Place 2 or 3 thicknesses of paper towels on the kitchen counter beside the stove. Keep another set of towels handy to use as a blotting pad.

2. Transfer the fried wafer to the paper towels on the counter, and cover it with the other set of towels. Press the wafer through the towels, using moderate pressure to blot up the excess oil. Do not apply too much pressure or you will break the wafer. Repeat with the remaining wafers the same way. This whole process should be carried out without interruption, while the wafers are still warm and pliable, because once they cool (in about 5 seconds) they turn brittle. Any pressure from that point on will instantly and most definitely crumble the wafers.

Frying a lentil wafer

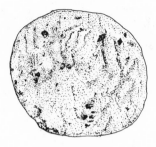

Lentil wafer
before cooking

Lentil wafer
after cooking

The wafers may be made ahead, and reheated just before serving, uncovered, in a preheated 375°F oven for 2 minutes. To keep them warm, turn off the oven and leave the wafers inside, covered, until needed. They may be left uncovered on the kitchen counter provided there is no humidity in the air to make the wafers limp. Just to be on the safe side, I would advise you to store them either in airtight containers or loosely wrapped and sealed in foil.

Puffy Lentil Wafers

(Puppadam)

For 8 persons

8 large (5-inch diameter) or 16 small (3-inch diameter) lentil wafers *(puppadam)*

Peanut or corn oil enough to fill a frying pan to a depth of 1½ inches

Follow the instructions for frying Lentil Wafers on page 425. Since these wafers puff up when fried, the alternate method for degreasing suggested in the Lentil Wafers recipe cannot be used.

Snowflakes or Tapioca Wafers

(Phool Badi)

For 8 persons

16 Sago wafers *(phool badi)*

  Peanut or corn oil enough to
    fill a frying pan to a depth
    of 1½ inches

Follow the recipe for Lentil Wafers (p. 425), using tapioca wafers instead of lentil wafers. The alternate method for degreasing the wafers suggested on page 426 does not work well with tapioca wafers, because of their uneven textured surface, and therefore should not be used.

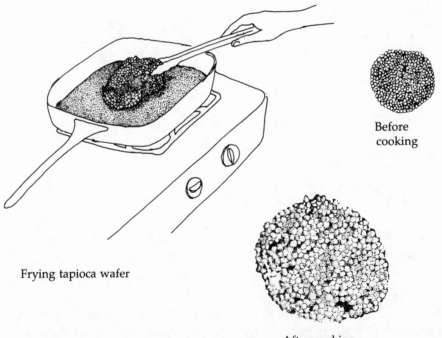

Before
cooking

Frying tapioca wafer

After cooking

Relishes

(Chutney)

VEGETABLE RELISHES

Raw Onion Relish   *(Kache Piaz)*
Onion Vegetable Relish   *(Kachoomar)*
Onion and Roasted Tomato Relish   *(Tamatarwale Piaz)*
Grated Cucumber Relish   *(Kheere ke Lachee)*
Shredded Carrot and Mustard Seed Relish   *(Koosmali)*

HERB RELISHES

Fresh Mint Relish   *(Podina Chutney)*
Mint Coriander Dip   *(Dhania-Podina Chutney)*
Coconut Relish   *(Narial Chutney)*
Sour Mango Relish   *(Aam Chutney)*

PRESERVED RELISHES

Sweet Tomato Relish   *(Tamatar Chutney)*
Hot Hyderabad Tomato Relish   *(Hyderabadi Tamatar Chutney)*
Sweet and Sour Tamarind Relish   *(Imli Chutney)*

Relishes can be grouped into three general categories: vegetable relishes, herb relishes, and preserved relishes.

Vegetable relishes are the quickest and simplest to make. They are nothing but chopped or grated salad vegetables flavored with a little salt, pepper, and lemon juice. Sometimes a spice or two is added to enhance the flavor. Vegetable relishes are usually very mild and frequently take the place of a green salad. They are often assembled just before serving.

Herb relishes are made with highly fragrant herbs, such as mint, coriander, and basil, and with pulpy vegetables, such as raw mango, grated coconut, and spices. They range from mild and highly aromatic to spicy and peppery hot. These relishes keep well for a couple of days in the refrigerator, after which they begin to lose their fragrance and turn dark.

Preserved relishes are made by cooking pulpy fruits, such as apples, pears, peaches, apricots, bananas, guava, and mangoes, or such vegetables as carrots, tomatoes, and tamarind. They are minced or chopped, cooked with sugar, vinegar, and spices, and turned into a sort of sweetish-sour spicy conserve. Major Grey's Chutney, which you see everywhere, falls into this category. Since preserved relishes, particularly those made with fruits, contain expensive ingredients, they are reserved for special occasions like wedding banquets. Because of their saucelike consistency, they make ideal dips to be served with such fried food as fried fish fillets (pp. 248 and 251) and Shrimp Fritters (p. 118). If properly cooked and bottled in sterilized jars, these relishes can be kept up to a year. Once opened, they must be stored in the refrigerator.

There are no rules as to which relish should accompany which appetizer. Some combinations, however, have become classics. Savory Pastries with Spicy Potato Filling (p. 125) are generally served with Tamarind Relish (p. 442), Vegetable Fritters (p. 113) with Fresh Mint Relish (p. 436) or Coriander Mint Dip (p. 437), and Silky Bean Dumplings (p. 123) with Coconut Relish (p. 438). Several of the vegetable relishes are so substantial, they are often served as vegetable side dishes.

Raw Onion Relish

(Kache Piaz)

In India, most dry meat preparations such as kabobs, *tandoori* food, and cutlets are eaten with raw onions, because the onions provide moisture against the dry meat. Besides, these meat dishes taste better with onions. The onion slices are often squeezed slightly to extract and remove some of the juices; this is done to reduce the impact of too sharp and hot a taste. The onions are washed in several changes of water to rid them of any clinging juices; this also makes them taste less sharp. If you want the onions even milder, soak the squeezed onions in salted water to cover (about ¼ teaspoon of salt per cup of water) for ½ hour, and drain. This will make the onions taste sweet, and best of all, there will be no onion odor lingering in your mouth. To make this salad more aromatic, add leaves from 2 or 3 sprigs of fresh coriander.

For 6–8 persons

3 medium-sized onions,
    preferably red
1 green chili, seeded and sliced
    (optional)

Juice of ½ lemon, or
    2 teaspoons cider vinegar
Kosher salt to taste

1. Peel onions, and cut them in thin slices. Separate the shreds, and wash them in several changes of cold water, squeezing them slightly. Be careful not to squeeze the shreds too hard, or you may crush them. Put them in a bowl, add chili, and sprinkle them with lemon juice or vinegar, and salt. Toss. Serve immediately.

Onion Vegetable Relish

(Kachoomar)

Kachoomar is a classic North Indian relish. It is made with onions, tomatoes, green peppers, and usually flavored with lemon juice, coriander leaves, and green chilies. Sometimes a little ground roasted cumin seed is sprinkled on top to give it an interesting texture and flavor. *Kachoomar* goes well with all North Indian dishes.

For 6–8 persons

2 medium-sized onions, preferably red, or 1 large yellow Spanish onion	1 small ripe tomato
½ teaspoon cider vinegar (optional)	½ cup loosely packed fresh coriander leaves
1 small green pepper	1–2 green chilies
	Juice of 1 small lemon
	Kosher salt, to taste

1. Peel the onions, and cut them in half from the top. Cut off the ends, and slice each half into ⅛-inch slices. Separate the shreds, and put them in a bowl. Add enough iced water to cover them by an inch. Stir in the vinegar, and refrigerate until needed.

2. Wash green pepper in cold water, and wipe dry. Cut off the stem and discard. Cut the pepper in half, and discard the seeds and spongy white interior. Slice the pepper into shreds, and put in a bowl.

3. Wash tomato in cold water, and wipe dry. Cut the tomato in half, and scrape the interior, removing the pulp (save it for some other use, such as making gravy for meat dishes). Slice the tomato halves into thin shreds, and add them to the bowl with the shredded pepper.

4. Chop coriander leaves coarsely. Seed and shred the green chilies. Add both to the tomato and peppers.

5. Do not mix the vegetables. Simply cover the bowl, and

refrigerate until needed. (The vegetables and onions can be pre-pared ahead and refrigerated for up to 2 hours.)

6. When ready to assemble the relish, drain the onions thoroughly and add them to the other vegetables. Squeeze the juice of the lemon over them, and add salt to taste. Toss the vegetables briefly, and serve immediately. The *kachoomar* must be served soon after it is assembled, or it will lose its crunchy texture.

Onion and Roasted Tomato Relish

(Tamatarwale Piaz)

This is my favorite relish. It is made with onions and the pulp of roasted tomato. My mother-in-law's mother-in-law, whose recipe this is, made it over the soft ashes of the wood fire. Because of its gentle smoky flavor, it is served with Lamb Pilaf (p. 189), Lamb Pilaf with Leftover Roast Lamb (p. 188), Meat Cutlets (p. 197), and Emperor's Layered Meat and Fragrant Rice Casserole (p. 192).

For 6–8 persons

2 medium-sized onions, preferably red	1 medium-sized ripe tomato Kosher salt

1. Preheat the oven to 500°F.

2. Peel the onions, and cut them in half from the top. Cut off the ends, and slice each half into ⅛-inch slices. Separate the shreds, and wash them in several changes of water, squeezing them slightly. Be careful not to squeeze too hard, or you may crush the shreds. Put them in a bowl, and set aside.

3. Wash the tomato, wipe dry, and smear a little oil over it. Place the tomato in a small oven-proof dish. Bake, uncovered, in

the middle level of the oven for 15 minutes or until the tomato is fully cooked and very soft and the skin is cracked and charred. Take the dish from the oven, and let the tomato cool briefly. Then carefully peel off the skin. Mash the pulp with a fork or spoon. Be careful not to overmash; the pulp must remain a little lumpy.

4. Mix onions and tomato pulp in a small serving bowl. Add salt to taste, and serve.

Grated Cucumber Relish

(Kheere ke Lache)

This simple yet very refreshing relish of grated cucumber is a marvelous snack for any time of the day. It is also good with any Indian meal.

For 6–8 persons

3 medium-sized cucumbers	Black pepper, to taste
1 tablespoon lemon juice	Kosher salt, to taste

1. Peel the cucumbers and cut in half. If the seeds look hard and mature, scrape them out and discard. Grate the cucumber into a bowl, using the coarse blade of the grater or food processor. Cover and refrigerate. (This can be done up to 4 hours in advance.)

2. When ready to serve, add lemon juice, and black pepper and salt to taste. Toss well, and serve.

Shredded Carrot and Mustard Seed Relish

(Koosmali)

This is a popular relish in the southern and southwestern parts of India. It is made with grated carrot (you may substitute cucumber) and mustard-seed-flavored oil. The carrots are briefly cooked in the oil to remove their raw taste. *Koosmali* may accompany Spicy Brussels Sprouts, Green Beans, and Lentil Stew (p. 276), Mixed Lentils and Vegetable Stew (p. 280), Goanese Hot and Pungent Curry (p. 199), or Shrimp Poached in Coconut Milk with Fresh Herbs (p. 243).

For 6–8 persons

6 medium-sized carrots (about 1 pound)

3 tablespoons *usli ghee* (p. 50), or oil (preferably light sesame)

½ teaspoon black mustard seeds

1–2 green chilis, seeded and sliced (optional)

6–8 fresh or dry kari leaves, or 2 sprigs fresh coriander leaves

Kosher salt to taste

1. Wash the carrots, scrubbing them under running cold water, and pat them dry. Grate them, using the coarse blade of the grater, or finely shred them.

2. Heat the *ghee* in a frying pan over medium-high heat. When it is very hot, carefully add the mustard seeds. Keep a pot lid or spatter screen handy, since the seeds may splutter and splatter. When the seeds stop spluttering and turn gray, add the chilies, stir rapidly for a moment or two, and follow at once with the grated carrots. Fry the carrots briefly to remove the raw taste (about 5 minutes), stirring constantly to prevent burning. Turn off heat, sprinkle with salt, and mix. When slightly cool, transfer the relish to a small serving bowl. Bury the kari leaves or coriander sprigs in the pile of shredded carrots. Cover and refrigerate. When ready to

serve, discard the kari leaves or coriander sprigs, and check for salt. Fluff the shreds, and serve.

Note: This relish can be made several hours ahead and refrigerated until you are ready to serve.

Fresh Mint Relish

(Podina Chutney)

This is the most popular of all relishes in North India. It is made year-round, since mint flourishes in the North all twelve months. This relish has the consistency of a thick *pesto* (the Italian basil sauce) and is generally served with such fried foods as Onion Fritters (p. 113), Shrimp Fritters (p. 118), Savory Pastries with Spicy Potato Filling (p. 125), Savory Meat Pastries (p. 130), Spinach and Mung Bean Dumplings (p. 120), and Chick-pea Batter Fish (p. 251). You may also serve this relish with a North Indian vegetarian meal.

Makes 1 cup

3 cups loosely packed mint leaves (without stems)
2–3 green chilies, seeded
3 tablespoons finely chopped onions
¾ teaspoon grated fresh ginger root

¾ teaspoon Kosher salt
1½ teaspoons sugar
1½ tablespoons lemon juice
3 tablespoons water

1. Put all the ingredients in the container of a food processor or electric blender, and blend until reduced to a fine, smooth puree. (This will take a few minutes more in the blender because of the lack of liquid. You will need to push the ingredients down, scraping the sides of the container from time to time.) Cover, and chill thoroughly before serving. Taste for flavoring, and if desired, add more salt and sugar.

Note: This relish keeps well in the refrigerator for a week. It also takes well to freezing, except that the liquid separates from the pulp. Therefore, be sure to stir the relish thoroughly before serving.

Mint Coriander Dip

(Dhania-Podina Chutney)

This relish is made with coriander and mint, and thinned with yogurt so that its consistency will resemble that of a sauce. It is ideal as a dipping sauce with most fried appetizers, such as Spinach and Mung Bean Dumplings (p. 120), Savory Meat Pastries (p. 130), Onion Fritters (p. 113), and Indian Cheese Fritters (p. 117). It is also good with fried fish, such as Chick-pea Batter Fish (p. 251) or Shrimp Fritters (p. 118).

Makes 1 cup

⅓ cup plain yogurt
2 tablespoons cold water
1 tablespoon finely chopped
   onions
⅓ teaspoon finely chopped
   fresh ginger root
1–2 green chilies, seeded
1 teaspoon Kosher salt

¾ teaspoon sugar
¼ small green pepper, cored
   and chopped
¼ cup packed fresh mint leaves
   (or substitute 2 teaspoons
   powdered dry mint leaves)
¾ cup packed fresh coriander
   leaves

1. Put all the ingredients in the container of a food processor or electric blender, and blend until finely pureed and reduced to a creamy sauce. Check for salt, and pour into a small bowl. Cover and chill thoroughly before serving.

Coconut Relish

(Narial Chutney)

This is the most popular relish of South India. Although its flavor will vary from state to state, it consists essentially of freshly grated coconut and mustard seeds. The mustard seeds are sizzled in hot oil and folded into the coconut. Some Indians flavor the relish with ground roasted yellow split peas *(bhona channa dal ka aata);* others with tomato. But the most refreshing and fragrant is the *Malayali* version from Kerala, which adds chopped fresh coriander. This herb also tints the relish a very appealing pale green color.

Coconut relish generally accompanies southern delicacies. Serve it with Silky Bean Dumplings (p. 123) and with southern or southwestern vegetarian meals that are characteristically flavored with black mustard seeds.

Makes 1¼ cup

1 cup packed fresh grated
   coconut
½ cup plain yogurt
2 tablespoons finely chopped
   fresh coriander leaves
   (optional)
2 green chilies (or ¼ small green
   pepper plus ¼ teaspoon red
   pepper)

½ teaspoon Kosher salt
2 tablespoons hot water
4 tablespoons *usli ghee* (p. 50),
   or oil (preferably sesame)
1 teaspoon black mustard seeds

1. Put coconut, yogurt, coriander leaves, chilies, salt, and hot water into the container of an electric blender, and blend until finely pureed. Pur into a small serving bowl.

2. Heat the *ghee* or oil over medium-high heat in a small frying pan. When it is very hot, carefully add mustard seeds. Keep a pot lid or spatter screen handy, since the seeds may splutter and splatter. When the seeds stop spluttering and turn gray, imme-

diately pour the *ghee* and seeds over the coconut puree. Mix thoroughly, check for salt, and serve.

Note: This relish may be prepared ahead and refrigerated for up to 2 days. Remove from refrigerator at least 15 minutes before serving.

Sour Mango Relish

(Aam Chutney)

This is a relish commonly seen on North Indian tables during the summer, when mangoes are in season. The traditional recipe is fairly hot, so serve only a few teaspoons per person. This relish may accompany a North Indian meal, particularly a vegetarian one. It is also very good with Savory Pastries with Spicy Potato Filling (p. 125), Onion Fritters (p. 113), and Indian Cheese Fritters (p. 117).

Makes 1½ cups

1–2 very green raw mangoes (about 1½ pounds altogether)	¼ teaspoon red pepper
	¼ teaspoon ground clove
	¼ teaspoon grated nutmeg
1 cup packed fresh mint leaves	1 teaspoon dry ginger powder
2 teaspoons ground cumin	2 teaspoons Kosher salt
2 tablespoons ground coriander	3 tablespoons sugar or molasses

1. Peel and seed the mango, and cut the pulp into ½-inch pieces (makes about 2 cups).
2. Put the mango, with all the other ingredients, in the container of an electric blender, and blend until reduced to a fine

puree. Taste, and if desired, add more salt and sugar. Pour the relish into a small serving bowl, and chill thoroughly before serving.

Note: For best results, the relish must be served within a couple of hours after being prepared, as the spices seem to lose much of their fragrance with keeping.

Sweet Tomato Relish

(Tamatar Chutney)

This bright-red tomato relish is perfumed with ginger and cloves. Its consistency is like ketchup, and it is excellent served with Shrimp Fritters (p. 118), Panfried Fillet of Sole Laced with Carom (p. 248), Meat Cutlets (p. 197), and Chick-pea Batter Fish (p. 251).

Makes 2½ cups

2 pounds red ripe tomatoes, blanched, peeled, and coarsely chopped
1 medium onion, peeled and finely chopped
1½ teaspoons finely chopped garlic
⅓ cup cider vinegar
¼ teaspoon ground clove (optional)
1½ teaspoons ginger powder
½ teaspoon paprika
¼–½ teaspoon red pepper
⅔ cup sugar
2 teaspoons Kosher salt

1. Put tomatoes, onion, and garlic in a heavy-bottomed enamel-coated pan, and bring to a boil. Reduce heat and simmer, uncovered, until the tomatoes are soft and reduced to a thick puree (about 45 minutes). Stir from time to time to prevent sticking and burning.
2. Strain the puree through a sieve into a small bowl. Discard seeds and any residue that may remain in the sieve.

3. Return the strained puree to the pan, add the remaining ingredients, and bring again to a boil. Reduce heat and simmer, uncovered, for 30 minutes or until the sauce turns thick and glossy and coats a spoon. Stir often throughout this time, especially during the last few minutes, when the sauce becomes considerably thick and sticks to the bottom of the pan. Turn off heat, and immediately pour into sterilized jars, and seal. Or alternatively, cool thoroughly, and freeze in airtight plastic containers. The relish may be refrigerated. Let the relish rest at least 2 days before serving. For best results, it must be refrigerated once opened.

Note: This relish will keep well for several months in the refrigerator.

Hot Hyderabad Tomato Relish

(Hyderabadi Tamatar Chutney)

This pulpy, saucelike tomato relish is piquant, garlicky, and delicious. A specialty from the city of Hyderabad, it goes well with Moghul dishes containing a cream and yogurt sauce, such as Lamb Braised in Yogurt Cardamom Sauce (p. 168), Lamb Braised in Aromatic Cream Sauce (p. 164), or Ground Meat with Potatoes in Scented White Sauce (p. 160). You can step up the peppery taste in this recipe by increasing either the red peppers or the green chilies, or both, to the desired amount.

Makes about 1 cup

4 medium-sized red ripe tomatoes (about 1 pound)	6–8 green chilies, slit open and seeded
⅓ cup light vegetable oil	1–2 teaspoons red pepper
⅓ teaspoon cumin seeds	1 teaspoon paprika
8 small garlic cloves, peeled	1 teaspoon Kosher salt

(continued)

1. Wash tomatoes in cold water, and wipe dry. Slice them into ¼-inch-thick wedges, and set aside.

2. Heat oil over medium heat in a heavy-bottomed enamel-coated pan. When the oil is very hot, add cumin seeds. When the cumin turns dark (about 10 seconds), add garlic and whole chilies, and fry for 1 minute. Add the tomato wedges and remaining ingredients, stir to mix, and cook for 2–3 minutes. Reduce heat, and let the tomatoes cook, uncovered, for 1 hour or until the tomatoes are reduced to a thick pulpy sauce and the oil has separated. Stir 3 or 4 times during this period to ensure that the sauce does not burn. The stirring should be very slow and gentle, as the tomato pieces break easily if roughly handled. Cool thoroughly, and serve at room temperature.

Note: This relish keeps well for up to a day if left at room temperature. In the refrigerator it keeps for a week, and it also freezes well. Defrost thoroughly, and bring to room temperature before serving.

Sweet and Sour Tamarind Relish

(Imli Chutney)

This tamarind relish has a sweet, sour, and hot taste. Its consistency is like a cream sauce. It best accompanies Savory Pastries with Spicy Potato Filling (p. 125). It is also very good served with Silky Bean Dumplings (p. 123).

Makes about 3 cups

1 large lemon-sized ball of
   tamarind (about ¼
   pound)
½ cup unsulphured molasses,
   or brown sugar
¼ cup golden raisins
¼ cup finely chopped pitted
   dates
1½ teaspoons ground roasted
   cumin seeds (p. 66)

1 teaspoon *Mughal garam*
   masala (p. 37), or *garam*
   masala (p. 38)
1 teaspoon dry ginger
   powder
¼–½ teaspoon red pepper
2 teaspoons Kosher salt
1 teaspoon black salt (*kala*
   namak, optional)

1. Put the tamarind in a bowl and add 1 cup of boiling water. Cover and let soak for ½ hour. Mash the pulp with the back of a spoon, or use your fingers, to make it into a thick pulpy sauce. Add 1½ cups of boiling water, mix well, and let stand until lukewarm. When cool enough to handle, mash the pulp again for a minute. Strain the juices through a sieve or cheesecloth into another bowl, squeezing as much juice out of the pulp as possible. Discard the fibrous residue.

2. Stir in the remaining ingredients. Cover and let rest at least 4 hours at room temperature, or overnight in the refrigerator before serving.

Note: This relish keeps well in the refrigerator for a week. It can also be frozen successfully. Defrost slowly and thoroughly before serving.

VARIATIONS:

Banana Tamarind Relish

Follow the instructions for making basic Tamarind Relish, except add 1 large ripe banana, thinly sliced, and reduce molasses or sugar to ¼ cup.

(continued)

Ginger Tamarind Relish

Follow the instructions for basic Tamarind Relish, except add 2–3 tablespoons shredded fresh ginger root and ¾ cup thinly sliced onions, and omit the dates.

Pickles

(Achar)

Sweet Lemon Pickle with Cumin   *(Meetha Sabat Nimboo Achar)*
Hot Lemon Pickle   *(Garam Nimboo ka Achar)*
Quick Mango and Shredded Ginger Pickle *(Aam ka Achar)*

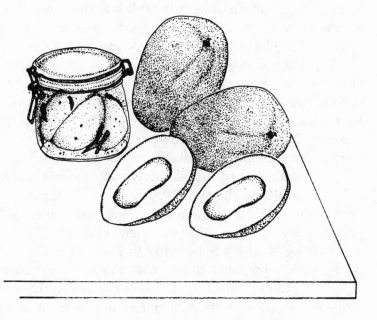

The Indian vegetarian meal almost always contains a pickle or two—a phenomenon not as common with nonvegetarian meals. In India, for poor farmers and laborers whose lunch consists of several thick breads, or rice mixed with a little plain yogurt, either staple accompanied by a chunk of spicy pickle, the pickle often takes the place of the side dish. Pickles are a very popular accompaniment for picnics and long journeys away from home. There are vast numbers of orthodox Indians who won't eat food cooked by people not of their sect. When they have to go on trips for two or three days, they would often go hungry if it weren't for the pickles they take along, with a stack of bread.

Indians pickle just about every vegetable, meat, fruit, nut, and berry. The most common, of course, are the vegetable and berry varieties, because they are inexpensive and plentiful. Except for a few sweet ones, most pickles range from mildly to very hot. All contain fragrant spices. The pickles are prepared by long marination in a spice-laced strong brine solution, with some pickles taking as long as half a year to mature. For this reason, the ingredients to be pickled are left whole or cut into large chunks.

Exposure to sunlight is an essential step in preparing pickles. This is done during the initial maturing period, because sunlight kills off bacteria, thus preventing mold and mildew from forming. To take advantage of the strong sunlight, pickles are generally prepared in summer, with the fortunate coincidence that during most of the pickling, vegetables are also in season.

All Indian grocery stores carry many varieties of pickles, from mild and sweet to fierce and peppery. Unfortunately, I have not found any worth recommending. I suggest you try a few, and if you find any one that suits your taste, stick with it.

Pickling is an art flourishing in the kitchens of Indian housewives, with whom the commercial establishment dares not compete. Each family has a special method and recipe for preparing pickles, a secret seldom divulged to outsiders. It is also believed that some have a natural hand for pickling. No matter what and how they pickle, it turns out just perfect. Such people often become the suppliers of pickles for the entire family of daughters, aunts, cousins, sisters, nieces and so on.

The lemon pickle recipes included in this chapter have been particularly chosen for their simplicity and superb flavor and appearance. Packed in attractive jars, they make excellent holiday gifts.

Although there are many interesting pickles made in India with raw mangoes, I have purposely avoided including the recipes, because the green raw pickling mangoes available in the United States lack the necessary tartness, close-grained texture, and intense flavor for pickling. There is, however, one interesting and easy-to-make mango pickle that uses mildly sour mangoes. It takes only a short time to make, and it needs to rest only half an hour before serving. The recipe for this pickle is included. The raw pickling variety of mango is widely available at greengrocers' stores, especially those selling Latin American produce. These mangoes are seasonal, however. They are in the market for 8 weeks from the middle of April to the middle of June.

Sweet Lemon Pickle with Cumin

(Meetha Sabat Nimboo Achar)

Makes about a quart

9 lemons (about 1½ pounds)	2 tablespoons seedless raisins
4 tablespoons Kosher salt	(optional)
1 tablespoon ground cumin	1 teaspoon black peppercorns
1 tablespoon black pepper	(optional)
3 cups sugar	5–6 dry red chili pods (optional)

(continued)

1. Wash the lemons in running cold water and wipe completely dry. (If there is moisture on the surface of the lemon, the pickle will spoil.)

2. Quarter 6 lemons from the top to within ½ inch of the bottom. Extract the juice from the other 3 lemons in a small bowl.

3. Mix salt, cumin, and black pepper in a small dish, and stuff the 6 cut lemons with it, making sure not to separate the wedges so much that lemons break open. Press the lemons slightly, to reshape them, and place in a ceramic or glass jar so that they fit snugly without crushing each other. Pour the extracted lemon juice over them. Cover the jar with a piece of cheesecloth, and tie a cord or rubber band around the jar so that the cover does not slip or blow away. (During this stage, the pickle should not be covered with the lid of the jar, or it may rot. The porous cheesecloth excludes dust and other foreign matter, while allowing full air circulation.) Let the lemons marinate in the salt and spices for 7 days. For best results, place the jar during the day in the sun (a sunny window sill is ideal.) This will prevent any bacterial growth.

4. On the eighth day, pour all the juices from the jar into an enamel pan, squeezing and pressing the lemons slightly. Add the sugar to the juices, and bring to a gentle simmer over low heat. Stir often to prevent sticking and burning. When the sugar has fully dissolved, add the lemons, and gently boil for 10 minutes or until the lemons are cooked and tender. Turn off heat, and if desired, stir in the recommended amounts of raisins, black peppercorn, and chili pods. Transfer the pickle to sterilized jars. When thoroughly cooled, cover jars with their lids. Let the pickle rest for at least 3 weeks before serving. (For full flavoring, the pickle should rest for 10 weeks.)

Hot Lemon Pickle

(Garam Nimboo ka Achar)

Makes about 1 quart

1½ teaspoons black mustard
    seeds
1 teaspoon fenugreek seeds
2 tablespoons red pepper
1 tablespoon turmeric

½ teaspoon ground asafetida
6 tablespoons Kosher salt
1 cup light sesame or peanut
    oil
6 lemons (about 1 pound)

1. Heat a small frying pan over medium heat. When it is very hot, add the mustard and fenugreek seeds, and roast until the mustard seeds turn gray and the fenugreek dark brown (about 5 minutes), stirring constantly to keep them from browning unevenly. Add red pepper, turmeric, and asafetida, all at once, and stir rapidly for 10–15 seconds to roast the ground spices slightly. Transfer the spices to a small plate or bowl, and let them cool briefly. Grind the spices to a fine powder in a coffee grinder, or use a mortar and pestle. Return the spices to the bowl, stir in salt, and set aside.

2. Wash lemons in running cold water, and wipe dry. (Make sure there is no moisture on the surface of the lemons that could cause the pickle to spoil.) Cut each lemon into 8 slices, and set aside.

3. Heat the oil in an enamel pan until very hot; then turn off heat. Add the spices, stir for a second or two, and follow at once with the lemon pieces. Stir to coat all the lemon pieces with the spices, and transfer to a sterilized jar. When thoroughly cooled, cap the jar with its lid. Let the pickle stand for 15 days, stirring once every day, before use.

Quick Mango and Shredded Ginger Pickle

(Aam ka Achar)

Makes about 3 cups

2–3 very green raw mangoes
⅓ cup shredded fresh ginger
　　root
1 tablespoon Kosher salt
1½ teaspoons red pepper

3 tablespoons light sesame oil
　　or light vegetable oil
1½ teaspoons black mustard
　　seeds

1. Wash the mangoes in running cold water, and wipe completely dry. (If there is moisture on the surface of the mango, the pickle will spoil.)

2. Cut the pulp, including the skin, into ½-inch cubes, and put it in a small bowl. Add ginger root, salt, and red pepper, and mix well.

3. Heat the oil in a small frying pan until very hot, and add mustard seeds. Keep a pot lid or spatter screen handy, since the mustard seeds may splutter and splatter. When the seeds stop sputtering and turn gray, pour the oil with the seeds over the mango pieces. Mix well. Let the pickle rest ½ hour before serving.

Desserts

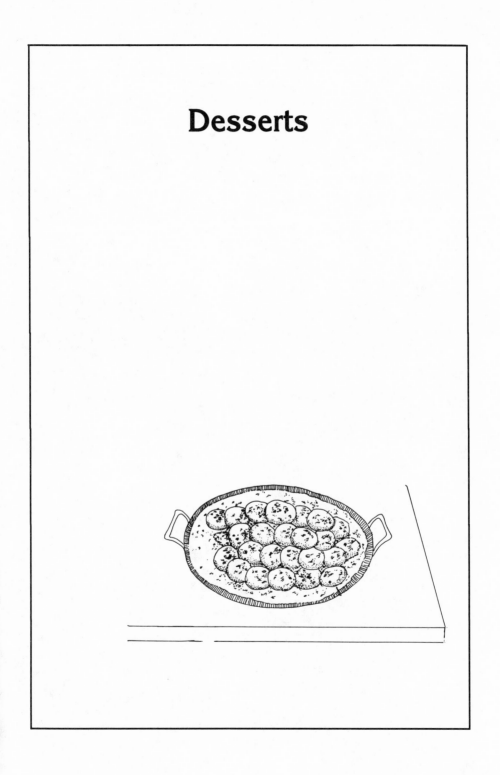

Desserts

(Meetha)

Cream Pudding   *(Basoondi)*
Carrot Pudding with Cardamom and Pistachios   *(Gajar ki Kheer)*
Saffron Almond Pudding   *(Badaam Kheer)*
Coconut Wedding Pudding   *(Payasam)*
Semolina and Raisin Pudding   *(Sooji Halwa)*
Almond and Rice Dessert   *(Firni)*
Whole Wheat Crepes Laced with Fennel   *(Malpoora)*
Cheese Dumplings in Pistachio-Flecked Cream Sauce   *(Ras Malai)*
Mangoes with Cream   *(Malai Aam)*
Mango Fool

Indian meals always conclude with a dessert. When the meal is served traditional Indian style in a *thali*, the dessert is put in one of the small bowls. When the meal is served Western style, on the other hand, the dessert is brought out as a separate course. Most Indian families, except the affluent, have given up this practice of serving desserts with every meal for economic reasons. They are now served on special occasions, such as formal dinners and parties.

Indian desserts are primarily milk-based, and their consistency is much like creamy pudding or foamy custard. Some are served fresh while they are still warm, others are frozen into ice cream, but most are served at room temperature or chilled.

Many of these glorious desserts with their seductive flavors have never come to public attention in the United States, largely because the established Indian restaurants served sweetmeats instead of desserts. (Sweetmeats are easy to prepare in bulk, and will keep well for several weeks without refrigeration. Indian desserts, on the other hand, are delicate preparations that stay fresh for only two to three days, properly refrigerated. Then too, most desserts have a puddinglike appearance, whereas sweetmeats with their impressive colors, shapes, textures, and breathtaking garnishes really steal the show.) Since the restaurants did not bother to clarify the distinction between desserts and sweetmeats, many were led to believe that Indian desserts are rich, syrupy, candylike concoctions, rather than the actual creamy, silky puddings with the mellow fragrance of crushed cardamom, rose essence, or saffron. All this by no means suggests that Indian sweetmeats are something less than Indian desserts. On the contrary, they are some of the finest confections in the world. It only means that each should be served at the appropriate occasion to be enjoyed to the fullest.

Several Indian restaurants that have opened in the last decade are making fervent attempts to restore the tradition of serving proper desserts, an innovation enthusiastically welcomed by the public.

Cream Pudding

(*Basoondi*)

Basoondi, a popular dessert in Uttar Pradesh and Rajasthan, is essentially sweetened *rabadi* (see page 55 for description) studded with pistachios and almonds. In India this dessert is served at room temperature, but I prefer to chill it before serving so that it will taste subtler and mellower.

For 4–6 persons

8 cups milk
3 tablespoons honey or sugar
2 tablespoons blanched
    almonds, cut into thin
    slivers

2 tablespoons unsalted
    pistachio nuts, blanched
    and cut into thin slivers
2–3 sheets silver foil (*vark*,
    optional)

1. Make *rabadi* following the directions on page 55, but reduce the milk only to 2¼ cups.

2. Stir honey or sugar and 1 tablespoon each of the almonds and pistachios into the *rabadi*.

3. Carefully spoon the pudding into individual dessert dishes. Garnish each dish with the remaining almond and pistachio slivers. If you are using the silver foil, decorate each serving with a small piece of it. Place the dishes in the refrigerator, and chill thoroughly before serving.

For flavorful variations, fold in 2 cups fresh pineapple chunks or cantaloupe balls, or stir in ½ teaspoon crushed saffron threads.

Carrot Pudding with Cardamom and Pistachios

(Gajar ki Kheer)

You don't have to be a carrot lover to like this luscious pistachio-laced pudding. Although this dessert is popular throughout the North, it is really the favorite of the Punjabis. It is made by cooking grated carrots with thick, creamy milk until the mixture reduces to the consistency of rice pudding. Sometimes a little rice is added to provide puffiness and body, and also to blend in flavors. This dessert is at its best when thoroughly chilled.

For 6–8 persons

4 cups milk
2 tablespoons long grain rice
2 cups firmly packed peeled
    and grated carrots (about
    1 pound)
½ cup sugar
2 tablespoons slivered blanched
    almonds

⅓ teaspoon ground cardamom
1 teaspoon rose water
¼ cup heavy cream
2 tablespoons chopped
    blanched raw pistachios

1. Bring the milk to a boil in a heavy-bottomed 3-quart pan. Add the rice, and stir for a few minutes to prevent its settling. Reduce heat to medium-low, and cook the milk at a bubbling boil for 20 minutes. The rice will be thoroughly cooked and the milk reduced by half. Stir often to ensure that no skin forms.

2. Add carrots, and continue cooking, uncovered, for 15 minutes or until the carrots are cooked and most of the milk has been absorbed by the carrots, stirring often to prevent burning. (The contents of the pan should reduce to a thick, pulpy sauce.)

3. Add sugar and almonds, and cook, stirring constantly, until the pudding is very thick and begins to stick to the bottom of the pan (about 10 minutes). Turn off heat, and let the pudding cool to room temperature.

4. Stir in cardamom, rose water, and cream. Cover with plastic wrap, and chill thoroughly. Check the consistency of the pudding before serving. It should be slightly thinner than American rice pudding, but not runny. If it looks very thick, add a little milk. Serve in individual dessert dishes, sprinkled with chopped pistachios.

Saffron Almond Pudding

(Badaam Kheer)

This silky-looking dessert, popular in the South, is made with a puree of almonds, whole milk, sugar, and farina. Its lovely sweet fragrance is due to the crushed saffron added at the end. This pale-yellow pudding has a consistency similar to *zabaglione* (the Italian Marsala dessert) or somewhat like vanilla pudding, but its texture is grainy. It is served either hot or chilled. I prefer it chilled, because the flavors of saffron and almond are too intense in a hot pudding.

For 8 persons

¾ cup blanched almonds
4½ cups milk
2 tablespoons *usli ghee* (p. 50), or light vegetable oil
3 tablespoons sliced or slivered almonds for garnish (optional)

3–4 tablespoons semolina (farina)
¾ cup sugar
½ teaspoon saffron threads

(continued)

1. Put almonds in a bowl, add enough boiling water to cover by 1 inch, and soak for a minimum of 2 hours. Drain, reserving ¾ cup of the soaking water.

2. Put the almonds with the reserved ¾ cup of water into the container of a blender, and grind to a fine paste. Add the milk, run the machine for a moment or two to blend, and set aside.

3. Heat the *ghee* over medium heat in a deep enamel pan, and add the slivered almonds. Sauté, tossing the nuts until they are golden (about 1 minute). Take them out with a slotted spoon, drain on paper towels, and set aside for the garnish. (If you are not using garnish, omit this step.)

4. Add the semolina to the pan, and fry over medium heat for 5 minutes or until lightly browned, stirring constantly to ensure even browning. Add the almond-milk mixture in a stream, stirring rapidly to prevent lumping and bring to a boil. Lower heat and cook, uncovered, for 20 minutes, stirring often to keep the milk from sticking and burning. Stir in the sugar, and continue cooking gently for an additional 5 minutes. Turn off heat. The pudding at this stage will have the consistency of a thin, grainy custard sauce. It will thicken considerably with cooling and chilling.

5. Crush the saffron threads to a powder with your fingers, and stir into the pudding until thoroughly blended. When the pudding is cool, transfer to the refrigerator and chill thoroughly. Before serving, check the consistency of the pudding. If it is too thick, thin with a little milk. Serve the pudding in individual dessert dishes sprinkled with the roasted slivered almonds.

Note: This pudding may be prepared ahead and refrigerated for up to 5 days.

Coconut Wedding Pudding

(Payasam)

The dessert traditionally served at wedding banquets in the South is called *Payasam*. It is made with mung beans, yellow split peas, and coconut milk. *Payasam*, generally flavored with crushed cardamom, is of the consistency of a light cream soup. This dessert is served warm (mostly because of the lack of refrigeration in India). I prefer it chilled, because the coconut tastes sweeter and more delicate.

For 6–8 persons

¼ cup yellow split mung beans
    (*moong dal*)
1 tablespoon yellow split peas
    (*channa dal*)
2 tablespoons *usli ghee* (p. 50),
    or butter
2 cups milk

1 cup coconut milk (p. 46)
½ cup light brown sugar
¼ teaspoon ground cardamom
2 teaspoons cornstarch
    dissolved in 2 tablespoons
    of milk or water

1. Pick over, clean, and wash mung beans and split peas following instructions on page 327. Pat them dry.

2. Heat the *ghee* in a heavy-bottomed pan, and add mung beans and split peas. Over medium heat, sauté the *dals*, stirring rapidly, for 2 minutes. Add 2½ cups boiling water, and cook over medium heat, partially covered, for 35 minutes or until the beans and peas are tender. Check often to make sure the water is not evaporating too fast.

3. Increase heat to high, add 1 cup of the milk, and continue cooking, uncovered, for an additional 5 minutes. Stir occasionally to prevent sticking. Turn off heat. Let the mixture cool briefly, then puree the *dals* to a smooth paste in an electric blender or food processor.

4. Return the puree to the pan, and stir in the coconut milk,

brown sugar, cardamom, the remaining 1 cup of milk, and the cornstarch mixture until thoroughly mixed. Simmer gently until the pudding is slightly thickened, stirring rapidly to prevent lumping. When the pudding is cool, transfer to the refrigerator and chill thoroughly. A skin will form over the pudding which is natural. Simply stir it in with a wire whisk. Serve in individual dessert dishes.

Note: This dessert keeps well in the refrigerator for up to 4 days, after which time the coconut milk in the dessert begins to develop a rancid smell.

Semolina and Raisin Pudding

(Sooji Halwa)

Although this pudding is called *halwa*, it is completely different in consistency and texture from the Middle Eastern or Turkish *halvah* candy we are all familiar with here. And it does not look like cooked breakfast cereal. *Sooji Halwa*, at its best, is like thousands of tiny beads, coated with *ghee* and light syrup, clinging together in a fragile mass. This wheat-colored dessert, studded with black raisins, is the most commonly prepared dessert in Indian homes. It is good served either hot or at room temperature.

For 6–8 persons

10 tablespoons sugar	¾ cup semolina (farina)
2½ cups water	¼ teaspoon ground cardamom
4 tablespoons seedless raisins	½ cup heavy cream (optional)
¾ cup *usli ghee* (p. 50) or Indian vegetable shortening	

1. Put sugar in a heavy saucepan with the water, and dissolve over low heat, stirring constantly, until no granules remain. Stir in raisins, and set aside.

2. Heat the *ghee* over medium heat in a large non-stick frying pan or skillet. When it is very hot, add semolina and fry until it is lightly golden brown (about 10 minutes), stirring constantly to ensure even browning. Watch carefully, as the semolina should not become too brown. Add the raisin-sugar syrup in a steady stream, mixing rapidly to prevent lumping, and bring to a boil. Lower heat and simmer, uncovered, for 8–10 minutes or until the water is fully absorbed and the semolina is cooked and puffed. The butter at this point will begin to separate from the pudding. Stir quite frequently during these 10 minutes. Add cardamom, mix well, and turn off heat. The pudding may be served piping hot, warm, or at room temperature, with a little cream spooned over it if desired.

Note: This pudding keeps well for several weeks in the refrigerator. It also takes well to freezing. Defrost thoroughly before reheating.

Almond and Rice Dessert

(Firni)

This is not the usual run-of-the-mill *firni* made with milk and rice-flour and tasting like a starchy, oversweet, pureed rice pudding. It is instead made with almond milk and cream and turned into a velvety smooth custard with a consistency like *pot de crème*. Its sweetness is just enough to satisfy. This *firni*, perfumed with the fragrance of roses, is garnished with slivered almonds and pistachios and crowned with ruby red pomegranate fruit. It looks stunning and tastes exquisite.

(continued)

For 8 persons

FOR ALMOND MILK:

⅓ cup blanched almonds
⅔ cup boiling water

5 tablespoons rice flour
1⅓ cups milk
2 cups light cream
10 tablespoons sugar
2 teaspoons rose water
2 tablespoons finely chopped
   or ground unsalted
   pistachios

2 tablespoons finely chopped
   or ground blanched
   almonds
8 tablespoons fresh
   pomegranate fruit, or 8
   firm ripe fresh
   strawberries

1. Make almond milk: Place blanched almonds in a small bowl, and pour the boiling water over them. Cover, and soak for at least 15 minutes. Put the almonds with their soaking water in the container of an electric blender, and finely puree. Strain the almond milk through a double layer of cheesecloth into a small bowl, squeezing the cloth to extract as much almond milk as possible. This will yield ⅔ cup.

2. Add the rice flour to the almond milk, stir well to mix thoroughly, and set aside.

3. Combine the milk, light cream, and sugar in a heavy-bottomed saucepan, and bring to a boil, stirring constantly. As the milk comes to a boil, reduce the heat. Give the rice and almond mixture a stir, because rice flour has a tendency to separate from the liquid and settle at the bottom. Add it to the milk and cream in the saucepan in a steady, slow stream, stirring rapidly with a wire whisk to prevent lumping. Cook over low heat until the mixture thickens and a thin custard is formed on the spoon. Continue cooking the custard, uncovered, for an additional 5 minutes. The custard should be quite thin. As it chills, it will thicken considerably. (If the custard should accidentally stick and burn, turn off the heat, and immediately pour it into another saucepan. *Do not scrape out the burnt residue;* it will release the burnt-custard smell and texture into the pudding.)

4. Cool the custard thoroughly. Check to make sure there are no lumps. If there are, pass the custard through a fine sieve. (Do not blend it in the electric blender or food processor, or it will become runny.) Stir in the rose water, cover, and refrigerate to chill thoroughly. A skin will form on the custard. No need for alarm. Simply stir it in with a wire whisk. To serve, pour into individual dessert dishes, sprinkle with chopped almonds and pistachios, and place a teaspoon of pomegranate or a strawberry in the center.

Note: This dessert can be made ahead and refrigerated for up to 4 days. It does not freeze well at all.

Whole Wheat Crepes Laced with Fennel

(Malpoora)

Traditionally, *malpoora* batter contains no eggs and is deep-fried. But personally, I prefer to add an egg (it helps to bind the batter) and to cook it like a regular crepe (since the batter is essentially a crepe batter), because deep frying makes it taste greasy and overly rich. Then too, I achieve a prettier-looking crepe.

(continued)

For 6–8 persons

½ cup whole wheat flour
½ cup all-purpose flour
   (both flours measured by
     scooping flour with
     measuring cup and
     leveling off with a spatula
     or knife)
¾ cup heavy cream
1 cup milk
4–5 tablespoons sugar
1 large egg

1 teaspoon fennel seeds,
   crushed
2 tablespoons melted *usli ghee*
   (p. 50), Indian vegetable
   shortening, or butter
Pinch of Kosher salt

½ cup *usli ghee*, Indian
   vegetable shortening, or
   butter for frying crepes

1. Mix all the ingredients, except the ½ cup *ghee*, in an electric blender or food processor, and process until thoroughly blended. Or blend the ingredients thoroughly with a wire whisk. Cover with plastic wrap, and let stand at room temperature for ½ hour, or refrigerate for 2 hours. (The batter may be prepared ahead and refrigerated for up to 1 day.)

2. When ready to fry the crepes, heat a small frying pan (about 8 inches in diameter) or a crepe pan over medium heat, and add a teaspoon of the *ghee*. Tilt the pan to coat the bottom and sides thoroughly. When the *ghee* begins to sizzle, add 2–3 tablespoons of batter to the pan. Lift the frying pan and tilt it from side to side until the entire bottom is covered with the batter. Return the pan to the heat, and cook until the edges begin to curl and brown (about 2 minutes). Turn the pancake with a non-stick spatula, or use your fingers to lift the crepe and turn. Cook the second side for ½ minute. Lift the pan and invert it quickly to drop the crepe onto a plate or a piece of foil. The serving side will be at the bottom; therefore fold the crepe in half to bring the serving side up. Continue with the rest of the batter the same way.

Note: These crepes can be made several hours ahead and reheated briefly in the frying pan just before serving.

The crepes can be served in one of the following ways:

• Arrange the folded crepes in a heated serving platter, and sprinkle them with a little ground cardamom and chopped pistachios.

• Brush each crepe lightly with molasses or honey, before folding and sprinkling with nuts.

• Dip the crepes in sugar syrup until they are fully soaked. Fold them in half, and arrange them on a serving platter. Serve sprinkled with chopped pistachios, and pass heavy cream on the side.

TO MAKE SUGAR SYRUP:

Combine 1 cup sugar and 6 green cardamom pods with 2 cups water. Boil briskly, uncovered, for 5 minutes. Let the syrup cool to room temperature before dipping the crepes.

Cheese Dumplings in Pistachio-Flecked Cream Sauce

(Ras Malai)

Ras Malai has a very intricate flavor, yet it is made with the most basic of ingredients—milk and sugar. Bengalis, known for their famous milk desserts, believe *Ras malai* is another of their wonderful creations, while the Punjabis claim it as *their* contribution to the culinary world. But one thing is certain—it is the most delicate dessert in Indian cooking.

The milk is used in two forms in *Ras malai:* as cheese (*chenna*) and as a thick milk sauce (*rabadi*). The cheese is formed into patties, simmered in syrup until they swell up and look like dumplings. These dumplings are served with the *rabadi* and garnished with pistachios and almonds. *Ras malai* tastes best when it is chilled.

For a fuller description of the uses of *chenna* and *rabadi*, see pp. 52 and 55.

(continued)

For 8 persons

FOR CREAM SAUCE:

5 cups milk

Bring the milk to a boil in a shallow pan, such as a chicken fryer. (This will hasten the process of evaporation.) Reduce heat to medium, and let the milk boil for 1 hour and 15 minutes or until it reduces to 1½ cups. Stir now and then to prevent its sticking to the bottom of the pan and forming a skin on the surface. (A skin will prevent steam from escaping; it also slows the evaporation process. To reduce the milk quickly the skin should either not be allowed to form, or be broken as often as possible. (See more on *rabadi*-making on page 55.) Cool the sauce briefly. If you want a smoother sauce, put it in the container of an electric blender or food processor, and blend until it is smooth. Transfer to a small bowl, cover, and refrigerate until needed. The cooling and chilling will further thicken the *rabadi* to 1¼ cups.

FOR CHEESE DUMPLINGS:

8 cups milk	2 teaspoons all-purpose flour
3–4 tablespoons lemon juice	⅛ teaspoon baking powder

FOR SYRUP:

8 cups sugar	1 tablespoon cornstarch
⅛ teaspoon cream of tartar	dissolved in 2 tablespoons
9 cups water	water

1. Bring the milk to a boil in a large heavy-bottomed pan. Reduce heat, and add 3 tablespoons of lemon juice. Stir gently until a white curd forms and separates from the greenish-yellow whey, about 10 seconds. If no curd forms, add a little more lemon juice.

2. Drain the curd through 3 or 4 layers of cheesecloth or a thin fabric, placed in a colander or sieve in the kitchen sink. Hold the colander or sieve under the tap, and let cold water run at medium

speed through the curd in the cheesecloth for 10 seconds. Bring up the four corners of the cheesecloth and tie them together. Gently twist to extract as much water as possible, and hang the cheese to drain for 1½ hours. There should be 10½ ounces of cheese.

3. Remove cheese from its cloth, and transfer to a butcher block or a marble surface. Working with the heel of your hand, break the lumps very gently. Knead the cheese for 5 minutes, or until it becomes somewhat doughy. Use moderate pressure; it is important not to destroy the grains of the cheese so that the curd does not become a paste. Form the cheese into a thin circle. Mix the flour and baking powder together and sift several times. Sprinkle the mixture evenly over the cheese and knead again for a few minutes to mix thoroughly. The kneaded cheese dough will be very soft, moist, and sticky.

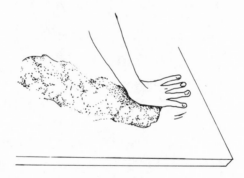

4. Divide the cheese dough into 16 equal portions, and roll the small pieces into balls. Flatten the balls into round 1¼-inch pillows with your hand, and set aside on the workboard while you make the sugar syrup.

5. Mix the sugar and cream of tartar with 9 cups of cold water in a 5-quart heavy-bottomed pan with a tight-fitting lid (a casserole is ideal). Bring to a boil, stirring now and then to dissolve the sugar. Boil the syrup rapidly, uncovered, until it registers 220°F on a candy thermometer (about 10 minutes). Add the cornstarch solution, stirring rapidly. Reduce heat to settle the syrup to a gentle boil.

(continued)

6. Gently slip the cheese patties into the syrup, being careful not to crack them. Let them simmer in the syrup, uncovered, for ½ minute. (This process heats the patties and cooks the outer layer so that they hold their shape and do not fall apart during the boiling which is to follow).

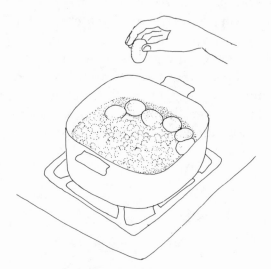

7. Increase the heat to maximum, and bring the syrup to a vigorous boil. Cover the pot with the lid, and let the patties cook in the boiling syrup for 20 minutes. It is essential to keep the temperature constant during these 20 minutes of cooking so that the syrup does not get too thick. This is done by adding 3–4 tablespoons of cold water every 3 minutes (you will use about a cup of cold water in all). If the syrup boils over, you may have to add cold water every 2 minutes, or turn down the heat just a little so that the syrup continues to boil vigorously without boiling over. The cooked patties will puff up like dumplings, and float just beneath the surface of the syrup. Turn off heat.

8. Gently remove 1½ cups of the syrup from under the floating dumplings, being careful not to break any, and pour it into a deep bowl. Thin this syrup with 3 cups of cold water. Transfer the dumplings to this diluted light syrup. When slightly cool, cover, and refrigerate until ready to assemble.

ASSEMBLING RAS MALAI:

16 cheese dumplings in light
    syrup
1¼ cups cream sauce
6 blanched almonds, sliced or
    powdered

1 tablespoon slivered unsalted
    pistachios
2 three-inch square pieces of
    silver foil (*vark*, optional)

1. Carefully take the dumplings out of the syrup, one at a time, pressing them lightly to extract excess syrup. Dip them in cream sauce, and arrange them in one layer in a shallow serving dish. Stir the almonds into the remaining cream sauce, and pour it over the dumplings. Cover, and refrigerate for at least 2 hours to cool thoroughly, turning the dumplings in the sauce a few times. Just before serving, sprinkle with pistachios, and if desired, decorate with silver foil.

Ras malai

Note: The assembled *Ras malai* will keep in the refrigerator, if tightly sealed, for up to 5 days, after which time the cream sauce will begin to taste sour. The cream sauce usually thickens with keeping; therefore, always check the consistency, and if necessary, add 2–3 tablespoons of syrup or milk.

(continued)

Hundreds of batches of *Ras Malai* are usually prepared every day in pastry shops in India. The syrup—gallons of it—is continuously used for subsequent batches of dumplings by thinning it with water to the appropriate consistency. When a certain amount of syrup has been used up, it is replenished with fresh syrup. With the syrup in this recipe, no more than two batches of dumplings can be made. Before starting a second batch, you first need to thin the syrup. Measure the remaining heavy syrup in the pot. To each 1 cup of syrup add ¼ cup of cold water. After cooking the second batch, the remaining syrup may be strained through a double layer of cheesecloth and used to make *Lassi* (p. 488), *Barfi* (p. 476) or Semolina and Raisin Pudding (p. 460). Or use it in fresh lemonade, in place of sugar.

Mangoes with Cream

(Malai Aam)

This is a light and refreshing dessert, good at lunch or Sunday brunch, particularly if you are fond of mangoes.

For 8 persons

2 large ripe mangoes (about 1½–2 pounds each), or 2 twenty-ounce cans of Alfanzo mango slices in syrup

3 tablespoons chopped unsalted pistachios or walnuts
1 cup thickened milk sauce (*rabadi*, pp. 55 and 466)
2 tablespoons sugar

1. Peel mangoes, cut the pulp into large pieces, and put them in a shallow serving bowl. (If you are using canned mangoes, drain, and arrange the slices in the shallow serving bowl.) Sprinkle with the pistachios or walnuts, cover with plastic wrap, and chill thoroughly.

2. Put the *rabadi* and the sugar in the container of an electric blender or food processor, and process until reduced to a smooth sauce. Transfer to a small bowl, cover, and chill thoroughly. Serve mango slices, and pass the *rabadi* sauce on the side.

Variation: Substitute for the *rabadi* ½ cup sour cream diluted with ¼ cup drained juices from canned mangoes (or any fresh or canned fruit juice), and sweetened with 2 tablespoons of sugar.

Mango Fool

Mango fool is made with mangoes, milk or cream, and sugar. Its consistency may vary from thin milkshake to thick custardlike dessert. This particular recipe produces a consistency similar to thin custard sauce. Generally, mango fool does not contain liquor, but I like to add peach or apricot brandy because it enhances the flavor of the mangoes, and livens up the dessert as well.

For 8 persons

2 cups canned mango pulp, or the pulp of 1 large ripe fresh mango weighing about 2 pounds
1 cup milk
3 tablespoons sugar
1½ tablespoons cornstarch dissolved in 3 tablespoons milk or water

1 cup heavy cream
½ teaspoon almond extract
¼ cup apricot or peach brandy
1 tablespoon lemon juice
8 small pieces of canned or fresh mango for garnish (optional)

1. Pass the mango pulp through a fine sieve to remove all the stringy fiber, and put it into a small bowl. Set aside.
2. Heat the milk and 2 tablespoons of the sugar in a small pan over medium heat. When the milk comes to a boil, stir in the cornstarch mixture. Cook until the milk is thickened and forms into

a custard (about 2 minutes). Let it cool thoroughly. Stir in the mango pulp and mix well. (Both the mango pulp and the custard may be prepared ahead and refrigerated for up to 2 days, separately or mixed together.)

3. Whip the heavy cream until it forms definite peaks. Stir in the almond extract and the remaining tablespoon of sugar. Cover, and refrigerate until the final assembly.

4. To assemble, stir the brandy and lemon juice into the mango-custard mixture. Gently and thoroughly fold in the whipped cream. Spoon the dessert into 8 individual dishes. (Or fold in only half the whipped cream, and spread the remainder over the mango mixture in a thin layer, covering it totally.) Garnish with a piece of mango. Chill thoroughly before serving.

Note: The Mango Fool may be prepared 2 hours before serving.

By American standards, this dessert will be considered more a sauce than a pudding. Its consistency, when chilled, is like cream soup. If you prefer a thicker consistency, add less brandy.

Sweetmeats and Beverages

All Indians seem to be born with a sweet tooth; a day isn't complete without a piece of candy. Indians crave sweets not because they love sugar but because Indian sweets are absolutely irresistible. They are sweet as sweetmeats should be but no sweeter than, say, the French *Savarin*, the Middle Eastern *baklava*, or even American pecan pie.

Hundreds of varieties of Indian sweetmeats can be made with fresh and dried fruits, nuts, vegetables, and legumes. Frequently milk fudge *(khoya)* is folded in to provide richness, body, and texture. Sweetmeats can be flavored with saffron, cardamom, rose or screwpine water, and decorated with silver foil *(vark)*, chopped nuts, and sugar glazes. Since most sweetmeats are cooked to a fudgelike consistency, they keep well for a long time.

To moderate the sweetness and wash them down smoothly, sweetmeats are generally eaten with a beverage. Often a savory snack like Savory Pastries with Spicy Potato Filling (p. 125) is eaten simultaneously to balance flavors. Snacking in this yin and yang way—a sweet with a savory plus a beverage—is a favorite Indian pastime. No particular hour is appointed for this; Indians snack when they are hungry—and that could be at any time of day.

Sweetmeats

(Mithai)

Foamy Coconut Fudge   *(Narial Barfi)*
Cashew Nut Fudge   *(Kajoo Barfi)*
Almond Milk Fudge   *(Badaam Barfi)*
Cheese Delights   *(Gokul ke Pede)*
Sesame Crunch   *(Gajjak)*

FUDGE

(Barfi)

In India, people eat fudge or *barfi* the way people here eat candies and cookies. Also, just as Americans take a box of candy when visiting someone, Indians take a box of *barfi*. *Barfi* can be made with several ingredients—nuts, vegetables, fruits, lentils, flour, and milk. The ground ingredients are cooked with sugar and, sometimes, fat, until they reduce to a fudgelike consistency. The fudge is then flavored with spices, perfumed with flower essences, and poured onto a greased plate. When slightly cool, it is decorated with silver foil *(vark)* and cut into neat diamond-shaped or square pieces.

Barfi made with nuts is generally less sweet than the other kinds. The following recipes show three distinct ways of cooking *barfi*. The first one, prepared with a heavy sugar syrup, is more like a candy. The second is made with a light syrup and yields a soft fudge. The third contains milk. All three are delicious and extremely simple to make.

Foamy Coconut Fudge

(Narial Barfi)

This coconut fudge, with its light, foamy texture, is an exquisite creation. Its special crumbly texture is achieved by adding toasted coconut to a very thick bubbling syrup, a technique popular in the south of India.

Note: Use only freshly grated coconut. The dry flaked coconut available in supermarkets simply does not taste as good. For a combination flavor, add two tablespoons of roasted unsalted chopped cashew nuts with the coconut.

Makes about 3 dozen pieces

3 cups well-packed freshly
    grated coconut (meat of 1
    medium coconut)
2 cups sugar
    Pinch of cream of tartar
    (optional)

¼ teaspoon ground cardamom
2 tablespoons *usli ghee* (p. 50),
    or light vegetable oil

1. Grease a 9-inch-square or 6-inch by 12-inch baking pan. Or cut out a 9-inch square of waxed paper, grease it, and place it on a work surface.

2. Heat a large heavy-bottomed pan with non-stick surface over medium-high heat for 1 minute. Add the grated coconut and fry, stirring constantly, until it looks dry and flaky but is still snow white (about 5–7 minutes). Transfer the coconut to a bowl.

3. Add sugar, cream of tartar if you are using it, and 1 cup cold water to the pan, and bring to a boil, stirring. Let the syrup boil over medium-high heat, uncovered, for 7–10 minutes or until the syrup is thickened and looks frothy and full of bubbles. Add the coconut and cardamom powder, and cook for 2–5 minutes, stirring rapidly and vigorously. Stir in the *ghee,* and continue cooking until the mixture begins to foam and stick to the bottom of the pan (about 1 minute). *Do not stop stirring the fudge during this last critical minute, for any reason whatsoever,* or you may end up with crystals of candy instead of flaky-textured fudge.

4. Immediately pour the mixture into the greased pan, or onto the greased waxed paper, and working deftly and quickly, spread the fudge to form an even layer, patting it gently with a flat spatula. (Do not pack too much or the fudge will become dense. The fudge should be light and foamy, filled with air pockets.) Let it cool for 5 minutes. Then cut into neat 1½-inch-square pieces.

Note: This fudge keeps well for several months if stored tightly sealed in containers.

Cashew Nut Fudge

(Kajoo Barfi)

This fudge is made with cashew nuts that have been soaked in water. The nuts are drained, ground to a paste, and cooked with sugar until the mixture reaches a fudge consistency. This technique, popular with Maharashtrians in southwestern India, produces a soft, chewy fudge with a grainy texture.

Note: Almonds, pistachios, or walnuts may be substituted for the cashews.

Makes about 3 dozen pieces

2 cups raw cashew nuts (½ pound)
¾ cup sugar
1 tablespoon butter

2 teaspoons rose water
3 three-inch-square pieces of silver foil (*vark*, optional)

1. Place the cashew nuts in a bowl. Pour boiling water over them to cover, and soak for 1 hour. Drain the nuts, put them in the container of an electric blender or food processor, and reduce them to a fine paste (adding a little milk or water if the paste begins to clog).

2. Grease a 9-inch-square baking pan, or mark and grease a 9-inch-square section of a cookie sheet.

3. Heat a non-stick frying pan (at least 9 inches in diameter) over medium heat for 2 minutes. Add the nut paste and the sugar. Reduce heat to medium-low and cook, stirring and scraping the sides and bottom of the pan constantly with a flat spatula for 20 minutes or until the fudge is thick and sticky. Stir in the butter.

4. Pour the fudge into the greased pan or onto the greased square of cookie sheet. Spread it evenly by patting it gently with the spatula. Let it cool thoroughly.

5. When cool, brush the top with the rose water, and let it dry

briefly. Press the silver foil over the fudge, and cut 1½-inch-square or diamond-shaped pieces, using a knife dipped in cold water.

Note: This fudge keeps well, if stored tightly sealed, at room temperature for 3 weeks and for several months in the refrigerator.

Almond Milk Fudge

(Badaam Barfi)

Makes about 4 dozen pieces

2 cups blanched almonds (about 1 pound)

2 cups milk

¾ cup sugar

2 tablespoons *usli ghee* (p. 50), or Indian vegetable shortening, or butter

2 three-inch square pieces of silver foil (*vark*, optional)

1. Put the almonds in the container of an electric blender or food processor, and powder them finely. Set aside until needed.

2. Mark and grease an 8-inch square on a cookie sheet, or on a sheet of waxed paper placed on the work surface.

3. Bring the milk to a boil in a heavy-bottomed non-stick pan. Cook over high heat, uncovered, for 10 minutes or until it has thickened to the consistency of a cream soup, stirring constantly to prevent burning.

4. Reduce heat to medium, add sugar, and cook for an additional 2 minutes or until all the sugar has dissolved. Add the powdered almonds and the *ghee*. Stir vigorously and constantly as the mixture begins to lump up and stick to the spoon. Release the fudge from the spoon by scraping it off with a knife or a teaspoon. Continue cooking the mixture for 3 minutes.

5. Pour the fudge on the center of the greased square, and

working deftly and quickly, flatten and spread it to an even thickness within the square. If you are using the silver foil, place it over the fudge, and gently press it to make it adhere. While the fudge is still warm, cut it into neat 1-inch by 2-inch diamond-shaped pieces, using a sharp knife dipped in cold water.

Note: This fudge keeps well, if stored tightly sealed, at room temperature for 3 weeks, and for several months in the refrigerator.

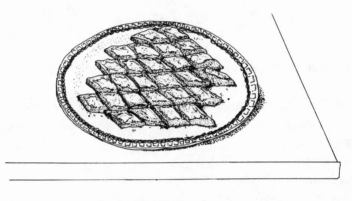

Barfi with silver *vark*

Cheese Delights

(Gokul ke Pede)

Peda is generally made with milk fudge—*khoya*—which is fried and mixed with sugar, nuts, and flavorings, and then formed into smooth one-inch pillows. Made with Indian cheese *(chenna)*, this dessert is a refreshingly different addition to any table. This *peda*, a specialty of Uttar Pradesh, has a coarse, grainy texture and is very light.

Makes about 2 dozen pieces

8 cups milk

3 tablespoons vinegar mixed
   with 3 tablespoons water

½ cup sugar

⅛ teaspoon cardamom powder

⅓ cup confectioner's sugar

2–3 teaspoons milk

1 teaspoon *usli ghee* (p. 50), or
   light vegetable oil

2 tablespoons finely chopped
   or powdered unsalted
   pistachio nuts

1. Make cheese *(chenna)* with 8 cups of milk and vinegar water mixture, following instructions on page 52.

2. Place the cheese in a large shallow bowl, and knead with the palm of your hand until it becomes a smooth dough. Add the sugar, and knead again for a few minutes to mix well. Set aside.

3. Heat a non-stick frying pan over medium heat for 1 minute. Add the cheese (the cheese will melt and become a thick paste) and bring to a boil. Cook the bubbling paste, stirring constantly to prevent sticking, for 5 minutes or until it begins to dry and starts to look crumbly. Reduce heat to medium-low, and continue cooking for an additional 3 minutes or until it looks very dry and grainy.

4. Return the mixture to the bowl, and sprinkle the confectioner's sugar and cardamom powder over it. When cool enough to handle, knead vigorously, using the heels of your palms to crush and break the cheese grains. As you knead, sprinkle in the milk to moisten the mixture. Add only enough milk to make the mixture adhere together and hold its shape when pressed into patties.

5. Wash your hands thoroughly, wipe dry, and grease them with the *ghee* or oil to prevent the cheese mixture from sticking to your fingers. Take out 1 tablespoon of the mixture, and roll it into a smooth ball. Press the ball between your palms to form a 1¼-inch to 1½-inch patty. Press the edges with your fingers to smooth them. (You may use a small greased cookie mold to press and mold the cheese mixture.) Make a gentle depression in the center of the patty, and place a pinch of chopped nuts in it. Press it slightly to ensure that the nuts adhere to the patty. Lay the shaped patty on a

platter, and continue with the rest of the cheese mixture the same way.

Note: These patties store well, if sealed, at room temperature for 3 weeks, and for several months in the refrigerator.

Sesame Crunch

(Gajjak)

This is a simple and popular candy, sesame crunch, known as *Gajjak* in India. I like to use natural, unroasted sesame seeds because they impart a lovely flavor and make the candy slightly chewy.

Makes about 6 dozen pieces

1 cup raw sesame seeds
1 tablespoon water
1 tablespoon sweet butter
½ cup sugar
½ teaspoon lemon juice

1. Grind the sesame seeds to a fine powder, using a coffee grinder or an electric blender.
2. Grease a section, about 9 inches square, of a marble or wooden board. Cut a 9-inch-square piece of waxed paper, grease it thoroughly, and set aside.
3. Heat the water and butter in an enamel pan over medium-low heat. When the butter melts, add the sugar, and cook until it melts and turns a butterscotch color (about 10–15 minutes), stirring constantly to prevent burning.
4. Add the lemon juice, and stir rapidly for 5 seconds (the melted sugar will sizzle), and then add the sesame powder. Mix vigorously for 15 seconds, and immediately pour the mixture on the

greased surface. Place the greased waxed paper (greased side down) over the sesame mixture, and using a rolling pin, roll into a ⅛-inch thick sheet. Working quickly, while the mixture is still warm, peel off the waxed paper, and using a sharp knife, cut it into one-inch squares or diamond-shaped pieces. *(The entire process— from pouring the sesame mixture onto the greased board through cutting the shapes—must be done very quickly, without interruption, because once the mixture cools it becomes brittle and impossible to handle.)*

5. When cool, separate the pieces. Wrap each one in decorative silver paper, or simply store them in an airtight container. *Gajjak* keeps indefinitely.

Beverages

(Thanda-Garam)

Spiced Tea   *(Masala Chah)*
Cardamom Tea   *(Ilaichi Chah)*
Rose-Flavored Yogurt Drink   *(Lassi)*
Minty Yogurt Refresher   *(Mattha)*
Indian Summer Punch   *(Thandai)*

Indian beverages are in a class by themselves. They are fragrant drinks, filled with nutritives, laced with such aromatic spices as cinnamon and cardamom, or herbs such as basil, or essences like rose and sandalwood. There is no tradition of serving a beverage after an Indian meal. Beverages are served at any time of day. They always accompany sweetmeats and savory snacks.

Spiced Tea

(Masala Chah)

Indians like to aromatize everything they eat and drink, and tea is no exception. Generally, cinnamon, cardamom, and cloves are added to give tea a spicy fragrance, but the addition of black pepper, ginger root, coriander, and fennel is not uncommon. The people in the cooler parts of India have traditionally added spices to their tea, not just for flavoring but also to induce heat in the body (see more on pages 3–4). Spiced teas are particularly welcome after an Indian meal, because they provide a gentle, more graceful ending to the intricately spiced Indian dishes. (A plain cup of coffee or tea, in my opinion, tastes bland and flavorless.)

The recipe below produces a wonderfully fragrant tea, richly accented with cinnamon.

Makes 8 six-ounce servings
For 8 persons

6 cups cold water	12 black peppercorns (optional)
⅓ cup milk, or to taste	12 teaspoons sugar, or to taste
1 stick cinnamon, 3 inches long	6 heaping teaspoons leaf tea, or
6 green cardamoms	9 tea bags (orange pekoe)
4 whole cloves	

1. Combine water and milk in a deep pan, and bring to a boil. Add the spices and sugar. Stir to blend, and turn off the heat. Cover the pan, and let the spices soak for at least 10 minutes.

2. Add the tea leaves or bags, and bring the water to a second boil. Reduce heat and simmer, covered, for 5 minutes. Uncover, check the color and taste, and if desired add more milk and sugar. Strain the tea into a warm teapot, and serve immediately.

This is the way the traditional spiced tea is made. You may, however, omit the milk or sugar, or both, in which case reduce the quantity of tea to 2 heaping teaspoons, or 3 tea bags.

Cardamom Tea

(Ilaichi Chah)

This tea is mellower than *masala* tea. It is flavored only with pods of green cardamom, which lend a tasty sweetness.

Makes 8 six-ounce servings
For 8 persons

6 cups cold water	1 1-inch by ½-inch piece of
12 green cardamom pods	lemon, lime, or orange peel
6 heaping teaspoons leaf tea, or	Scalded milk and sugar, to be
9 tea bags (orange pekoe)	served on the side

1. Combine water and cardamom pods in a deep saucepan, and bring to a boil. Reduce heat and simmer, covered, for 5 minutes. Turn off heat, and let soak, covered, for 10 minutes.

2. While the cardamom is soaking, rinse the teapot with boiling water. Add the tea leaves or bags and the peel to the pot.

3. Bring the cardamom water to a full boil, and pour it, pods and all, into the teapot. Let the tea brew for 2–3 minutes before serving. Pass the scalded milk and sugar on the side.

(continued)

This is the way Indians enjoy cardamom tea. You may, if you wish, omit the milk and sugar altogether, in which case reduce the tea to 2 heaping teaspoons or 3 tea bags, or else the brewed tea will be too strong and bitter.

Rose-Flavored Yogurt Drink

(Lassi)

A familiar sound in the streets of Delhi in the summer months is the rhythmic juggling of liquid and ice from one jug *(loota)* to another. What is being prepared is the heavenly yogurt drink called *lassi*. This foamy and frothy liquid, besides being so tasty, is perhaps the most healthful and nutritious drink in the world.

For a classic *lassi*, the quality of the yogurt is of prime importance. It should be slightly sour, so that when it is diluted it still retains a strong yogurt flavor. Also, it is essential that the yogurt be rich and creamy, or else the *lassi* will taste watery. Since American yogurt lacks the right creaminess, you will need to add a little cream to enrich it. *Lassi* is especially refreshing on a hot summer afternoon to accompany a Sunday brunch. It's also wonderful before an Indian breakfast or after a good game of tennis.

Makes 2 eight-ounce servings
For 2 persons

1½ cups plain yogurt	6 tablespoons sugar
3 tablespoons heavy cream	9–10 standard-size ice cubes
1 tablespoon rose water	

1. Put yogurt, cream, rose water, and sugar in the container of an electric blender, and blend for ½ minute or until the sugar is fully dissolved. Add ice cubes, and continue blending for another ½ minute or until the yogurt drink is frothy (the ice cubes will not

disintegrate fully). Pour the drink, with the ice cubes, into 2 tall glasses, and serve.

Note: Lassi may be made ahead and kept refrigerated for 2–3 days. Just before serving, run it through the electric blender for a few seconds to froth it up. Do not add more ice cubes, as they will dilute the *lassi*.

Minty Yogurt Refresher

(Mattha)

Mattha, literally translated, means buttermilk. Its taste and consistency, however, bear no resemblance to American buttermilk. Indian buttermilk is much thinner, more like skimmed milk, and has a buttery-yogurt flavor. *Mattha* is so flavorful that it is frequently served just by itself, though it is quite common to add a little salt, crushed cumin, and a few fragrant herbs. It is a perfect drink for beating the summer heat, or serving before an Indian breakfast or brunch. For the best flavor, the yogurt should be a little tangy.

Makes 2 eight-ounce servings
For 2 persons

1 cup plain yogurt	½ teaspoon Kosher salt
¾ cup cold water	8–9 standard-size ice cubes
12 fresh mint leaves	
½ teaspoon ground roasted cumin seeds (p. 66)	

1. Put yogurt, water, and 8 mint leaves in the container of an electric blender, and blend for ½ minute or until the mint is finely chopped.
2. Add cumin, salt, and ice cubes, and continue blending for

an additional ½ minute or until the yogurt drink is frothy (the ice cubes will not disintegrate fully). Pour the drink with the ice cubes into two tall glasses. Squeeze the 4 remaining mint leaves slightly in your fingers, to release the fragrance, and place them on top. Serve immediately.

Note: This yogurt drink may be made a day ahead and refrigerated. Just before serving, blend again to froth the drink. Do not add more ice cubes, or it will taste weak and flavorless.

Indian Summer Punch

(Thandai)

Writing about *thandai* brings back sweet memories of my childhood in Kanpur. Summer vacation was always a very special time of the year; that was when various candies and pickles were prepared and different spice blends ground and mixed. Every day a fresh beverage was made especially for us while we played in the yard with the sun beating down. The most flavorful of all these was a cardamom-scented almond drink called *thandai*. It is a specialty of Uttar Pradesh and its preparation was, I remember, a long drawn-out process. First, different nuts and seeds were carefully measured. Then each was cleaned and blanched. Then the nuts were mixed and ground to a paste, with a little milk or water, on an Indian stone grinder. This paste was then blended into milk, sweetened with sugar, and poured into tall glasses filled with crushed ice.

Thandai can be made quite effortlessly, in a fraction of the time it takes by the traditional method, by using an electric blender. The results are very good. This beverage is perfect for warm, sultry days. It is a particularly good nonalcoholic drink to serve at cocktail time.

Note: It isn't necessary to make *thandai* with milk—you can use cold water instead, as is often done—though the milk tends to mellow the spices, giving the drink a more delicate taste.

Makes one quart of thandai *concentrate*
8 ten-ounce servings

2 tablespoons fennel seeds
   Seeds from 8 green
     cardamom pods
6 whole cloves
12 peppercorns
½ cup blanched almonds

1 cup raw seeds (such as
   sunflower, pumpkin, or
   papaya)
   boiling water
1 cup sugar
4 cups milk or water

1. Grind fennel, cardamom, cloves, and peppercorns into a fine powder, using a coffee grinder or a mortar and pestle. Set aside.

2. Place almonds and raw seeds in a bowl, add boiling water to cover, and let soak for ½ hour. Drain.

3. Put the soaked almonds and seeds, along with 2 cups of boiling water, in the container of an electric blender, and blend until the almonds and seeds are reduced to a fine paste. Add sugar, and spice mixture, and continue blending until sugar is thoroughly dissolved (about ½ minute).

4. Pour the punch mixture into a bowl. Add 2 more cups of boiling water to the blender, and run it through briefly to release any paste clinging to the sides. Add this to the punch mixture, and stir to blend.

5. Strain the punch mixture through 3 layers of cheesecloth, squeezing to extract as much liquid as possible. (The pulp may be saved and used in nut fudges.) Transfer the concentrate to a bottle or pitcher, and chill thoroughly.

To make individual drinks, pour ½ cup of *thandai* concentrate into a tall glass. Add ½ cup whole milk or water, stir well, add 3 or 4 ice cubes, and serve.

Note: Thandai concentrate will keep in the refrigerator up to a week. It also freezes well. Defrost thoroughly before serving.

Mail Order and Shopping Guide

Below is a list of stores that are well equipped with Indian spices. Most carry canned goods, *dals, basmati* rice, essences, silver foil (*vark*), such spices as black cumin seeds, asafetida, saffron, black cardamom pods, tamarind, mango powder, onion and black mustard seeds, kari leaves, *sambaar* powder, and fresh herbs. Most carry a variety of Indian utensils and cooking tools. And they accept mail orders.

CALIFORNIA

Bazaar of India
1331 University Avenue
Berkeley, California 94702
Tel: (415) 548-4110

Bezjian Groceries
4725 Santa Monica Boulevard
Los Angeles, California 90029
Tel: (213) 663-1503

Bombay Bazaar
1034 University Avenue
Berkeley, California 94710
Tel: (415) 848-1671

India Gifts and Food
643 Post Street
San Francisco, California 94109
Tel: (415) 771-5041

Mr. K's Gourmet Foods & Coffees
Stall 430, Farmer's Market
Third and Fairfax
Los Angeles, California 90036
Tel: (213) 934-9117

CONNECTICUT

India Spice and Gift Shop
3295 Fairfield Avenue
Bridgeport, Connecticut 06605
Tel: (203) 384-0666

DISTRICT OF COLUMBIA

Spices and Foods Unlimited, Inc.
2018A Florida Avenue NW
Washington D.C. 20009
Tel: (202) 265-1909

FLORIDA

Indian Grocery Store
2342 Douglas Road
Miami Beach, Florida 33134
Tel: (305) 448-5869

ILLINOIS

Conte Di Savoia
555 West Roosevelt, #7
Chicago, Illinois 60607
Tel: (312) 666-3471

India Gifts and Foods
1031 West Belmont Avenue
Chicago, Illinois 60650
Tel: (312) 348-4392

India Groceries
5010 North Sheridan Road
Chicago, Illinois 60640
Tel: (312) 334-3351

Oriental Foods & Handicrafts, Inc.
3708 North Broadway
Chicago, Illinois 60613
Tel: (312) 248-8024

MARYLAND

Indian Emporium
68-48 New Hampshire Avenue
Tacoma Park, Maryland 20012
Tel: (301) 270-3322

Indian Super Bazaar
3735 Rhode Island Avenue
Mount Rainier, Maryland 20822
Tel: (301) 927-2224

Indian Sub-Continental Store
908 Philadelphia Avenue
Silver Spring, Maryland 20910
Tel: (301) 589-8417

MASSACHUSETTS

India Tea and Spice, Inc.
453 Common Street
Belmont, Massachusetts 02178
Tel: (617) 484-3737

MICHIGAN

Gabriel Importing Co.
2461 Russell Street
Detroit, Michigan 48207
Tel: (313) 567-2890

India Foods and Boutique
37-29 Cass Avenue
Detroit, Michigan 48201
Tel: (313) 831-0056

India Grocers
35-46 Cass Avenue
Detroit, Michigan 48201
Tel: (313) 831-5480

MINNESOTA

International House of Foods
75 Island Avenue West
Minneapolis, Minnesota 55401
Tel: (612) 379-2335

MISSOURI

Seema Enterprises
10612 Page Avenue
St. Louis, Missouri 63132
Tel: (314) 423-9990

Quality International
3228 Ivanhoe
St. Louis, Missouri 63139
Tel: (314) 781-2444

NEW JERSEY

Bombay Bazaar
797 Newark Avenue
Jersey City, New Jersey 07306
Tel: (201) 963-5907

India Bazaar
204 Hudson Street
Hoboken, New Jersey 07030
Tel: (201) 653-8116

Krishna Grocery Store
103 Broadway
Passaic, New Jersey 07057
Tel: (201) 472-3025

NEW YORK

America India Traders
139 Division Street
New York, New York 10002
Tel: (212) 226-0467

Annapurna
127 East 28 Street
New York, New York 10016
Tel: (212) 889-7540

Aphrodisia Products, Inc.
28 Carmine Street
New York, New York 10014
Tel: (212) 989-6440

Beirut Groceries
199 Atlantic Avenue
Brooklyn, New York 11201
Tel: (212) 624-9615

Foods of India
120 Lexington Avenue
New York, New York 10016
Tel: (212) 683-4419

House of Spices
76-17 Broadway
Jackson Heights, New York 11373
Tel: (212) 476-1577

India Food and Gourmet
110 Lexington Avenue
New York, New York 10016
Tel: (212) 686-8955

India Spice Store
135 Lexington Avenue
New York, New York 10016
Tel: (212) 254-1055

Kalpana Indian Groceries and Spices,
    Inc.
42-75 Main Street
Flushing, New York 11355
Tel: (212) 961-4111

Kalpana Indian Groceries and Spices,
    Inc.
2528 Broadway
New York, New York 10025
Tel: (212) 663-4190

K. Kalustyan, Orient Export Trading
    Corporation
123 Lexington Avenue
New York, New York 10016
Tel: (212) 685-3416

Maharaj Bazar
665 Flatbush Avenue
Brooklyn, New York 11225
Tel: (212) 941-2666

Patel Discount Center
74-17 Woodside Avenue
Elmhurst, New York 11373
Tel: (212) 478-4547

Sahadi Importing Company, Inc.
187 Atlantic Avenue
Brooklyn, New York 11201
Tel: (212) 624-4550

Seema Sweets and Snacks
41-17 Union Street
Flushing, New York 11355
Tel: (212) 358-8805
*Varieties of Indian sweetmeats,
snacks, savories, and* chat.

Shaheen Sweets
99 Lexington Avenue
New York, New York 10016
Tel: (212) 683-2139
*Large variety of Indian sweetmeats,
snacks, savories, and* chat.

Spice and Sweet Mahal
135 Lexington Avenue
New York, New York 10016
Tel: (212) 683-0900
*Spices, groceries, utensils, sweetmeats,
savories, and snacks.*

Thomas Zarras, Inc.
92 Reade Street
New York, New York 10013
Tel: (212) 227-5278
*Freshly made almond butter and
cashew nut butter.*

OHIO

India Gift Center and Indian Grocery
1568 North High Street
Columbus, Ohio 43085
Tel: (614) 291-0213

OKLAHOMA

Indian Foods and Spices
13125 East 36 Street
Tulsa, Oklahoma 74134
Tel: (918) 665-3184

OREGON

Porter's Foods Unlimited
125 West 11th Avenue
Eugene, Oregon 97401
Tel: (503) 342-3629

PENNSYLVANIA

Bombay Emporium
3343 Forbes Avenue
Pittsburgh, Pennsylvania 15213
Tel: (412) 682-4965

House of Spices
716 West Wyoming Avenue
North Philadelphia,
Pennsylvania 19140
Tel: (215) 455-6870

House of Spices of New York
4101 Walnut Street
West Philadelphia,
Pennsylvania 19104
Tel: (215) 222-1111

India Bazaar
3358 Fifth Avenue
Pittsburgh, Pennsylvania 15213
Tel: (412) 682-1172

India Foods and Exhibits
11619 Penn Hill Shopping Center
Pittsburgh, Pennsylvania 15235
Tel: (412) 242-9977

TEXAS

Jay Store
4023 West Himier Street
Houston, Texas 77027
Tel: (713) 871-9270

Yoga and Health Center
2912 Oaklawn Avenue
Dallas, Texas 75219
Tel: (214) 528-8681

WASHINGTON

De Laurenti International Food
    Market
1435 First Avenue
Seattle, Washington 98101
Tel: (206) 622-0141

Specialty Spice House
Pike Place Market
Seattle, Washington 98105
Tel: (206) 622-6340

Specialty Spice House
Sea Tac Mall
Federal Way, Washington 98003
Tel: (206) 839-0922

Specialty Spice House
Tacoma Mall
Tacoma, Washington 98049
Tel: (206) 474-7524

WISCONSIN

Indian Gifts and Food (Chadda
   Imports)
1450 East Brady Street
Milwaukee, Wisconsin 53202
Tel: (414) 277-1227

Indian Groceries and Spices
4807 West North Avenue
Milwaukee, Wisconsin 53208
Tel: (414) 445-9202

International House of Foods
440 West Gorham Street
Madison, Wisconsin 53703
Tel: (608) 255-2554

CANADA

S. Enkin, Inc.
1203 St. Lawrence
Montreal, Quebec H2X 2S6
Tel: (514) 886-3202

House of Spice—Kensington Market
190 Augusta Avenue
Toronto, Ontario M5T 2L6
Tel: (416) 363-8544

India Food Center
802 Somerset Street, West
Ottawa, Ontario K1R 6R5
Tel: (613) 234-2606

India Food Center
2204 Dundas Street West
Toronto, Ontario M6R 1X3
Tel: (416) 533-9144

Kohinoor International Foods
1438 Gerrard Street East
Toronto, Ontario M4L 1Z8
Tel: (416) 461-4432

Glossary

Aam	ripe mango fruit	AHM
Aata	flour; whole wheat flour	AH-dah
Achar	pickle	ah-CHAR
Adrak	fresh ginger root, also known as green ginger	ah-DRUK
Agni	God of fire worshiped by Vedic Indians	ahg-NEE
A-himsa	nonviolence; the doctrine of refraining from the killing of animals or insects	ah-HIM-sah
Ajwain	carom seeds, also known as lovage	aj-WINE
Akhroot	walnut	ak-ROHT
Aloo	potato	AH-loo
Amchoor	mango powder made from raw sour mangoes	ahm-CHOORR
Anardana	dried edible seedlike fruit of the pomegranate	ah-NAHR-dah-na
Anda	egg	AHN-dah
Appalam	lentil wafers	AHP-blahm
Arbi	Indian starchy root vegetable	AHR-bee
Arhar Dal	lentils	AHR-haar DAHL
Arwa Chawal	long grain rice	AHR-wa CHAH-val
Aur	and	OUH-re
Badaam	almond	ba-DAHM
Badaami	meat or chicken, cooked with ground almonds and spices	ba-dah-MEE or ba-DAH-mee
Bade	small doughnut-shaped fried bean dumplings	ba-RRAY
Badi Elaichi	black cardamom pods	ba-RREE eh-LIE-ee-jee
Badshahi	emperor's	bahd-SHAH-hee
Bag Bazaar	famous market in Calcutta	BAHG bah-ZAHR

499

Bagda Jheengari	giant prawns	BAHG-da JEEN-ga-ree
Baghar	spice-perfumed butter used for flavoring *dal*, yogurt salads, vegetables, relishes, and some meat and poultry preparations	bag-HAAR
Baigan	eggplant	BANG-gun
Bakara or *bakari*	goat	BAH-ka-rah or BAH-ka-ree
Bakare ka Gosht	goat's meat	bah-ka-RAY ka GOHSHT
Bandh Gobhi	cabbage	BAND-d go-BHEE
Bara Jheenga	lobster	BAH-ra JEEN-gah
Barfi	fudge	BAHR-fee
Barista	crisp fried onion shreds used in Moslem cooking	bahr-RIH-stah
Barra Kabab	thin strips of boneless loin or rib meat, marinated, skewered, and grilled	bah-RAH ka-BAHB
Bartan Maanjhane Wali	paid worker who cleans dishes, pots and pans twice a day	BAHR-ten MAHN-jha-nay WAH-lee
Basoondi	dessert made with *rabadi*, sweetened with honey or sugar, and garnished with nuts	bah-SOON-dee
Basmati	generic name of a variety of Indian long grain rice	BAHS-mah-tee
Beans	green beans	beh-LAHN
Besan	chick-pea flour	BAY-sahn
Bhara	stuffed	BHAR-ah
Bharta	smoked eggplant fried with onions, tomatoes, and herbs	BHAR-tah
Bharva	same as *Bhara*	BEHR-vah
Bhatoora	leavened dough made of yogurt, potatoes and white flour, rolled into circles and deep fried	bheh-TOO-rah

Bhindi	okra	BHIN-dee
Bhojia	vegetables stir-fried with spices and seasonings	BHOO-jee-ah
Bhona	fried	BHOO-nah
Bhonao	the technique of frying onions, and meat	bhoo-NAW-oo
Bhone Piaz ke Lachee	crisp fried onion shreds used as garnish for pilafs	BHOON-eh pih-YAZ kay LAH-che
Bhorji	scramble, generally applied to scramble of eggs	BHOOR-jee
Biriyani	an elaborate pilaf made by cooking meat or chicken sep-arately as *korma* and then folding fragrant rice into it. Lamb *biriyani* is generally flavored with saffron and screw-pine essence, and gar-nished with nuts and silver foil.	bih-ree-YAH-nee
Biswa Tulsi	sweet basil, the common su-permarket variety	BIS-wah TUHL-see
Bombil, or *Bombay Duck*	small transparent fish (found along the western coast of India), sun-dried, and sold as a wafer	bohm-BIL
Boti Kabab	boneless pieces of meat, mari-nated, skewered, and grilled	BOH-tee ka-BAHB
Brahma	the supreme Hindu God, the creator of the universe	BRAH-ha-mah
Brahmin	priestly class, or person be-longing to priestly class—the topmost of the four Hindu castes	BRAH-ha-min
	(others being, in order of im-portance, *kshatryas* (the war-rior class),	KSHAH-tree-yah
	vaishya (trader),	VEH-she-ah
	and *shudra* (cultivator or ar-tisan).	SHOO-drah

	Untouchables are outcastes, and include *chamaar*(leather worker),	ja-MAHR
	bhangi (sweeper),	BHUN-ghee
	and *dhobi* (laundryman)	DHO-bee.
Chah	tea	CHAH
Chakki	grain mill	CHAH-kee
Chakko	knife	CHAH-koo
Chakla	marble or wooden board for rolling bread	CHAH-klah
Chalni	strainer, sieve, sifter	CHAL-nee
Channa	dried chick-peas, garbanzos; also cooked chick-pea dish with spices	CHAH-nah
Channa Dal	yellow split peas	CHAH-na DAHL
Chapati	thin griddle-baked whole wheat bread	cha-PAH-tee
Chapli Kabab	ground meat mixed with spices, herbs, and season-ings, shaped into patties and shallow fried	CHAH-plee ka-BAHB
Chat	a cold dish made with vegeta-bles, fruits, and spices, eaten as a snack or appetizer	CHAHT
Chaunk	same as *baghar*	CHAWNK
Chaunk Gobhi	Brussels sprout	CHAWNK GOHB-hee
Chawal	rice	CHAH-val
Chenna	Indian cheese	CHAY-nah
Chimta	tongs	CHIM-tah
Choolha	coal- or wood-burning Indian mud stove	CHOOL-ha
Chota Piaz	shallot	CHO-tah pih-YAZ
Choti Elaichi	green cardamom; also white bleached cardamom	CHO-tee ee-LIE-a-chee
Chotoo Jheengari	large shrimp or prawn	CHO-too JEEN-ga-ree
Chukandar	red beet	choo-KAHN-dahr

Dahi Bhalle	fried bean dumplings in spice- and herb-laced yogurt, specialty of Punjab State	da-HEE BHAH-lay
Dal	legumes (lentils and dried peas and beans)	DAHL
Dalchini	cinnamon	dahl-CHEE-nee
Deghi Mirch	Indian paprika made from mild Kashmiri pepper pods	DAY-ghee MEERCH
Dhakkan	lid	DHAH-kahn
Dhania	coriander	DHAH-nee-yah
Dhan-sak Masala	spice blend used for making *Dhan-sak,* a chicken, lentil, and vegetable stew	DHAHN-sahk ma-SAH-la
Dhooli Urad	white split gram bean	DHoo-lee OO-rd
Doodh	milk	DOOHDT
Doodhwala	milkman	doohd-WAH-la
Do-piaza	literally translated, means meat, chicken, or shellfish, cooked in double its weight of onions	doh-pih-YA-za
Ducan	shop	DOO-kahn
Dum	Indian technique of pot-roasting	DUMB
Durga Pooja	festival during the months of September and October to worship the Goddess Durga, also known as Kali or Parvati, the consort of Lord Shiva	DOOHR-gah POOH-ja
Elaichi	cardamom	ee-LIE-a-chee
Eleesh	fatty fish found in Hoogli river in Calcutta, Bengal	EH-lesh
Firni	pudding made with rice flour, almonds, and creamy milk	FIHR-nee
Gajar	carrot	GAH-jar
Gajjak	sesame brittle	GUH-JUK

Ganth Gobhi	kohlrabi	GAHNT GOHB-hee
Garam	warm, hot	ga-RAHM
Garam Masala	spicy and highly aromatic blend of roasted spices used in popular cooking of North India	ga-RAHM ma-SAH-la
Geela Masala Bhoonana	brown-frying onion, garlic, and ginger root	GHEE-lah ma-SAH-la BHOO-na-nah
Geela Masala Tay-yar Karana	preparing onion, garlic, and ginger root for cooking	GHEE-lah ma-SAH-la TIE-yahr KAHR-nah
Ghara	pottery or metal jug for storing water	KHAH-rah
Ghat	meaning "steps," generally applied to the chain of hills along the western coast of India which rise sharply on the East and slope gradually toward the coast	KHAHT
Ghee	fat	KHEE
Gingelly	light sesame oil	JIN-jeh-lee
Gobhi or *Phool Gobhi*	cauliflower	POOL GOHB-hee
Gochian	black beehive-shaped mushrooms from Kashmir region, similar to French morels	GOO-chee-an
Gol	round	GOHL
Golda Jheengari	lobster	GOHL-da JEEN-ga-ree
Gosht	meat	GOHSHT
Ground Nut Oil	peanut oil	
Gujjia	crescent-shaped sweet pastries filled with nuts and coconut	Goo-jee-ah
Gulab	rose	GOO-lab
Gulab Jal	rose water	Goo-lab JEHL
Gulkand	rose petals preserved in heavy sugar syrup	goohl-KAND
Haldi	turmeric	HAL-dee

Halwa	vegetables, lentils, nuts, and fruits, cooked with sugar and *ghee* to the consistency of plum pudding	HAL-vah
Halwai	pastry chef	hal-WIE-ee
Halwai ki Ducan	pastry shop	hal-WIE-ee kee doo-KAHN
Hara Dhania	fresh coriander leaves	HA-rah DHAH-nee-ah
Hara Piaz	scallion	HA-rah pih-YAZ
Hari Chutney ka Pullao	pilaf made with fresh mint, coconut, and spices—a specialty of Andra Pradesh	HA-ree CHUT-nee ka POOL-aw-oo
Hari Gobhi	broccoli	HA-ree GOHB-hee
Hari Mirch or *Simla Mirch*	green pepper	HA-ree MEERCH; SIHM-la MEERCH
Heeng	asafetida	HEENG
Hindi	the most widely spoken Indo-european language in India, originally from Uttar Pradesh	HIN-dee
Hindu	follower of Hindu religion, with Brahma as the supreme God, and worshipping the God Vishnu or the God Shiva	HIN-doo
Hussaini Kabab	ground meat shaped into thin sausages, stuffed with nuts and raisins, and panfried or broiled	hoo-SIE-nee ka-BAHB
Imli	tamarind	IM-lee
Jain	follower of Jain religion (primarily centered in the state of Gujrat), founded by Mahavira (599–527 B.C.) with *Agamas* as their sacred scriptures	JAYN ma-ha-VEE-ra AH-ga-mah

Jaiphul	nutmeg	JAY-fehl
Jal Toori	literally translated, cucumbers of the sea—a fish	jal-TAW-ree
Javitri	mace	ja-VIH-tree
Jeera	cumin	JEE-rah
Jheenga or *Jheengari*	shrimp or prawn	JEEN-gah; JEEN-ga-ree
Kabab	kabob	ka-BAHB
Kabab Masala	spice blend used for making kabobs	ka-BAHB ma-SAH-la
Kabadiwala	person who buys used clothes and gives in return new stainless steel utensils	ka-BAR-ee-WA-lah
Kacha	raw	ka-CHAH
Kachauri	fried puffy bread stuffed with spicy bean mixture	ka-CHAW-ree
Kachoomar	chopped or sliced onions, tomatoes, and green pepper, flavored with lemon juice	ka-CHOO-mahr
Kaddoo-kas	vegetable grater	ka-DOOH-kahs
Kadhi	dumplings made with chick-pea flour and simmered in yogurt with spices and vegetables	kahr-HEE
Kadhai	Indian cooking utensil similar to Chinese wok, used for frying food	KAH-DHAH-hee
Kajoo	cashew nut	KA-joo
Kala	black	KA-lah
Kala Channa	small black chick-peas that also yield chick pea flour *besan*	KA-lah CHEH-nah
Kala Namak	black salt	KA-lah NEH-mek
Kalaiwala	person who lines or recoats copper and brass utensils	kah-LAY-ee-WA-lah
Kalaunji	onion seeds	ka-LAUN-jee
Kali Dal	rich dish of black whole gram bean (*sabat urad*) cooked with sweet butter, spices, and fresh herbs	KA-lee DAHL

Kali Mirch	black pepper	KA-lee MEERCH
Karchi	stirring spoon	KAR-chee
Kari	curry; also, sweet aromatic leaves of the kari plant	KAH-ree
Kari Podi	curry powder	KAH-ree PO-dhee
Kashmiri Pandit	Hindu from the state of Kashmir	KA-shmih-ree PUN-diht
Kasoori Mathari	savory crackers made with rich dough and dry fenugreek leaves	ka-SOOH-ree MAH-tih-ree
Kasoori Methi	dry fenugreek leaves	ka-SOOH-ree MAY-tee
Katch	lamb	KAHCH
Katoori	small metal bowls for serving individual portions of dishes	ka-TOH-ree
Keema	ground meat; also the gravy dish cooked with the ground meat	KEE-mah
Kekada	crab	KAY-krah
Kesar	saffron	KAY-sahr
Kewra	screw pine	KAY-rah
Khansaama	cook, chef	kahn-SAH-ma
Khara	plain, unelaborate, with few spices	KAH-ra
Khas-khas	white poppy seeds	KAS-KAS
Khasa	special	KAH-sah
Khatte	sour	KAH-teh
Kheer	pudding, rice pudding	KEERH
Kheera	cucumber	KEER-ah
Khichari	a porridge made with rice, yellow split mung beans, and spice-perfumed butter	KIH-chihr-ree
Khoobani	apricot	koo-BAH-nee
Khoshboo	aroma	KUSH-boo
Khoya	milk cooked down to fudgelike consistency	KOY-yah
Kofta	kafta—ground meatballs simmered in sauce with spices	KOHF-tah

Koosmali	relish made with raw grated carrots and fried black mustard seeds	KOHS-ma-lee
Korma	braising, braised, to braise	KOOR-mah
Kulcha	leavened white-flour dough shaped into rounds and baked in the *tandoor*	KULL-cha
Kulfi	Indian ice cream made with cooked-down milk, frozen in special conical molds called *Kulfi ka saancha*	KULL-fee
Lobhia	black-eyed peas	LHOB-hee-ah
Lal Mirch	red pepper	LAHL MEERCH
Lassan	garlic	LA-sahn
Lassi	yogurt thinned with water, sweetened, and flavored with rose essence or rose water	LA-see
Laung	clove	LONGH
Maalik/Maalkin	master/mistress	MAH-lik/MAHL-kin
Maan Dal	black whole gram bean	MAHN DAHL
Maanz	meat	MAHZ
Maharaj/Maharajin	male Brahmin cook/female Brahmin cook	ma-ha-RAJ/ma-ha-rah-JIN
Machi	fish	MAH-chee
Makhan	butter	MAH-kehn
Makhani Murgh	cooked *Tandoori* chicken pieces simmered in creamy tomato sauce with butter and spices and flavored with fresh coriander leaves	ma-KAH-nee MOORGH
Malai	cream (heavy, light, sour, and coconut)	ma-LIE-ee
Malai Kofta	meatballs simmered in creamy, buttery tomato sauce with spices	mal-LIE-ee KOF-tah

Malpoora	sweet whole wheat crepes fla-vored with crushed fennel	mal-POOH-rah
Masala	spice, spices, spice blend, blend of seasonings and spices	ma-SAH-la
Masala Bhoonana	roasting spices	ma-SAH-la BHOO-na-nah
Masala Musulana	crushing spices	ma-SAH-la MUH-suh-leh-nah
Masala Peesana	grinding spices	ma-SAH-la PEE-sa-nah
Masalchi	cook's assistant	ma-SAHL-chee
Masar Dal	pink lentils	MA-sahr DAHL
Masoor Dal	same as *Masar Dal*	ma-SOOHR DAHL
Matar	peas, chick peas	MA-tehr
Matar Shufta	vegetarian counterpart of *Keema Matar* (the gravy dish of ground meat and green peas) made with fried milk-fudge grains, a specialty from the state of Kashmir	MA-tehr SHOOF-tah
Mattha	yogurt drink flavored with salt, roasted cumin, and fresh mint leaves	MAH-tah
Meetha	sweet	MEE-tah
Mithai	sweetmeat, sweets	mit-HIE-ee
Meethe Neam ke Patte	kari leaves	MEE-tee NEEM keh PAH-teh
Methi	fenugreek seeds, fenugreek greens	MEHT-hee
Mirchi ka Achar	fresh red-hot chilies, slit, stuffed with spices, and pickled in mustard oil	MEER-chee ka a-CHAHR
Mirchi ki Bhaji	mild green chilies cooked in butter with molasses, tomatoes, and spices, a spe-cialty of Rajasthan State	MEER-chee kee BHAH-jee
Moolee	in coconut sauce	MO-lee

Moong Badian	fried mung bean dumplings made with pureed yellow mung beans and spinach greens	MOONGH BEH-ree-ahn
Moong Dal	yellow split mung beans	MOONGH DAHL
Mughal	Moghul—Turks, Mongol by origin and Moslem by religion, brought Persian culture, food, cooking techniques, and garnishes to India in the sixteenth century.	MUH-gehl
Mughal Garam Masala	classic blend of highly fragrant and mild-tasting spices used for flavoring dishes of Moghul origin	MUH-gehl GEH-rem ma-SAH-la
Mughalai	in the Moghul tradition	moo-GLIE-ee
Muharram	the day of observation of Saint Hussain's death	moo-HA-ram
Mullagatanni	*Mullaga* (black pepper) *tanni* (water or broth), the origin of Mulligatawny Soup	mool-ah-ga-TAH-nee
Mungaude ki Bhaji	*Moong Badian* simmered with tomatoes, seasonings, and spices	mung-gaw-RAY kee BHA-jee
Murgh or *Murghi*	Chicken	MOORGH or MOORGH-ee
Musalmaan	Moslem—follower of Islamic religion with Mohammad (A.D. 570–632) as prophet.	moo-sal-MAHN
Namak	salt	NAH-mek
Namaste, Namaskaar	Indian word of greeting	nah-ma-STAY;nah-ma-SKAHR
Nan	teardrop-shaped bread made with leavened dough and baked in the *tandoor*	NAHN
Nandi	sacred bull—carrier of Lord Shiva	NAHN-dee

Nargisi Kofta	meatballs stuffed with whole eggs, fried, cut in half to expose the egg, and simmered in onion gravy	NEHR-geh-see KOF-tah
Narial	coconut	NAH-ree-el
Narial-kas	coconut grater	NAH-ree-el KAS
Naukar/Naukarani	male servant/female servant	NO-kar/no-ka-RAH-nee
Nimboo	lemon, lime	NIM-boo
Obla	boiled	OH-blah
Oobalana	to boil, boiling	oo-BAH-la-nah
Op-phul	by-products	oop-FAHL
Paan	leaves of the betel pepper plant *(piper betle);* also the digestive preparation made with betel leaf *(paan ka patta,* BAHN-ka BA-ta),lime paste *(choona,* CHOO-nah), catechu *(kattha,* KA-tah),and betel nut *(sopari,* soo-pah-REE), which may also contain coconut flakes, fennel, clove, cardamom, tobacco, and *gulkand* (GULL-kahnd), and be covered with silver foil	PAHN
Paani	water	PAH-nee
Pachadi	yogurt salad made with raw vegetables and yogurt, flavored with fried black mustard seeds	PAH-cha-ree
Pakode	fritters	pah-KOOH-ray
Palak	spinach greens	PAH-lek
Paneer	*Chenna* compressed into a cake and cut into small pieces	pah-NEER
Papad	lentil wafers	PAH-per
Papeeta	papaya	pa-PEE-tah

Paraath	large high-rimmed platter used for mixing and kneading dough, cleaning *dal* or *basmati* rice, and preparing and cutting vegetables	pa-RAHDH
Paratha	griddle-fried whole wheat flaky bread	pa-RAHT-ha
Parsee	follower of the Persian Zoroastrian religion (primarily centered at Bombay in the state of Maharashtra), with Zoroaster as prophet. Parsees fled from their Persian homeland between the eighth and twelfth centuries to escape religious persecution by Moslem rulers.	PAR-see
Pasanda Kabab	same as *Barra Kabab*	PAH-sehn-dah ka-BOHB
Pateela	handleless saucepan used for general cooking	pa-TEE-lah
Payasam	pudding made with yellow mung beans, split peas, and coconut milk, a specialty of the southern regions	PIE-ya-sahm
Peda/Pede	milk fudge molded into small pillows and garnished with pistachio nuts	PEH-rah/PEH-ray
Peela	yellow	PEE-lah
Phool Badi	tapioca or sago wafers; rice wafers	POOL buh-REE
Phool Gobhi	cauliflower	POOL GO-bhee
Phulka	baked whole wheat puffed bread	PUHL-kah
Piaz	onion	pih-YAZ
Pista	pistachio	PIH-stah
Pitthi	spicy bean stuffing used in *Kachauri*	PIH-tee
Podina	mint	poh-DEE-nah

Pomfret	non-oily firm-fleshed fish with size and bone structure similar to flounder	POHM-freht
Poori	deep-fried puffy bread	POOH-ree
Pullao	pilaf—*basmati* rice cooked in *ghee* or oil with spices, meat, chicken, or vegetables	poo-LAW-oo
Punch-phoron	spice blend used for flavoring vegetables in the eastern regions of India	punch-POOH-rahn
Puppadam	puffy lentil wafers, a specialty of Malabar in South India	PA-pa-rahm
Rabadi	thickened milk sauce made by cooking down milk	RA-bhree
Rabadi Dooth	milk enriched with *rabadi*	RA-bhree DOOD
Rai	mustard	RAH-ee
Raita	raw or cooked vegetables or fruits mixed with seasoned yogurt	RIE-ta
Raja	king	RA-ja
Rajma	red kidney beans	RA-jeh-mah
Ram Tulsi	white basil	RAHM TOOL-see
Rang	color	RUHNG
Ras Malai	dessert of cheese dumplings in pistachio-flecked cream sauce	RAHS ma-LIE-ee
Rasam	spicy lentil broth, a specialty of the South	REH-sahm
Rasedar	vegetables in thin gravy	reh-seh-DAHR
Rasooi	kitchen	reh-SO-ee
Rogan Josh	Lamb braised in yogurt and cream with Moghul spices, a Kashmiri specialty	RO-gahn JOOSH
Rogani Gosht	rich meat dish made with cream, *usli ghee*, and spices	RO-gah-nee GOHSHT
Roi	a local fish sold in *Bag Bazaar* in Calcutta	RO-ee
Roti	bread	RO-tee

Ruh	essence	ROOH
Sabat Moong	green whole mung beans	SAH-bat MOONGH
Sabat Urad	black whole gram beans	SAH-bat OO-rahd
Sabzi	vegetables; also, stir-fried vegetable preparation from North India	SAHB-zee
Sabziwala	vegetable seller	SAHB-zee-WA-lah
Sada	plain	SA-dah
Safaid	white	sa-FIE-id
Saag	greens	SAHG
Salan	spicy gravy	SAH-len
Sambaar	vegetable and lentil stew with tamarind, flavored with spices	SAHM-bahr
Sambaar Podi	blend of hot spices used for flavoring *sambaar*	SAHM-bahr PO-dhee
Sambhar Namak	white salt, table salt	SAMB-her NAH-mek
Samosa	triangular savory pastries filled with potatoes or meat	sa-MO-sah
Sarsoon	mustard greens	Sahr-SOHN
Saunf	fennel; anise	SOHNF
Seek Kabab	thin sausage-shaped kabobs of broiled ground meat and fresh herbs	SEEK ka-BAHB
Selha Chawal	converted rice	SEHL-ha CHAH-vel
Sem	same as *beans*	SAYM
Sendha Namak	rock salt	SAYND-ha NAH-mek
Shahi	royal	SHAH-hee
Shamme Kabab	ground meat and yellow split peas, flavored with mint, ginger root, and spices, shaped into small patties and fried	SHAH-mee ka-BOHB
Sharbat	fruit punch	SHER-beht
Shorva	soup	SHOOR-wah

Shiva	the God of destruction or power	SHIH-va
Sikh	bearded and turbaned follower of Sikh religion (primarily centered in the state of Punjab), founded by Guru Nanak (A.D. 1469–1538), with *Granth Sahip* (GRAHNT SAH-hip) as principal scripture	SICKH
Sil-batta	grinding stone	SIL-BHA-tah
Sonth	dry ginger powder	SAWNT
Sookha Dhania	coriander seeds	SOO-kah TAH-nee-yah
Sookha Masala Bhoonana	frying spices	SOO-kah ma-SAH-la BHOO-na-nah
Sooji	semolina, farina	SOO-jee
Sopari	betel nut	soo-PAH-ree
Srikhand	dessert made with drained yogurt, sugar, nuts, and saffron	shree-KAHND
Tadka	same as *Baghar*	TAHR-ka
Tahari	spicy rice-and-peas dish with turmeric and herbs	TEH-ha-ree
Tala	deep-fried	TEH-lah
Talna	deep frying	TELL-na
Tamatar	tomato	ta-MAH-tehr
Tandoor	Indian clay oven	tan-DOOR
Tandoori	food cooked in a *tandoor*	tan-DOO-ree
Tandoori Masala	spice mix used for flavoring *Tandoori* Chicken	tan-DOO-ree ma-SAH-la
Tari	gravy	TEH-ree
Tava	handleless iron griddle	TAH-vah
Tej Patta	bay leaf	TAYJ PAH-tah
Tel	oil	TAYL
Thal	metal platter	TAHL
Thali	metal dinner plate	tah-LEE
Thandai	summer punch made with ground seeds, almonds, spices, sugar, and whole milk	tahn-DA-ee

Tinda	round gourd, a vegetable belonging to the cucumber family	TIN-dah
Tikka	cutlet	TIH-ka
Toor Dal	red lentils	TOOR DAHL
Toovar Dal	same as *toor dal*	Too-var DAHL
Topshe	a local fish sold in *Bag Bazaar* in Calcutta	TOHP-chee
Urad Dal	white split gram bean	OO-rahd DAHL
Usli Ghee	Indian clarified butter	AHS-lee KHEE
Vanaspati Ghee	vegetable shortening	va-NAHS-pa-tee KHEE
Vark	silver foil	VAHRK
Veda	literature of the ancient Indians, compiled between 1500 and 500 B.C.	VAY-dah
Vedic	referring to the period of the *veda*	VEH-dik
Vendaloo	Goanese hot and pungent curry	VEN-deh-loo
Vishnu	the God of preservation	VISH-noo
Ya	or	YAH
Yakhni	meat broth	YAHK-nee
Yerra	same as *Jheenga*	YEH-reh
Zaffran	same as *Kesar*	ZAH-frohn
Zarda	sweet saffron pilaf, traditionally made on *Muharram*	ZAHR-dah

Index

Page numbers in **bold face** refer to recipes.

517

ABOUT THE AUTHOR

Julie Sahni was born in India in 1945 and grew up in Kanpur (Uttar Pradesh) and in New Delhi. She graduated as an architect from Delhi University and spent almost a decade as a professional dancer, performing the classical Indian repertoire throughout her own country and abroad. In 1968 she moved to the United States, where she earned a master's degree in Urban Planning from Columbia University. She is an American citizen and works with the New York City Planning Commission as an urban designer. Mrs. Sahni is the founder of the Indian Cooking School in New York City and also gives courses in Indian cooking at the New School for Social Research. She has traveled extensively in all the regions of India and is familiar with the many traditions of Indian cooking. While Indian food is her specialty, the author is equally comfortable with French, Chinese, and Italian cuisines. Julie Sahni lives in Brooklyn Heights with her husband, Viraht, a theoretical physicist, and their young son, Vishal Raj. When they visit India to see family and friends, they stay in New Delhi.

ABOUT THE ILLUSTRATOR

Marisabina Russo is a graduate of Mount Holyoke College. Her drawings appear regularly in *The New Yorker* and in other magazines. Among the many books she has illustrated is *More Classic Italian Cooking* by Marcella Hazan.